# THE GOSPEL
## *according*
# TO WOMAN

*Karen Armstrong*

# THE GOSPEL

*according*

# TO WOMAN

*Christianity's Creation
of the Sex War
in the West*

ANCHOR PRESS/DOUBLEDAY
GARDEN CITY, NEW YORK
1987

Originally published in Great Britain in 1986
by Elm Tree Books/Hamish Hamilton, Ltd.,
Garden House, 57–59 Long Acre, London WC2E 9JZ

Anchor Press edition published with permission

*Library of Congress Cataloging-in-Publication Data*
Armstrong, Karen.
The Gospel according to woman.
Bibliography: p. 347
Includes index.
1. Women in Christianity.   2. Woman (Christian
theology)—History and doctrines.   3. Sex religious
aspects—Christianity.   I. Title.
HQ1394.A75   1987     270′.088042     86–26610
ISBN 0-385-24078-3 (pbk.)

# CONTENTS

# CONTENTS

# ACKNOWLEDGMENTS

I should like to thank Kyle Cathie, my editor, for her encouragement while I have been writing this book and for her invaluable suggestions, and I must also thank her assistant, Judith Hannam, for her excellent work on the manuscript. Finally, many thanks to Michael Jones for his important and helpful criticisms and encouragement.

NOTE

All Biblical quotations have been taken from *The Jerusalem Bible.*

# INTRODUCTION

This book can most simply be seen as the history of women in Christianity. Because in traditional Western Christianity women have been kept out of the male world of action and thought, it cannot be a conventional history which proceeds chronologically, describing a sequence of events. There have been no great Events in this history of women and no great intellectual movements. That kind of activity was the preserve of the male saints and the male theologians. However, sometimes women did penetrate this male world of action and thought, and they did so in ways that often seem very different on the surface but are really deeply similar. This book will examine the way that men regarded women in Western Christianity and the ways that they coped with their view of women. It will also look at the solutions that women found for the problems that were created for them by the particular neuroses of Christianity.

The idea of neurosis is important. Christian dogma has officially been quite positive about women, although the implications of some of the teachings of Christianity have been sinister and suspect. However, there is an underlying emotion in Christianity which surfaces violently and repeatedly in its history that has no connection with the dogma, just as in our own personal lives our emotions often bear little resemblance to the beliefs and opinions we hold intellectually. Thus the Crusades, when Christians savagely butchered Moslems and Jews, completely contradicted Christianity's doctrine of love. They were an emotional explosion that proceeded from some quite separate part of the Christian mind that had nothing to do with doctrine. Christian attitudes to sex and to women are similarly irrational and inconsistent and have from time to time exploded violently. They continue to explode.

Neuroses are much more difficult to get rid of than beliefs. We can all change our opinions more easily than we can eliminate destructive patterns in our lives, however hard we try. It is the same with a religion and, surely, the same with a culture. Our religious beliefs may have changed, but our emotional compulsions have remained. Western society was created and formed by Christianity. When the culture of Late Antiquity was lost during the Dark Ages, it was the Church which preserved learning and cultural values. The Church dominated the life of Europe politically and emotionally until this century. For a long time there was no life and no learning possible in Europe outside the Church. It is perhaps only in this century that the Christian religion has ceased to influence the minds and hearts of many Western men and women. In some ways we could be said to be living in a Post-Christian society. During the last hundred years or so since the scientific revolutions of the 19th century, which deeply shook the basis of Christian belief, a secular society has been slowly evolving which is independent of any Church. Our politics, our education, our "charitable" social work are no longer undertaken as they were for nearly two thousand years by dedicated Christians intent on bringing about the Kingdom of God on earth, but by dedicated secular experts who often have no religious belief at all. It is no longer necessary in England, as it was until the late 19th century, to subscribe to the 39 Articles of the Church of England to be admitted into Oxford or Cambridge University or into the Civil Service, and no undergraduate would today be expelled from a university, as Shelley was in the early 19th century, for holding atheistic beliefs. Religion, it could be said, has become irrelevant to the mainstream of life in the 20th century, and the fact that many of the Christian Churches are fast being emptied of committed believers shows that Christianity has been pushed to the sidelines because it no longer has anything to say to our liberated and secular world where, in certain parts of society, a lack of Christian belief and a skepticism about conventional religion is often taken for granted and even encouraged.

If it is true that we are living in a society which seems to have outgrown Christianity, then why is it important to think about the Christian history of women? Surely such archaeological delving in the rubble of a dead religion is irrelevant to the woman of today, who has often liberated herself from the shackles of an outworn religious faith? Yet while it is true that parts of our society could well be described as having moved into a Post-Christian era, Christianity is far from being a dead letter. In the first place, a good deal of lip service is still paid to traditional Christian beliefs in the public life of Europe and America. State weddings and funerals often take a conventional Christian form, and politicians, however skeptical they may privately be, still invoke God or at least are chary about taking His name in vain. In England schools still have to have some kind of "prayers" or religious service—however anemic—and have to give some sort of religious instruction. We still stand to attention and sing "God Save the Queen" or "God Bless America" even if we no longer believe in the Deity. And of course many people still do believe in Him.

In the 1960s it seemed impossible that religion would ever play an important role in the public life of a nation again. There was increasing interest in the West in Eastern religions and in meditation, but such practices were very private and, indeed, often embraced by people who had dropped out of the political and social system. Conventional Christianity seemed to belong to an order that was passing away. Yet today in the 1980s there seems to be a religious revival, with people returning to strongly fundamentalist Christian belief. In the United States Jerry Falwell's Moral Majority has seized the imaginations of many citizens, including, it is said, Reagan's. In England people are flocking in large numbers to charismatic or pentecostal sects which hold—often very aggressively—traditional Christian beliefs. It may be too soon to say that we have moved once and for all into a Post-Christian era, but we are perhaps in a state of transition, and it is certainly true that Western society is deeply divided about the relevance of Christianity. Programs in the media which criticize traditional doctrines cause an emotional explosion from all parts of society, which in itself shows that people feel very strongly indeed about the traditional Christian faith.

Even those aspects of Western Society which may have entered a Post-Christian era are affected by Christianity, albeit unconsciously. We have not yet learned how to be entirely secular, and continue to reproduce Christian patterns of thought and behavior in secular ways. It has been said by Jewish scholars, for example, that although Nazi anti-Semitism had nothing whatever to do with Christianity on one level, at a deeper level it was merely repeating in a secular mode the patterns of Christian anti-Semitism which surfaced in Europe at the end of the 11th century during the First Crusade and which has continued in sporadic explosions ever since, especially in Germany. Anti-Semitism, which kills and destroys thousands of our fellow men, is an excellent example of the way a Christian neurosis can completely contradict the essence of the Christian faith but which is so fundamentally written into the hearts of men in the Christian West that it had to find expression in a secular mode when Christianity had been left behind. I would argue similarly that the Christian view of women and the Christian emotion about women still affect us at a very deep level.

A good deal of work has been done on the history of women, but until recently, when Marina Warner, Mary Daly and Rosemary Radford Ruether pioneered the subject, there was little understanding of the Christian history of women. What I am attempting in this book is to show how women still owe a great deal to our Christian past for good and for ill. Women still behave in ways that Christian women behaved for centuries, even if they hold no Christian beliefs and have little technical knowledge about the Christian faith. They are translating, subconsciously, Christian myths about women into a secular idiom. Some of these myths are more healthy and helpful than others.

It seems important to be very clear about Christianity's contribution to—I would say creation of—women's problems in the West, if only because of the dominant role Western women are taking as self-styled leaders of the oppressed women of the world. It often surprises me that people who are usually quite antagonistic toward Christianity are often extremely chauvinist about it once they start comparing it to other religions, especially in this matter of the treatment of women: Christianity may be bad, they say, but Judaism or Islam are definitely worse. Comparisons are often not only odious but the result of ignorant prejudice. I make no great claims for any religion's attitude to women. Most religions have been male affairs and have kept women in a subordinate position. The only point that I would make is that they all did this in very different ways. Christianity had a particular difficulty with women, and its solutions to this problem and the neuroses arising from it are quite peculiar to Christianity. It is important for us to be clear about that difference and that distinction. The West is the society that has pioneered the liberation of women. This is no accident, for the peculiar neurotic problems it developed led Christianity from its very earliest days to produce an ideal of liberated and autonomous women who were independent of and equal to men. The West is very anxious to spread this gospel of liberation in other cultures. However, it is no good taking our particular views of oppression and our particular solutions to women of other cultures because their views and solutions will be different. We have had very different cultural histories and will therefore have very different values and priorities. In *Sex and Destiny* Germaine Greer tells us how angry Third World women tend to become when Western women explain their own cultures and their own problems to them, usually with great inaccuracy. Women need to be free of oppression, and Western women are right to worry about abominable habits like Islamic clitoridectomy and problems of contraception in the Third World. However, we are now very sadly aware in this country of our disastrous policy of Colonialization when we chauvinistically imposed our culture on worlds that were quite alien to it. Women are fond of citing the mistakes men have made in history, but in this matter of spreading the good news of liberation they are in danger of repeating this particular male mistake. Certainly pooling of resources and ideas must go on, and we can and must do a good deal to help women in other cultures. However, it is not sufficient to seize upon a few superficial likenesses which reassure us and confirm our own view of the problems *we* have, and assume that their problems are *precisely* the same as ours. There are probably subtle differences that are crucial. To appreciate these subtle distinctions we must first learn about our own cultural heritage and our own peculiar Western problems. I have, therefore, confined myself to a study of Western Christianity and have not included Eastern or Russian Orthodox Christianity which has dominated Greece, parts of Eastern Europe and the Near East and large areas of what is now the Soviet Union. For the last thousand years, largely due to the aggressive behavior of Western Churches, there has been a division between Eastern and Western Christianity, and from the beginning of the Christian era in the East Christians developed their own problems and their own solutions which were very different from Western answers. Here in the West we must confront our own heritage.

Christianity does not emerge well from this story of Western women. It is not, however, my intention to offend anybody or to denigrate the whole Christian contribution to civilization. We are still expressing in purely secular ways excellent Christian ideals like concern for the underprivileged, equality and justice for all and world peace. Religious people must above all be concerned about truth even if this truth is sometimes uncomfortable. Some of the Churches are trying to change their attitudes and prejudices about women and are clearly aware that all was not well in the past, even though sadly some Churches are more aware of this than others. Old prejudices and neuroses die hard, and having a good long look at them can be a step in the right direction of healing. As long as Christians continue to dance defensively around the problem of women, they will simply reproduce the system of double-think which has for so long bedeviled the matter.

I have called this book *The Gospel According to Woman* because it is the story of the way women lived out the gospel of Jesus Christ. The word "Gospel," of course, means good news, and although at the very beginning of its history Christianity did offer women a positive message it has to be said that since the 2nd century Christianity has been anything but "good news" for women. Today women are very conscious of the suffering and damage wrought upon them by Western values and myths about the role of the sexes. However, it is true that in this century women have managed to change things for the better, and they owe this achievement in large part to their Christian heritage, though they may be unaware of this. Christianity has been extremely damaging to women, but there are elements in Christian modes of thought and feeling that could be used more creatively. It is now surely time for women to begin to capitalize on the improvements in their position instead of merely bewailing their sufferings. This must be the next essential step to complete liberation. In this sense Christianity can offer a message of glad tidings to women, as long as women are clear which of the cultural habits of mind that Christianity has taught us in the West they want to cultivate and which they want to jettison. That is why we need to understand our Christian past, and in any case to re-create the past can sometimes, somehow, redeem it.

# THE GOSPEL
*according*
# TO WOMAN

# 1

# THE PROBLEM: SEX

Women's main problem in the Western world has always been sex. It is no accident that the latest wave of feminism coincided with the sexual revolution of the 1960s and 1970s. Once women started to feel sexually freer, they began to reappraise their position in society as a whole. The wonders of contraception had given them freedom to enjoy their sexuality without fear of unwanted pregnancy. The theory was that this gave them the same sexual freedom as men. They then started to campaign for greater freedom and equality in other spheres. If sexual freedom and a more sexually permissive atmosphere gave women intimations of liberation, it is also true that in our culture sexual guilt and repression have put women in an impossible position. In all cultures women have been seen as inferior beings: they are men's chattels and have no independent rights; they are considered spiritually and intellectually weaker than men; their whole duty in life is to pander to male comfort. To be a wife and mother is a woman's whole fulfillment and she must not ask for anything more. Her place is in the home. Women have shared this burden of inferiority in all cultures. However, in the West women have had a specially difficult problem that has made the usual oppression especially onerous. It is a problem that Jewish and Islamic women, for example, do not share. The Christian world of Europe and America has been permeated by a hatred and fear of sex. Because men have been taught to think of sex as something evil, they have feared and hated women who have tempted them into this dangerous sexuality. Christianity has formed Western society and Christianity has been the only major religion to hate and fear sex. Consequently it is in the West alone that women have been hated because they are sexual beings instead of merely being dominated because they are inferior chattels.

Other cultures and other religions have been very harsh and oppressive to women, but not because of sex. The world of Islam is the misogynist culture that first springs to mind. We see it as harsh and cruel—the epitome of male domination. However, Moslem women are not subjugated because Islam hates sex but because in Islam women are the valued possessions of men. Islam has always appreciated sexuality. Mohammed was a passionate and erotic man; in his view women were the best gift God had given to man. Chauvinist that remark may be, but there is no hint in Mohammed's thought that sex is evil. He had no time for celibacy and there was, he said, to be "no monkery in Islam." The ascetics and mystics of Islam, the Sufis, have not been celibate, because sexual contact with women was not seen as a hindrance to union with God as it was in the West. Before having sex, the Koran tells the Moslem to thank Allah for the great gift of sexuality. Men are allowed to have up to four wives, but each wife is to be cherished and valued. Mohammed was clear that if a man cannot be fair, sexually and emotionally, to more than one wife, then he should be monogamous. Mohammed certainly did not think that women were sexually disgusting. When his wife had her period he used to make a point of reclining in her lap, of taking his prayer mat from her hand, saying for the benefit of his disciples, "Your menstruation is not in your hand." He would drink from the same cup, saying, "Your menstruation is not on your lips." The

Koran says nothing about women having to be veiled or locked away in harems. In fact, in the early period of Islam, women had a good deal of freedom. Veiling came in during the third and fourth generation after Mohammed, and it has been suggested that Islam acquired the practice from its contact with Christian Byzantium, which had always treated its women this way. Harsh sexual punishments are meted out to sexual offenders in some Islamic countries because sexuality is valued and the ideal has been debased, not, as in the past in the West, because sexuality is abhorrent.

However, simply to mention Islam calls to mind the barbaric practice of clitoridectomy. Yet we in Britain cannot afford to be too chauvinist about this because in the 19th century British doctors also performed clitoridectomy on girls who used to enjoy their sexuality too much by masturbating. In England the operation was justified by the myth current in Victorian society that sex was evil. Islam would never subscribe to that. Islam performs the same operation on girls not because their sexuality is evil but because they are the property of men. They belong first to their father and then to their future husbands. In the same way, the Crusaders used to lock their wives into appalling chastity belts to ensure their fidelity while they were away in the Holy Land. Western women have also always been the chattels of their husbands. Yet Islamic girls and Victorian English girls would have experienced clitoridectomy very differently. In both cases the effects would have been deeply traumatic and the scars would physically have been much the same, but the psychological scars would have been different. To be mutilated because you are a chattel and to be mutilated because you are sexual and therefore evil are very different experiences. Neither is desirable, and this kind of suffering should not be weighed and compared, but, if healing were possible, each would have to be treated differently. Much of the Islamic world, for all its new-found 20th-century wealth in oil, is still culturally in the 19th century. We should be quick to deplore the practice of clitoridectomy as mutilating to women, but we should be chary of apportioning all the blame to Islam when we, in the last century, were performing the same operation with the full support of society.

Similarly, Judaism is seen as being oppressive, and certainly Israeli men tend to be extremely chauvinist. Yet again, this is not because of sex. Judaism has never hated sexuality in the way that Christianity has done, because it is a racial religion. The Chosen People have to propagate themselves, and so women, as mothers, have a particularly important, even crucial religious role. The purity laws of Leviticus made women "impure" while they were menstruating as though they were dirty and sinful, but it is not usually realized that exactly the same prohibitions and legislation apply to a man who has had a nocturnal emission or has a venereal discharge. It is an issue of ritual purity, and there are times when semen can be as impure as menstrual blood. Again, although there have been Jewish celibates—like Jesus and St. Paul, for example—celibacy came very late to Judaism. People who practiced it, like the Essenes at Qumran by the Dead Sea, were only a tiny minority. Celibacy has never been considered valuable by the majority of Jews, because continuing the Chosen Race has been too important. It has never been a requirement for the Jewish mystic, as it has traditionally been in the Christian world. Indeed it used to be the case that a young man was not allowed to embark on the mystical study of the *Kaballah* until he was married: the mystical path, it was believed, had many psychological perils, and this could be very dangerous if there was an unhealthy sexual repression.

Judaism values sex. This is true also of other religions. The Buddha may have told his monks to shun women, but no Buddhist would force celibacy on another. It has to spring from a man's own free choice: any involuntary repression (such as exists in the Catholic priesthood, for example) can only induce what Buddhists call an "unskillful state," a state of mind which will embed a man in his own ego and prevent Enlightenment. Sexual guilt, for example, is an "unskillful state" because it is unproductive and makes a man too conscious of himself, so it must not be induced by forcing him to a celibacy that is unnatural or uncongenial to him. Certain sects in Buddhism and Hinduism have used sex as a mystical activity. Everybody has heard of the *Kama Sutra,* but not everybody is aware that this is not just a sex manual, but a method of achieving transcendence and spiritual enlightenment. Christianity is unique in having hated and outlawed sex and in making people feel guilty because they are sexual beings.

There are two things that can be said against this. Firstly, it could be argued that although in the past Christianity certainly did have an unfortunate and damaging effect on the sexuality of the West, we have now shed these unhealthy values. The majority of people in our society are no longer Christians, and are therefore no longer subject to the sexual guilt of Christianity. Therefore, it must follow that the sexual wisdom we have recently acquired will necessarily free women from any oppression and prejudice that may have injured them in the past. Now that we have liberated sexuality from the oppressions of Christianity, liberation for women will also occur and we do not need to worry about what happened in our past, when the Church enshrined values and beliefs that most people no longer share. The second more important objection is that the sexual neurosis of the West is not the fault of Christianity. It may be true that a few Christian cranks in all ages have said some extremely unfortunate things about sex, but the Churches have always officially upheld sex, marriage and the family as things that are holy and good. To blame Christianity for the sexual muddles of Europe and America is unfair. It is just as unfair to blame Christianity for the oppression of women. After all, the Churches have declared since the time of St. Paul that men and women are equal in the sight of God, and indeed the cult of the Virgin Mary in Catholic Europe did great things for the position of women. Christianity, both sets of objectors would say, is irrelevant to the position of women today and is certainly not responsible for any sexual neuroses we might have in our society—if indeed, in these days of sexual permissiveness, we have any sexual problems left at all.

The first objection—that sexuality has now been liberated from Christianity and that people today no longer think about sex in Christian terms—is based on a romantic notion about sexuality which has recently come in for a good deal of criticism. Michel Foucault in his book *The History of Sexuality* has shown that sexuality is not an innate "natural" force inherent in every one of us, which is yearning to break free of social constraint. On the contrary, sexuality is formed by society. Just as every one of us has been affected sexually by the way we were taught about sex, the same applies in a larger way to society as a whole. Society creates sexual attitudes which obviously affect the sexuality of the individuals in that society. Indeed, society actually creates sexualities. Foucault cites homosexuality as an example of this. A hundred years ago women had intense and passionate friendships with one another; they even lived and slept together, and nobody thought very much about it or paused to wonder what they did in bed together. Today such women are called lesbians and the fact that they have now acquired a distinct sexual identity affects their whole lives: it must have a profound effect also on their sexual lives. The same applies to male homosexuals. A man who is "gay" today has a very different attitude to himself and his sexuality from the furtive homosexual of a hundred years ago. Certain pressures and influences in society have produced a new form of sexuality. There is nothing new about homosexuality as such, but the way it expresses itself, sexually as well as socially, is now quite different from the way it expressed itself in the Victorian period or in ancient Greece. Homosexuality is not a great natural force that has suddenly sprung forth in a liberated way in its essential form.

One can say the same thing about the sexuality of women also. In the Victorian period a woman was told that she had no sexual feelings; if she did have sexual pleasure there was something wrong with her. She was an "Angel" and angels didn't have bodies; she was too pure and sacred to share in the disgusting lusts that afflicted men. Men and women were told this by sex "experts," by religious teachers and priests and by the popular literature and poetry of the day. It was an entirely new phenomenon in Western society, because hitherto women were thought to be sexually insatiable. Certain needs and pressures in Victorian society created this new "angelic" woman who was sexually frigid. Because women were told that they would and should not experience sexual pleasure, they didn't, or if they did, suffered such agony of guilt that it destroyed their sex lives altogether. Women became weak and ailing creatures in the 19th century because they were told that they were delicate, especially when they menstruated. Consequently they felt terrible during their periods, and perhaps many of the Victorian ladies who took to their sofas were suffering from the repressions involved in their sex lives. Today women are told that it is all right for them to have orgasms, indeed it is vital for them, and so they are either having them or are locked in a desperate pursuit of the elusive prize. This view has entirely changed the way women behave and feel sexually. The new sexual identity of women, however, is not something that has suddenly sprung forth in the 20th century after being distorted by the Victorians. It is not that women have suddenly got in touch with their "true" sexuality today, but that forces and needs in society have made us construct a late-20th-century sexuality for women which responds to the unique pressures and drives of Western society in the 1980s and which, as these forces change, will change with it to be replaced by yet another form of sexuality.

It is a mistake to see sex apart from culture and society as a whole. Since the time of D. H. Lawrence we have tended to have a romantic view of sex as a great natural force, throbbing in some pure way in each one of us. If only we could let it burst free in its essential form! On that glorious day we should see Sex as It Is in Itself! This is an idealistic dream. There is no such thing as Essential Sexuality, any more than there is an Essential Justice, Essential Freedom or Essential Love. These ideals are constructed differently in different societies. Democracy in ancient Athens was not the same as democracy in the West today, for all our tendency to view Greece as the "Cradle of Democracy." We are quite aware that it would be impossible and undesirable to recreate Athenian democracy in the 20th century. Sexuality is no different in this respect from any other aspect of human behavior. It is a social construction manufactured by our culture and society.

Until this century, our society was essentially Christian. It was the Church which preserved Western culture during the Dark Ages, and in the Middle Ages the Church dominated society. It was not merely that outside the Church there was no salvation, but outside the Church there was no political life, no education, no career. The Church gave you what education you had and much of your entertainment too. Popular preachers like Vincent Ferrer drew huge crowds when they visited a town. People camped outside, listening to sermons that lasted three or four days. It was like a modern pop festival. The Church was the central pivot of each community. Its festivals, rituals, sermons and rhythms of mourning and joy shaped the lives of ordinary people. So important and vital a role did religion play in the lives of ordinary people that when the first Crusade was preached thousands of ordinary peasants simply took off on a hideous journey to the East where nearly all of them were eventually massacred. Hitherto they had probably not gone beyond a twenty-

mile radius of their village, but for the honor of the Church they
were prepared to tramp hundreds of miles to Jerusalem, which must
have been a very shadowy reality to most of them geographically,
though a very vivid emotional reality. Religion continued to play an
important role in Europe after the Renaissance and the Reformation,
as witness the great religious wars of the 17th century. The coloniza-
tion of America was also fundamentally affected by religious vision.
Many of the Christian denominations were attempting to build
God's Kingdom in the American wilderness and, in places like California and New England, so dominated the early settlements that
consequently Christianity is embedded in the national identity of
every American. We cannot simply cast off two thousand years of
cultural formation in a mere fifty years of a more secular approach,
even if we are deeply opposed—and therefore, we think, unaffected—
by Christianity. Christianity still affects our thinking in matters of
ethics and justice. It is inevitable therefore that our Christian culture
has also formed our Western attitudes to sex and to women, and that
these attitudes are present, even if in a submerged form, today.

The second objection is that Christianity is not hostile to sex. It is
certainly true that the major theologians of the Church have said
that sex within marriage was part of God's plan and was therefore
permissible—some would even say holy. Yet even this apparently
obvious fact is not as simple as it looks. Whatever Christianity may
have said, especially after the Reformation, about Matrimony being
Holy and the Family a sacred institution, it has, from the very earliest days, shown itself to be hostile to the family and in favor of the
liberation of women from petty domesticity and the burdens of married life. Furthermore, later Churches have all taught Christians to
have a most negative view of sex. Even though orthodox Christians
have never said that to have sex was a sin (provided that sex takes
place within marriage), they have always associated it strongly with
sin. We now think of Christianity as the religion of the family, but
until the Reformation it was thought holier to be celibate and marriage was not considered a valuable Christian vocation. For all that
the theologians taught that marriage and sex were part of God's plan
for mankind, in practice they did not think that it had a place in the
true Christian life. The great Reformers, Luther and Calvin, did not
change the fundamental Catholic teaching on marriage very much,

and they certainly had very little time for sex. The ideal of "Holy Matrimony" which most Christians now take for granted as essential teaching came into Christianity late in its history. It was not until the Anglican and Puritan theologians of the 17th centuries began to push the ideal with such extreme efficiency that marriage got a new profile.

Today it is often said that family life in the West is in trouble. Divorce rates are soaring: some people are seeking alternative ways of living together and are fleeing the nuclear family. People usually blame modern movements like the "Permissive Society" or "Women's Liberation" for this destruction of "old" values. In fact these values are not very old at all. Some three hundred years ago the Churches decided to "baptize" the family and make it a "holy" Christian vocation, but the older, hostile official view of marriage was never lost. As valued institutions, marriage and the family are very new in our Western society. In Islamic or in Jewish cultures on the other hand they have always been respected and their value taken for granted in a way that has simply not been the case in the West, where they always sustained a barrage of criticism. Certainly, if it is true that marriage and the family are in trouble today, modern trends in sexuality and the new position of women have contributed to this decline, but present criticism simply repeats an old Western tradition of criticism. We are still having teething troubles when we try to appreciate marriage in our society.

This rejection of marriage and the family is an extraordinary phenomenon, and unique to the West and the Christian religion. How did it come about, when Christianity had its roots in Judaism, which, as is well known, values the family very highly? In most cultures, such as Judaism or Islam, it is true that women play little part in life outside the home, but as wives and mothers they do have respect and authority. Arabs, for example, deeply respect their mothers in a way that Western men rarely do. Patronizing attitudes to "Mother" are all too common in some sectors of Western society, but are quite alien to the esteem and respect with which Moslems approach their mothers. The power of the Jewish Mother is a byword. If Christianity has for centuries denigrated marriage and the family as second-class or even irrelevant vocations, this will strip its women of the power that the institution of the family has brought to women in other cultures.

The disparagement of the family can be traced right back to Jesus, although later Christians would reject marriage for very different reasons. No preacher would be able to get up into the pulpit today and give Jesus' views on family life and family relationships. Jesus himself never married and seems not to have considered the family to be an important or significant institution. In this respect Jesus was a most unusual Jew. He seems to have been, if not exactly antagonistic to his own family, at least fairly indifferent to his mother and brothers and sisters. This is not because he thought sex was evil, as the great theologians St. Augustine or St. Jerome would teach later. Jesus rejected the family because it was a distraction from an urgent mission. He believed that he had come to inaugurate the Kingdom of God in Jerusalem, whereby the Jews would triumph over their enemies and rule over the Gentiles, the non-Jews. It would be a cosmic and political triumph. The prophets had foretold that in this Kingdom there would be an entirely new world-order—lions would lie down with lambs, children could put their hands into the lairs of dangerous snakes with impunity. Pain and violence would disappear in a new order of peace. Some Jews even believed that the virtuous dead would rise again to enjoy this new triumph of Israel. Jesus believed that he was the Messiah and that his job was to inaugurate this new Kingdom, this new world-order. When he began to preach, Mark tells us, his message was "The Kingdom of God has already arrived." Jesus believed that he was living in a time of crisis and urgency. There was no time to get saddled with a family and the claims of a wife and children—there was work to be done, and soon, anyway, the Kingdom would be established when there would be no marriage nor giving in marriage. As the Messiah, Jesus could not allow his own family to impede his work by the usual claims that families make on people.

Jesus' own family do not seem to have been very supportive to him, and we see him sometimes shaking them off as a nuisance. There is a story that when he first started preaching and healing in Galilee "his relatives heard of this and set out to take charge of him, convinced that he was out of his mind" (Mark 3:21). On one occasion they actually arrived at the house where he was preaching and interrupted him:

> His mother and brothers now arrived and, standing outside sent in a message asking for him. A crowd was sitting round him at the time the message was passed to him, "Your mother and brothers and sisters are outside asking for you." He replied, "Who are my mother and my brothers?" And, looking round at those sitting in a circle about him, he said, "Here are my mother and my brothers. Anyone who does the will of God, that person is my brother and sister and mother."
>
> (Mark 3:31–35)

His family's special claims to attention had to be put aside if they got in the way of his mission, even if he appeared ruthless and callous in his rejection. Furthermore, Jesus here appears to be abolishing a family based on kinship in favor of a wider family bound together by obedience to God. He is quite clear that the real disciple has to be ready to throw his family over out of zeal for the Kingdom. Any shrinking back out of love for close relations means that one cannot be a Christian. "If any man comes to me without hating his father, mother, wife, children, brothers and sisters, yes and his own life too, he cannot be my disciple" (Luke 14:25 and 18:29). Any Christian today who left his wife and children in the lurch because he felt he had a vocation to be a missionary would be denounced by his fellow Christians for un-Christian callousness. The addition of "wife" to the list of people the Christian disciple has to be prepared to desert, if necessary, is peculiar to Luke. Matthew only puts parents, siblings and children on his list of the family that the Christian must be prepared to forsake. Even so, that list is austere enough for modern taste. Who would think himself justified today in abandoning his children to fulfill a personal Christian vocation? Matthew tells us that when a man offered to follow Jesus, saying, "Let me go and bury my father first," Jesus ruthlessly replied: "Follow me, and leave the dead to bury the dead" (8:22). It is unlikely that the father's corpse was already awaiting burial (though if it were that would be shocking too), but the disciple is probably asking Jesus if he could stay at home until his old and sick father died. Jesus' answer in today's terms would be: "Put him in a geriatric home and come and follow me." Duties that *we* consider Christian and humane had no place in Jesus' list of priorities. To bring about the Kingdom demands a man's full commitment, and he no longer has time for the luxuries of family life. This is a time of crisis, and terrible, urgent measures are necessary. Far from setting up a religion of the family, therefore, Jesus seems to have been intent on abolishing it, seeing its day as over. This ruthless attitude towards the family is something that later Christianity never entirely lost, even though the later rejection of family as a second-class Christian vocation would be based on very different premises.

This rejection of family did not mean that Jesus saw women as useless burdens. Jesus' treatment of his own mother would seem, at first sight, to indicate that she had lost her power as a good Jewish mother, because he literally had no time for her. In St. Luke's gospel there is a story that Jesus disappeared for three days during the family visit to Jerusalem for the Passover and was discovered in the Temple talking to the scholars there. When Mary reproached him for causing them so much anxiety, he coldly replied, "Why were you looking for me? Did you not know that I must be about my father's business?" His mother's feelings were no longer of any concern to him when God, his divine "father," called him. At the wedding feast of Cana when Mary told him that the wine had run out, Jesus at first impatiently swept her aside, sounding very much like an irritated modern man brushing off a mother's fussing: "Woman," he said, "what is that to you or to me?"—a Hebrew idiom that is commonly used to reject interference or to reject overtures of any kind. When one of his women listeners was so entranced by his teaching that she cried out, "Happy the womb that bore you and the breasts that you sucked!" Jesus shrugged off this praise of his mother. She was irrelevant: "Still happier those who hear the word of God and keep it" (Luke 11:27–28). The power that Judaism gave to women as wives and mothers seems, in Jesus' view, to have been lost.

Yet though St. Luke seems to denigrate women, it is he, more than any other Evangelist, who exalts Mary. When Mary sings the *Magnificat,* her great hymn of praise after Jesus' conception, she proclaims "from this day forward all generations will call me blessed" (1:48). God, she says, has exalted "his lowly handmaid" and there has been a revolution—a new order in which the poor, the lowly and the hungry and even women are exalted, and the mighty and the rich pulled down from their thrones and sent empty away. Former values have been reversed. In fact, in the Gospels as a whole women have rather a good press. They are not seen as irrelevant impediments. Some of Jesus' best friends were women. The women don't run away at the crucifixion, for instance, as do most of the male disciples. Often Jesus gives some of his most important teachings to women, like the outcast woman at the well in Samaria. He had a band of women followers in the tradition of the holy men of Galilee who had usually worked alongside women. Elijah and Elisha, for example, the two great Galilean prophets, had both had women disciples. Luke tells a story which is very instructive about the way Jesus saw women. He was friendly with a family in Bethany, near Jerusalem, consisting of two sisters, Mary and Martha and their brother Lazarus:

> In the course of their journey he came to a village, and a woman named Martha welcomed him into her house. She had a sister called Mary, who sat down at the Lord's feet and listened to him speaking. Now Martha who was distracted with all the serving said, "Lord, do you not care that my sister is leaving me to do the serving all by myself? Please tell her to help me." But the Lord answered: "Martha, Martha," he said, "you worry and fret about so many things, and yet few are needed, indeed only one. It is Mary who has chosen the better part; it is not to be taken from her."

(Luke 10:38–42)

Just as the male disciple had to be absolutely single-minded about his following of Jesus, even if that cut across his traditional male responsibilities as a husband, father or son, so too the woman has to pursue the only thing that is necessary: the message of Jesus. She has to do this even if that means neglecting her traditional responsibilities, leaving the kitchen and sitting at Jesus' feet, just as rabbinical students would sit at the feet of the great scholars in the Yeshivahs. Hitherto this kind of study had been for men only; the woman would be expected to do what Martha is doing—tiptoe around and make sure everybody is comfortable, while the men talk. Jesus' new world-order, which reverses old positions, is liberating women from domes-

tic triviality and giving them a place equal to men. It is in this light
that we can see some of his remarks to his mother. Women should no
longer waste their energies fussing about the catering arrangements
at parties. The idiom "what is that to you or to me?" for once has its
full meaning. To both men and women this kind of triviality is irrelevant, and they should seek the one thing necessary. Again a woman's
main glory is now no longer motherhood, even if she is the mother of
the Messiah (a glory still coveted by many Jewish women).

St. Paul is usually blamed for bringing the hatred of sex and the
consequent denigration of women into Christianity. However, if we
look at the passages where he appears to deride marriage, we shall
see that his views are far more lenient than Jesus'. His rejection of
marriage was not based on a hatred of sex, and like Jesus he believed
that in the new Christian order there was sexual equality. It is not
surprising, of course, that his views should resemble Jesus' and differ
from them only in their leniency. St. Paul's Epistles were written
before the Gospels—at least twenty years before the earliest Gospel,
St. Mark's. They were written by the Churches he founded, and
consequently they reflect his theology. However, in the time that
elapsed attitudes hardened among the Christians and became more
extreme as Christianity encountered more and more hostility in the
world. Like Jesus, Paul believed that the Kingdom of God was at
hand. It would certainly arrive during his own lifetime. Like Jesus,
he regarded his own time as a time of crisis. He calls the Christian
era "these present times of stress" (1 Corinthians 7:26). It is therefore pointless to get, literally, bedded down in family life and sexual
relationships. Nothing was going to last. However, unlike Jesus, Paul
thinks that if a man or woman is already saddled with a family he or
she shouldn't desert them. He should continue as he is (1 Corinthians 7:17). Paul is also a realist. Certainly it is better to be celibate but
if somebody is widowed and they find celibacy too hard, then it is
perfectly all right for them to marry again, and if a father feels that it
is not fair to deprive his daughter of the chance of marriage, then
again that is quite permissible. It is, Paul is adamant, "no sin" (1
Corinthians 7:6–28). Celibacy is not preferable to marriage because
sex is evil; celibacy leaves a man freer for the affairs of the Lord and
for prayer. To attempt celibacy if you are not naturally inclined to it
is only asking for trouble:

Yes, it is a good thing for a man not to touch a woman; but since sex is always a danger let each man have his own wife and each woman her own husband. The husband must give his wife what she has the right to expect, and so too the wife to the husband. The wife has no rights over her own body; it is the husband who has them. In the same way, the husband has no rights over his body; the wife has them. Do not refuse each other except by mutual consent, and then only for an agreed time, to leave yourselves free for prayer; then come together again in case Satan should take advantage of your weakness to tempt you. This is a suggestion not a rule; I should like everybody to be like me, but everybody has his own particular gifts from God, one with a gift for one thing and another with a gift for the opposite.

(1 Corinthians 7:1–7)

It is worth pausing for a while to consider Paul's teachings, because later Christians, down to our own day, totally misunderstood his lack of enthusiasm for sex, and theologians like the early Fathers of the Church who formed Christianity and who lived in a very different world and in a very different time would use his words to back up their own sexual neuroses. Paul is very clear that he is only making a suggestion about the advisability of celibacy and the role of sex in the Christian life. All he will be definite about is that sex is not sinful, that anybody who cannot be celibate should get married and that no married person should desert his sexual or his family duties and ties. "The rest," he says, "is from me and not from the Lord." It is his own personal opinion, not a divine decree:

Brothers, this is what I mean: our time is growing short. Those who have wives should live as though they had none, and those who mourn should live as though they had nothing to mourn for; those who are enjoying life should live as though there were nothing to laugh about; those whose life is buying things should live as though they had nothing of their own; and those who have to deal with the world should not become engrossed in it. I say this because the world as we know it is passing away.

I would like to see you free from all worry. An unmarried man can devote himself to the Lord's affairs, all he need worry about is pleasing the Lord; but a married man has to bother

about the world's affairs and devote himself to pleasing his wife:
he is torn two ways. In the same way an unmarried woman, like
a young girl, can devote herself to the Lord's affairs; all she need
worry about is being holy in body and spirit. The married
woman, on the other hand, has to worry about the world's affairs and devote herself to pleasing her husband. I say this only
to help you, not to put a halter around your necks, but simply to
make sure that everything is as it should be, and that you give
your undivided attention to the Lord.

Still, if there is anyone who feels that it would not be fair to
his daughter to let her grow too old for marriage, and that he
should do something about it, he is free to do as he likes; he is
not sinning if there is a marriage.

(1 Corinthians 7:29)

Paul is usually presented as the sexual rigorist who ruined the gentle
and loving gospel of Jesus. In fact, Paul has far more concern for the
stresses and strains of his disciples than his later followers, the Evan-
gelists, would show Jesus having in the Gospels. However, Paul's
letters show clearly that for the Christians of the first century the
family could only be secondary to the pressing urgency of preparing
for the Kingdom.

It seems then that first-century Christians did not value the family,
and saw celibacy and freedom from family ties as a preferable state.
However, this denigration of the family did not downgrade woman,
but tried to alter her role in life. She was no longer to find her chief
glory in marriage and childbearing. She, like her husband, had as her
first duty to be busy for "the Lord's affairs." It is noteworthy that in
both the passages I have quoted Paul is careful to give to women
equal rights and equal consideration. A wife owns her husband's
body just as much as he owns hers. Celibacy is not just an ideal state
for a man; it is better for the woman too not to be saddled with the
bother of looking after her husband and children. Paul is usually
seen as a misogynist, firmly preaching a woman's basic inferiority,
yet this is not fair. He, just as much as Jesus is seen to do in the
Gospels, was convinced that Christianity had liberated women from
their old roles and given them complete sexual equality with men.
"In Christ," he wrote, "there is neither male nor female" (Galatians

3:28). The Epistles and the Acts of the Apostles both make it clear that women, like Lydia, the seller of purple dyes in Philippi, were of the greatest help to Paul in his mission. They put their houses, their wealth and their inspiration at his disposal, and he was very dependent upon them. Many women of the upper classes were, the Acts tell us, extremely supportive to Paul. In those passages of his epistles where Paul sends his greetings to the various Christians in the Churches he is writing to, he mentions women just as frequently as men and scatters his praise and loving gratitude indiscriminately between the sexes. When he sends his love and thanks to the famous missionary couple, Aquila and Prisca, who were extremely valiant and important Christians, he mentions Prisca before her husband, against all common usage of the time. Later Christian writers in the New Testament would be far more misogynistic and dogmatic about a woman's place. The Epistles to Titus and to Timothy and, almost certainly, the Epistles to the Ephesians and Colossians (some of which contain teaching about women's basic inferiority) were not written by St. Paul, but a long time after his death by writers who saw themselves as Paul's successors and who, in the Biblical tradition, wrote in his name. By that time attitudes had hardened and the circumstances of Christians had changed.

Nobody is perfect, however, and there is one occasion when Paul's Jewish chauvinism does burst through. In the first epistle to the Corinthians where he is careful about giving women equality, Paul also writes tetchily about women who were not wearing their veils when they prophesied and prayed under the inspiration of the Spirit:

> What I want you to understand is that Christ is the head of every man, man is the head of woman, and God is the head of Christ. For a man to pray or prophesy with his head covered is a sign of disrespect to his head. For a woman, however, it is a sign of disrespect to her head if she prays or prophesies unveiled; she might as well have her hair shaved off. In fact, a woman who will not wear a veil ought to have her hair cut off. If a woman is ashamed to have her hair cut off or shaved, she ought to wear a veil.
>
> A man should certainly not cover his head since he is the image of God and reflects God's glory; but woman is the reflec-

tion of man's glory. For man did not come from woman; no,
woman came from man; and man was not created for the sake
of woman, but woman was created for the sake of man. That is
the argument for women's covering their heads with a symbol of
the authority over them, out of respect for the angels. However,
though woman cannot do without man, neither can man do
without woman, in the Lord; woman may come from man, but
man is born of woman—both come from God.

(11:3–12)

This piece of traditional Jewish teaching is quite at odds with the rest
of Paul's thoughts about the relations between the sexes and the role
of authority in the Church. In the very next chapter he writes his
famous passage about the Church as the Body of Christ, which absolutely rejects this kind of hierarchical thinking. It is noteworthy,
however, that by the end of his outburst against women, Paul is
coming round to his usual way of speaking about husbands and
wives, seeing an equality and interdependence of need. Later in the
same epistle, he says that when women are *not* inspired by the Spirit,
they should keep silent, and he backs this ruling by reference to the
Law of Moses:

As in all the churches of the saints, women are to remain quiet
at meetings since they have no permission to speak; they must
keep in the background as the Law itself lays it down. If they
have any questions to ask, they should ask their husbands at
home: it does not seem right for a woman to raise her voice at
meetings.

(14:34–35)

These rather bad-tempered remarks constitute the whole of Paul's
misogyny and are not characteristic of his usual egalitarianism. They
*are* characteristic of this particular epistle, however, and must be
seen in the context of Paul's relationship with the whole of the
Church of Corinth. The Corinthians were causing Paul a good deal
of anxiety, and later Christians in the city would begin a smear
campaign against him which would elicit his second letter to the
Corinthians, which is a passionate and personal defence of his position. There was a movement in Corinth which was preaching abso-

lute libertarianism. Each Christian felt that because he was inspired
by the Spirit he was a law unto himself and that anything he felt like
doing—even visiting prostitutes, getting drunk at the Eucharist and
taking part in idolatrous pagan feasts—was perfectly all right because he was already redeemed. Paul's letter shows that the Corinthians were becoming extraordinarily competitive about their special
gifts of the Spirit and were vying with one another about which gifts
were the most valuable. It is in this general context that we must see
Paul's remarks to the Corinthian women. It may well have been that
the women were also flinging themselves into the competition for
Prophet of the Year and defying the authority of the Church leaders.
For a woman in this atmosphere to throw off her veil while she was
inspired by the Spirit or to voice her opinions at a meeting could
have been a competitive challenge, which in Paul's teaching about
the Body of Christ in chapter 12 of the epistle and in his famous
hymn to charity in chapter 13 he shows to be ruining the religious
lives of the Corinthians and to be absolutely opposed to the true
Christian spirit, where everybody had his own part to play and competition about who worked the most miracles or whether the gift of
prophecy was "better" than the gift of tongues was ludicrous.

Paul was trying to pull the Corinthian men and women back to a
greater sense of responsibility. The early Church had a class of people who were "prophets," directly inspired by the Spirit and en-
trusted with divine messages to the Church. Paul fully accepted that
women, like men, could be prophets and that they too, with their
husbands, were directly in contact with the Spirit of Jesus. It may
have been that this was going to the heads (literally) of some women
and that the prestige that they gained by their prophecy meant that
they had started throwing their weight about at home in a way in
which Paul, who when all is said and done was deeply Jewish, could
not approve. That is why he tells them to wear their veils as a sign of
their subordination to their husbands and, when they are not inspired by the Spirit, to keep their mouths shut. In this Paul was just
like many men today in the modern world who may agree fully with
the principles of women's liberation, but whose inbuilt prejudices
break out unexpectedly on occasion, triggered off by the sight of a
woman being "too independent." While the outburst in I Corinthians is not characteristic of Paul's general attitude toward women,

later Christians, inspired by the sexual and misogynistic neurosis that crept into Christianity after Paul's time, would make great capital out of it and use it to keep women in their place.

It is due to Paul that Christianity moved away from Judaism and became firmly embedded in the Gentile world, where it remained. Inevitably, as more and more non-Jews flocked into the Church, they would bring their own pagan attitudes, prejudices and preoccupations with them. Inevitably also, as Jesus failed to return and establish the Kingdom of God, Christianity became more and more involved with this world. This Gentile pagan world was the world of the late Roman Empire, which was beginning its slow decline and fall. (Nero was the Emperor in whose persecution of Christians Paul is believed to have died.) Many people in the Empire were, naturally enough, reacting against the excesses—sexual and otherwise—of the late Empire and there were, in the religious and philosophical life of the time, movements of asceticism. The Stoics, for example, preached self-control, and the mystery cults of the period seem sometimes to have recommended periods of abstinence as a preparation for their secret rites. Inevitably Christianity was affected by this atmosphere. Western Greek-trained theologians had very different insights and neuroses from Paul, the Jewish Rabbi. For example, they misunderstood some of his Jewish terms. As the atmosphere in the West darkened and Rome began to fall to the Barbarians, the trauma would deeply affect influential theologians like Augustine, who would see rational self-control as a bulwark against the inchoate and savage forces of passion which could drag a man down toward bestiality, just as the Vandals and the Goths were destroying Greco-Roman civilization and pulling the West into the obscurity of the Dark Ages. As the atmosphere in which Christianity lived changed, so too did the neuroses and anxieties of Christianity itself. Although neither Jesus nor Paul had preached very enthusiastically about marriage, most Christians were married and, as the Kingdom didn't seem to be coming, were not so ready to be celibate as Paul's converts had been. Theologians had to come to terms with the place of marriage in God's plan, but Paul's injunctions to celibacy were never forgotten. The Fathers began to show a divided thinking. Marriage was part of God's plan, but sex was evil and should be avoided. The neurosis of Christians who couldn't cope with their sexuality in this frightening world, where excess seemed to have caused decline and fall and ruin, conflicted with their official teaching, and the conflict is still present in Christianity and in the West today.

It is very important to distinguish between official Christian doctrine on the one hand, and what I should like to call the Christian neurosis on the other. Paul had preached that marriage was permissible, and theologians have usually endorsed this. However, the Christian neurosis has led them to seize far more enthusiastically upon Paul's cautious words about the desirability of celibacy. The Christian may assert that the official doctrine of Christianity says that sex within marriage is good and can quote a long and distinguished tradition of theology which has upheld this. However, very often he *feels* that sex is shameful in some way, and this emotion has a long and distinguished tradition. This tradition of neurotic emotion has been transmitted steadily, throughout the two thousand years of Western Christian history, alongside official doctrine. We all have neuroses and emotional complexes which often contradict our rational beliefs and make us act destructively and in opposition to our ideals. In fact, the higher our ideals are, the more likely we are to be neurotic about putting them into practice. Christianity's ideals are supernatural and it was, perhaps, inevitable that it should produce neuroses which bear little relation to its dogma and beliefs. Our emotions and neuroses also tend to inform our thinking, and Christian dogma has also been penetrated by the Christian neurosis.

A good example of the way Christian emotion contradicts doctrine and still affects us in quite secular ways today is the matter of the human body. By the 3rd century, Christianity was committed to the *doctrine* of the Incarnation. This doctrine teaches that God, the second person of the Trinity, came down from heaven and took a human body. Jesus Christ was God and yet he was born of a woman, lived in the world in a human body, eating, drinking and sleeping like all the rest of us. For just over thirty years he led a normal physical life. He died physically, and the death of his human body redeemed the world. Three days later he rose again, but was not a ghost. His body rose again from the dead, triumphant now over sin and death. Jesus was at pains to show that his glorified body was not a mere spiritual thing: it could eat and drink and be touched and embraced. When he says the Creed a Christian not only believes in the resurrection of Jesus, but he proclaims his faith in the resurrection of his own body. The body, therefore, since the 3rd and 4th centuries has been absolutely central and crucial to Christian doctrine.

It should surely follow from this that Christianity of all the religions of the world should be the religion that values the body most. Because God valued the body enough to take it himself and use it to redeem the world, the Christian should value his own body as something sublime, not something that he will discard contemptuously after death, but which will be glorified eternally. However, merely to say this shows us how far the doctrine departs from the practice. Nobody would say that Christianity has taught us to love, cherish and value our bodies. In fact, most Christians have seen the Christian life in terms of a war against the body and the physical. Despite our zealous efforts to rectify this, we are still far from happy or at ease with our bodies. We tend to slouch around, presenting our bodies apologetically rather than proudly. Men stand with hunched shoulders, lolling against walls with their hands in their pockets, and women tend to twist themselves into strange contortions out of physical embarrassment. Very few girls stand up straight and confidently once they have attained puberty. When they speak to you or to each other they stick one hip out, hunch their shoulders, twist their legs around one another or stand so badly that their bosoms are concealed. This is very different from the way Arab or Indian women hold themselves. Despite the restrictions of their lives they are not physically abashed or ashamed in the way we Western women are, unless we make a special effort. Whether or not we accept the Christian message, we have been affected by Christianity's dislike of the body. We still tend to divide ourselves into body and soul; our spirits are the important and valuable parts of ourselves and our bodies are rather gross and shameful things which must not be pandered to.

Neither Jesus nor St. Paul would have understood this separation between body and soul because Judaism at that time did not divide people up in this way. When Paul decries the "flesh," as he so often does, he doesn't mean the body as opposed to the soul. In Jewish thought "flesh" meant man (soul and body together) in all his physical and moral frailty. When Job said that all "flesh" was grass and would wither away like the grass of the field, he was not speaking of man's physical body eventually dying. He was saying that the part of man which separates him from God and turns him away from true goodness is frail and doomed to destruction. For Paul "flesh" is not the body but man as he exists (body/soul together) unredeemed by Christ. The separation of man into body and soul came from the Greeks, but we also know that the Greeks thought of the body as something divine if it was beautiful. When later Greek-trained theologians read Paul's words about the "flesh" they naturally thought he was talking about the body, and that gave them a handle on which to hang their own neuroses about their bodies. Very early in Christianity the salvation offered by Jesus was seen as a liberation from the body. St. Ambrose, the 4th-century bishop of Milan, preached the idea of a wholly spiritual God, which was a revolutionary and inspiring idea to his disciple, the great St. Augustine, who later became bishop of Hippo in North Africa and who was, after St. Paul, probably the most influential theologian in the whole of Christian history. "Think of the soul," Ambrose wrote "rising free of the body, having turned away from sensuality and the sweet pleasures of the flesh, and cast off the cares of this worldly life" *(De Isaac,* iii, 18). For Ambrose the body was simply a soiled, tattered garment to be thrown aside when man was united to the wholly spiritual God. Augustine constantly echoed this idea. "Oh take from me this body," he prayed, "and *then* I will bless the Lord!"

In the lives of all the great Christian saints, we find this distrust of the body. Francis of Assisi used to call his body "Brother Ass," as though the body were some rather stupid and randy beast of burden which impeded the finer part of him, his soul. Often saints have undertaken a daily assault on the body in hair-raising mortifications. It is now deeply implanted in the Western consciousness that the body has to be disciplined and controlled. In English public schools boys take cold showers instead of lolling luxuriously in a warm bath, because such effete behavior is considered weakening. Girls when they are menstruating are told briskly not to "give in" to the pain. If we are tired or ill we force ourselves grimly and proudly to "carry on" even though our bodies are telling us very clearly that we ought to stop. The most surprising people raise disapproving eyebrows when you say that you want a taxi; it would be much better "for your soul" to walk or endure the discomforts of public transport. I would suggest that this punitive attitude toward the body and pride in physical discomfort is part of our Christian inheritance.

When we read the lives of some of the early saints it is tempting to wonder how Jesus would have reacted to the offensive they neurotically directed against their bodies. St. Jerome's account of his days as a hermit is very far in spirit from Jesus' life in Galilee. In the Gospels there is evidence that Jesus was considered rather a *bon viveur*. He would surely have been bewildered by this new Christian way of life which is now simply a way of starving and mortifying the body:

Oh how often, when I was living in the desert, in that lonely waste, scorched by the burning sun, which affords to hermits a savage dwelling place, how often did I fancy myself surrounded by the pleasures of Rome! I used to sit alone; for I was filled with bitterness. My unkempt limbs were covered in shapeless sackcloth; my skin through long neglect had become as rough and black as an Ethiopian's. Tears and groans were every day my portion; and if sleep ever overcame my resistance and fell upon my eyes, I bruised my restless bones against the naked earth. Of food and drink I will not speak. Hermits have nothing but cold water even when they are sick, and for them it is sinful luxury to partake of cooked dishes. But though in my fear of hell I had condemned myself to this prison house where my only companions were scorpions and wild beasts, I often found myself surrounded by bands of dancing girls. My face was pale with fasting; but though my limbs were cold as ice my mind was burning with desire and the fires of lust kept bubbling up before me when my flesh was as good as dead.

And so, when all other help failed me, I used to fling myself at Jesus' feet; I watered them with my tears, I wiped them with my hair; and if my flesh still rebelled I subdued it by weeks of fasting. I do not blush to confess my misery, nay rather, I lament that I am not now what once I was. I remember that often I joined night to day with my wailings and ceased not from beating my breast until tranquillity returned to me at the Lord's behest. I used to dread my poor cell as though it knew my secret thoughts. Felled with stiff anger against myself, I would make my way alone into the desert; and when I came upon some

hollow valley or rough mountain or precipitous cliff, then I
would set up my oratory, and make that spot a place of torture
for my unhappy flesh. There sometimes also—the Lord Himself
is my witness—after many a tear and straining of my eyes to
heaven, I felt myself in the presence of the angelic hosts.

(Letter xxii: To Eustochium)

Far from "not blushing" to reveal all this, Jerome positively revels
in this neurotic account, looking back to his desert days with a definite nostalgia. His oratory was quite simply a "place of torture for
[his] unhappy flesh." It does not need much psychological perception
to see that what is being set up before us as virtue is extremely
perverse and masochistic behavior. It is clear too that this massive
assault Jerome is waging day by day against his body is deeply sexual. Jerome, a typical "born-again" Christian, cannot come to terms
with his past unregenerate life when he was "surrounded by the
pleasures of Rome." The bevies of dancing girls that flaunt themselves before the crazed hermit and rage through his sick mind are,
we feel, an inevitable result of such a way of life. The body has a life
of its own and if you ill treat it like this it will kick back; sexuality is
not something that you can simply lock away and forget about. Either it will erupt in sick hallucinations or it will fester and go bad.
There is something repulsive about the relish with which Jerome
describes the hideous vitality of his sexuality—it is like raging
"fires," it "bubbles"—coursing through his emaciated and corpse-
like body. Jerome may seem extreme—even mad—but his hatred of
the body is by no means eccentric. It is not unusual in the lives of the
saints, who discovered most ingenious ways of torturing the body
and putting it to death, which is what the word "mortification"
means. The body is hated because it is sexual, and in a vicious circle
this hatred of the body increases the Christian sexual disgust, for in
sex man is at his most physical and so furthest from God. John
Colet, the humanist of the New Learning, loathed the obscurantism
of medieval and scholastic Christianity, yet in the matter of sex he
simply parrots the old view:

For while this sin is peculiarly a sin of the body, so is it a
turning away of the body from the soul in a peculiar degree, and
a dissolution of it in endless death. No transgression, accord-

ingly, is so specially ascribed to the body as fornication, seeing
that this is its own proper act; the one which loosens it from
continence and enslaves it to fall to ruin. In other cases the body
appears rather as the *instrument* of sin; in this of fornication, as
the very originator and agent.

*(On I Corinthians,* Chapter VI)

The female body was regarded with especial disgust, and it was a
source of deep embarrassment to the Fathers that Jesus was born of a
woman. They laid great stress on the fact, in sermon after sermon, in
treatise after treatise, that Mary remained a virgin not only before
the birth of Christ but afterward as well. Her hymen remained unbroken, her body remained sealed off and intact, unravaged by the
mess and bloody violence of childbirth. "To embrace a woman,"
wrote Odo of Cluny in the 12th century, "is to embrace a sack of
manure." The messy and mysterious innards of woman with her
voracious womb was particularly filthy, and the Fathers wanted to
make sure that Jesus had as little contact with this repulsive body as
possible. We try hard now to bring girls up to love their bodies, to
understand and feel proud of them. Some women even give puberty
parties when their daughters start menstruating. Yet at the same time
every Christmas women are expected to sing to listen to—in however
secular a context—the words from the *Adeste Fideles,* "Lo! he abhors
not the Virgin's womb," as though Christ's tolerance of a woman's
body was an extraordinary concession on his part. The fact that we
no longer even notice the words shows just how deeply they have
found acceptance in our minds.

Today we are making great efforts to make friends with our bodies.
We soak them and steam them in Jacuzzis and saunas, exercise them,
massage them, fill them with health-giving food and flaunt them on
nudist beaches. But there is something frantic and a little self-conscious about this sudden adulation of the body. There is also something poignant and ridiculous about the way women at feminist
meetings examine and admire each other's vaginas and naked bodies.
We are having to woo our bodies, reestablishing contact with them
after centuries of neglect. We are mounting a benign campaign to
befriend our bodies with as much zeal as Christianity mounted a
campaign to alienate and destroy them.

Sometimes we fall into patterns of behavior, however, which are disturbingly reminiscent of the Christian patterns. Our obsessions with health can make us as deeply intolerant of other people's physical habits as Christians have been to heretics or nonconformists. People get quite vicious about smokers, for example. We are making a religion out of our cult of health, and proselytize and excommunicate with all the zeal of our Christian forefathers who had found the path to salvation. It may be true that, now that our faith in the afterlife has weakened so much, the cult of health *is* a way of salvation because it will preserve us in this life for as long as possible.

The Christian attitude to sex and the body has been plagued by a process of doublethink. Christian hatred of the body does not cohere with the Church's condemnation of heretics who said that the body was evil any more than it coheres with the doctrine of the Incarnation. Dogma seems to exist in one part of the Christian mind, but alongside it exist neurotic emotions which, logically, completely contradict it but which still have a strong authority over the Christian and influence his behavior just as deeply, if not more deeply, than official doctrine.

Theologians have often defended the dogma of the holiness of married sexuality, but then, in an off-guard moment, have shown that emotionally they feel that sex is evil and abhorrent. Thus Augustine said that marriage was a Sacrament, because it was a symbol used by St. Paul to express Christ's love of the Church. However, Augustine also said: "We ought not to condemn wedlock because of the evil of lust, but nor must we praise lust because of the good of wedlock." It is an uneasy conundrum which shows the depth of his confusion. His teacher, St. Ambrose, has often been praised for his preaching of the holiness of marriage, but he was also called "the Doctor of Virginity," and said, "Virginity is the one thing that keeps us from the beasts." In the 13th century, the great Scholastic theologian St. Thomas Aquinas, who dominated Catholic thought until very recently, said that sex was always evil, but not always morally evil. This negative attitude was not confined to Catholicism, however. Luther and Calvin were both deeply indebted to Augustine and carried his negative attitudes towards sexuality and marriage right into the heart of the Reformation. Luther particularly hated sex, even though he himself got married and abolished celibacy in his

Christian movement. "No matter what praise is given to marriage,"
he wrote, "I will not concede it to nature that it is no sin." All
marriage could do was provide some poor remedy for man's uncontrollable lust: "How foul and horrible a thing sin is," he cried, "for
lust is the only thing that cannot be cured by any remedy! Not even
by marriage, which was expressly ordained for this infirmity of our
nature" *(Commentary on Genesis,* 3:9).

Luther's emotional revulsion from sexuality is profoundly Christian. It links sin and sex; furthermore, it views sex as something that
is uncontrollable and incurable in man, like a rampant cancer. "We
are so made," wrote Luther, "that when once our passions are
aroused we forget everything." This terror of sex derives from the
Christian connection which exists between sin and sex, and which
finds its most powerful expression in the doctrine of Original Sin.
This doctrine is now crucial to Christianity, and crucial also to the
Christian view of women. By the doctrine of Original Sin, Christianity teaches that God created men and women innocent and free from
sin. There was no human evil in the world, and man lived in a state
of Paradisal bliss. Adam and Eve lived joyfully and virtuously in the
Garden of Eden without sin and also without all the disorders that
now plague human life, like sickness and death. Alas, this happy
state did not continue, the Book of Genesis tells us. Satan tempted
Adam and Eve in the form of a serpent. He told Eve that if she ate
the fruit which God had forbidden them to eat she would be like a
god herself, knowing good and evil. Eve fell. She ate the fruit, gave
some to her husband and instantly their innocence was lost for ever.
They did indeed know good and evil, and saw at once that they were
naked. Horrified by their genitals, they covered them up with fig
leaves and trembled under God's condemnation. They were now subject to pain, sorrow, exhaustion and death. Further, they had let sin
loose into the world and could never regain their lost innocence.
What was worse was that all their descendants were similarly afflicted. It is not only that since the Fall of Man into sin everybody
will suffer sickness and pain and will ultimately die: we are all also
enslaved by sin. It is impossible for us to act correctly all the time
and we "fall" time and time again into wrongdoing, however hard
we try. Our nature has been profoundly damaged by the Original Sin
of Adam and Eve. But it could have been far worse. Because all of

Adam's descendants were born thus damaged, they were also doomed to eternal separation from the pure and sinless God who can tolerate no evil. This separation is called Hell, and over the centuries Christianity has built up terrifying pictures of this as a place of endless torment. If God had not been merciful every single human being born into the world would automatically have gone to Hell because of the sinfulness of the nature which he inherited from Adam. Fortunately, however, God promised that he would send a Redeemer, who was, of course, Christ. By his death on the cross, Christ atoned for the Original Sin of Adam and won for man the possibility of union with God. At Baptism, every Christian receives this "salvation" won by Christ, and even though many of the effects of Original Sin remain—we still get sick, we still die and, worst of all, we still commit sins in spite of all our good intentions—we are now "saved" from Hell and can live in union with God in this life and in the next if we sincerely try to live a good Christian life.

It is obvious that the doctrine of Original Sin is crucial to Christianity as we now understand it. However, it did not appear in its final form until the 4th century. In the Gospels Christ never once talks about the sin of Adam or about the effects of Original Sin in every one of us. He would probably have been rather startled by the doctrine as I have described it. Jesus, of course, was Jewish, and even though the Book of Genesis is a Jewish scripture there is nothing like the doctrine of Original Sin in Judaism. It is an entirely Christian invention. Judaism is a very pragmatic religion and has never been interested in working out all the knotty philosophical problems involved in the paradox of the existence of evil in a world created by a wholly good God. It prefers to cope practically with sin and evil as they crop up. Until quite late in its history, Jewish thinkers never once considered the question of how evil came into the world. Some two centuries before the birth of Jesus, the Rabbis began speculating about it for the first time and came up with some solutions which show how very differently Judaism and Christianity regard sin.

When the story of Adam and Eve was included in the Jewish scriptures, it was not at first seen by the Jews as an account of the First Sin in the Christian sense; for centuries it was considered to be a morally neutral myth. Other Jewish legends and writings refer to Adam without any mention of his "sin" and without any condemnation whatsoever. The story of the Garden of Eden expresses a very primitive Hebrew theology, found constantly in the first twelve chapters of Genesis. It is a story about the end of the Golden Age, when mankind acquired knowledge that God didn't want him to have. In the first chapters of the Bible, God seems a rather peevish and insecure deity, who is very jealous of man's knowledge and power. The story of the Tower of Babel, for example, shows God frightened both by man's technical skill and by men's ability to unite against him.

> Now Yahweh came down to see the town and the tower that the sons of men had built. "So they are all a single people with a single language!" said Yahweh. "This is but the start of their undertakings! There will be nothing too hard for them to do. Come, let us go down and confuse their language on the spot so that they can no longer understand one another."
>
> (Genesis 11:5–7)

The story of Adam and Eve was originally a similar myth. The serpent actually tells Eve the truth, and God seems to have told Eve a lie. Eve says that God has told her that if they eat the fruit they will die, but the serpent contradicts her. They will not die, he says, but become like gods, acquiring a god-like knowledge of good and evil. Sure enough, they do not die, but they do know good and evil. When, centuries after the story was written down, the Jewish Rabbis began to consider the moment when evil came into the world, some of them picked on the story of Adam and Eve as an account of the first sin, but this was by no means everybody's choice. Jews were not used, at this point, to reading the story as the story of the Fall of Man, and no matter how obvious such an interpretation seems to Christians, who have been conditioned to this particular reading by two thousand years of Christian teaching, many Rabbis discounted the story of Adam and Eve and chose another story in Genesis as a description of the moment when evil entered the world:

> When man had begun to be plentiful on the earth, and daughters had been born to them, the sons of God, looking at the daughters of men, saw they were pleasing so they married as many as they chose. Yahweh said, "My spirit must not for ever be disgraced in man, for he is but flesh; his life shall last no more

than a hundred and twenty years." The *Nephalim* were on the earth at that time (and even afterwards) when the sons of God resorted to the daughters of man, and had children by them. These are the heroes of days gone by, the famous men.

(Genesis 6:1–4)

This mysterious fragment was filled out in Jewish legends and appears in a number of apocryphal Jewish writings. Heavenly beings, like angels, mated with earthly women, and produced a race of giants, the *Nephalim,* who were like the Titans of Western myth. The "angels" brought mankind skills and knowledge from heaven and taught him civilization. They also brought man crafts like metal work, which enabled him to progress into the Iron Age. Like the story of Adam and Eve and the Tower of Babel, it is about the end of the pastoral Golden Age, but it is also very well qualified to stand as the story of the first sin. In Genesis because of this "sin" God sent the Flood, and therefore many of the Rabbis preferred this story to that of Adam and Eve, despite its prior position in Genesis, as an account of man's first sin.

A third group of Rabbis discounted both stories and came up with a third solution about the origins of human evil, which still shares the particularly Jewish view of sin. On one of the days of creation, they taught, God said, "It is very good" instead of merely "It is good" when he surveyed his handiwork. Why? Because on this day, God created the *yecer,* the evil impulse in man. Thus, Rabbi Samuel ben Nahman:

> *And behold it was very good.* This is the evil impulse. Is the evil impulse good? Yet if it were not for the evil impulse no man would build a home, nor marry a wife, nor beget children, nor engage in trade. Solomon said, "All labour and all excelling in work is a man's rivalry with his neighbour."
>
> *(Genesis Rabbah Ecclesiastes,* 4:4)

In other words the *yecer* theory persists, with the other theories, in linking the coming of sin with the coming of progress and civilization. You can't make an omelet without breaking eggs, nor can man progress and build a civilization while remaining in a state of childish pastoral innocence. Sin, for the Jew, may be very unfortunate in many of its aspects, but in another sense it is "very good" because it is the source of much of man's energy and creativity. The *yecer* is very similar to the concept of *libido* invented by that great Jew, Freud. It follows, then, that sin in Judaism is a very different matter from Christian sin. It is not a total disaster, and even though God punishes Jews in the Old Testament when they sin, he will always forgive them. There is absolutely no idea that all men inherit an innate sinfulness which will damn them eternally in the torments of Hell unless God sends a Redeemer. Some Jews at the time of Christ were certainly waiting for a Messiah, but no Jew was waiting for a Messiah to "take away the sins of the world."

The doctrine of Original Sin is, therefore, an invention of Christianity, and it has had a profound effect on Western culture. It teaches us that our "natural" state is evil and hopeless and has made religion for many people a desperate affair: a guilty battle with a self that seems to refuse salvation, a terror of "Hell" (which does not appear in the Christian sense in the New Testament) and finally, because of the way it was formulated, a fear of sex and a hatred of women. It was St. Paul who bequeathed the doctrine to Christianity, but even Paul would have been extremely surprised at the way the idea developed later. Paul took Christianity into the Gentile world. He believed that Christ had died for all men; the Kingdom of God would not simply be a Jewish triumph but a new type of existence for all mankind under the leadership of Christ. Christ had died to free men from sin and death. The controversy about when sin first entered the world was still going on among Jewish scholars and Paul, who was a serious scholar and a member of the progressive Jewish party, the Pharisees, before his conversion, was clearly of the Adam and Eve persuasion. When he writes about Christ's salvation, he says that as all men died in Adam, so all men would rise again to new life in Christ, thus using the kind of parallelism that a lot of Jewish scholars enjoyed. He did not mean that all men were literally condemned by the sin of Adam and "in" him were lost and wallowing in a damned state. He never discusses the ways that this Original Sin was passed on from one generation to another; he never discusses Eve's part in the Fall and he never links "Original" sin with sex. All these later developments were brought in by the Fathers of the Church during four centuries of discussion and speculation.

The Eastern Churches and the Western Churches took very different lines about Original Sin, and this is the origin of their fundamental differences about the role of sex and women in the Christian life.
Suffice it to say that the Western Fathers interpreted the Bible literally: the Adam and Eve story, for example, was not a myth to be
interpreted symbolically as it was for many of the Eastern Fathers, it
actually happened. It is therefore unfortunate that Western Fathers
like Tertullian and Augustine could not read Greek, the language of
the New Testament; instead they had to rely on translations like that
of St. Jerome, which was a brave attempt but often unsatisfactory. It
is also unfortunate that the most influential Western Fathers were
neurotic and highly emotional men. Tertullian, Jerome and Augustine were all Christians who were converted in a violent and explosive type of religious experience, people whom William James in his
classic work *The Varieties of Religious Experience* calls "twice-born."
James calls these people "sick souls," because their conversions were
often preceded by a morbid struggle with themselves and a very
gloomy outlook on life. The "once-born" soul on the other hand is
not converted in a traumatic experience, but approaches religion
much more peacefully, progressing quietly and logically in his religious life, without having recourse to exotic psychological experiences. N. P. Williams, in his book *The Ideas of the Fall and of
Original Sin,* notices that these "twice-born" people tend to adopt
theologies which are fundamentalist and literal, just as the emotional
Western Fathers did, and that they are unable to come to terms
peacefully with their sexual lives prior to conversion, as we have seen
in St. Jerome. Augustine saw his conversion in terms of a sexual
struggle. He prayed before his conversion: "Lord, give me chastity,
but not yet!", realizing that as far as he was concerned Christianity
meant celibacy. He sees his conversion entirely as a decision against
sex: at the moment he was "convinced" he noted that Christ had
taken away his desire for sex and family life.

Thus the Western Fathers of the Church who were most influential
because of their intellectual brilliance and forceful personalities were
all of a religious "type" which inclined them towards fundamentalist,
aggressive and anti-sexual theologies. They are not called Fathers for
nothing: from them was born Western Christianity. They were
deeply infected by the atmosphere of asceticism in Late Antiquity,

and their emotional temperaments together with their misunderstanding of certain subtle points in the Greek words of the epistles of St. Paul (like *sarx* [flesh]) meant that they were ill-equipped to provide the new Church with a healthy sexual rationale. Once-born Greek theologians, like Cyril of Alexandria, were developing far less frightening interpretations of the doctrine of Original Sin and were much less anti-sexual. For the Western Fathers, like Augustine, sex and sin became inextricably entwined for reasons that were personal and peculiar to the time and place but which had no real warranty from the New Testament. It is Augustine who finally formulated the doctrine, and it was the theology of Augustine which dominated the Church through the Dark Ages until he was superseded by the Scholasticism of Thomas Aquinas. However, Augustine's theology was given a new lease of life at the Reformation by Luther and Calvin: his sexual disgust, which informs Luther's theology, and his horrifying tendency towards Predestination, which influences Calvin. It was Augustine who formulated the doctrine that Christians still believe today:

> God indeed created man upright, being Himself the author of natures not of vices. But man, having of his own free-will become depraved, and having been justly condemned begat a posterity in the same state of depravity and condemnation. For we all were in that one man (Adam) seeing that we all *were* that one man who fell into sin through the woman, who was made of him before the sin.
>
> *(The City of God,* xiii, 14)

This view, that we were all "in" Adam when he sinned, derives from a misunderstanding and a far too literal interpretation of St. Paul's use of the word "in," which in Greek does not imply physical presence, but merely some loose and symbolic unity. Man is now depraved; there is nothing he can do about it. Because he was physically and potentially "in" Adam in the Garden, he is born into sin. And it is noteworthy too that in this first classic formulation of the disastrous doctrine of Original Sin, there is the woman, Eve, the cause of the sin of the man, Adam.

Eve appears again in another formulation of the doctrine by Augustine, which was to be seminal in Europe, inspiring Calvin among others. It is here too that we see sex as inherently evil. It is not that the first sin was sex. Augustine was a literalist: the sin was disobedience—Adam took the apple even though God had told him not to. However, the result of that sin is that although the Christian is "saved" by Baptism, he is still plagued by what Augustine calls "concupiscence." Concupiscence means the desire man has, against all reason, to take pleasure in mere creatures instead of in God. Concupiscence forces us to sin, when we desire something like an apple which cannot possibly satisfy us wholly and which God has forbidden. When do we experience concupiscence more powerfully than in sex, when two creatures take such passionate and violent delight in each other? God had created man as a deeply rational being: sin made him irrationally choose things that are less than God. Concupiscence is the essence of sin, because it makes us lose our reason and nowhere is the loss of rational control more acutely felt than in sex. It follows, for Augustine, that every child born into the world has sin passed on to it by its copulating parents and is thus doomed to eternal damnation. Sex is the means whereby Original Sin is transmitted (like a venereal disease which infects man's deepest nature) because it is now impossible for people to have sex without concupiscence. Adam and Eve had had sex *before* the Fall, Augustine says, but it was a very different matter then. It was a totally rational act, performed in obedience to populate the earth. "Away with the thought," Augustine cries in horror, "that there should have been any unregulated excitement or the need to resist desire!" Adam did not ejaculate in pleasurable orgasm, Augustine insists, but his semen was as calmly and as pleasurelessly discharged as urine or menstrual blood. This happy state of affairs came to an abrupt end, alas, once their natures were vitiated by irrational concupiscence. Sex had now got out of hand and become a raging and irrational force—concupiscence in its most basic and classic form, a mindless, bestial enjoyment of a creature instead of God who in the heat of passion is quite forgotten. It was sexual concupiscence which so often interfered with the contemplation of God, holding a man back "by a pressing throng of desires" which he cannot control. And because of sex and also because of Eve all men are doomed:

Banished (from Paradise) after his sin, Adam bound his offspring also with the penalty of death and damnation, that offspring which by sinning he had corrupted in himself, as in a
root; so that whatever progeny was born (through carnal concupiscence, by which a fitting retribution for his disobedience was
bestowed upon him) from himself and his spouse—who was the
cause of his sin and the companion of his damnation—would
drag through the ages the burden of Original Sin, by which it
would itself be dragged through manifold errors and sorrows,
down to that final and never-ending torment with the rebel angels. . . . So the matter stood; the damned lump of humanity
was lying prostrate, no, was wallowing in evil, it was falling
headlong from one wickedness to another; and joined to the
faction of the angels who had sinned, it was paying the most
righteous penalty of its impious treason.

*(Enchiridion,* 26, 27)

Sex, then, was created as something rational and good by God.
Sin, however, has so vitiated it that it is now impossible without
concupiscence. Every flicker of desire is an experience of essential sin
and a reminder of our "naturally" sinful nature. Augustine bequeathed to the West a terror of sin as a raging and ungovernable
force. And there, at the heart of each formulation of the doctrine, is
the woman Eve, the "cause" of all that misery, all that burden of
guilt and evil, all that human wallowing in sin. Sin, sex and woman
are bound together in an unholy trinity. For the celibate male like
Augustine the three elements of the trinity are inseparable. In the
West woman is forever Eve, luring man to his doom. Childbearing,
which in other cultures is a woman's chief pride and source of what
power she has, has been tainted with evil; it is the means whereby sin
is transmitted.

In the West guilt seems to be part of the female condition. When
we women have cause to feel guilty we wallow in it, and when we
have no cause we manufacture one, in a way that men simply do not
do. Many women who return to work after having a baby will tell
you that they feel guilty about their children, guilty about their husbands and guilty about the job because they are distracted from its
demands by their husbands and children. Other women feel guilty

because they are staying at home and enjoying being mothers and wives and know that they "shouldn't" want to do this at all in these liberated days. Mothers feel guilty eternally about their children, and this is hardly surprising. Modern psychology and popular manuals of childcare all insist that if a child is neurotic this is somehow the mother's "fault." Mothers also make their daughters feel guilty or somehow a failure if they have in some way not fulfilled parental expectations. Even in social gatherings or in office situations women are quick to blame themselves if anything goes wrong, feeling that somehow it is all their fault. Men also are in the habit of encouraging this guilt. They often imply in all sorts of ways that the women around them are inadequate. If they get upset, that is because their wives or lovers have wounded them, and even when this has not happened and the man gets upset for reasons quite extraneous to his woman, both of them will really believe that it is still her fault. Women spend their lives apologizing in ways that men never do. We are trained not to be assertive and to prelude a criticism or to herald our presence with an apology that might be verbal ("I'm sorry to disturb you . . . sorry to insist on this . . . sorry to have to tell you that your work is appalling") or might simply be a deprecating smile or apologetic shrug. We tend to define ourselves in terms of guilt, and our guilt blows our importance up out of all proportion. How can the average suburban housewife, who has been deprived of any real power and influence, be so totally responsible for the welfare of her children and her husband? How can *their* failures throughout life really be *"her* fault?" Where did women get all this power to effect disaster when society has stripped them of power and excluded them from offices of power? Women know the answer, but only in a confused way. We know that we are Eve, guilty and responsible.

When Europe fell into the intellectual abyss of the Dark Ages, it was Augustine's theology which dominated Christian thinking and it was the Church which was the only guardian of culture left in a world of barbarians. When Christianity arrived in Central and Northern Europe, the Germanic peoples would not have been particularly amenable to receiving Augustinian teaching. For one thing, they simply did not have the intellectual equipment to cope with the subtleties of his thought and his tortuous arguments. For another, they seem, as one would expect, to have been a randy lot who would not take kindly to all this talk of celibacy. Thus the 8th-century missionary St. Boniface writes in disgust about the English, who, he says, "utterly despise matrimony." They continue in their illicit relationships stubbornly "after the manner of neighing horses and braying asses." A century later, the monk Alcuin wrote that England "has been absolutely submerged under a flood of fornication, adultery, incest, so that the very semblance of modesty is entirely absent." The famous knights who, cleaned up and Christianized, would later inhabit the legends of King Arthur and his Round Table get a very different treatment in the writings of the Christian historian, Gildas. They are "sanguinary, boastful, murderous, addicted to vice, adulterous and enemies of God," and ". . . although they may keep a large number of wives, they are fornicators and adulterers." Rescuing damsels in distress meant something very different before these knights were Christianized, if we are to believe Chrestien de Troyes:

> The usages and rules at that time were that if a knight found a damsel or wench alone he would, if he forced her against her will . . . have been scorned in every court. But on the other hand, if the damsel were accompanied by another knight, and if it pleased him to give combat to that knight and win the lady by arms, then he might do with her as he pleased.

Neither the sexual nor the intellectual climate seemed hospitable soil for Christianity. In addition, for the peasants particularly, life was extremely hard. Famine and starvation were ever-present realities and agriculture was incompetent. The mortality rate was high. Few people had time for theology. The barbarian world, with its savage customs and desperate lifestyle, would, however, be tamed and civilized by the Church and would emerge in the late 11th century as Christendom, united under the Pope and dominated by Christian belief.

It was the Church which preserved the culture of the fallen Roman Empire in the Dark Ages; the Church alone could offer some hope or solution to a desperate, famine-ravaged Europe. The Papacy began a reform movement, cleaning up its own clergy and trying to reach the common people. Slowly the people learned the rudiments of the Christian faith. They did so not by reading theologians like Augustine for themselves, of course. They had a variety of teaching aids. During the Middle Ages the art of the great churches and cathedrals visually instructed men and women and impressed upon them the great images of Christianity. The medievals saw sculptures and frescoes of Adam and Eve clutching fig leaves to their genitals, and learned the Augustinian emotion of shame: sin, sex, sorrow and death were subliminally associated in the Christian, Western mind. The miracle and mystery plays also taught the Christian stories, but above all there was the sermon. During the Middle Ages originality was not prized as it is today. Just as the sculptors and painters did not sign their creations, a preacher would not be expected to stamp his sermon with his own insights. A preacher preached as scholars studied at that time, by constant deference to authorities. In a sermon the views of Augustine, Tertullian and Jerome were quoted. Other great sermons were quoted which also discussed these Church Fathers' views and slowly the Christian teaching, imbued by Christian neuroses, was spread among the population. It took a long time, and until the Reformation pagan ideas coexisted with orthodox Christianity in the popular mind in a pious muddle. Nevertheless, as Christianity spread, slowly too did the misogynism and sexual hatred of Christianity. Preachers were always male, of course. Increasingly, too, they were either celibate or being unwillingly forced into celibacy, so had a complicated attitude to sex. Nowhere is the sexual message, as it touched the ordinary people, more bleak and negative than it is in the directives for confession in which the Church tried to control the sex lives even of married people. Thus the Penitentials (guides for the clergy about how to judge the various sins of the faithful) show that in the early Middle Ages the Church was trying to enforce total abstinence on married couples. Sex was forbidden while a woman was pregnant, menstruating or breastfeeding, which was very prohibitive considering the extreme frequency of pregnancy, because, of course, contraception was forbidden. Sex was also forbidden during Lent and Advent, on Ember days and also on Sundays, Wednesdays and Fridays. It was also forbidden before receiving communion. By the time a virtuous and law-abiding couple had found a spare Tuesday which did not fall into any of these forbidden periods they were probably sexually paralyzed. The Penitentials are very concerned about the frequency of the sin of masturbation (in the five short Penitentials we possess there are twenty-five sections devoted to masturbation and another twenty-five about masturbation of the clergy). This could indicate that people were trying to keep the rules and were driven to masturbation because any other sexual outlet was forbidden.

The later Middle Ages added some refinements to the list of forbidden days. Different writers and sermons recommended different days, but the list was formidable. Thus sex was forbidden: on Thursdays in honor of Jesus' arrest, on Fridays because of his death, on Saturdays because it is Our Lady's day, on Sundays because of the Resurrection and on Mondays in commemoration of the dead. Fasting was recommended on these days also, thus reinforcing the neurotic linking of food and sex in the minds of the faithful. These rules were not compiled in a spirit of cold, ruthless calculation. They were flung together in desperation by the celibates, who found the very idea of sex going on on Holy Days intolerable even within marriage. Marriage may have been a "sacrament," but sex was unholy. Whether the laity actually obeyed these regulations or not, the constant recommendation of abstinence would have slowly impressed upon them that sex was a sinful activity that had nothing to do with the holy Christian life. Sex stood outside the idea of Christian holiness and the Christian life.

In the climate in which we now live, it seems extraordinary that confessors and penitents should have taken such directives seriously, yet it is salutary to remember that until about the 18th century, the sexual expectations of ordinary people were far lower than they are for the average person today, not because of any particular ideology, but for more basic, physical reasons. In his book *The Family, Sex and Marriage in England, 1500–1800,* Lawrence Stone has pointed out that very few of the masses of peasants and ordinary townsfolk remained sexually interested or attractive for long in their lives. It is not simply that people aged far more quickly than we do now and that by the time they were eighteen few people would have many teeth left, for example. There were other physical hazards. Malnutrition deriving from deprivation as well as from an inadequate diet was rife in Europe for long periods, and it is well known that this lowers libido. Also, unhealthy diet meant that many people suffered from appallingly disfiguring skin diseases. Women suffered from many vaginal and ovoid complaints which made intercourse frequently painful or impossible, and venereal disease was very common. In addition to this, men and women smelled. Even allowing for the fact that we are speaking about a society which did not value washing as much as we do, English women seem to have acquired a reputation among foreigners for being particularly smelly. It is also true that people were very basic about sex in Europe. Contemporary observers note that among the peasants foreplay was unknown in both France and England. It is likely then that the average person expected very much less pleasure from sex than we do today, when our expectations are sometimes rather too high. There was too the constant danger of pregnancy in an age when childbirth was perilous for a woman and often also resulted in the death of the child. It could well be that the spate of anti-sex propaganda put out by the Church struck a chord with many people, who probably did not see sex as something either fulfilling or life-enhancing, but rather as an appetite which had to be satisfied by any means at hand, just as their hunger for food was not satisfied by a *cordon bleu* meal, but by much cruder, unsatisfactory and even unpleasant food.

It is, of course, impossible to tell how seriously these directives to chastity were taken. None of the couples who were thus advised have left us any record of their reactions, their struggles or their rebellions. There is evidence that the Church took some time to impose her sexual views on the laity and that the older, healthier pagan attitudes survived for some time, alongside the new Christian views. However, as Europe emerged from the Dark Ages, a change in the climate of opinion in Europe does seem to have been effected by the Church. In the 10th century, the Church initiated a movement of reform, trying to clean up the morality described by Gildas and Alcuin. In particular, she wanted the clergy to live chaste lives, not simply because sex was evil and incompatible with the priesthood, but also because a celibate clergy was a powerful tool in uniting the Church and centralizing it under the Pope. Without a family and without dynastic interests, a priest would owe all his loyalties to his religious superiors. He would be less likely, for example, to be worried about his property if he had no children to leave it to. It is interesting that the Popes who pressed hardest to impose celibacy on the clergy were often popes like Gregory VII and Innocent III who were most successful in extending the temporal power of the Church.

Nevertheless, it took the Church a long time before she was able to make her clergy celibate. The clergy resisted furiously this attempt to regulate their sex lives—at one point they actually founded a rival Church with their own anti-Pope. If the priests were resistant, it is reasonable to assume that the laity were even more opposed to sexual control. Nevertheless, after several abortive attempts, Innocent III did finally manage at the Lateran Council in 1215 to make a ruling about obligatory clerical celibacy that was at last effective. It was effective because this time it was supported by the laity, who now themselves, after centuries of complete apathy on the subject, wanted a chaste clergy and were not prepared any longer to accept married priests. The long process of Reform had at last changed sexual attitudes, so that the ordinary Christian now felt that sex and marriage did not befit the holy vocation of the priesthood.

Yet still we occasionally see glimpses of a healthy sexuality which has refused Christian baptism. Juliet's nurse or Chaucer's Wife of Bath are fictional examples of the type of personality which managed to remain quite unaffected by the teachings of the Church. A real historical character who shared this attitude appears in the records of the Inquisition during the 14th century. Since the 12th century the southern region of Europe had been affected by the heresy of Catharism, which believed that Evil was as absolute as Good and that matter was evil and tainted. The body, sex and marriage were also condemned as physical and sinful, but Catharists held that if you could not be one of the celibate *Perfecti,* the top rank, it was better to be promiscuous than to marry, because marriage gave a legal blessing to something inherently Godless. In the French village of Montaillou, which was strongly infected by the Cathars, a woman called Fabrisse married into a heretical family, but because she herself had not joined the heretics she was thrown out of her husband's home and had to live in extreme poverty, earning her living in the local tavern. When her daughter Grazida was twenty-one she was called before the Inquisition not only because she was suspected of the heresy but also because she had been the mistress of the parish priest Pierre Clergue, who was both a Catharist and an Informer. Grazida's evidence has been recorded for us, and is a fascinating picture of a woman who has been entirely untouched by either orthodox or heretical views on sexuality:

Seven years ago, or thereabouts, in summer, Pierre Clergue came to my mother's house—she was out reaping—and incited me to let him make love with me. I consented; I was still a virgin then, fourteen years old, I think, or perhaps fifteen. He took me in the barn where the straw is kept, but not at all violently. Afterwards he made love with me often, till the next January, and this always in my mother's house. She knew and tolerated it. It was mostly in the daytime.

Then in January he gave me in marriage to Pierre Lizier, my late husband. And after that he still often lay with me, in the four years my husband was alive: my husband knew about it, and did not put up any resistance. When he asked me about our love-making, I said yes, it was true, and he told me to take care it should be with no other man. But Pierre and I never made love when he was at home, only when he was out.

I didn't know Pierre Clergue was, or was said to be, a cousin of my mother, Fabrisse: I had never heard anyone say so. I didn't know she was related to him by blood in any way. Had I known she was a cousin of his—though an illegitimate one—I would not have let Pierre near me. Because it gave me joy and him also when we made love, I did not think that with him I was sinning.

At the time we made love together, both before I was married and after, as our love-making in all that time gave joy to us both, I did not think I sinned, nor does it seem so to me now. But now there'd be no joy in it for me—so, if I were to make love with him now, I believe it would be a sin.

When I was married and made love with the priest Pierre it did seem more proper to make love with my husband—all the same it seemed to me, and I still believe, it was as little sin with Pierre as with my husband. Did I have any qualms at that time, or think that such deeds might displease God? No I had none, and did not think my lying with Pierre should displease any living being, since it gave joy to us both.

If my husband had forbidden it? Supposing he had—even though he never did—I still would not have thought it a sin, because of the shared joy of love. If any man whatever lies with any woman (unless she is related to him by blood), whether

she's a virgin or has been seduced, whether in marriage or outside it—all such coupling of men and women gives displeasure
to God, and yet I still do not think the partners sin, insofar as
their joy is mutual. . . .

I don't know, but I've heard it said that there is a paradise,
and I believe it; I've also heard there is a hell, but that I don't
believe, though I won't urge it is untrue. I believe there is a
paradise for it is something good, as I've heard tell; I don't
believe in hell (though I don't argue against it), for that is something evil as people say. I've often heard that we shall rise again
after death—I don't believe that, though I don't discredit it.

I still believe it is no sin when love-making brings joy to both
partners. I have believed that ever since Pierre first knew me.
No one taught me these ideas except myself. I haven't taught
them to others—no one has ever asked me about them.

        (P. Dronke, *Women Writers of the Middle Ages*, p. 205)

Grazida has not only been totally untouched by the Church's teaching about sex; she is quite ignorant about basic Christian teaching
like the existence of Heaven and Hell, which she has "heard about"
vaguely. About her sexual beliefs she can simply say "no one has
ever asked me about them." It was precisely to combat this kind of
ignorance, which left the common people wide open to heresy, that
St. Dominic founded the Order of Preachers—mendicant friars who
would wander about the countryside, preaching and teaching the
ordinary people the basic truths of Christianity. It was also this kind
of ignorance of course which contributed to the superstition that was
rife in the Catholic Church, where the magical reliance on relics and
incantations contains a good admixture of pagan beliefs. The Inquisition was set up to try to stamp out error and ignorance and to
correct people like Grazida, but there is evidence that Catholicism
was never very effective in spreading Christian teaching until after
the Protestant Reformation.

It was Protestantism and Puritanism which most efficiently and
effectively controlled the sexuality of the populace according to
Christian ideals. Protestants believed that every Christian was responsible for his or her own salvation, so they were much more
zealous about instructing the ordinary people in the basic teachings

of Christianity than the Catholics had ever been. Thereby they also spread Christian sexual guilt very efficiently—more efficiently than the Catholic Church. Protestant sexual teaching simply reverted to the old teachings of Augustine, which some Catholic theologians like Duns Scotus had shown signs of rejecting. The Reformers and after them the Puritans were able to enforce their rigid sexual morality on the ordinary people by judicial shaming punishments. A "sinful" woman had to stand in the Church wearing a white sheet, for example, and a couple who had produced an illegitimate child were flogged through the village. In *The Scarlet Letter* Nathaniel Hawthorne shows how this morality was imposed in the early days of New England. Hester has to stand in shame on the public pillory in acknowledgment of her sexual sin, which is treated not as a private matter but as a crime against the law of the land. She then has to wear perpetually a scarlet letter "A" on her chest as a token of her adultery and is cast out of the community. It is usually thought that Protestantism is more sexually lenient than Christianity. After all, Luther wanted to abolish clerical celibacy, and Protestant Churches now allow contraception whereas the Catholic Church continues to condemn it. This refusal to allow married couples to practice birth control springs from the Catholic refusal to admit that sexual pleasure is a good in itself; its only justification is procreation. A married couple must not copulate unless there is a possibility of a child being conceived, because otherwise they are indulging themselves by having sexual pleasure for its own sake. The Protestant admission of contraception certainly shows a more positive vision of the role of lovemaking in married life. However, Protestantism has consistently adopted more cruel and ruthless policies against sexual offenders than Catholicism during its history. Its policies have often been far removed from Jesus' treatment of the woman taken in adultery.

The Catholic Church was simply not efficient enough to enforce its sexual ideals as strongly as Protestantism. Perhaps this is the reason why in Catholic countries like Italy there is a greater appreciation of sex and, in some respects, a greater appreciation of women than there is in countries that are traditionally Protestant. Despite the proximity of the Pope the people have been left, sexually, to their own devices, as Grazida was. The Italian mother, deeply respected and powerful within her family, resembles non-Christian women of the Mediterranean world like the Islamic Arab mothers far more than she resembles her Christian sisters in England or Germany, where mothers simply do not enjoy the same prestige. It is impossible, however, to generalize too much about the sexual freedom of the populace in Catholic countries. Ireland is a Catholic country where the sexual teachings of Catholicism seem to have definitely taken. Spain, which was strongly affected by Islamic occupation, has been affected sexually and in its attitude to women by Moslem ideals, for better and worse. Spanish women tend to be guarded and shielded from the world in quasi-harem conditions that are clearly reminiscent of the way Moslem women are shielded. However, it is also true that they and their menfolk often exude a passionate sensuality which is also Arab and alien to traditionally Protestant Christian countries. Seclusion from the world is a sign that the Moslem respects his women too much to let them mingle with the sordid and dangerous world of the market place. There is evidence that Western women who settled in the medieval Crusader Kingdom of Jerusalem gained a respect that their sisters were certainly not enjoying in Europe in the misogynistic 12th century, and that they gained this respect from their contact with Islam. Many Crusader women took to wearing the veil, seeing the prestige and respect it afforded Moslem women. Spanish women too have derived a similar mystique that is alien to their treatment in Protestant countries, even though this does also mean that their lives are far more circumscribed.

There is, however, one phenomenon that shows that despite the real inefficiency of the Catholic Church, Christianity was still managing to create a very unhappy sexual climate which made ordinary people rush in droves to adopt extreme and even eccentric solutions to their sexual problems. Time and again, from the 2nd century on, heresies have sprung up within Christianity which say that sex and the body are evil. Repeatedly people who have called themselves Christians in both the Catholic and the Protestant worlds have denounced and outlawed sexuality or else have advocated promiscuity. So ingrained and so widespread was the sexual disgust of Christianity that heresies were constantly trying to find better solutions to the problem than those supplied by Orthodoxy. One of these heresies was Catharism, which proved so powerful that after gentler methods had proved unavailing and Catharism had spread rapidly throughout southern France, the Church eventually summoned a Crusade against the heretics and put them to death by the sword. The first of these anti-sex heresies, however, was Encratism, which sprang up during the 2nd century. It produced a number of scriptures, like the *Acts of Thomas* and the *Acts of Paul,* which all say that sex is degrading and that it is only celibacy which will bring us to the Kingdom of Heaven. These scriptures were read and enjoyed for a long time by perfectly orthodox Christians. It has been said that because these texts were heretical and unofficial—the mere Sunday afternoon reading of Christians—they should not be taken seriously, but it seems that precisely for this reason they should be taken very seriously indeed. Devotional works like the lives of the saints and the *Imitation of Christ* have had far more influence on ordinary Christians than Aquinas' *Summa Theologica.* That these texts were read for centuries by non-Encratists, who found nothing extraordinary in the idea that sex is evil and that married couples must abstain from "this filthy intercourse" *(Acts of Thomas* xiv), shows that the average Christians were getting a very negative message about sex. Indeed, it is difficult to see how Encratists differed from the Orthodox. When the *Acts of Andrew* says that marriage is a "foul and polluted way of life," is that really very different from St. Jerome's remark: "If we abstain from coitus we honor our wives; if we do not abstain,—well, what is the opposite of honor but insult?" *(Adversus Jovinian,* I, 7). When the Encratist *Acts of John* says that sexual intercourse is "an experiment of the serpent . . . the impediment which separated from the Lord," we are getting very near to the eventual Orthodox view which linked sin and sex. When Martin of Tours, a perfectly Orthodox saint, compares the pure ungrazed field of virginity to the field of marriage which is torn up by the pigs and cattle of fornication, it seems an Encratist remark. The trouble was that these heresies—Encratism, Montanism, Catharism, Manichaeism—were more orthodox than the Orthodox. Instead of hedging round the worrying neurosis of sex with Orthodox doublethink, they made it explicit and so could focus on it clearly. The fact that they attracted large followings also shows that they appealed to a common anxiety. The antisexual neurosis flares up again and again within Christianity powerfully and repeatedly. It is impossible to stamp out. Manichaeism is still rife in Eastern Europe and perhaps has affected our present

Polish Pope's sexual rigorism. The Church may condemn it, but ultimately she cannot deal with this anti-sexual heresy except by neurotic violence. People were clearly made worried about sexuality from as early as the 2nd century within Christianity. Even if ordinary Christians did not observe all the Forbidden Days and Practices of the Penitentials, it would seem, by the extraordinary recurrence of this heresy in its various forms, that the sexual climate of Europe was becoming increasingly unhappy.

Perhaps the most astonishing manifestation of the heresy was the Shakers. Their leader was the English woman Mother Ann Lee, who in the late 18th century discovered that celibacy was the answer to her own sexual problems. She had been married to a man of whom she was very fond, but she bore four children with considerable pain and danger and then lost all of them in infancy. This made sex terrifying and intolerable to her. Her husband and the Church authorities told her that she must return to her conjugal "duty," but she was too afraid to do so. She also had to do battle with her own sexual needs, and spent night after night calling out to God for deliverance. Ultimately she found relief by joining a branch of the Quakers, called Shakers, because of their ecstatic singing and dancing: in this tranced dancing and the release it engendered Ann discovered a way of coping with her celibacy. After one of these noisy sessions, Ann Lee was imprisoned for disturbing the peace, and in a jail in Manchester she had a vision. She saw Adam and Eve copulating in the Garden of Eden, and realized that sex was the sin which had caused the Fall. It must therefore be absolutely prohibited. Later Jesus appeared to her and told her that she was right to shun sex: he gave her a mission to spread the gospel of celibacy throughout the world. Ann Lee converted her fellow Shakers to her beliefs and took control of the movement. It was to accomplish her mission that she emigrated with her first followers to America, where the Shakers enjoyed spectacular success and founded several colonies where men and women—many of them married—lived together in total chastity.

It is most unlikely that Ann Lee, who was a dynamic and capable but quite uneducated woman, had read either Augustine or Luther, but she reproduced their views exactly. Benjamin Seth Young, her disciple who expressed her message for her in *The Testimony of*

*Christ's Second Appearing*, had also probably never read any of the great theologians, but here we find views that exactly reproduce Luther's terrors of the uncontrollable dangers of sex:

> What is there in the universe, within the comprehension of man, that has so sensible, so quick and ravishing an operation, as a corresponding desire of the flesh in the different sexes? . . . As a gushing fountain is more powerful in its operations than an oozing spring; so that desire of carnal enjoyment, that mutually operates between male and female, is far more powerful than any other passion in human nature. . . . Surely then, that must be the fountain-head, the governing power that shuts the eyes, stops the ears, and stupefies the sense to all objects of time or eternity, and swallows up the whole man in its own peculiar enjoyment. And such is that feeling and affection which is formed by the near relation and tie between male and female; and which being corrupted by the subversion of the original law of God, converted that which in the beginning was pure and lovely, into the poison of the serpent; and the noblest of affections of man into the seat of human corruption.

It would be hard to find a better description of concupiscence. It could almost have been written by Luther or Augustine, yet it is spontaneously produced centuries later by simple people who almost certainly had no intellectual training, but who knew very well how Luther and Augustine *felt* about sex.

America was suffering an extreme sexual crisis in the 19th century. Many Americans felt such intense sexual disgust that they were quite prepared to disrupt their entire lives. Married couples with their children moved into the Shaker colonies, selling up their homes and embracing total celibacy. Men and women lived side by side during the day, but slept apart in separate dormitories at night. As though celibacy were not difficult enough, new Shakers had to learn to live an entirely communal life, to give up domestic privacy and submit entirely to the total authority of the Shaker leaders—who were, to add to the difficulty, often women. Their sexual desperation must have been great indeed. Shakerism had a long history. Mother Ann arrived in America in the 1770s, and the movement was very strong until the 1840s. New recruits flocked in to the colonies and Shaker children grew up to form a second and third generation. Although it slowly petered out, there are a few Shakers still living in New England.

Shakerism clearly fulfilled a need for many Americans. There were also many other sects which experimented with celibacy like the Shakers or flirted with "free love," showing that the sexual malaise had crossed the Atlantic. The sexual crisis in America expressed itself in a variety of religious visions, and indeed was inspired by a religious revival in the country. The area around New York State was swept so frequently by the flames of revivalist ardor that it became known as the Burnt Over district. It was a Christianity that was charismatic, visionary and revivalist in tone, and Evangelical preachers preached a highly charged and emotional creed, which was in sharp contrast to the more restrained, conventional Congregationalism and Episcopalianism of Eastern America. At the same time as America was undergoing its explosion of sexual distress, England was in the grip of the sexual nightmare of Victorianism. This too coincided with a surge of religious fervor which swept away the cool rationalism of the 18th-century Enlightenment. It is as though the Age of Reason in Europe simply pushed the irrationality and neuroses under the carpet, where they festered and gained new life to break out again in the 19th century more violently than ever before. Indeed, the history of the Protestant West has been characterized by these extreme and unhealthy alternations between sexual libertinism and sexual repression, and these alternations have always coincided with the decline and the rise of religious fervor. It is a phenomenon that is peculiar to the West and which historians of sexuality have only been able to attribute to Christianity. Christianity has created a climate where sex can never be regarded simply as play. You have to love it or hate it passionately. Either it is an activity that is brimful of sin and corruptive concupiscence, or it is a functional exercise in which pleasure must be subordinated to procreation. The ban on contraception, still advocated in the Catholic Church, springs from this horror of sexual pleasure, which is as old as Augustine. It has sometimes led Catholics to ludicrous extremes, as when the great 17th-century Casuist Suarez speculates tortuously on the plight of a man who is having sex with a whore and who is suddenly overcome with remorse: should he withdraw or should he continue? To withdraw would, perhaps, make him guilty of a worse sin than mere fornication—contraception. This absurd lack of humor characterizes the desperate Western attitude to sex. Even in those periods of sexual relaxation, as in the 18th century for example, there is something frantic in the constant rutting of a Don Juan, and the perversions of the Renaissance period, with its cruelty and sadism ever in the background, are reminders that even when the West is sexually at play sickness is never far away. Sex is too serious and too dangerous to play at.

Never has the explosion of sexual hatred expressed itself so acutely as it did in Victorian England. Evangelicalism had become a powerful force, spreading from the newly emerging middle classes into the upper classes. It was a form of Christianity which was deeply Calvinist in its distrust of pleasure. Thus the Evangelical Sir James Stephen once smoked a cigar and found it so delicious that he never smoked one again. Yet Evangelicalism was not the only form of repressive religion current in Victorian society. The puritanism of Methodism and the nonconformist sects was as morally earnest and ascetic in tone as the Oxford Movement. The asceticism was indeed a reaction to the apparent permissiveness of the 18th century, but it was not a new phenomenon in the country, as has often been argued. Rather, Victorian hatred of sex was as old as Christianity itself. When we read a passage like this one, from the popular work *The Duties of Parents: Reproductive and Educational* (1872), we find ourselves in a very familiar world:

> Our children must be taught, from the earliest periods at which their minds can grasp such teaching, the inviolable sanctity of their sexual nature—the irreparable ills which follow its abuse. They must be saturated with the conviction that impurity is a foul and hateful sin, that the perversion of these instincts through whatever agency is a plunge into a fathomless abyss of turpitude from which they will never emerge with a clean soul.
> (pp. 132–33)

It is the world of Luther and of Augustine. Sex is an uncontrollable force which will sweep the hapless Christian child into an abyss of depravity. There is also the typical Christian doublethink: sex is holy and yet at the same time profoundly dangerous. It has acquired an almost pagan danger: it is so "holy" that any small sullying of this awful power will result in appalling requitals, as the sacred instinct revenges itself. Children must be watched over scrupulously, the Evangelical writer Elisabeth Sewell maintains. If they start chattering impurely, God will forgive them but the effects will stay with the child forever:

> The scars will always remain; visible to the inward eye, though unseen by man, and, as we may humbly trust, blotted out by God. And they will not only be seen as scars, disfigurements, but they will be felt as wounds; they will give the pain of wounds; an ever-increasing pain as the spirit longs more and more intensely for that purity of heart bestowed upon them who shall hereafter "see God."
>
> (*Principles of Education*, 1865, II:81)

The confusion of thought here echoes that of the Early Fathers. It is an appalling world-view. It represents a God who will punish the idle chatter and sexual curiosity of a child with lifelong wounds and disfigurement. This portrait of God entirely contradicts the Christian teaching about a God of Love who is ever ready to forgive sins, which can only be because the Christian emotion about sex as inherently sinful is more powerful than the mere dogmas of the Churches.

The fear of sex, accentuated on the one hand by the religious revival of the period and on the other by the threats that science offered to religion, invaded even the political sphere in Victorian England. Darwinism had shown man's animal origins, and where, as Augustine and Ambrose had said centuries before, is man more bestial and irrational than in sex? A form of moral "evolution" had become popular even before *On the Origin of Species*, however. As Tennyson put it in that quintessential poem of the period, *In Memoriam*, man has evolved from the animal, and now each man must

> Arise and fly
> The reeling Faun, the sensual feast;
> Move upward, working out the beast,
> And let the ape and tiger die.
>
> (cxviii)

It was a human's duty to shun his lower animal, sensual nature and scale the spiritual heights of true humanity. At the same time the threat that scientific discoveries could overthrow the claims of religion threw Victorians into a state of panic. If man were not a divine and spiritual being with no immortal or eternal destiny after this life, then he was no better than the beasts, and love became simply brutish lust, swallowed up in oblivion.

> And Love would answer with a sigh,
>     "The sound of that forgetful shore
>     Will change my sweetness more and more,
> Half-dead to know that I shall die."
>
> O me, what profits it to put
>     An idle case? If Death were seen
>     At first as Death, Love had not been,
> Or been in narrowest working shut,
>
> Mere fellowship of sluggish moods,
>     Or in his coarsest Satyr-shape
>     Had bruised the herb and crushed the grape,
> And basked and battened in the woods.
>
>                        (xxxv)

Here in Tennyson's great doubtful poem, we see the transition between the age of faith and the age of doubt. If the doctrine passes, the emotion of Christianity remains. The Victorian did not stop to consider that if there were no longer a Heaven or a Hell, he was free to enjoy himself here, without the restrictions of Christian belief and the threat of punishment in the next world. The emotion of sexual disgust persists, indeed is intensified as faith in Christian teaching crumbles. This terror of unbridled sensuality meant that anybody who professed a sexual liberalism was suspected also of political and revolutionary extremism. To let rip the sensual beast in man would produce just the same social anarchy as would occur if the bestial proles took over. If the sexual line over which it was dangerous to cross were not observed, not only would each man be sucked into a whirlpool of meaningless moral anarchy, the whole of the social order would crumble into mindless, sensual chaos.

The vision of sex as the activity which brings us closest to beasts and which makes us less than human had been bequeathed to the West centuries before. Victorianism was not an aberration, it was merely an extreme expression of a well-established neurotic tradition. Sex was dangerous. It was even physically dangerous. A sexual disease called spermatorrhea was invented, whose symptoms were premature ejaculation, wet dreams and imperfect erections. It became the bogey of Victorian men. Any sexual activity which seemed beyond a man's control became a symptom of this imaginary illness. "Hundreds of young men are driven to suicide by the disease," said the contemporary writer T. L. Nichols. Terrible contraptions were invented for men to wear at night to control seminal emissions. The seed must not be spilt frequently—the physical consequences could be fatal. On the other hand, the Victorian sexologist Drysdale painted an equally terrifying picture of too much chastity. If a man didn't get enough sex he could become dangerously ill or at least develop spermatorrhea and impotence, but it was a very fine line, because too much sex was equally fatal. On no account must it occur more than twice a week, Drysdale decreed. You couldn't win. As one would expect, the Victorians developed an absolute terror of masturbation. As the sex historian of the period, Dr. Acton, explains:

> Few young persons, perhaps, come into contact with so many conscience-stricken young men as I do. If a youth has abused himself, as soon as he learns the consequences, he becomes alarmed, and sets down all his subsequent ailments to the particular cause which is uppermost in his mind.

Sex was invested with a horrifying power of life and death, as Eric Trudgill explains in his book *Madonnas and Magdalens, The Origins and Development of Victorian Sexual Attitudes:* "Sex is thought of as a universal and virtually incurable scourge. It cannot ultimately be controlled and serves as a kind of metaphor for death in the way that cancer does today" (p. 54). This power had been handed to it by Christianity.

We are fond of saying today that we have still not fully recovered from the repressions and terrors of the Victorian period and that the desperation of contemporary sexual permissiveness is both a natural and inevitable reaction to it. However, it is not simply an aberration of seventy years in the 19th century that we are fighting today. It is two thousand years' worth of cultural conditioning that we have to reckon with. It is not a question for us in England of "recovering" from a temporary disease that afflicted our country and returning to the jollity of Pepys' London or the sexual frolics under the Greenwood Tree in Merrie England. Those periods had the same old sexual problems. The 18th century produced de Sade as part of its sexual reaction to Puritanism, and the swiftness of the West to respond to this perversion speaks volumes for our attitude to sexuality. Merrie England was riven not only with aggressive religious persecutions and factions but with personal strife and bitter feuds in the villages in which love was very difficult to cultivate. Sex, we have seen, was never considered "Merrie." It would soon be overtaken by the rigorism of the Protestant/Puritan Ethic. It has always been difficult to shed the sexual neurosis of Christianity even when a society is confident that it has done so successfully.

There is every evidence today that we are returning to a period of relative sexual repression and are abandoning the apparent liberation of the 1960s. Perhaps the current religious revival is yet again bringing the sexual pendulum swinging towards restraint. Yet even in the height of the so-called Permissive Society there were signs that all was not as liberated as it might seem on the surface. There was and is still a good deal of the old Christian doublethink about sex. Nancy Friday in her book *My Mother/My Self* has shown that mothers often pass a sexual neurosis to their daughters without realizing that they have done so. The mothers *think* that they have told their daughters how wonderful and fulfilling sex is, but when interviewed it is clear that the daughters have "heard" the feeling that exists behind the words. What the daughters quite genuinely claim to have been taught is that sex is frightening and dangerous. They have picked up the neuroses of their mothers, which are more powerful than any cheering words and positive sermons about sex.

Michel Foucault has suggested that the Penitentials and the Confessional actually paved the way in Europe to the discussion of sexuality that characterizes the present scene. Certainly we have remained very willing to hand our sex lives over to be examined by experts, in the same way as Christians used to let their sex lives be examined by priests. It is true too that we still seek orthodoxy in sex even when we are trying to be liberated. The most famous sex manuals of the 60s, like Reuben's *All You've Ever Wanted to Know About Sex* and *Every Woman Can* and "J's" *The Sensuous Woman,* seem very frank and free, but these so-called experts are actually merely reinforcing old orthodoxies. Thus homosexuality is still seen by Reuben as something that needs to be "cured" by the priest/doctor, the missionary position is still *the* best position, other more experimental forms are relegated to the sidelines of the sexual experience and people are urged to strive for sexual "normality." So conservative and orthodox are the manuals that *Every Woman Can* does not mean that every woman can have an orgasm, but that every woman can have a husband! Orthodoxy in sexual matters persists, for all our talk about freedom. Most people continue to think that there is only one way to manage sex and that every other way is wrong. It has been said that sexual prejudice is the last prejudice to be condoned in our society. We "know" that racism and classism are wrong now, but a lot of people remain convinced of the need to "draw the line somewhere" in matters of sexual freedom, and there is still the fear that once that line is crossed, then all hell will be let loose. We persist in thinking of sex as something powerful and dangerous which has, somehow, to be rigidly controlled and kept within bounds. We have also given sex too much power, just as Augustine, Luther and the Victorians did. Sex for them was powerfully present, a constant and looming danger. Today we have gone rather to the other extreme. Sex is wonderful, we proclaim loudly, but we are perhaps investing it with power it cannot have. It has been presented to us since the '60s as the universal Panacea and as the Answer to Life, raising expectations that it cannot possibly fulfill.

It is quite clear to me that despite all the positive remarks Church leaders have officially made about the holiness of married sex, Christianity created a most unhappy sexual atmosphere in much of Europe and America that would have astonished Jesus and St. Paul. It is obvious how this would affect women. For an Augustine, struggling with celibacy, women could only be a temptation, luring him away from his safe and holy sexlessness. That the sexual neurosis of Christianity deeply affected the status of women can clearly be seen in the fact that when women joined the anti-sex heresies and became celibate they very often enjoyed a prestige and respect that they would never have enjoyed in Orthodoxy. It is clear in the case of

Mother Ann Lee and her successor to the Shaker leadership, Lucy Walker. In Catharism too women were deeply respected. The Catharist élite included men and women, and the activities of certain Catharist women like Esclarmade de Foix scandalized the orthodox clergy. On one occasion during a debate between the Catholics and the heretics, a monk shouted out "Go, madam, spin at your distaff! You know nothing of such matters." In these anti-sex heresies women enjoyed equality. It seems that once a woman shed her sexuality she was accepted as a perfectly respectable human being.

# 2

# THE RESULT: EVE

"Women have very little idea of how much men hate them," Germaine Greer wrote in *The Female Eunuch*, in what has become a very famous sentence.

> Any boy who has grown up in an English industrial town can describe how the boys used to go to the local dance halls and stand around all night until the pressure of the simplest kind of sexual urge prompted them to *score a chick*. The easier this was the more they loathed the girls and identified them with the guilt that their squalid sexual release left them. "A walk to the bus-stop was usually good for a wank," they say bitterly.
>
> (p. 293)

The frequency with which that opening sentence has been quoted shows that it struck a chord of recognition in many women, even if we have not personally been "scored" in this particular way. It is often surprising how even a most gentle and friendly man can come out with a hostile remark that is breathtakingly unkind, and then continue in appreciative and affectionate conversation, quite unaware of what he has said. Of course it doesn't apply to all men, but it is a rare woman who can lay her hand on her heart and say that she has never encountered an irrational male hostility. Even the wolf whistles that echo from building sites as a hapless female walks past have about them something jeering and scornful. It is interesting that Germaine Greer, after making her arresting opening sentence, instantly identifies this "hatred" with sex. The atmosphere in a strip club in Soho and Amsterdam is a very different thing from the more ebullient atmosphere in an Arab belly-dancing show. In London and Amsterdam there is contempt for men in the way a woman takes off her clothes and a definite hostility in the way she is often presented for men's delight with a halter round her neck or weighed down with chains. This may be an extreme situation, but it is often the case that the extreme can throw light on the more mundane. The way models are photographed to sell products in advertisements also often reflects this sexual hostility between men and women. The women glare into the camera sullenly and sexily or gaze contemptuously past the viewer into the middle distance as though he did not exist. Often two girls have their arms round each other as they pout seductively, as though the sexy female race is linked against the male world in a threatening solidarity, or they gaze yearningly at one another in a sexual rejection of men. This new unsmiling sexiness is the traditional scowl that girls formerly wore only in pornographic photography, but which has now spread from the pages of *Playboy* out onto the billboards and into the Sunday color supplements. The hatred and contempt that men feel for women in pornography is now becoming more and more a common image of woman: pouting, scowling, hostile and seductive. We are not happy about sex in our culture and this must affect the way women see themselves and the way that men and women view each other.

From almost the earliest days of Western Christianity, men started to see women as sexually dangerous and threatening, and in the grip of this fear they started a process which would eventually push women away from the male world into a separate world of their own. This might at first seem an odd development: neither Jesus nor Paul had pushed women away, but had worked closely with them and granted them full equality with men. However, later books of the

New Testament, particularly the First Epistle to Timothy, which was probably written at the beginning of the 2nd century some sixty years after Paul's death, have a very different message. By this time Christianity is coping with the Gentile world of the late Empire and its terrors of sexual excess. A fear of sexuality had changed official Church policy toward women:

> I direct that women are to wear suitable clothes and to be dressed quietly and modestly without braided hair or gold and jewellery or expensive clothes; their adornment is to do the sort of good works that are proper for women who profess to be religious. During instruction, a woman should be quiet and respectful. I am not giving permission for a woman to teach or to tell a man what to do. A woman ought not to speak, because Adam was formed first and Eve afterwards, and it was not Adam who was led astray but the woman who was led astray and fell into sin. Nevertheless, she will be saved by childbearing, provided she lives a modest life and is constant in faith and love and holiness.
>
> (1 Timothy 2:9–15)

When Paul had told the women in Corinth to keep quiet in Church, there was no hint of sexual disgust, nor was there any idea that women were potentially wicked (they just have to remember their place!). In 1 Timothy we have something different and sinister. Woman is not just inferior, she is wicked also, because of Eve. Eve fell into sin first and led Adam into sin. This is a theme which will recur again and again in the writings of the Early Fathers, and is also a deeply sexual idea.

The author of 1 Timothy begins his remarks about women with directions about the sort of clothes they should wear. Glancing through the works of the Fathers, it is extraordinary how much time they devoted to writing about women's dress—a concern that should have been beneath them. Diatribes about the way women load themselves with jewelry, cake their faces with makeup and douse themselves with perfume crop up with extreme frequency. One of the first was written by Tertullian in the 3rd century. In a treatise written to his "best beloved sisters" in the faith, Tertullian glides from affection and respect to an astonishing attack:

If there dwelt upon earth a faith as great as we expect to enjoy in heaven, there wouldn't be a single one of you, best beloved sisters, who, from the time when she had first "known the Lord" and learned the truth about her own condition, would have desired too festive (not to say ostentatious) a style of dress. Rather she would have preferred to go about in humble garb, and go out of her way to affect a meanness of appearance, walking about as Eve, mourning and repentant, so that by her penitential clothes she might fully expiate what she has inherited from Eve: the shame, I mean, of the first sin, and the odium of human perdition. *In pains and anxieties dost thou bear children, woman; and toward thine husband is thy inclination and he lords it over thee.* * And do you not know that you are each an Eve? The sentence of God on this sex of yours lives in this age: the guilt must of necessity live too. *You* are the devil's gateway: *you* are the unsealer of that forbidden tree: *you* are the first deserter of the divine law: *you* are she who persuaded him whom the devil was not valiant enough to attack. *You* destroyed so easily God's image, man. On account of *your* desert—that is death— even the Son of God had to die. And do you think about adorning yourself over and above your tunics of skins.

*(On Female Dress,* I:i)

It is exactly the same complex of ideas that we find, less clearly articulated, in 1 Timothy: female appearance, Eve, childbirth. It seems at first sight strange that this enormous attack—each woman is completely responsible for destroying men and crucifying Christ— should start and finish with something as apparently unimportant as women's clothes. What prompts Tertullian's virulent attack is pure irrational fear. As the treatise goes on, we see that it is wholly about sex. Woman is as much of a temptation to man as Eve was to Adam, not because she is offering him an apple but because she is offering the forbidden fruit of sex. She can cause a man to lust after her just by walking around looking beautiful. "You must know," Tertullian insists, "that in the eye of perfect Christian modesty, having people lusting after you with carnal desire is not a desirable state of affairs but is something execrable" (II, ii). He is thinking of Jesus' words

* Genesis 3:16. Tertullian quotes God's words to Eve after the Fall.

when he said that a man who looks at a woman lustfully has already committed adultery in his heart. Jesus was not making a particular issue of lust here, but was illustrating his admirable religious insight that mere external conformity to a set of rules is not enough for the truly religious man. It is the attitude in his heart that counts, not a meticulous performance of burdensome commandments. Tertullian twists this potentially liberating idea into a truly frightening view of the moral world. "For as soon as a man has lusted after your beauty, he has in his mind already committed the sin which his lust was imagining and he perished because of this, and you [women] have been made the sword that destroys him" (II, ii). A man's lustful glance may be entirely involuntary, but he still perishes. The woman is guilty of destroying him just as Eve was guilty of destroying Adam. She may have had absolutely no intention of tempting him— she may not even realize that she has caused any lustful thoughts at all, but she is still guilty. Both the man and the woman have sinned even though what happened was quite beyond their control.

Tertullian is quite clear that women are to blame: "even though you may be free of the actual crime, you are not free of the odium attaching to it" (II, ii). This means that, far from dressing up and making herself look pretty and desirable, a woman has a duty to look as unattractive as she possibly can:

> . . . it is time for you to know that you must not merely reject the pageantry of fictitious and elaborate beauty, but even the grace and beauty you enjoy naturally must be obliterated by concealment and negligence, because this is just as dangerous to the people who glance at you. For even though comeliness is not to be censured exactly, because it is certainly a physical felicity and a kind of goodly garment of the soul, but it is to be feared, because of the injury and violence it inflicts on the men who admire you.
>
> (II, ii)

This is an oft-repeated theme for Tertullian. In his treatise *On the Veiling of Virgins,* it surfaces in a particularly disturbed form. St. Paul had said that women had to wear veils in Church "because of the angels." Here he was referring to the legend of the "Sons of

God," the "angels" who lusted after earthly women and came down from heaven to mate with them.

> For if it is "because of the angels"—those beings of whom we read as having fallen from God and from heaven because of lusting after women—who can presume that it was bodies already defiled and relics of human lust which the angels yearned after, but that rather that they were inflamed for virgins, whose bloom pleads an excuse for human lust? . . . So perilous a face, then, ought to be kept shaded, when it has cast stumbling stones even so far as heaven. This face, when it stands in the presence of God, at whose bar it already stands accused of driving the angels from their heavenly home, may blush before the other angels who didn't fall as well.
>
> *(On the Veiling of Virgins,* VII)

There is something extremely unpleasant here. It is not simply the view that sex always defiles a woman, so that afterward she is merely a "relic of human lust," a memory of a shameful act. There is also a horrible leering prurience about unsullied virgins being especially lustworthy, and there is a real terror in the idea that a woman's beauty is so dangerous and powerful that it can even cause angels to abandon heaven and fall irretrievably into sin. If even angels are not safe from a woman's beauty, then what hope is there for mere men? A woman must keep her "perilous" face hidden. She must disguise her beauty, or she will destroy men just as surely as Eve destroyed Adam. Already, years before Augustine would finally formulate for the West the doctrine of Original Sin, the emotional trinity which exists at the heart of that doctrine has been formed in the Christian neurosis of Tertullian: woman, sex and sin are fused together in his mind indissolubly. The only hope for man is that women hide themselves away—veil their faces from man's lustful eyes, hide their beauty by disfiguring themselves and make themselves ugly and sexless in the penitential garb that befits each woman as an Eve.

Christian men were told to inhabit a separate world from women. When Jerome wants to defend his friendship with the noble Roman lady St. Paula, who became one of his staunchest disciples, he stresses the fact that he was scrupulous about keeping away from women:

Before I became acquainted with the household of the saintly
Paula all Rome was enthusiastic about me. Almost everyone
concurred in judging me worthy of the highest office in the
Church. My words were always on the lips of Damasus of
blessed memory. Men called me saintly: men called me humble
and eloquent. Did I ever enter a house of any woman who was
inclined to wantonness? Was I ever attracted by silk dresses,
flashing jewels, painted faces, display of gold? No other matron
in Rome could dominate my mind but one who mourned and
fasted, who was squalid with dirt, almost blind with weeping.
All night long she would beg the Lord for mercy, and often the
sun found her still praying. The psalms were her music, the
Gospels her conversation: continence was her luxury, her life a
fast. No other could give me pleasure, but one whom I never
saw munching food.

(Letter xiv: To Asella)

For Jerome the only good woman is a sexually repulsive one. Paula
has made herself "repellent." When Jerome went to visit her, he felt
disgusted by her and his virtue was quite safe. He was in no sexual
danger. Paula herself would have been delighted by this appalling
description; she was only one of the new breed of Roman ladies who
were taking up the ascetic life and mutilating themselves physically
and spiritually in this way. This pattern of mutilation is one that
recurs in all sorts of psychological and physical ways among the
women of Western Christianity. By telling a woman that she should
not be physically attractive if she wanted to consort with men and
still be virtuous, Jerome and his like were deeply damaging the
women who obeyed them.

If a woman is not repulsive then she must be isolated and ostracized. In his letter to Nepotian, a young priest, Jerome tells him that
he must be careful to keep himself away from women, even the most
innocent and virtuous women, unless they are sexually repellent:

A woman's foot should seldom or never cross the threshold of
your humble lodging. To all maidens and to all Christ's virgins
show the same disregard or the same affection. Do not remain
under the same roof with them; do not trust your chastity. You
cannot be a man more saintly than David, or more wise than

Solomon. Remember always that a woman drove the tiller of
Paradise from the garden that had been given him. If you are ill
let one of the brethren attend you, or else your sister or your
mother or some woman of universally approved faith. If there
are no persons marked out by ties of kinship or reputation for
chastity, the Church maintains many elderly women who by
their services can both help you and benefit themselves, so that
even your sickness may bear fruit in almsgiving. . . . There is a
danger for you in the ministrations of one whose face you are
continually watching. If in the course of your clerical duties you
have to visit a widow or a virgin, never enter the house alone.
. . . Never sit alone without witnesses with a woman in a quiet
place. If there is anything intimate she wants to say, she has a
nurse or some elderly virgin at home, some widow or married
woman. She cannot be so cut off from human society as to have
no one but yourself to whom she can trust her secret.

(Letter lii)

Merely sitting with a woman or letting her nurse you is to put yourself in grave danger. Women, therefore, have to be shunned, even if
they are in trouble and need help. A woman is to be avoided and left
alone in a world which is quite apart from men.

It becomes part of the advice that is given to young aspirants of
both sexes who want to lead virtuous Christian lives. Men are to
shun women, and women are urged to withdraw from the world and
take themselves off into a separate and totally female existence. Inevitably that will be maiming, even without the fasting and the deliberate physical mutilation that the woman is urged to undertake in the
name of physical penance. Simply by being deprived of the realities
of the male world, by being deprived of education and normal activity, women were only being able to function in half the world. However, the most destructive thing of all was the sexual disgust which
drove women into their separate worlds. There is a continual process
of repulsion which we have already seen in Tertullian, a process
which is neurotic and probably not even conscious. You begin speaking lovingly to your "best beloved sisters" and you end up castigating
"Eve." Jerome has exactly the same reaction. Here he is writing to a
young girl who has written asking for his advice about the Christian

life. Jerome urges her to lock herself away from the world. Simply by walking around she will inspire male lust, however virtuous she is. In fact, virtue itself can turn a man on:

> What will you do, a healthy young girl, dainty, plump, rosy, all afire amid the fleshpots, amid the wines and baths, side by side with married women and with young men. Even if you refuse to give what they ask for, you may think that the asking is evidence of your beauty. A libertine is all the more ardent when he is pursuing virtue and thinks that the unlawful is especially delightful. Your very robe, coarse and sombre though it be, betrays your unexpressed desires if it be without crease, if it be trailed upon the ground to make you seem taller, if your vest be slit on purpose to let something be seen within, hiding that which is unsightly and disclosing that which is fair. As you walk along your shiny black shoes by their creaking give an invitation to young men. Your breasts are confined in strips of linen, and your chest is imprisoned by a tight girdle. Your hair comes down over your forehead or over your ears. Your shawl sometimes drops, so as to leave your white shoulders bare, and then, as though unwilling to be seen, it hastily hides what it unintentionally revealed. And when in public it hides the face in a pretence of modesty, with a harlot's skill it shows only those features which give men when shown more pleasure.
>
> (Letter cxvii)

It is not surprising that Jerome doesn't let himself near women, because this letter shows him to be sexually obsessed and one of the great voyeurs of all time. He has obviously studied women minutely, and is pruriently eager to pick up each and every movement, every mannerism. He is even excited by the creaking of a woman's shoe. Watching a woman walk down the street, he immediately imagines her underwear; his eyes are skinned to catch a glimpse of her white shoulders. It is taken for granted that she is teeming with lust. Every movement, intentional or unintentional, is a sign of her "unexpressed" sexual desire. What Jerome is doing is over-sexualizing women because of his own sexual repression. *He* is rampantly frustrated so he tells women that *they* are sexually insatiable. He has forgotten here that he is writing to a good little girl, who has asked him for advice. He is so lost in his fantasy that by the end of the paragraph he is comparing her to a harlot. In just the same way Tertullian begins by calling his readers "best beloved" and ends by calling them "Eve." Christian love for women easily modulates into sexual hatred.

Woman then is man's deepest enemy. She is the harlot who will lure a man to his doom because she is Eve, the eternal temptress. Just as Original Sin comes to be linked with sex, so woman is Eve because she is sexual. Jerome's pathological disgust with sex is shown in his letter to Furia, who had written to seek his advice about getting married again:

> The trials of marriage you have learned in the married state: you have been surfeited to nausea as though with the flesh of quails. Your mouth has tasted the bitterest of gall, you have voided the sour unwholesome food, you have relieved a heaving stomach. Why would you put into it again something which has already proved harmful to you. *The dog is turned to his own vomit again and the sow that was washed to her wallowing in the mire.*
>
> (2 Peter 2:22)

What must Furia have felt like when she received this letter? Again she seems to have been a virtuous woman, a genuine and enthusiastic Christian, but because of her sexuality she would have been made to feel foul and sinful. Jerome is clear that she is sexually obsessed and voracious. As a widow she must be inflamed by the "pleasures of the past." The widow "knows the delights that she has lost and she must quench the fire of the devil's shafts with the cold streams of fast and vigil." Jerome sees a woman as having such strong sexual cravings that if she dresses attractively she is crying out for sex, her "whole body reveals incontinence." Again he sees her as luring poor unsuspecting men into sex and sin. Woman is Antichrist:

> What have rouge and white lead to do on a Christian woman's face? The one simulates the natural red of cheeks and lips, the other the whiteness of the face and neck. They are fires to inflame young men, stimulants of lustful desire, plain evidence of an unchaste mind. How can a woman weep for her sins when

tears lay her skin bare and make furrows on her face? Such
adorning is not of the Lord, it is the mask of Antichrist.

(Letter liv)

Reading this one might assume that Jerome is writing about prostitutes whose garish makeup advertises their availability. In fact here,
as elsewhere, he was writing about ordinary Roman matrons who
used frequently to wear cosmetics at this time.

This hostility and fear of women's sexual powers we see again and
again. Augustine sees danger even in the virtuous women of the Old
Testament, sometimes with ludicrous results. Trying to come to
terms with the sex lives of the Patriarchs, he presents Abraham and
Isaac copulating with their wives dutifully but with enormous distaste, in order to obey God's command to found the Chosen Race.
They would far rather have abstained. Abraham, Augustine says,
had to go on copulating with his wife Sarah for years before he
managed with God's help to conceive his son Isaac. Abraham, who
seems to have been a highly sexed man, would have read all this with
considerable bewilderment. Isaac, Augustine continues, was more
fortunate. The Bible only mentions his having sex once, and he was
lucky enough to produce the twins, Esau and Jacob, straight off so he
never had to do it again. When he came to Jacob, however, who had
twelve sons, Augustine is in a bit of a quandary. This looks like zeal
in excess of duty. However, he decides that Jacob would gladly have
followed the example of Isaac and only had sex once in his life, but
his two wives, Leah and Rachel, kept pestering him because of their
excessive lust and sexual greed, forcing the holy Patriarch to abandon his high ideals. Yet Rachel and Leah are good women. For
Augustine, as for his predecessors Jerome and Tertullian, all women,
however virtuous, are men's enemies. "What is the difference," he
wrote to a friend, "whether it is in a wife or a mother, it is still Eve
the temptress that we must beware of in any woman." (Letter 243,
10)

There is no room for this enemy in the male world. Indeed, there
is no room for her at all in God's plan. Augustine seems puzzled
about why God made women at all. It is not possible that she was a
friend and helpmate to man. After all, "if it was good company and
conversation that Adam needed, it would have been much better

arranged to have two men together, as friends, not a man and a woman" *(De Genesis ad Litteram* IX, v, 9). The only reason he made women was for the purposes of childbearing. Luther shared this view. The only vocation he could see for a woman was to have as many children as possible, so that all the more people could be led to the Gospel. It didn't matter what effect this might have on women: "If they become tired or even die, that does not matter. Let them die in childbirth—that is why they are there." There was no other way that a woman could help man. Her place was "in the home" (the famous phrase was actually coined by Luther). There was no place for her in the male world of affairs. Similarly Calvin, who is virtually the first Christian theologian to speak favorably of women, might insist that woman *was* created to be a companion to man and that marriage was instituted by God precisely for that companionship, but his Geneva was entirely male dominated, and women's role as a companion was confined to the domestic female world of the home. Protestantism shared fully the misogyny that the Fathers had bequeathed to the Catholic Church. When Lutherans at Wittenberg discussed the question whether women were really human beings at all, they were not discussing anything new. Theologians had always been perplexed about women's place in God's plan. Thomas Aquinas was as puzzled as Augustine had been about why God had made her at all and decided that woman was a freak in nature:

> As regards the individual nature, woman is defective and misbe-gotten, for the active force in the male seed tends to the produc-tion of a perfect likeness in the masculine sex; while the produc-tion of woman comes from a defect in the active force or from some material indisposition, or even from some external influ-ence.
>
> *(Summa Theologica,* IV, Part I. Quaest. XCII, art 1, 2)

It does not help that Aquinas decides that womankind in *general* is human. The "individual nature" of women is a defect, an idea he picked up from Aristotle's biology. The norm is the male. Every woman is a failed man.

*     *     *

Women are therefore emotionally excluded from the male world, for all that Paul had originally insisted upon sexual equality. Even now that we are breaking into the male preserves we still tend to feel ill at ease in it. Recent surveys show that college women are even more afraid of success today than they were when Betty Friedan did her original survey in the early 1960s. Dons at Oxford and Cambridge have complained about the quality of women who are gaining admission to the colleges that used to be all-male. They have asked schools to stop sending them girls who are polite, efficient and well-behaved, and instead send them students who will argue with them as aggressively as the boys do. Breaking into the male world is not simply a matter of opportunity. It is a question of attitude on the part of both men and women. Women are still ambiguous and fearful in these new male worlds that have recently been opened to them. They are still maintaining their guilty apologetic stance. For centuries they have been excluded not simply because they were supposed to be inferior but because they inspired sexual fear and disgust in men. Marilyn French's novel *The Women's Room* puts this humorously when she imagines the male world of Harvard terrified to admit women in case they drip menstrual blood all over this pure male preserve. Where Moslems have traditionally locked their women into harems inside their homes because they owned and valued them, men in the Christian West have locked their women outside their lives because they hate them, exiling women to a lonely, separate world.

The loneliness is still with us. If men have traditionally castigated women, women have learned the trick from them and are very ready to castigate one another. It used to be fashionable for women to proclaim loudly how much they loathed other women. Women used roundly to attack the boredom of gatherings where there were only women, used to say that women were bitches, that it was impossible to have good women friends because women were so petty and small-minded, that institutions of women—like women's clubs—were utterly deadly and life in an institution of women like the ATS or the WAACS during the war was unalleviated hell because women could not live happily together. Many of us grew up hearing our mothers make these appalling remarks about our sex as a matter of course. Now such remarks are socially unacceptable. The Women's Movement has taught women to talk to one another and to appreciate each other. Sisterhood is an ideal. Yet it is an ideal that has not wholly been attained, for all our new enthusiasm about women supporting one another with love and the richness of friendships between women. As yet we do not have Sisterhood but Sectarianism. Women are certainly banding together, but they are only banding with other women who share their opinions. Women who disagree with other women are often as cruel and as dismissive as the most chauvinist male. Feminists scorn women who are happy in a traditional role, and vice versa. Some feminists disagree vociferously with other feminists. We still feel wary with one another, and this is surely one of the saddest legacies from our Christian past. It is not surprising, however, that women should still be suspicious of one another, because our culture has told us so many terrible things about our sex. At the Council of Mâcon in the 6th century the bishops had to vote to decide whether women had souls. The motion was carried by one vote. With a background of such misogyny, who can blame us for disliking each other?

One of the things that women tend to be most intolerant about is the sexuality of other women. Monogamous women tend to be shrill in their condemnation of women who have more than one lover, married women intolerant of women who are not and do not want to be married. The heterosexual shudders at the "unnatural sexuality" of the lesbian and the feminist lesbian denounces her heterosexual feminist "sisters" for consorting with the enemy, man. There is no need to belabor this point. Sexual prejudice particularly afflicts women and their relationships with other women who do not share their sexual preferences. Women believe passionately that there is *one* best way to live a sexual life and are quick to condemn anybody who doesn't do it that way. This is not because women are constitutionally unable to get on with one another nor because they are right and there really *is* only one way for a woman to enjoy her sexuality. It springs, like all prejudice, from fear and insecurity. Women even more than men are afraid of their sexuality; if they find something that works for them they cling to it as a drowning man clings to a raft, and fight off anyone who threatens their lifeline.

Even when women have been particularly interested in promoting the cause of women, an enjoyment and a toleration of the diverse sexuality of women has never been very high on their agenda. The early feminists of the 19th and early 20th centuries were women of their time: Victorian women who were still imbued with the Victorian myth that women hated sex. These early feminists also hated sex. Thus Helen Thompson, the American feminist who was one of the first to explore the idea that there was little difference between the mental capacity of women and men, was so embarrassed by sex that she could never speak of it or explain it to her daughters, and during her engagement she was so physically repelled by her fiancé that he despaired of the marriage and nearly broke it off. Another American, Mary Roberts Smith, who was one of the first women to pioneer sex research, was very ambivalent about her own sexuality: although she usually had orgasm and found sex "agreeable," she also found that it was accompanied by neurotic symptoms like backaches and "often a very great nervousness." Olive Schreiner, who spent her life working for women, actually hated her own sex. She had clearly been influenced by her Calvinist upbringing which stigmatized sexual pleasure as evidence of sin and concupiscence. Throughout her life she suffered from psychosomatic aches and pains that seem symptomatic of sexual disgust, and in her novels women's bodies often appear as bloated and swollen with a fearful reproductive sexuality. It comes as no surprise then to read of her frank dislike of women. "Oh, it's awful to be a woman," she wrote to Havelock Ellis in 1888. "These women are killing me. . . . Please see they bury me in a place where there are no women. I've not been a woman really, though I've seemed like one." Modern feminists may not share this Victorian disgust, but it is true that the Women's Movement has concentrated far more on the sufferings than on the pleasures of women's sexuality. It has explored the damage women have suffered, the hatred shown them in pornography and the dangers and iniquities of the laws regarding rape. It has done much valuable work here but, as some feminists are beginning to discover, not nearly enough work on women's sexual pleasure. Indeed, it has tended to erect new dogmatisms about sex, drawing up new "lines" of sexual behavior which the committed feminist may not cross. Instead of certain sexual practices being "perverse" or socially unacceptable, they are now politically unacceptable for the feminist because they pander too much to the patriarchal ideals of male supremacy and the exploitation of women.

At a conference of feminists held recently at Columbia, this idea was explored and the papers were published in a volume called *Pleasure and Danger* edited by Carole S. Vance. In her paper "Desire for the Future: Radical Hope in Passion and Pleasure," Amber Hollibaugh was very revealing about the intolerance that feminists feel for certain sexual ways of life. Now a radical lesbian feminist, she is totally acceptable to the sisterhood, but before her enlightenment she had been a nightclub dancer. As she points out, it can make more sense for a working-class woman to strip in a club for a few hours a week than to endure the backbreaking sweated labor of the factory. However, her white middle-class feminist sisters were unable to understand this. The only time Hollibaugh is made to feel ashamed of her "wicked past," she says, is at feminist gatherings:

> There are many assumptions at work behind feminist expressions of surprise and horror: I must be stupid or I could have done something better than that; I must have been forced against my will or I was just too young to know better. I have prefeminist consciousness; I had a terrible family life; I must have hated it; I was trash and this proved it; and finally, wasn't I glad I'd been saved.
>
> (p. 404)

It is very sad that women who are trying to be particularly supportive of other women should show such unkind intolerance, but many of us, who may be neither lesbians nor nightclub dancers, have encountered much the same kind of attitude with regard to our sexuality. It is particularly and understandably true across generations: mothers gaze despairingly at daughters who seem to have abandoned the principles which were axiomatic for them. Daughters shudder at their mothers' sexual repressions and "hypocrisy." But it also happens among peers. Because women are so frightened and ignorant about women's sexuality, they cannot afford the security and pleasure they have discovered to be threatened by different standards and different lifestyles.

Men have told many terrible stories about women's sexuality during the last two thousand years. We have been told that it is impossible for us to have orgasm at all, that all our orgasms are vaginal or, the latest craze, that they are clitoral. Male researchers in laboratories and conservative sex manuals tell us what we like and enjoy. Yet we ourselves enclose our sex lives within a wall of privacy which entails extreme loneliness. The only thing we are prepared to discuss about our sexuality is what we *couldn't* tolerate: women frequently say, often quite proudly, that they simply *couldn't* have an affair with a married man, have a male/female lover, have two lovers at once, practice fellatio, get married, or have a lover of a race other than their own. This is all right as far as it goes, and it is important that women are honest about the things they do not want to do sexually, as long as these taboos are not just prejudiced and conditioned responses. What women should surely not do, in these days when we are trying to band together to improve our lot, is be unkind and intolerant of women who actually *do* like some of the things they don't. To confine a woman's sexuality to one's own rigid little orthodoxy is in fact to whittle it away and limit it. To say that orgasm has to be either vaginal *or* clitoral is a similar limitation. We simply don't know enough about women's sexuality yet to make such insecure and dogmatic claims; it could be something far richer than our frightened visions allow.

One of the things women should be doing is discussing with one another the things they *do* like sexually, instead of concentrating on the things they don't. We very rarely do. Either we shrink in horror from discussing what we like to do in bed, or we primly say that it is all too private or personal to discuss. However, as long as we concentrate on negatively restricting our discussion of female sexuality to what is wrong and unnatural, we are continuing the long tradition of sexual fear and intolerance imposed by men on our society. We need to take our sexuality into our own hands and out of the hands of men. Most women have a very isolated sexual journey. Either a woman is totally dependent upon the experience of her mate and is therefore often educated by a man who all too frequently has his own sexual problems, or she has a solitary quest for her own sexual identity, worrying if her likes and dislikes are "normal" or not. If she is fortunate enough to find a partner who can educate her successfully, then she may expand her sexual horizons, but she may not have the chance to do this. Women's sexual education is almost entirely confined to the functions of reproduction rather than instruction about the mysterious ways the female body gives us pleasure. Paula Webster, in her article on women's sexuality "The Forbidden: Eroticism and Taboo," makes this point forcefully.

> Our mothers, to whom we often dedicate our [women's] movement, if not our lives, were either bizarrely matter-of-fact when they told us about sex, or bitter and resentful. Either your father wanted too much or too little, and she had to put up with "it." Needless to say, she never told you *if* she masturbated (or how, when or where) or *how* she felt about it. Nor did she tell you if she liked rough or gentle sex, being on top or bottom, whether she read pornography, or had fantasies about the milkman, her brother-in-law, her best girlfriend or her own children. Sexually mute and mysterious, our mothers observed the taboo imposed by motherhood, and presented us with little or no knowledge of what women's sexuality was like or could be. We have no documented erotic heritage, and the exploration is made even more difficult by our mother's sacrifices. We may feel that we betray her when we want more than she had.
>
> *(Pleasure and Danger,* p. 394)

The fact that the very idea of such a sexually frank discussion with our mothers puts most of us into a state of nervous hysteria shows just how taboo we feel the topic of our own sexual pleasure really is. From the beginning of our lives, erotic pleasure is something that is unmentionable for women. For centuries the male world pushed it away into this isolation and we are each one of us condemned to discover our sexuality alone. We are not even helped by our own fantasies, because many women don't have very explicit fantasies: it is one of the things that women like to say categorically separates the sexuality of men and women. It may be, however, that women are too wary to allow themselves to fantasize: such a liberation of the sexual imagination could cross that "line" which we have drawn so ruthlessly for ourselves, leading us toward sexual desires which might be socially, morally or politically unacceptable.

But what about love? Surely the great force which is supposed to relate the sexes is romantic love, which has inspired the fairy stories, plays and poetry which condition us all to believe that men and women love one another, and that a woman will, like Cinderella, be rescued by her prince. There is a good deal of controversy at the moment about the evolution of love in our culture and about how it relates to marriage. The notion of love has always been a very important ideal in Christianity. Jesus had said that the distinguishing mark of his followers would be the love they bore for one another. St. Paul praised love or charity above all the more spectacular gifts of the spirit. Without it a Christian was only a hollow shell, a sounding brass or a tinkling cymbal. St. John insisted that only by loving his neighbor could a Christian truly love God. Jesus had even said that love for friends was not enough. A Christian must also love his enemies but love is not an easy ideal to practice. It has to be said that, whatever its official theology of love, in reality Christianity has been conspicuous less for its love than for its hatred. We are very happy to stigmatize the violence we see in Islam, but conveniently forget that our own Christian history has been a disedifying story of crusade and persecution. For two centuries Christians in Europe believed that it was their religious duty to slaughter Moslems and Jews in the Crusades. Killing the enemies of Christ and Christendom was seen as a meritorious and holy act, a way for the layman to practice the perfect love of God that a monk practiced in the religious life. Later Christians would launch crusades against other Christians; not only in the Inquisition but after the Reformation, Catholics and Protestants would murder one another. Even where there has been no question of actual persecution Christianity has been cruelly callous, brutally indifferent and hypocritically exploitative of many groups of people.

Women are certainly not the only ones who have suffered at the hands of Christianity, but it is true that they were one of the earliest "enemies" that Christianity created. This hatred of women springs from a projection of the fears and insecurities that existed in the minds and hearts of Christian men. Throughout its history Christianity has created similar images of enemies which likewise evolve by a process of projection. Thus from the 9th century the Moslem became an Enemy of Christians and the image of the Moslem that Christians had in Europe bore no relation at all to reality but shows the mixed fear and admiration that they felt towards Islam as well as buried worries about Christianity itself. Thus, at a time when Europe was plagued by feudal wars and was building up the concept of holy violence that ultimately exploded in the Crusades, Islam was presented (quite wrongly) as a violent and intolerant religion which slaughtered people of other faiths. Again, at a time when Europe was wracked with sexual insecurity, the Moslem was seen as abominably sexually permissive—also quite wrongly. This was not just a matter of ignorance; even when people had access to accurate knowledge about Islam they can be seen reproducing the old prejudices which were an emotional need for the West for centuries. The Jews also suffered in the same way from the end of the 11th century. Later, similar projections which produced distorted images of the Outsider were directed against other Christians—against heretics like the Cathars and Waldenses. Such a process of projection was not an established mode of Christian life until the Middle Ages, whereas it was a habit to make an Enemy of women from the 2nd and 3rd centuries of the Church. And women were not merely an exploited class like the slave or the poor man whose sufferings Christians not only did nothing to alleviate but actually sometimes increased. The poor have always been told to keep in line by the Church: Luther would even urge princes to murder rebellious peasants, but they had to *be* rebellious. The peasant was not wicked simply because he was a peasant, as a Jew was wicked just because he was a Jew and as a woman was wicked because she was Eve. Alongside the exploitation and cruelty many Christians have shown toward the poor, there has existed a veneration of the Poor Man and a theoretical tradition of Christian charity towards the poor. Sometimes the Christian poor were actually able to exploit their poverty to gain a practical power. This power of the poor becomes very evident during the First Crusade: they had definite power over the Crusading Barons and clergy and could dictate policy, because of their status as the poor who would inherit the Kingdom of Heaven.

Women, however, were not merely a group whom Christians mistreated. They were one of the very first of the Christian enemies who were associated with Satan for the overthrowing of men. During the 12th century a secular movement sprang up, possibly in reaction to this, which attempted, for the first time, to accord to women the spiritual status and veneration that, for example, the poor enjoyed. However, it did nothing for the position of women any more than the veneration of the poor had elevated their status or practically relieved their poverty. The Courtly Love cult which idealized women was confined to a very small area geographically, and socially it encompassed only the upper class. It has to be seen against the misogyny of the 12th century as the period also saw Christian hatred of Woman the Enemy rising to a crescendo. Thus a French bishop of the time wrote that all women without exception were whores, who, like Eve, were the cause of all the evils in the world: women came between old friends, separated lovers, set children against their parents, destroyed villages, cities and whole peoples. A Benedictine monk, Bernard de Moraix, said flatly in his poem *De Contemptu Mundi* that there was no good woman on earth. The English monk Alexander Neckham said that because a woman was sexually insatiable she would often have to drag some poor wretch into bed with her to satisfy her on the spot, if her husband wasn't instantly available. The result of this was that husbands were frequently having to bring children up who were not their own. The myth of women's voracious sexuality was so well established that by 1621 Robert Burton could refer to it as a universal complaint in *The Anatomy of Melancholy* ". . . of women's insatiable lust, what country, what village doth not complain" (iii). The terrors and neuroses of the Jeromes, Tertullians and Augustines had been stamped on the consciousness of Western Europe so that Chaucer could satirize the form that this misogyny traditionally took in *The Nun's Priest's Tale:*

> Wommennes conseils been ful ofte colde;
> Wommannes conseil broghte us first to wo,
> And made Adam fro Paradys to go,
> Ther as he was ful myrie and wel at ese
> But for I noot to whom it myght displese
> If I conseil of wommen wolde blame
> Passe over, for I seyde it in my game.
> Rede auctours, where they trete of swich mateere,
> And what they seyn of wommen ye may heere.

The conventional diatribes against women listed the wicked women of antiquity, starting with Eve and working through to Delilah and Jezebel, showing that women had always been the ruin of man. They followed a typical form and cropped up again and again in literature, with the same irrelevance and pedantry that Chaucer is laughing at in his satire of the rhetoric of his day. The Fathers had impressed the

notion of woman as Eve firmly on the minds of Europe. It is against
this background of sexual prejudice and hatred of women that the
cult of "Courtly Love" grew up and bequeathed to us our myth of
Romantic Love.

The cult of Courtly Love was probably inspired by Arab love
poetry which Christians encountered in Spain and Southern Europe.
The Troubadours wandered from one great house to another singing
mournful songs about their Lady, their *Domna*. She inspired them to
goodness and was the goal of their lives. A notion of Chivalry grew
up, which existed to serve the desires of women. A knight was supposed to right the wrongs of the world to please his virtuous lady.
This "love" he felt for his *Domna* made the Troubadour idolize her;
she was the possessor of all the virtues, and thus led him to virtue.
Yet this love was sexless. The lover rarely wanted to possess his
*Domna*'s body. As the Troubadour Arnault Daniel writes:

> I love and seek her so eagerly that I believe the very violence of
> my desire for her would deprive me of all desire whatever, could
> one lose aught by loving well. For her heart drowns mine in a
> never-diminishing flood.

(Quoted by Denis de Rougemont, *Passion and Society*, p. 90)

This love and desire is so pure that it kills off any other erotic desire;
ultimately it puts love above the reach of vulgar sex. Bernart de
Ventadour writes, "She has taken my heart, she has taken my self,
she has taken me from the world, and then she has slipped away
from me, leaving me with only my desire and my parched heart"
(ibid. p. 89). Love has become a form of religious experience; just as
in mystical religion the self and the world are left behind, so now the
Lady by her sublime but distant presence could effect what hours of
meditation in a solitary cell was doing for monks and nuns of the
period. Dante took this ideal as the motif of his *Divine Comedy*. He
had fallen in "love" with Beatrice Portinari when she was a child of
eight and he was a grown man. It was a cataclysmic revelation, just
as "falling in love at first sight" is supposed to be today. Dante saw
Beatrice only a few times in his life, and each time the experience
was a religious revelation; the perfection of Beatrice was an affirma-
tion of the goodness of God. Dante was not interested in knowing
the "real" Beatrice. That was irrelevant. He certainly didn't desire

her erotically, but was married quite amicably to somebody else. After Beatrice's early death, he wrote the *Divine Comedy*. From Heaven Beatrice summons him on a mystical journey through Hell and Purgatory to Paradise, where she is reunited with him and leads him to the vision of God. Thus from the beginning of its history the European cult of the love of men and women had little to do with sex, and it also had nothing to do with women as they really were. Neither did it have anything to do with marriage—the *Domna* or Beatrice was married to another man. There was no thought of a man falling in love with his wife and taking her as the lodestar of his life.

By being sexless a woman could be an inspiration to men. The only woman a man would "fall in love" with was a woman he never slept with, a woman he barely knew and a woman he could never hope to marry. In the 12th century the Catharist heresy was gaining many adherents in exactly the same areas of Southern Europe that were affected by the Courtly Love ideal. Catharism is clearly close to the Courtly Love ideal in matters of sexuality: it exalts sexless and chaste women; it decries sexual desire and marriage. The similarity between the two as well as the geographical coincidence has led Denis de Rougemont to suggest that Courtly Love was a cryptic branch of Catharism. I think this is most unlikely; what seems more probable is that both flourished as another form of the sexual disgust and hatred of the time, a disgust that either produced misogyny or the pure women of the Cathari and the pure unsexual love for an idealized woman of the Troubadours.

Petrarch shows how deep hatred of women could lie at the heart of Courtly and Romantic Love. His sonnets to Laura are classic examples of the cult of love. He had once written of her that she was "all virtue, all beauty, all nobility, bound in one form in wondrous unity." But he felt no difficulty about writing this:

> Woman is a real devil, an enemy of the peace, a source of provocation, a cause of disputes, from whom a man must hold himself apart if he wishes to taste tranquillity. Let them marry, those who are attracted by the company of a wife, by nightly embraces, the screaming of children and the torments of insomnia. As for us, if it is in our power, we will perpetuate our name

through talent and not through marriage, through books and
not through children, with the co-operation of virtue and not
that of a woman.

*(De Remediis utriusque Fortunae)*

Women might be all right if you can put them on a pedestal and
idealize them; in real life, however, they can only drag you down into
a sordid mediocrity. To have such high ideals about women, as Petrarch did in his sonnets, certainly can lead to increased hostility
when the real flesh and blood women fail—as fail they must—to
measure up to the ideal. Faced with an image of perfection, women
can only disappoint. To idealize women can sometimes be an act of
alienation. Ruskin is a classic case here, of course. He saw women as
ideal beings, and physically he was so enamored of the ideal woman
as she was portrayed by painters that the sight of his wife's real body
on their wedding night seems to have filled him with disgust and
made it impossible for him to consummate the marriage. For all his
eulogies on the noble nature of woman, he was extremely cruel to his
own wife, who through no fault of her own could not measure up to
this pinnacle of perfection.

To say that a woman is an island of perfection in a dark world is
certainly better than to say that she is Eve, but there are some dangers in this courtly myth of the perfect woman. By making women
perfect, men were making them freaks of impossible virtue. By depriving them of sexuality, men were also depriving them of an important and essential part of their nature. During the period of Courtly
Love, the cult of the Virgin Mary was spreading from the East into
Western Europe. She was the Church's answer to Catharism and its
pure and powerful women. She was also the religious answer to the
secular Courtly Love ideal. In one respect this was harmful to
women. Mary was both a virgin and mother, something that is naturally impossible. She was therefore another freak. Hitherto the Virgin Mary had not played an important part in Christian thought and
in Christian emotion. By bringing her into the market place, the
Church was popularizing the ideal of the perfect and sexless woman.
It was a very compelling image and inspired massive devotion among
laymen and clerics alike. The Virgin Mary has continued to play a
huge part in the religious lives of the populace—to some, she is a

more real and immediate figure than Jesus himself. However, the myth could be used to make women feel inadequate. As a role model the Virgin Mary is impossible. With the best will in the world no woman can imitate the Virgin Mary. She cannot be a virgin and a mother at the same time. She cannot be without sin or imperfection. To hear too much about these idealized Marys, Lauras and Beatrices could make their sisters in the real world feel failures.

Yet the Courtly Love ideal and the cult of the Virgin Mary do show some kind of rejection of the overwhelmingly masculine world of the early Middle Ages. In the 11th century religion had been martial and masculine: the patron saint of France was St. Michael, the substitute for Woden, the pagan god of War. In popular poems like *Le Chanson de Roland* love of God is seen as inseparable from love of war. When Roland is dying he never thinks of his beautiful fiancée, Aude. Instead, he lovingly apostrophizes his sword, Durandel. It was the era of the Crusades; new soldier saints appeared —saints who were holy not in spite of being soldiers, as the earlier, more pacific Christianity had said, but precisely because they were soldiers. Into this aggressive and masculine religious world, strictly for men only, came the cult of the Virgin Mary. Cathedrals were built all over Europe in her honor. She replaced St. Michael as the focus of popular devotion and in legends, not endorsed by the Church, she becomes a rebel against the harshly masculine world of Jesus and God the Father. Mary is on the side of the poor and dispossessed. She can get people whom God has assigned to Hell into Heaven. She alone can force God to do what she wants; she can, as it were, twist his arm because of her holiness and specially privileged position. This new female revolt remained at a purely popular level. The people in power clung to the older masculine ideals. In Courtly Love circles there was a similar rejection of the purely masculine; women were trying to refine the coarse and butch image of the knight. In Courtly romances the knight is no longer the brash warrior like Roland; he also has to be the lover of a woman. Courtly Love was a secular reaction against the brutal and cruel religion of the period, and can be seen as a desire to feminize the world. It is certainly true, however, that neither Courtly Love nor the cult of the Virgin Mary influenced the actual position of women in society, and certainly neither of them halted the official misogynist propaganda that the Church continued to put out. St. Bernard, who did most to spread the cult of Mary in the Church, was a bitter misogynist. When his sister came to visit him in his monastery, Bernard flew into a rage because she was wearing a new dress: she was, he said, a filthy whore and a clod of dung. The new cult did nothing to temper his view of flesh and blood women, which remains exactly in the old tradition of Tertullian. The fate of Abelard shows how little the Church and society valued real sexual love as opposed to courtly platonic love between men and women at this time. Abelard and Héloïse themselves saw their love as sinful and their tragedy as richly deserved.

Sometimes Europe did see powerful women in the flesh. The most obvious example is Eleanor of Aquitaine, who was closely associated with the Courtly Love ethic: she was the granddaughter of the first great Troubadour, William of Poitiers, and she was a great patron of Troubadours. She was also the most powerful woman of her time, not because she gained confidence from the idealization of women in Courtly Love, but because she had inherited a very great deal of important land. The landed heiress, because of Europe's system of primogeniture, enjoyed great power because land was the basis of the social and political system. St. Bernard of Clairvaux, the most powerful Churchman and politician of his day, was not able to oppose Eleanor when she engineered her divorce from Louis VII of France and took her patrimony off to Henry II of England. Similarly, in the Crusading Kingdom of Jerusalem, because of the dearth of male heirs to the throne, women held a great deal of political power. Eleanor of Aquitaine's opposite number in Jerusalem was the powerful and often pernicious Queen Melisande. However, Eleanor and Melisande were, literally, in a class of their own, and it is interesting to notice how in popular legend Eleanor becomes a wicked woman, sexually unfaithful and the murderer of Fair Rosamund. Even powerful women were not wholly immune to the climate of misogynism, though it is doubtful that Eleanor lost much sleep over the misogynistic propaganda of her time. She could literally afford not to. Eleanor's very real influence may have given her time a powerful image of woman, but her lot was so different from that of the vast majority of men and women that she probably seemed to belong to a different species, as different as Laura, Beatrice and Mary.

The powerful and challenging aspects of the cult of the Virgin Mary and the cult of Courtly Love did not survive. The idealized and sexless woman lost her threatening qualities when she surfaced again in Victorian England as the Angel of the House. It is interesting that in England in the anti-Catholic 19th century the Madonna image was very important, stressing a traditional link with older Christian ideals which transcended dogma and doctrinal controversy. Yet when Hippolyte Taine, the French writer, describes the typical British beauty of the period, he certainly does not have a *Domna* like Eleanor in mind, nor the Virgin Mary who challenged the decrees of God the Father. Instead, he presents us with a submissive and rather gutless Madonna:

> The fair maiden—lowered eyes, blushing cheeks, purer than a Raphael Madonna, a kind of Eve incapable of Fall, whose voice is music, adorable in her candour, gentleness and kindness; one is moved to lower one's eyes respectfully in her presence.
>
> (Quoted by E. Trudgill, *Madonnas and Magdalens*, p. 258)

The Victorian ideal woman exacts male respect not by her confidence or by her self-assertiveness, but by her submission. The potential for defiance that the myth once had has now gone. The Victorians revived only the myth of the idealized Virgin Mother and said that the only good woman was a sexless one. The woman remains a virgin, no matter how many children she has, because she remains sexually unaroused. Her nature is essentially virginal and impenetrable by foul male lust. It was only wicked and lascivious women who felt sexual pleasure. "There are many females who never feel any sexual excitement whatsoever," asserted Dr. Acton:

> The best mothers, wives and managers of households, know little or nothing of sexual indulgences. Love of home, children and domestic duties are the only passions they feel.
>
> As a general rule, a modest woman seldom desires any sexual gratification for herself. She submits to her husband, but only to please him; and but for the desire of matrimony would far rather be relieved from his attentions.
>
> (p. 101)

Just as men had for centuries told women that they were sexually insatiable, so now men asserted that women "pass through life without ever being cognizant of the prompting of the senses. Happy for them that it is so!" (Dr. W. R. Greg, *Westminster Magazine,* July 1850). It is the old process of projection, but this time in reverse. Men cannot cope with *their* sexuality, so they assure themselves that the women can cope with it even less than they can. Nobody thinks to ask the women themselves. It shows a fundamental lack of respect in the male Christian for his women. Women have no existence outside male needs and consciousness. They have to change their natures, leaping from one sexual extreme to another, simply to fit in with the men's emotional needs at the time.

A good woman, according to Dr. Acton, lays her suffering sexuality on the altar of male need. The ideal woman has no needs and no passions of her own, she simply submits to her husband. W. R. Greg expands this sacrificial idea even more pruriently; when he describes a virtuous woman's initiation into the horrors of sex:

> The first sacrifice is made and exacted . . . in a delirium of mingled love and shame. The married woman feels shame, often even remorse, and a strange confusion of all her moral conceptions.

Christianity had been busy for hundreds of years making women feel shame about their sexuality. Women knew very well, as Augustine and Luther had said centuries before, that the institution of marriage was only a very poor "remedy" for the evils of sex. A woman told Dr. Greg: "It is not a quarter of an hour's ceremony in a Church that can make *that* welcome or tolerable to pure and delicate feelings which would otherwise outrage their whole previous notions and their whole natural and moral sense" (see E. Trudgill, pp. 56–61). It is needless, surely, to point out how damaging this new myth of virginal frigidity was for women. The old myth of her sexual insatiability had its benefits—at least women were expected to enjoy sex; such enjoyment might be wicked but at least it *was* pleasurable. In the Victorian period they were denied pleasure, and many women today are still suffering from the consequences of this and find sexual satisfaction difficult. Yet even more damaging—to men as well as to women—is this idea that the marriage bed is now a sacrificial altar where the woman suffers the sexual attentions of her husband. There is an unhealthy enjoyment on both sides of the woman shrinking in horror from brutal male lust, a prurient dwelling on the horror of the experience which men are forcing upon women. The sexual lives of married people have become a nightly violation of a virgin. Apart from the falsehood of acting out unnatural roles, this type of scenario could only damage still further the relations between men and women and widen the gulf between them at a time when they were supposed to be most intimate. Men were pushing women away into a sexless world and encouraging women to reject them emotionally. Dora Langlois, in her floridly named treatise *The Child: Its Origin and Development; A Manual Enabling Mothers to Initiate their Daughters Gradually and Modestly into All the Mysteries of Life,* remarks, on the subject of sex instruction, that a husband will not want his wife to be ignorant of the fate that awaits her, but for very dubious reasons.

> I incline to the belief that any right-thinking man would prefer to feel that his bride knew the sacrifice she must make of her person to his natural demands, and that her confidence in him was sufficient to enable her to face the necessary ordeal.
>
> (p. 27)

Because sex was seen as being incompatible with True Love and because by this time men and women were expected to marry for love, married sex was abhorrent. The lofty ideal of Christian love had been kept apart from sexual enjoyment in Western Christianity, but now the wife's love is seen in terms of Christian sacrifice. She lays her delicacy and her person in the marriage bed to be constantly impaled. The Christian ideal of selfless sacrifice has here been perverted into a sick act where both men and women wallow in their sexual disgust, with a good deal of sado-masochistic pleasure.

Given this sexual climate, it is no wonder that so many eminent Victorians preferred the love of little girls to grown women. The child, the pre-Freudian Victorians fondly believed, had no sexuality. Neither did angels, because they had no bodies, and Victorian women were seen in terms of Coventry Patmore's popular poem "The Angel in the House." Victorians like Ruskin and Ernest Dowson preferred to turn away from mature women, and pursue the feminine sexual ideal in children, where the sexual ideal was more perfectly enshrined. Wives were encouraged to be childlike and innocent. However, grown and mature women are not sexless children, and to expect them to behave like little girls was damaging. Women were being asked to play an unnatural role, and inevitably this Little Girl act alienated their husbands, as Dickens shows in *David Copperfield.* Copperfield becomes more and more frustrated and irritated by his child-wife, Dora.

Copperfield is fortunate in one sense, in that his child-wife dies, appropriately in childbirth. The adult state of motherhood was impossible for the retarded woman who is clinging to a trivial innocence. Yet Copperfield's ultimate fate is the boring and saintly Agnes, who announces Dora's death to David by walking into the room with a mournful expression and her hand pointing upward (to indicate the flight of Dora's soul to the heaven). The novel finishes on this lofty domestic note:

> And now, as I close my task, subduing my desire to linger yet, these faces fade away. But one face, shining on me like a Heavenly light by which I see all other objects is above and beyond them all. And that remains.
>
> I turn my head and see it, in its beautiful serenity, beside me. My lamp burns low, and I have written far into the night; but the dear presence, without which I were nothing, bears me company.
>
> O Agnes, O my soul! so may thy face be by me when I close my life indeed; so may I, when realities are melting from me like the shadows which I now dismiss, still find thee near me, pointing upward!

This type of sentiment could be illustrated from very many novels written by men in the Victorian period. Women, now freed from sex, have become the Virgin Mary indeed, heavenly beings, pointing upward to another world. Having sex with the saintly Agnes would seem a sacrilege. At a time when religion was being discredited and men were beginning to live in a new secular age, a woman was being asked to step into the place that religion had previously filled. She was the guardian of male virtue. Ruskin, in his famous essay "On Queen's Gardens," says that woman is "incapable of error, enduringly incorruptibly good, instinctively infallibly wise." What real woman could live up to this? She would be a monster of smugness and complacency. Falling in love once again has become a religious experience. However, idealizing a woman from afar as the Troubadours did was one thing. Being married to her quite another. Irritation or disillusion were inevitable in domestic proximity. Even though this adulation might seem flattering, men were really relegating their women to a world which they had outgrown or rejected. Instead of a woman being a real companion to her man in the real world, she was only a delightful anachronism in a world of her own. Such an act of love is really an act of war. It does not result in a closer union but in deeper alienation. Even the most atheistic or agnostic of men wanted their women to become "religious experiences" for them. Thus Leslie Stephen wrote to his fiancée, Julia Duckworth:

> You must let me tell you that I do and always shall feel for you something which I can only call reverence as well as love. Think me silly if you please. . . . You see, I have not got any saints and you must not be angry if I put you in the place where my saints ought to be.
>
> (Noel Annan, *Leslie Stephen,* London, 1951, p. 51)

Not only did the woman stand in for the saints; she also stood in literally for Christ. Holman Hunt's models for Christ in his classic Victorian religious painting *The Light of the World* were Lizzie Siddal and Christina Rossetti. Such spiritual adulation is an attack on woman. She has been put away into an ideal world where she does not belong because it bears no relation to her reality.

It is also a physical act of alienation. Men like Ruskin not only shut a woman away in a separate world from men by making her unnaturally good and spiritual, but shut her away physically too in the great Victorian institution of The Home:

> By her office, and place, she is protected from all danger and all temptation. The man, in his rough work in the open world, must encounter all peril and trial: to him, therefore, the failure, the offence, the inevitable error. Often he must be wounded, or subdued, often misled, and *always* hardened. But he guards the

woman from all this; within his house, as ruled by her, unless she herself has sought it, need enter no danger, no temptation, no cause of error or offence. This is the true nature of home—it is the place of Peace; the shelter, not only from all injury, but from all terror, doubt and division. In so far as the anxieties of the outer life penetrate into it, and the inconsistently-minded, unknown, unloved, or hostile society of the outer world is allowed by either husband or wife to cross the threshold, it ceases to be home; it is then only a part of that outer world which you have roofed over and lighted fire in. But in so far as it is a sacred place, a vestal temple, a temple of the earth watched over by Household Gods, before whose faces none may come but those whom they can receive with love, so far it vindicates the name and fulfills the praise of Home.

And wherever a true wife comes, this home is always round her. . . . This then, I believe to be—will you not admit it to be —the woman's true place and power?

("Of Queen's Gardens")

Ruskin has given a new twist to the Protestant ideal that "a woman's place is in the home." The Home, for the Victorians as well as for the Americans of the period, became a shrine, removed from the male world of ideas and action. Ruskin and his contemporaries saw a woman presiding over the Home as a guardian spirit, a vestal virgin. But she is still a prisoner; she cannot get away from it—"this home is always around her" wherever she goes. The outer world of male affairs cannot "penetrate" into it. The sexual innuendo is not accidental. The Home is to be as Virginal as it is Vestal. It is to be sealed off from the male world in an unrealistic perfection. Such a home would be so utterly boring that most men would find themselves escaping from it as often as possible into the nearest brothel or all-male club where they could get a little earthy sex and reality. The Americans saw exactly what they were doing to their women. They said that men and women occupied "separate spheres." Their cult of "true womanhood" was almost exactly equivalent to the damaging myth of the Angel of the House. The men dealt with external, political and worldly matters in their sphere, and the women with the spiritual, the domestic and the vaguely cultural in theirs. The idealization of women in the 19th century sprang from the same sexual hatred and fear which had made the old Christian misogynists push women away from them by projecting their own disturbances upon them so that they became monsters of sexual depravity. The Angel-Child and the True Woman are well within a long tradition which Christianity has bequeathed on the West.

Many women still suffer from the same problem of idealization. The Angel of the 19th century became the "nice" girl of the 20th. The nice girl, many of us were told in the '40s and '50s, was taught to distinguish between "real love" on the one hand, and "just sex" on the other. Sex and love had to be in separate spheres. The nice girl was taught to distrust and discount her sexuality nearly as much as the Child-Angel had been before her. She could admit sexual advances so far and no further. Many women were told by their mothers that men would never "love" or respect a girl they had sex with before marriage. Such a girl had "made herself cheap." This of course was not true. Our mothers probably knew many women who had had sex before marriage and who were now perfectly respectable matrons. It was not simply that they wanted to protect their daughters from an unwanted pregnancy; they needed to believe in the myth that the fast, sexy girl would come to a sticky end in much the same way as the Victorians needed to believe that all prostitutes ended up in the river or in Australia. Novelists like Dickens helped to keep this myth alive even though there was plenty of contemporary evidence that the Victorian prostitute often married and that prostitution frequently helped the working-class girl to move up in society and gain affluent respectability, as a pop singer or a model does today. It was, however, culturally important to believe that sex leads women to ruin and degradation, so the myths have remained. The frequency with which the "nice" girl appears in popular novels today shows that she has been a real problem for women who have had to struggle to get away from this "nice" conditioning.

Similarly, many women are still troubled by the myth of female perfection. Women often try to attain impossibly high standards. They want to be "perfectly" beautiful, to be "perfect" wives, mothers, housekeepers, career women. It is the ideal of the "Superwoman" who is so proficient in so many spheres (men may want to be perfect careerists, but are not so worried about domestic perfection) that she is superhuman. Such perfection is unnatural, and in striving for it women can irritate their men as much as the Child-Wife antagonized Victorian husbands. Once women felt guilty because they were Eve; next they felt guilty because they were not the Virgin Mary. Now a woman feels guilty for not being perfect in everything she does.

Secular women have certainly seen themselves as damaged by the system which pushes women away into a separate world. Eleanor of Aquitaine and powerful rich women like her would have experienced the misogyny of Western Europe very differently from the ordinary woman. Other women were certainly aware of the injustice of Christianity's position. The voices of two distinguished Christian women of the 15th and 16th centuries have come down to us, showing the distress women felt at the virulent Christian misogyny, and they show us also the two chief ways that women felt able to cope with the hatred of the male world.

Teresa of Avila, the 16th-century Carmelite nun, was a woman who won considerable respect from the male world of her time. She became a leading figure in the Counter-Reformation, and by her own efforts was responsible for the widespread reform of the Carmelite order of nuns and friars. Yet it is clear that she suffered acutely from the restrictions and the charges laid at women's door:

> When thou wert in the world, Lord, thou didst not despise women, but didst always help them and show them great compassion. Thou didst find more faith and no less love in them than in men. . . . [Now] we can do nothing in public that is of any use to thee, nor dare we speak of some of the truths over which we weep in secret, lest thou shouldst not hear this, our petition. Yet, Lord, I cannot believe this of thy goodness and righteousness, for thou art a righteous Judge, not like judges in the world, who, being after all men and sons of Adam, refuse to consider any woman's virtue as above suspicion. Yes, my King, but the day will come when all will be known. I am not speaking on my account, for the whole world is already aware of my wickedness, and I am glad that it should become known; but, when I see what the times are like, I feel it is not right to repel

spirits which are virtuous and brave, even though they be the
spirits of women.

*(The Way of Perfection,* III)

There is a defiance in Teresa's complaint to her God. Men are not
being Christian in their behavior to women. She foresees a time when
the unjust and uncharitable judgments of these men will be over-
thrown. Teresa's own life was an example of the way that women
could defy the male world of Christendom. But defiance and challenge could be very dangerous for women in the Christian world.

Most women chose to retreat. The male world pushed them away
and the women cooperated by withdrawing into a different world.
Most women disappeared into the anonymity of marriage and were
never heard of again. Other women, however, sought independence
and autonomy by entering into exclusively female worlds. A particularly interesting case is the 15th-century writer Christine de Pizan, a
well-to-do and highly educated woman, who gives an account of her
distressing conversion to the cause of women in her *Book of the City
of Ladies.* In all her wide reading, she tells us, she could find nothing
but hatred of women. All the authorities "concur in one conclusion:
that the behavior of women is inclined to and full of every vice."
When Christine carefully examined her own life and the lives of her
women friends, she could find nothing to justify this conclusion.
However, she could not simply shrug this off as typical male prejudice. It was too deeply engrained in her culture, it had too respectable a pedigree for her to sweep it aside as so much male nonsense.
Christine could not trust her own perceptions, and her account
makes it clear how pervasive was this damaging misogyny and how
powerful an influence it exerted over the minds of women themselves.

Yet I still argued vehemently against women, saying that it
would be impossible that so many famous men—such solemn
scholars, possessed of such deep and great understanding, so
clear-sighted in all things, as it seemed—could have spoken so
falsely on so many occasions that I could hardly find a book on
morals where, even before I had read it in its entirety, I did not
find several chapters or certain sections attacking women, no
matter who the author was. This reason alone, in short, made

me conclude that, although my intellect did not perceive my own great faults and, likewise, those of other women because of its simpleness and ignorance, it was however truly fitting that such was the case.

*(Book of the City of Ladies,* I:1:i)

Christine had the opportunity to work out her own position with scholarly clarity and logic. Yet it was not a position arrived at without pain. Her studies induced in her a crisis of self-hatred:

> I was so transfixed in this line of thinking for such a long time that it seemed as if I were in a stupor. Like a gushing fountain, a series of authorities, whom I recalled one after another, came to mind, along with their opinions on this topic. And I finally decided that God formed a vile creature when He made woman, and I wondered how such a worthy artisan could have deigned to make such an abominable work which, from what they say, is the vessel as well as the abode of every evil and vice. As I was thinking this, a great unhappiness and sadness welled up in my heart, for I detested myself and the entire feminine sex, as though we were monstrosities of nature.

(Ibid., I:1:i)

The views of Aquinas, of Augustine and so many others had made Christine convinced that she was something "abominable" and unnatural. Why, she asks passionately, did God make such a horrible creation, such a vicious thing as a woman must be? It almost led her into a blasphemous rejection of God's goodness, she recalls, because it seemed impossible to believe that a good God had made such a creature as woman. It is interesting and tragic that for a long time it never occurred to Christine to challenge the male authorities as Teresa did; for her it was more logical to challenge God Himself. Despite her own perception of women as innocent she was deeply convinced that women must be as evil as her society and culture told her they were:

> "O God, how can this be? For unless I stray from my faith, I must never doubt that Your infinite wisdom and most perfect goodness ever created anything which was not good. . . . Yet look at all these accusations which have been judged, decided,

and concluded against women. I do not know how to understand this repugnance. If it is so, fair Lord God, that in fact so
many abominations abound in the female sex, for You Yourself
say that the testimony of two or three witnesses lends credence,
why shall I not doubt that this is true? Alas, God, why did You
not let me be born in this world as a man, so that all my inclina-
tions would be to serve You better, and so that I would not stray
in anything and would be as perfect as a man is said to be? But
since Your kindness has not been extended to me, then forgive
my negligence in Your service, most fair Lord God, and may it
not displease You, for the servant who receives fewer gifts from
his lord is less obliged in his service." I spoke these words to
God in my lament and a great deal more for a very long time in
sad reflection, and in my folly I considered myself most unfortunate because God had made me inhabit a female body in the
world.

(Ibid., I:1:ii)

One of the most distressing aspects of Christine's plight is her
isolation. Locked alone inside her female body, outside God's plan,
outside the concern of the male world, she feels that the whole world
is armed against her. When she has her "vision" of the three ladies
who console her and give her her mission, it is significant that her
solution is not defiance but defense. She will build in her "City" a
"refuge and defence" for women against all their assailants. For too
long women have been vulnerable, "exposed like a field without a
surrounding hedge." It will be Christine's job to build "a particular
edifice, built like a city wall . . . where no one will reside except all
ladies of fame and women worthy of praise" (ibid. I:1:iii). For Christine, the women's answer is to retreat. The best they can do is to
create a separate world for themselves where there are no men.

However, this female stronghold is not without its dangers. One of
the precursors of her "City," Christine writes, is the tribe of the
Amazons, the mythical race of female warriors that fascinated Christendom. This tribe arose in Scythia during the Classical period, when
all the men in their country had been killed in war. Their women
banded together, Christine explains, in a "new domination by themselves without being subject to men, and they promulgated a new

edict whereby no man was allowed to enter into their jurisdiction" (I:16:i). It is no wonder that the classical story of this aggressive tribe of women, who were so powerful that they even defeated Hercules himself, was so deeply fascinating to the Christian mind. It clearly fitted the male view of women as strongly inimical and dangerous to men, and yet, at the same time, ideally separate from them, living in their own self-contained world. However, this separation was mutilating. The Amazons literally deformed themselves, just as for centuries people like Jerome and Tertullian had been urging women to make themselves repulsive and deform their female bodies:

> And in this way the women of Scythia began to carry arms and were then called Amazons, which actually means the "breastless ones," because they had a custom whereby the nobles among them, when they were little girls, burned off their left breast through some technique, so that it would not hinder them from carrying a shield, and they removed the right breast of commoners to make it easier for them to shoot a bow.
>
> (Ibid., I:16)

The idea of a separate world of deformed women was appealing to both men and women in the Christian world. Christine herself is so used to the female body being something deformed and repellent that she sees nothing abhorrent in the Amazons' self-mutilation. Women were already freaks. A further deformity would make no difference, especially if it deprived them of something as specifically female as a breast.

Most women have not had the opportunity Christine had to study the misogyny of Christian scholars and leading theologians. It is difficult to illustrate the effect official Christian hatred of women had on ordinary women, because unlike Teresa, Christine and, later, the great women novelists like George Eliot, who showed how damaging it was to push women into a different world from men, most women have not been able to record their feelings. Uneducated women would also have found it difficult to assess their feelings as accurately and intelligently as a Christine de Pizan and a George Eliot. For a long time it seems likely that women remained as untouched by Christian misogyny as Grazida of Montaillou had been untouched by the Christian hatred of sexuality. The Catholic Church has never been very efficient about spreading its doctrines among the masses, and, as we have seen, in Mediterranean countries which have been traditionally Catholic, saner and healthier attitudes to both sex and women prevail. Victorianism and the Cult of the True Woman in America are products of Protestant Christianity and Protestantism and Puritanism were both far more efficient about promoting Christian doctrines and Christian attitudes. In all cultures some people remain impervious to all forms of propaganda, and it is likely that many women were not hurt and damaged and that many men and women loved each other more than they hated each other. The anguish that characterizes the male/female relationship exists side by side with the earthy fun men and women have together in Breughel's paintings, for example. However, while certain peasant cultures may have remained healthily immune to the sick misogyny of Christianity, the late 15th century saw the explosion of the Christian hatred of women taken to its most extreme form. In the literature of the Great Witch Craze that raged in Europe for over two hundred years there is evidence that the view of women as evil and dangerous had left the cloisters and was deeply affecting ordinary men and women. The Craze also helped to imprint this portrait of woman as man's diabolic enemy more powerfully and more popularly than ever before. Ordinary and uneducated women really believed that they were witches, and ordinary men seem to have become terrified sexually of women.

# 3

# THE FINAL SOLUTION FOR MEN: THE WITCH

The repressions of Western culture are nowhere more clearly shown than in the great panics of persecution that erupt from time to time with astonishing violence and subside just as suddenly, leaving everybody bewildered and embarrassed by the temporary madness that has gripped society. The Nazi persecution of the Jews and McCarthy's persecution of communists and homosexuals for un-American activities are obvious examples. The craze of persecution is not directed at real culprits or real enemies of society, but the victims act as scapegoats for neuroses which society has repressed and can only express in this violent and irrational way. We often call these crazes "witch hunts," because of the great craze for persecuting witches that raged throughout Europe during the 16th and 17th centuries. It is a classic example of these irrational panics, and has named them with good reason. Yet the great Witch Hunts did more than give a name to a curious and disturbing Western phenomenon. They have profoundly damaged the relationship between the sexes in our society.

The Witch Hunts brought together all the buried sexual fears that had been developing in the Christian West. By the late 15th century the Church had clearly impressed Europe with a terror of sexuality and a hatred of women that exploded in the first sporadic Witch Hunts. The panic grew during the 16th century, reaching its zenith in the late 16th century and continuing until about 1680, when the fury had spent itself. America, the New World, had its own Witch Craze in Salem in 1692, yet again reproducing the neuroses of Europe on the other side of the Atlantic. The Witch Hunts were a religious phenomenon and were engineered by the Church and supported both by the beliefs of devout people and the fears of the "witches" themselves. There was no political or commercial motive such as contributed to the persecution of the religious order of the Templars or the persecution of Roman Catholics during Queen Elizabeth's reign. The Witch Hunts were purely the product of Christian zeal. It was an exclusively Western phenomenon. The parts of Eastern Europe and Greece which came under the aegis of Orthodox Christianity (which had always been a little more sane about sex and women) were quite unaffected. The panic was equally intense in Catholicism and in Protestantism. Some parts of Europe suffered more badly than others: Spain, Italy, Portugal and Holland had only limited and sporadic witch hunting. There was little mass witch hunting in England; though hundreds of women were executed for dabbling in the occult, this was a quite separate phenomenon from witchcraft proper. The craze was worst in Scotland, France, the German States and Switzerland. It would flare up violently in one area, then cease with unnatural suddenness, only to break out again in the same place years later.

During the Witch Hunts, it was believed that certain women had sex with a devil, called an *incubus*. These witches would fly through the air at night to attend a sabbath, where they worshipped the Devil and indulged in cannibalistic rites and perverted sexual orgies. Witches could also have magic powers; they were in league with Satan for the ruin of mankind. Witches could raise storms and ruin crops; they could cause impotence, sterility and even death. The witch was a Christian creation; she was seen as a heretic of the most dangerous sort, because she was giving to the Devil the honor that was due to God. It was therefore the duty of all good Christians to hunt out these enemies of society and of God. The conspiracy had to be uncovered and witches had to be made to confess their guilt and reveal their colleagues and fellow-conspirators. Torture was justifiable to this end and was applied brutally so that women "confessed" that they were indeed witches, described their sexual intercourse with the Devil and what happened at the Sabbaths, prompted by the questions of the Inquisitors. The Inquisitors were not involved in a cold manufacture of an untruth. They passionately believed in witchcraft; learned and sophisticated men were convinced it was their duty to hound witches to death and to hunt them out of their hiding places among virtuous Christians. It was not a logical belief; indeed, it contradicted many tenets of Christianity, including Jesus' command to love enemies. It was an emotional conviction proceeding from the repressions that Christianity had imposed on Europe. For centuries sex had been seen as evil and women as the enemies of man. Now sex became diabolical and women the arch-enemies of society.

In reality, of course, there were no witches. According to Margaret Murray's researches, there *were* pagan cults in Europe at that time, which were believed to be Satanic by Orthodox Christians. These pagans held their rites secretly in the woods at night. Belief in this theory, which was popular and widely accepted for a very long time, meant that many people still think that there were witches. Modern "witches" trace their origins back to the "witches" described by Margaret Murray. However, Murray's theory has now been discredited. She was wrong: there were no pagan cults, no sabbaths and no magic rituals. The "witch" was far more pernicious than a secret society. She existed only in the emotions and imaginations of Christians, but so powerfully that many women genuinely believed that they were witches. They believed that the dreams they had of having sex with the Devil (dreams which were fuelled by the panic and propaganda of the Church) had actually happened. Other people believed so strongly in the witch that they thought it their duty to kill thousands of women. It is difficult to know how many people died in the two-hundred-year craze. Some scholars have claimed that as many people died in the Witch Hunts as died in all the European wars up to 1914. In some Swiss villages there were hardly any women left alive. It is impossible to estimate numbers with any real accuracy, but it seems that the numbers were horrifyingly high.

Witchcraft then was a giant collective fantasy of Western Christians, expressive of their deepest fears. It was an international sickness inspired by a religion of love. Today it has become fashionable to deny that there was any particularly anti-woman bias in the Witch Craze because men died as witches as well as women. However, far fewer men than women were accused, and most of the great writers on witchcraft at the time were insistent that it was essentially a woman's vice. If some men did die, believing that they were witches, it is evidence of the power the panic exerted over the popular imagination. However, a neurotic panic like the Witch Craze cannot afford to be too specific in the way it expresses itself. Men had been taught to hate women and regard them as their enemy. However, they also knew that it was their Christian duty to love their enemies, and that hatred was wrong. The persecutors needed to hide from themselves the unedifying and un-Christian fact that men hated all women. Just as "token" women today sit on committees and directorial boards, so in the Witch Craze "token" men were executed. If only women had died, it would have expressed men's terror and hatred of women too nakedly and unacceptably. For centuries Christian theologians and preachers had been isolating women so that their contaminating and sinful sexuality should not draw men into sin. The Witch Craze simply took this ostracism to its emotionally logical conclusion. Christians had been told that women were abominable beings who were sexually depraved. The witch was the ultimate depravity, and her diabolic sexuality was truly monstrous.

Norman Cohn, in his excellent book *Europe's Inner Demons,* shows the different ingredients that made up this new Christian witch. There certainly had been "witches" before the late 15th century, but up until then the Church had condemned belief in witches as a pagan superstition. The witch was part of the pagan world that had preceded Christianity in Europe. Peasant communities believed that certain old women had the power of the evil eye and could cast spells on their enemies, damaging their crops and raising storms. If you suspected that one of these old witches had put a curse on you, you could bring a legal action against her for *maleficium,* the technical legal term for these evil spells. There were also old pagan beliefs that certain women could fly through the air at night with a goddess, who is sometimes called Diana, sometimes Hecate and at other times Herodias, and take part in cannibalistic rites. The Church condemned these beliefs, but some simple women really thought that they did take part in these nocturnal adventures. That this belief was rife among women is shown in the list of questions that the 10th-century Penitential of Burchard, of Wörms, suggests a woman be asked in confession:

> Have you believed what many women, turning back to Satan, believe and affirm to be true; as that you believe that in the silence of the night, when you have settled down in bed, and your husband lies in your bosom, you are able, while still in your body, to go out through the closed doors and travel through the spaces of the world, together with others, who are similarly deceived; and that without visible weapons, you kill people who have been baptized and redeemed by Christ's blood, and together cook and devour their flesh and that where the heart was, you put straw or wood or something of that sort, and that after eating these people you bring them to life again and grant them a brief spell of life? If you believe this, you shall do penance on bread and water for fifty days, and likewise in each of the seven years following.

(V:170)

It may seem incredible that anybody could actually believe what is so obviously a dream. However, anthropologists tell us that primitive people find it very difficult to distinguish between dreams and reality. Indeed, the most sophisticated of us sometimes have difficulty when we wake up after a particularly vivid nightmare in convincing ourselves that it didn't "really" happen. The dream experiences of witches would be crucial in the Witch Craze. At first the Church was absolutely clear that these dreams were simply dreams. In his *Canon Episcopi* of 906, Regino, Abbot of Prüm, is very scornful about people who can't distinguish between these flying dreams and reality: "who would be so foolish as to think that things that happened only in the mind have also happened in the flesh?" Later, witch hunters would find Regino's and Burchard's condemnations of witch beliefs an embarrassment. These old pagan superstitions were the basis of their own creation of the witch who flew through the air not with Diana but with Satan, who participated in orgiastic sabbaths and copulated with demons.

The essential ingredient for this transformation of the pagan witches into the Christian heresy was the unique Christian invention of Satan. In no other religion is there anything comparable in power and fearful monstrosity to the Christian Devil. There are certainly devils in other religions, but these are usually rather playful creatures, who possess none of the near omnipotence of Satan. Satan in his full horror was a fairly late development in Christianity, and did not begin to terrorize the imaginations of Christians until the Middle Ages. When Jesus and St. Paul talked about demons and about Satan they meant something rather different from what we mean by devils. They were speaking of the spiritual beings who had crept into the cosmogony of Judaism at that time and who were creatures of the upper air. They were no threat to the all-powerful God of monotheistic Judaism. St. Antony and the early ascetics in the desert were plagued by quite different demons, the demons of Late Antiquity who were seen as extensions of their own personalities. Each man was connected to a good spirit or a "genius" and a bad spirit. A great man was connected to a great "genius." Antony was wrestling with the shadow-side of his personality, albeit in a very neurotic way. These sophisticated distinctions got lost during the Dark Ages, when the refinements of Jewish and Greco-Roman culture were lost. As the repressions of Christianity spread through society to the common people, the Devil became the arch-projection for all the "evil" that they could not accept in themselves. It has been argued that belief in the Devil is the final triumph of ethical monotheism. Other religions see the Absolute God as beyond Good and Evil. The Hindus, for example, see Evil as one of the masks behind which the absolute God hides himself. However, in Christianity good and evil, as we limited human beings conceive them, become absolute forces in themselves. God is Absolute Good and can accept no evil in himself, no shadow side. The Devil gradually emerges as God's shadow, the evil that we know exists but for which God refuses responsibility. This means that we cannot accept the evil in ourselves. We disown the "evil" and project it outwardly on the Devil because evil can find no acceptance by the good God. The Christian creation of the Devil in fact makes Evil absolute. Sexuality was one of the "evils" that Christian men could not accept, and so they repressed it and projected it on women, who became unnaturally sexual in the Christian imagination. Sexuality also becomes diabolic in the Middle Ages, and Satan is represented as a vast animal with a priapic sexual appetite and huge sexual organs. It could only be a matter of time before the two monstrous sexual projections of medieval Christianity came together. Women and the Devil finally merged in the late 15th century, and the impact of their coming together exploded in the Witch Craze.

The old pagan belief in witchcraft received its Christian baptism in 1484, when Pope Innocent VIII brought out an astonishing Bull, *Summa desiderantes,* where it appears that an epidemic of sexual anxiety had sprung up in Germany. Men were becoming impotent and their wives unable to conceive. This was accounted for by the witches who "have abandoned themselves to devils, to incubi and succubi" and who have bewitched their neighbors. The Pope commissioned two Dominicans, Jacob Sprenger and Heinrich Kramer, to take the matter in hand. The result of this partnership was Sprenger's *Malleus Maleficarum (The Hammer of Witches),* which was a handbook to help Inquisitors in the investigation of witchcraft. The *Malleus* received a reluctant endorsement by the University of Cologne in 1487 and became a major text of the Inquisition, going through nineteen editions. In the *Malleus,* the creation of the witch is still in its infancy: there is no mention of the Sabbath and very little discussion of sex with devils. Sprenger concentrates on the *Maleficia* which women inflict upon men, especially the sexual disasters which had so suddenly erupted. After the publication of the *Malleus* there was only sporadic witch hunting, and the Craze did not really get under way until the early 16th century. However, Sprenger's document did influence the later writers on witchcraft, and its influence still lingers today in the myth of the castrating bitch which bedevils the relationship of men and women.

Sprenger is quite clear that witchcraft is a woman's vice. Women, he says, are either very good or very evil: there is no halfway state. This is a preoccupation of Western thinking about women: they are either Eve or the Virgin Mary. Women, he argues, are far more likely to be seduced by witchcraft than men, because they are essentially perverse creatures. Sprenger develops Aquinas' theory of women being essentially misbegotten human creatures:

> And it should be noticed that there was a defect in the formation of the first woman, since she was formed from a bent rib, that is, a rib of the breast, which is bent as it were in a contrary direction to a man. And since through this defect she is an imperfect animal, she always deceives . . . and this is indicated by the etymology of the word; for *Femina* comes from *Fe* and *Minus,* since she is ever weaker to hold and to preserve the faith. And this as regards faith is of her very nature.
>
> *(Malleus Maleficarum,* p. 44)

Women's inferior humanity, therefore, makes her far more vulnerable to the suggestions of the Devil than a man is. However, what particularly inclines women to witchcraft is, as by now we should expect, her insatiable sexuality: "All witchcraft comes from carnal lust," writes Sprenger, "which in woman is insatiable. 'There are three things that are never satisfied, yea a fourth thing which says: it is not enough.' (Proverbs xxx). That is the mouth of the womb. Wherefore for the sake of fulfilling their lusts, they consort even with devils" (p. 4). Just as sex had always been seen as deeply linked with sin, so now it is essentially linked with the power of the Devil. It is the means Satan uses to gain power over men and women:

> . . . God allows the Devil greater power against men's venereal acts than against their other actions; and [St. Thomas] gives this reason, that this is likely to be so, since those women are chiefly apt to be witches who are disposed to such acts.
>
> For he [St. Thomas] gives this reason, that since the first corruption of sin, by which man became the slave of the Devil,

came to us through the act of generation, therefore greater power is allowed by God to the Devil in this act than in all others.

(Ibid., p. 48)

The *Malleus* continues the tradition of laying the responsibility for sexual desire at the door of women. Sprenger thanks God devoutly that men are free of this cursed sexuality and therefore free of witchcraft, "for since He was willing to be born and to suffer for us, therefore He has granted to men this privilege." The astonishing implication of this is that God did *not* save women or die for women, and therefore He has abandoned them to sex and thus to the Devil. There had always been a tendency to push women outside God's plan for the world; now they have been not only excluded but made to assume the position of an enemy, in alliance with the enemy of God and man.

What emerges very clearly in the *Malleus* is the widespread sexual fear and neurosis which is manifesting itself in a regular epidemic of symptoms. Men were finding sex more and more of a problem. They were complaining of impotence and of premature ejaculation; they complained of frantic sexual passion which could only express itself in perversity. The anti-sex propaganda that the Church had been putting out for centuries was taking its toll. The fault was woman's, of course. Just as she had been responsible for luring men to sin by her sexual power, now she was maiming men sexually by diabolic magic. Sprenger lists seven ways in which women who are in league with Satan attack men, nearly all of them sexual:

Now there are, as it is said in the Papal Bull, seven methods by which they infect with witchcraft the venereal act and the conception of the womb: first by inclining the minds of men to inordinate passions; second by obstructing their generative force; third by removing the members accommodated to that act; fourth by changing men into beasts by their magic art; fifth by destroying the generative force in women; sixth by procuring abortion; seventh by offering children to devils.

(Ibid., p. 47)

There was a strong tendency in Christianity to see sex as an uncontrollable force within men. Now the new witchcraft scare showed that this wild sexual longing was falling upon men from the outside. It was the result of a malignant force, an evil spell inflicted upon men without any fault of their own by wicked witches. The old Christian projection had taken a further step forward: women have acquired a new and sinister power, which forces sexuality on unwilling men and reduces them to a state of passivity in the face of women's malign force.

The *Malleus* illustrates this point by a short history which is instructive:

> There was in the town of Marburg in the diocese of Constance a certain young man who was bewitched in such a way that he could never perform the carnal act with any woman except one. And many have heard him tell that he had often wished to refuse that woman and take flight to other lands; but that hitherto he had been compelled to rise up in the night and to come very quickly back, sometimes over land and sometimes through the air as if he were flying.
>
> (Ibid., p. 118)

Clearly, all that had happened was that the man had got sexually fixated on one woman so that he was impotent with his own wife. His vivid dreams about her (flying, as we all know, is about sex) are so real that he thinks he has actually been to bed with her and has traveled back to his own bed over huge distances. What is most interesting is that he feels "compelled" from without. When we feel passion for somebody we do feel possessed by a compulsion that seems beyond our control, but the implication in the *Malleus* is that this violent affection has been inflicted on the young man by the woman herself. It is she who forces him, however reluctant he might be, to copulate with her night after night; it is she who makes him impotent with other women. Women have always been sexual temptresses, but now their powers have increased. The Holy Patriarch Jacob was seduced by his wives, but he was only dragged into his own bed, in Augustine's view. Now the power of women is so great that a woman can bewitch a man and force him to travel through the air to come to her bed at night, hundreds of miles away. A man's sexuality is projected onto a woman's evil powers, which have now grown to such proportions that a Papal campaign has been launched in Europe to combat them.

The *Malleus* shows that there is a good deal of anger between the sexes. Men are seen as the hapless victims of these witches, who have to be cajoled or appeased into good humor. Women are seen as angry creatures, boiling and brooding with hatred and resentment. This may reflect a real state of affairs and may not be a piece of prejudiced misogyny. After all, being constantly vilified in sermons as Eve cannot have made women feel very good about themselves. If Christine de Pizan, some few years after the publication of the *Malleus,* could be reduced to a crisis of self-loathing because of the misogyny she had encountered in her studies, women who were not so educated may well have felt a confused anger and unhappiness at the hostility that the Church encouraged their men to feel for them. The fact that women are so often seen at this time as "scolds" with vile tempers and evil tongues may mean that this was the only way a woman could express the confused resentment she felt. The *Malleus* shows that this anger is especially furious when it is sexually linked, and indeed if men were really showing the degree of sexual disturbance that Sprenger suggests, this was almost certainly because of the Church's negative teaching about sexuality. It must have affected the sexual relationships of men and women, and women must have felt bewildered about their own role in the sexual act, which is now acquiring a depth of evil which is identified with Satan. The *Malleus* describes a woman as simmering with rage: "When she hates someone whom she formerly loved then she seethes with anger and impatience in her whole soul, just as the tides of the sea are always heaving and boiling" (p. 44). There is a state of war between men and women, especially when a woman has been divorced by her husband or rejected by a lover. Sprenger quotes from the Bible to show how women have always loved to take revenge on the men who have scorned them, as Potiphar's wife persecuted Joseph when he rejected her attempts to seduce him. But a woman is so angry and resentful, Sprenger continues, that in sexual matters even the good women in the Bible are consumed with hatred and jealousy: "For you see in Genesis xxi how impatient and envious Sarah was of Hagar when she conceived: how jealous Rachel was of Leah because she had no children: and Hannah who was barren of the fruitful Penninmah" (p. 45). Women are possessed of "inordinate affections and passions," Sprenger concludes, and "they search for, brood over and inflict various vengeances either by witchcraft or some other means. Wherefore it is no great wonder that so great a number of witches exist in this sex" (p. 45).

These women, for whom sexual rejection carried additional traumas in such an age of sexual guilt and resentment, may have really believed that they could bewitch the men who had injured them. After all, witchcraft was part of their culture: the Church had not been able to stamp out belief in the old pagan power of *maleficium*. It would have been one way of getting back at the male world which she must have felt, in however unformed a way, was unfairly weighted against her. A curse, believed in so readily by the men concerned, could well have frightened him into a temporary impotence. The widespread symptoms show an almost epidemic sexual anxiety among men. The "curse" of a "witch" could have added a last explosive element to an already dangerous situation. Worst of all, women could actually castrate a man, Sprenger insists. A witch "can actually take away the male organ, not indeed by actually despoiling the human body of it, but by concealing it with some glamour." It is worth noticing what has happened to that word "glamour," which now refers to an exotic and powerful feminine beauty, sought after and admired by men and women alike. It was originally a witch word: it was a magic power that could castrate hapless men who had the misfortune to cross a woman.

From as early as the 3rd century, people like the great Christian thinker Origen had felt that the only way to free themselves of the irresistible danger of their sexuality was by castrating themselves. Later, more spiritual forms of castration became fashionable. The *Malleus* quotes the old story of St. Helias, the early Christian ascetic. He had ruled a convent of nuns, but found that he had to flee because he was overcome by sexual temptation. However, he was saved by divine intervention. Angels appeared to him "and made him an eunuch. For one seemed to hold his hands, another his feet and the third to cut out his testicles with a knife, though this was not really so, but only seemed to be" (p. 94). Helias had no more trouble with sex and was able to go back to his virgins without any fear of being lured by them into sin. The story shows utter despair in the face of sex. Man cannot control his sexual urges, and God has to step in violently to control it for him. Sprenger also quotes the more recent story of Blessed Thomas, the Dominican, whose brothers wanted to prevent him joining the order. They locked him up with a prostitute, certain that the temptation would be quite irresistible, and indeed Thomas can't have been quite as cool as he might have wished about the lady as he had to resort to violence to get rid of her. He seized a lighted torch and drove out "the engine of the fire of lust" from the prison. He then fell into an exhausted sleep and had a dream in which angels girded him with the girdle of chastity. As soon as he felt the touch of this girdle in his dreams he became so chaste that for the rest of his life "he abhorred all the delights of the flesh, so that he could not even speak to a woman except under a compulsion" (p. 94). This kind of sexual trauma shows how extreme were the means thought justified to preserve male chastity. Castration, however spiritual and symbolic, is hardly a healthy way to deal with sexual temptation. Chastity has to be imposed by some form of mutilation, physical in the case of Origen and spiritual in the case of Helias or Thomas. The castration fear shows how men were being mutilated by the sexual neuroses of the Christian world as well as women. The result for women is the kind of isolation that Jerome had recommended centuries before in his letter to Nepotian. The virgins in St. Helias' convent may have had no sexual designs upon him, but because *he* felt tempted, they had to be abandoned. Any woman who wanted to speak to Blessed Thomas and seek spiritual advice would also be shunned. In the interests of male purity all women, prostitute or nun alike, have to be unfairly ostracized.

What was new in the 1480s was that it was now not only celibates who were having these castration fantasies. Married men were having them too. Men believed that the witch had literally castrated them by her evil spells. Sprenger gives a telling account of one such case of glamour:

> In the town of Ratisbon, a certain young man who had an intrigue with a girl, wishing to leave her, lost his member; that is to say some glamour was cast over it so that he could see or touch nothing but his smooth body. In his worry over this he

went to a tavern to drink wine; and after he had sat there for a while he got into conversation with another woman who was there, and told her the cause of his sadness, explaining everything and demonstrating in his body that it was so. The woman was astute and asked whether he suspected any one; and when he named such a one, unfolding the whole matter, she said "If persuasion is not enough, you must use some violence, in order to induce her to restore to you your health." So in the evening the young man watched the way by which the witch was in the habit of going, and finding her, prayed to her to restore to him the health of his body. And when she maintained that she was innocent and knew nothing about it, he fell upon her and winding a towel tightly round her neck, choked her saying "Unless you give me back my health, you shall die at my hands!" Then she, being unable to cry out and with her face already swelling and growing black, said "Let me go and I will heal you." The young man then relaxed the pressure of the towel and the witch touched him with her hand between the thighs, saying, "Now you have what you desire." And the young man, as he said, plainly felt before he had verified it by looking or touching, that his member had been restored to him by the mere touch of the witch.

(Ibid., p. 119)

It is not difficult to imagine how the unfortunate "witch" managed, out of pure desperation to "cure" her ex-lover by the "mere touch" of her hand, but women clearly believed in their castrating powers. This "glamour" was a woman's only weapon in a sexual atmosphere which was so unfairly weighted against her, and which could so suddenly erupt into violence. The clergy encouraged this belief in "glamour." Thus Sprenger tells how one of his fellow Dominicans in Spires had a young man come to him in Confession who "woefully said that he had lost his member." The priest was astonished at this, but obtained "proof of it when I saw nothing on the young man's removing his clothes and showing the place." The skeptical priest himself, if we are to believe Sprenger's story, immediately joined in with the young man's fantasy to the extent of hallucinating along with him. He instantly asked the young castratee whom he suspected of bewitching him, and on being told that the girl was now living in Worms, he said, "I advise you to go to her as soon as possible and try your utmost to soften her with gentle words and promises." The woman had to be appeased. Fortunately, the young man returned from Worms cured, though what method the girl used has been left to the imagination.

Castration did not just happen on a one to one basis. There were some witches whose glamour was so strong that they were mass castrators:

> And what, then, is to be thought of those witches who in this way sometimes collect male organs in great numbers, as many as twenty or thirty members together, and put them in a bird's nest, or shut them up in a box, where they move themselves like living members and eat oats and corn as has been seen by many and is a matter of common report.

(Ibid., p. 121)

The penis in such a grotesque and humiliating position is clearly a horrified male fantasy of the time. It is also interesting that a matter of such "common report" represents a widespread view that the penis has a life of its own; it does not need to be joined to a man. Augustine had seen the independent life of the penis with its involuntary erections as one of the punishments of the Fall. Now men believe that they are not essentially connected with their penises which can get on perfectly well without them. Women's sexual glamour can mutilate and castrate a man and the absurd position of the penis, trapped in a bird's nest, shows the contempt he feels for his discarded sexuality. Not even celibates were exempt from this castrating glamour of the woman. Sprenger goes on to tell the story of a young man who had lost his penis and went to the witch who had castrated him to ask for it back. She told him to climb up the tree where she kept her stock of members and choose one for himself from the nest. When the young man "tried to take a big one the witch said: you must not take that one, it belongs to the parish priest."

Many of the women who died in the later holocausts were old and crazy, Cohn tells us. However, there is nothing old or ugly about these witches in the *Malleus*. They are all women who had been

attractive enough to induce a young man to have sex with them or to
have had long involvements with them. Indeed, the *Malleus* is quite
clear that part of a woman's danger is her beauty. Sprenger quotes
Valerius' remark to Rufinus about the Chimera, that mythical beast
who was a lion, a goat and a viper all at once.

> You do not know that woman is the Chimera, but it is good that
> you should know it; for that monster was of three forms; its face
> was that of a radiant and noble lion, it had the filthy belly of a
> goat and it was armed with the virulent tail of a viper. And he
> means that a woman is beautiful to look upon, contaminating to
> the touch and deadly to keep.

(Ibid., p. 46)

Yet again woman is seen as a monster, which is beautiful and seductive, foul and dangerous all at the same time. Women are like the
Sirens who sang so sweetly that they lured sailors to their death:
"For as she is a liar by nature, so in her speech she stings while she
delights us," and woman tries very hard to delight men, Sprenger
says indignantly. "There is no man in the world who studies so hard
to please the good God as even an ordinary woman studies by her
vanities to please men" (p. 46).

It is obvious where Sprenger's witches are to be found today.
Women today desire "glamour" and its glossy, artificial beauty to
enslave men. The beautiful woman, the vamp who seduces a man so
that he becomes so obsessed by her that he gives up "all for love" is
deeply familiar to us as part of our mythology in plays, novels and
films. Shakespeare drew a portrait of a witch like this in Cleopatra,
who unmans Antony so that he neglects his empire and even runs
out of the battle of Actium in pursuit of her. Such a *femme fatale* is
literally fatal to men, not just because she can cause his death (as
Cleopatra caused Antony's), but because she has in some sense castrated him. Antony has been seduced away from his former manly
life of war and endurance and has come under the mysterious sexy
power of a woman. Constantly his relationship with Cleopatra is
referred to as an "enchantment." Cleopatra has true glamour. She
can even seduce Enobarbus, her greatest critic, to utter uncharacteristic praise when he recalls his first sight of her:

> *Enobarbus:* The barge she sat in, like a burnish'd throne,
> Burn'd on the water. The poop was beaten gold;
> Purple the sails, and so perfumed that
> The winds were love-sick with them; the oars were silver,
> Which to the tune of flutes kept stroke, and made
> The water which they beat to follow faster,
> As amorous of their strokes. For her own person,
> It beggar'd all description. She did lie
> In her pavilion, cloth-of-gold, of tissue,
> O'er picturing that Venus where we see
> The fancy out-work nature. On each side her
> Stood pretty dimpled boys, like smiling Cupids
> With divers-colour'd fans, whose wind did seem
> To glow the delicate cheeks which they did cool,
> And what they undid did.
>  *Agrippa:*      O, rare for Antony!
>  *Enobarbus:* Her gentlewomen, like the Nereides,
> So many mermaids, tended her i'th' eyes,
> And made their bends adorings. At the helm
> A seeming mermaid steers. The silken tackle
> Swell with the touches of those flower-soft hands
> That yarely frame the office. From the barge
> A strange invisible perfume hits the sense
> Of the adjacent wharfs. The city cast
> Her people out upon her; and Antony,
> Enthron'd i' th' market place, did sit alone,
> Whistling to th' air; which, but for vacancy,
> Had gone to gaze on Cleopatra too,
> And made a gap in nature.

Glamour is both erotic and exotic in our present use of the word, and Enobarbus dwells on the rich and foreign glossy quality of the opulent scene and its essential unnaturalness. Nature is "out-worked" by fancy and artifice. Glamour throws a carefully woven web of artificiality over a woman, and thus conceals her. The interesting thing about this famous account of Cleopatra is that she herself is absent from the description. Cleopatra is hidden by her accessories and dazzling ambience. Glamour conceals the "real" woman, and from the start this glamour makes a fool of Antony, who is left deserted and abandoned by the admiring crowds who have rushed out to look at Cleopatra.

Cleopatra is a secular version of the witch who was persecuted by the Churches during Shakespeare's time. Europe would eventually disown the old witch of the *Malleus*, but other slightly disguised versions of this castrating witch appeared instead. The witch constantly surfaces in literature. She is present in de Sade. His Juliette is a true *femme fatale* because she does literally destroy the men with whom she comes in contact. The Sadeian libertine is a hideous inversion of the Christian ascetic: both try to kill passion in themselves systematically and both live in a prison of solitude, whether it is actually a prison as in de Sade's case or in the hermit's cell. De Sade's heroines have entered the Western imagination and powerfully but tacitly reinforced the myth of the castrating woman. Huysmans also reinforced the witch fantasy and showed how psychologically he had been affected by religion in his fantasies of female degradation and female erotic power, when he finally converted to Catholicism. In *A Rebours* he has a perfect description of the sexy witch and the *femme fatale:*

> In this she was altogether female, obedient to her passionate, cruel woman's temperament; active and alive, the more refined, the more savage and the more hateful the more exquisite; she was shown awakening man's sleeping passions, powerfully bewitching and subjugating his will with the unholy charm of a great venereal flower sprouting in sacrilegious beds and raised in impious fields.*

The witch is the essence of woman—cruel, sensual and dangerous.

In general, the 19th century with its cult of the sexless woman was not a period when one would expect to find many sexy witches, but in fact the myth continued. Becky Sharp in Thackeray's *Vanity Fair* is a malevolent witch, whose sexy charm even makes her a murderess. Yet Thackeray was clearly attracted to her far more than to the saintly Amelia, the epitome of the good Victorian woman. The witch in the painting of the time shows that she continued to exert the

---

* See W. R. Hays, *The Dangerous Sex*, pp. 218–20, for Huysmans and the *femme fatale.*

same attraction over the imaginations of men. Rossetti's powerful portraits of women who have all proved dangerous, like Pandora or Lucrezia Borgia, are both erotic and threatening. Above all, the women of the late Burne-Jones are beautiful and destructive to men. One thinks especially of the mermaid pulling the dead body of a man down to *The Depths of the Sea,* as the painting is called—smiling out of the canvas with an amoral glee. Victorian men tried to neutralize women's power by making them sexless, making them into angelic children of otherworldly goodness, but in their imaginations they were as aware as ever of their fear of women and of their powerful sexuality.

Our own century has of course pushed the glamorous woman forward as the ideal woman of male fantasy. The film star and the cover girl have the same kind of impenetrability as Cleopatra. Her glamour makes her invulnerable and untouchable. However, glamour is also a quality that can make men feel inadequate and potentially impotent. On our television screens at present we have a perfect witch in Joan Collins as Alexis Colby in *Dynasty.* Alexis is essentially glamorous. She has a glittering and exotic ambience which is expensively erotic. She is shielded by glitzy clothes which often sheathe her like armor, and for all their contrived sexiness they actually say "touch me not." She is a real *femme fatale,* using her glamour to entrap and enslave men, castrating them emotionally and in the business world. All the women in the series share the same touch-me-not glamour and the same manipulative sexuality, using their eroticism as a means of power and control. In the world of Big Business and Oil Wells it is their strongest weapon, and they use it skillfully.

It is interesting how many witchcraft terms have survived in language describing the way a sexy woman gains power over men. Besides "glamour" there is "fascination," which in the language of witchcraft is magic communicated by the evil eye. In the *Malleus,* Sprenger quotes Thomas Aquinas to the effect that "fascination cast by the eyes over another person" can transmit a "subtle influence" over them. People can gain power over other people by looking at them in a certain way.

For the eyes direct their glance upon a certain object without taking notice of other things and although the vision be perfectly clear, yet at the sight of some impurity, such as, for example, a woman during her monthly periods, the eyes will as it were contract a certain impurity . . . and thus if anybody's spirit be inflamed with malice or rage, as is often the case with old women, then their disturbed spirit looks through their eyes, for their countenances are most evil and harmful and often terrify young children of tender years, who are extremely impressionable. And it may be that this is often natural, permitted by God; on the other hand, it may be that these evil looks are inspired by the devil.

(p. 17)

Here Sprenger is still puzzling over the former pagan witchcraft, which attributed to old women the power of casting a spell over their enemies and inflicting bad luck—*maleficium*—upon them. He is still, at the outset of his thesis, in the old pagan world, but as he baptizes the old pagan witchcraft and makes it Christian the witches become, as we have seen, much more sexy. *Fascination,* like *glamour,* is seen as something deeply malevolent. Gradually both these words have lost their obvious edge of hostility. When today we say that a woman is fascinating we mean that she is irresistibly and mysteriously attractive. The fascinating look has changed over the centuries, but it is still hostile. The cool, dangerous aloofness of the Burne-Jones woman or the long, challenging stare of the fashion model or the seductress is always malevolent, and men expect this and tell themselves they love it. A woman who sets out to fascinate a man like this wants to bring him under her spell.

It is no accident that we continue to use these magic terms to describe sexually powerful women. Men often hate the glamorous woman at the same time as they drool over her, because she is not for them. She is too expensive and out of their sexual class. Her extreme sexuality can make a man feel castrated and inadequate: he has a terrible suspicion that if he got her, he wouldn't be able to cope. Glamour also protects the "real" women from men. The vamp who offers an apparent invitation by her glamorous appearance and fascinating stare is often as absent from this invitation as Cleopatra was absent from Enobarbus' description. It is not a real invitation so much as a contemptuous challenge. Other women hate the vamp because she makes them feel sexually second or even third class. Witch words like "magical," "enchanting," "ravishing," "bewitching" preserve the hostility felt for the witch underneath the apparent admiration.

Not all women can be glamorous witches, simply because they lack the potential for gloss in their appearance, even though many women try to polish their looks as much as possible. However, if a woman cannot be Elizabeth Taylor, she can cultivate "charm." Women are taught to be charming far more than men. It is, of course, another of those hostile witch words, which has lost its original malevolent meaning on the surface but which still, while being apparently positive, is ambiguous in both its origin and in its present application. To say that a woman is charming is a compliment. We rarely think of the original meaning of the word whereby to "charm" somebody is to put an evil spell upon them. It is pure *maleficium* and it used to be punishable by law. Nowadays it is an asset that is painstakingly acquired. The *Malleus* had complained that women spend too much time and effort trying to please men. We still do. When we set out to be charming we are being placatory. Charm, like glamour, is the response of an oppressed woman to the male world which she feels, either consciously or in a confused way, is hostile to her. Charm is something that protects us from this hostility, a magic amulet against harm. Behind this barrier of charm women can be "themselves" and think their own thoughts. For many women charm becomes quite "natural," just as glamour is a "natural" way of life for others. Both are protective camouflage. Cleopatra's glamour meant that she herself remained mysterious in the midst of her minutely described exotic equipment in the barge. Those of us who can't be glamorous usually have to work very hard at charm as a substitute. If the world doesn't stop breathlessly when we walk into a room, we try to make ourselves magical in other ways. Charm is a way of neutralizing enmity before it has time to emerge.

Yet perhaps the way women charm men reveals contempt: butter him up—that's all he can cope with. It is quite possible also that men sense this disdain. In a way charm can be as castrating as glamour. To charm a snake is to subdue it so that it is no longer dangerous but completely under the charmer's power. To charm a man can be an attempt to subdue him to our female needs with a web of sweetness, blunting his aggressive edge, just as Delilah unmanned and castrated Samson when she cut off all his hair, after luring him to sleep and inattention by her soft flattery. Men may feel in some inchoate way threatened and despised by our charm. Women too belittle themselves by being endlessly placating and endlessly charming, as we have been taught by our mothers. Perpetually charming behavior reinforces within us the fear of a potentially hostile world and perhaps thus makes the world more hostile than it need be. The charming woman often finds it extremely difficult to lay aside her protective camouflage if she needs to be tough or direct. This web of artifice has become natural. However, it is important that she learns to be able to abandon charm when necessary, as men have always been able to do.

What is sad about the *Malleus Maleficarum* is that it reveals such a confused and unhappy picture of the relationship between men and women. Clearly it was as possible then as it is today for ordinary men and women to conduct a perfectly amicable relationship. There are even little glimpses of this in the *Malleus,* when, for example, the man who thinks he's lost his penis goes into the pub to cheer himself up and soon finds himself pouring out the whole story to a woman he meets there. Again, when another castratee goes to the witch to ask for his penis back, she is perfectly pleasant about returning it. Obviously men and women weren't in a state of out-and-out warfare, any more than we are today. However, the sexual neurosis which the Church had been trying to spread for centuries was certainly manifesting itself in these castration terrors and fears of impotence, and the picture the *Malleus* gives us of embittered women who will roundly "curse" men when they are hurt. The neuroses are all confusions and misdirections of natural impulses. The men hadn't really lost their penises, they only felt that they had. The women couldn't really make men who had hurt them impotent, but a lot of them thought they could. Today we are similarly confused. The way witchcraft has survived in the words we use to describe women shows that there is the same latent hostility as ever there was. Of course men can be glamorous and charming too, but for them glamour and charm are optional extras. Everybody expects a man to get tough, but when a woman does she runs the risk of being called a castrating bitch, even though she is perhaps being even more castrating when she is being charming.

The fact that we prefer to call a woman a castrating bitch rather than a castrating witch is instructive; so is the way we have completely buried the witchy meaning of words like glamour and charm, while at the same time we have both—men and women—decided to use these words instead of discarding them for something more neutral. It shows the way we have chosen in our day-to-day lives to "forget" the Witch Holocaust; like all the great panics, once it is over we feel only embarrassment at the mania that swept through our culture. The Witch Hunts happened a long time ago, but at some level we still remember them in shame and in fear, so that we don't want to think what we are really saying when we praise a woman for being "enchanting" or "bewitching." They have scarred the relationship between men and women in the West, but perhaps the most horrifying thing is that they were deeply typical of the relations between the sexes, and still continue to be so subliminally today.

The Witch Hunts, which really got under way in the 16th and 17th century, were conducted as a ruthless program of extermination of the enemies of society. Women were rounded up and tortured until they confessed to having intercourse with the Devil and having attended sabbaths; their bodies were pruriently searched for the stigma of witchcraft; they were tortured until they betrayed other women who were hunted up in their turn. Confession did not mean pardon and the witches were burned as heretics—many of them reneging on their confessions at the stake, even though they stood to gain nothing by this.

The most frightening thing about the *Malleus* is not the pathetic fantasies men and women were suddenly having about each other, but the cold and merciless way Sprenger, in the service of the Church, organized this neurotic confusion into a systematic persecution. What Sprenger began to do was to systematize the traditional Christian hatred of women, and the later Witch Hunts built on his work. The old misogynistic charges were now insufficient. Besides all their traditional faults, women now became truly diabolical—having sex with the Devil and worshipping him in huge orgiastic sabbaths. This extraordinary charge was not new. In his book *Europe's Inner Demons,* Norman Cohn has brilliantly shown that for centuries the

Church had developed a standard set of charges against heretics and
outsiders. The early Christians had been accused by the Roman authorities of having cannibalistic feasts and sexual orgies. Such
charges were useful to authorities when they wanted to suppress
their enemies. They made the outsider monstrous to people and justified persecution. In 1022, for example, Adhemar of Chabannes described the practices of the Cathars who were burned that year in
Orleans: they carry about with them the ashes of murdered children,
he says, they adore the Devil who appears to them at first like a
dusky Egyptian and later as an angel, and who daily brings them
huge supplies of money; at the command of the Devil the Cathars
entirely reject the mysteries of Christ, and even though on the outside they appear to be good Christians, in secret they commit
"crimes and atrocities which it is shameful even to speak about." It
was not enough for the Church to condemn the Cathars' heretical
opinions: they had to be feared by the people as abominable enemies
of society. There is a real paranoia about the enemies hidden in the
midst of society that characterizes all true Western witch hunts. The
same complex of accusations: cannibalism, Satanism, orgies and sodomy was brought up against a number of heretics including the
Cathars, the Waldenses and the Fraticelli. When in the 14th century
Philip IV of France wanted to destroy the powerful and wealthy
Order of Knights Templar for entirely political reasons, he had to
show they were heretics by bringing up this standard list of charges.
The wretched Templars were tortured and forced to admit these
accusations of sodomy, cannibalism and devil worship. Like the
witches, many of them reneged on their confessions at the stake and
maintained their innocence. Later, when the same cluster of accusations was brought against witches, it was with the same unconscious
aim of creating a stereotype which was so inhuman that the strongest
measures were justified to exterminate these evil enemies of society.
It is surely significant that this complex of charges was used most
intensively of all against women. The witch craze takes to its logical
extreme the gradual Christian ostracizing of women, so that woman
is now The Great Outsider in league with the Inhuman Satan.

The witchcraft craze was, however, not merely the final act of
hostility against women, it was also an unconscious and compulsive
revolt against a religion which everybody accepted intellectually

without question but was too repressive and unhealthy emotionally. Inquisitors and "witches" together in the torture chambers, in their dreams, in their fears created a fantasy which was a deliberate inversion of orthodox Christianity. Thus the Black Mass became a horrifying but perversely satisfying ceremony where the Devil was worshipped instead of Christ; where instead of Communion there was a cannibalistic feast and instead of sexual repression a giant orgy where every type of sexual perversion so strongly forbidden by the Church could be enjoyed in fantasy (both by the witch, by those who dreamed about sabbaths and, still more significantly, by the Inquisitor). The panic spread like wildfire because the neurosis had been so effectively, and yet in so submerged a way, prepared for over the centuries. At last men and women were sexually cooperating and creating a giant international fantasy. The result was that women revealed themselves, under torture, to be as evil and perverted as Christians had always believed them to be. They had always been outside God's plan; now it was shown that they were the friends and lovers of the Devil.

It was a deeply sick process, where one fantasy, one dream fed another, one account of an inquisition fed another. If the creation of the Sabbath showed how deeply people wanted to reject Christianity and showed in fantastic and detailed form exactly what they felt emotionally about its repressions and restrictions, the Incubus fantasy showed what the Christian world really thought of sex. It was now convenient for the Church to believe the flying fantasies of women it had previously condemned (it explained for one thing how the women managed to attend these huge mythical sabbaths, which were often held miles away, and get back safely afterwards to their husband's beds). It also suited their detestation of sexuality to believe that demons really did copulate with men and with women. There already existed a strong Christian connection between sin, sex and women, and the idea that a devil really did come down and have sexual intercourse with women was simply an aspect of this deep complex, which had exploded into a perverse neurosis. Pruriently the Inquisitors tortured every detail of these imaginary diabolic couplings out of the unfortunate women, who, crazed with pain, guilt and sexual dreams, fed their curiosity. The Devil's penis was foul to touch and icy cold; it was so unnaturally huge that it could not be inserted without excruciating pain. Sex was now being rejected as monstrous, evil and diabolic in a fantasy which was the logical outcome of everything that theologians and preachers had been saying about it for centuries.

In one respect, the devils were actually more virtuous than women, some of the writers on witchcraft declared. Nider, the Dominican Inquisitor, says that the devils themselves hate sex and find it repulsive "because of the abomination and shame of the sin. The Wicked Angels, because of the nobility of the state in which they were created, abhor having to undertake these foul sins, whether it is sodomy or even simple fornication." Only the very lower orders of devils, he declares, as does Henricus Institoris, will take on this job. It is because women are so lewd and foul in their insatiable lust that the devils find it a convenient way of enlisting them in the service of Satan. These incredible theories sound like the ravings of lunatics, but the writers of these treatises on witchcraft were, in all other respects, sophisticated and learned men. Girolamo Visconti, for example, who published his treatise *Lamiarum sive Striarum Opusculum* in 1490, was of a very noble family, became a Dominican Provincial of Upper Lombardy and was Professor of Logic of the University of Milan. He was not a crazed religious fanatic or a wandering lunatic preacher, but a scholar of renown. Yet he could write that to dismiss the incubus theory as a mere fantasy was "an extremely dangerous opinion, one which was opposed to the faith and against the honour of almighty God Himself." They are not the fantasies arising out of a melancholic humour, but actual events. Devils are summoned to women "because of their carnal desires."

Visconti concludes by remarking that although there are male witches, witchcraft is predominantly a female heresy. The *Malleus* would reinforce this attitude, and quickly influenced other writers on witchcraft who make the same identification of witches and women. Thus Sylvester Prierias, writing his *De Strigmagarum Daemonumque Mirandis* in the early 16th century, is fully imbued with the doctrines of the *Malleus*. It is women who attract demons, because of their abominable lust, he asserts, but he is afraid that if women are told about witchcraft even more women will invoke demons to gratify their passions. Later in the century, Arnaldo Albertini published his very influential and esteemed *De Agnoscendis Assertionibus*

*Catholicis et Haereticis Tractatus,* where he stated categorically that witchcraft is called a heresy *maleficarum* not *maleficorum* because it consists far more largely of women than men because of the frailty of the female sex and because of the insatiable lust of women who, besides raising storms and damaging men's property, also have the power to make men impotent. The Jesuits Peter Thyraeus and Paul Laymann, whose witchcraft treatises both went through numerous editions in the 16th century, both stress that it is a women's heresy because of the filthy lusts of the female sex. To deny, as male scholars like Norman Cohn or Keith Thomas have both done recently, that the Witch Craze bore any special malevolence to women is to ignore a substantial amount of evidence in the principal writers on witchcraft at the time of the craze. It is true that men were also executed, but witchcraft is seen as a woman's vice. The list of reasons for this are perhaps best summarized by Lupa da Bergamo, whose treatise *Nova Lux* was published in 1648 and was reissued by the Inquisition twice yearly. Why, he asks, are women more susceptible to witchcraft than men? Because they are talkative and garrulous, and can thus corrupt a whole neighborhood with their gossip and malevolence; because they are mean spirited, so that when they get depressed they can't shake off their depression and so are wide open to the temptations of the Devil. Women are deeply vindictive by nature and the Devil offers them the means of revenge; they are credulous and ignorant so that devils can easily delude them. Like Eve, they are curious and long to know about hidden things. They are, therefore, specially tempted by the occult. Women are softer than men and more impressionable: if they are taught by good spirits they are very devout, but if they fall under the influence of evil spirits they are more wicked than the most wicked men. What sort of women become witches? he asks. Some people say that they are women whose faith is weak, others say that it is ambitious women who are more susceptible to witchcraft. His own feeling is that it is those women "who are given to carnal vices, like adulterous wives and prostitutes. I agree with this last for they principally seek to make men impotent."

There was a good deal of skepticism about the incubus theory, but very often skeptics used their doubts to make another attack on women. Thus in his *De Spirituum Apparationibus* (published in 1597)

Peter Thyraeus says that he thinks that many people, especially
women, imagine the whole thing because women have such particularly filthy minds. There was no way for women to win. You could be
a good and pious woman but still deeply susceptible to witchcraft
however virtuous you tried to be. Thus Nicholas Remy, whose
*Demonolatria* (1595) became one of the most important books in the
movement, declares that judges must not be deceived by a woman's
piety. There was, he says, a case of a woman in Metz: she was always
first in Church and the last to leave it, was always praying and
crossing herself and yet she was burned as a witch. Convents were
certainly no havens from witchcraft. Jean Bodin, writing in 1581,
says that women often flee to monasteries to hide their witchcraft
under the guise of sanctity. The German Jurist Justus Oldekop, who
was a fierce critic of the Witch Hunts, showed caustically how a
woman could do nothing to help herself, once accused, because the
case was rigged against her no matter what the evidence or what her
character was like. Everything proved her guilt:

> . . . if a woman is especially regular in public worship, it is
> argued that the worst witches make the greatest show of piety—
> and if she is neglectful, it is the same. So with morals—an ir-
> reprehensible life is an *indicium* and so is an evil one. According
> to the absurd judgements of these judges everything is an excuse
> for torture and condemnation. So it is that if a woman brought
> before the judge has an assured or unchanged countenance, it is
> said that only witches carry so bold a front. If she is terrified
> and cast down, it is the consciousness of guilt and the pangs of
> conscience.
>
> *(Observationes Criminales Practicae,* 7, 8, 1640)

There were a few brave men like Oldekop who stood out against
the belief in witchcraft, though not as many as one might have
hoped. Perhaps the best known of these was the German physician
Johann Weyer, who wrote his famous critique in 1563, when the
Craze was at its height. Weyer still believes in the Devil, but thinks
that the Devil has caused this fantasy in men's minds. He is certain
that all the tales of witches, about their night flights, their sabbaths
and their intercourse with demons, come from sick bodies and sick
minds. If witches really are so dangerous to the human race, he asks,

then why doesn't Germany employ one full time to work against the national enemy, the Turks? Weyer bitterly attacks priests and monks who have no medical knowledge but who rush in as soon as a woman falls ill and start trying to prove that she is bewitched. He ridicules the book of a German priest of the town of Gueldres, where Weyer himself was practicing medicine. One of the young nuns in a very strict convent fell slightly ill. The priest declared that she could not be cured unless the Mass was performed on her belly. In an age of faith this would not just be a disturbing and kinky experience for a girl, but a deeply traumatic one, so it is not surprising that after this Mass she became much more sick than before.

What Weyer shows us is that many women really did believe that they were witches and had intercourse with the Devil and worshipped at sabbaths. He had himself been called into many convents where there was an epidemic of possession by the Devil, and had usually found that the cause of the possession symptoms was all too natural. The classic case that he investigated was at the Convent of Nazareth in Cologne in 1565. What he discovered was that many of the nuns had had lovers from the town, who used to steal into the convent at night. When this scandal was discovered and the lovers were kept out, nuns began to be "possessed" by the Devil. It began with a fourteen-year-old nun called Gertrude, whose lover had been particularly assiduous so that she was now particularly frustrated. In her sleep she would go through all the motions of violent sexual intercourse, and her dreams convinced her that she was being visited by an incubus. Her roommate observed Gertrude's antics and began to reproduce the symptoms herself. The symptoms then spread through the convent like wildfire. There was nobody left to satisfy Gertrude and her fellow nuns but the Devil.

Sometimes, however, the cause of these fantasies seems to have been pure loneliness instead of sexual frustration. The Bishop of Trier, Peter Binfield, writing in 1623, tells the story of Anna of Rover, who was denounced by her son and burned at the stake in 1590. Anna claimed that she had been ill treated by her husband. She was lonely and distraught. When one of her children was dying she believed that she had been abandoned by God also. There was nothing in orthodox religion that could comfort or satisfy her. In her despair she felt there was nothing left for her but the Devil. She called upon him, and he immediately appeared at her call. Her son's account is equally eloquent of the sexual guilt that caused witchcraft to thrive—it is just like a story in the *Malleus*. He had seduced a young girl, and after having sex with her, he dreamed that he was visited by a succubus. In horror he told Anna all about it, and she consoled him by "taking him with her" to a sabbath. Just as the possession had swept all through the Convent of Nazareth, so did witchcraft sweep through Anna's home. All her children fell victims to the craze and started dreaming of sabbaths, identifying with their mother because of their own loneliness or sexual guilt. The two oldest children were burned with Anna and the youngest two, who were still minors, were imprisoned for life.

Another story of a loneliness that led to a woman embracing witchcraft is the sad story of Jeanne Harvilliers, whose case came before the Parlement de Paris in 1578. Her mother had been burned as a witch when she was a child and she herself, as the daughter of a witch, had been scourged by order of the Parlement. The trauma did not end there. The stigma of her mother made Jeanne a complete outsider. Constantly forced to move house and change her name to escape the disgrace of witchcraft, Jeanne eventually became so lonely that she felt she had no one to turn to but the Devil. Like Anna of Rover, she felt that God was not interested in her and that conventional religion—which, after all, was responsible for her sufferings—had no comfort to offer her. Jeanne became convinced that her mother had consecrated her to the Devil, when she was twelve years old. She confessed freely, without torture, that a devil used to appear to her as a tall man, dressed in dark clothes, booted and spurred and wearing a sword. He became her only friend, promising to take care of her and to make her happy. He also became her lover, and Jeanne had intercourse with him until she was fifty years old, when she was finally accused by her neighbors of witchcraft. By that time Jeanne had got married, but her husband was clearly not as supportive as her handsome devil with whom Jeanne described having sex while her husband lay asleep beside her in the same bed. The devil would leave his horse at her door, she said, but nobody but herself could see it. Clearly, all that Jeanne was doing was creating for herself an imaginary companion to assuage her loneliness. The isolation of Anna and Jeanne shows that women turned to witchcraft for simple human comfort: they had no hope in God, no hope in their husbands or in the Church. Even though Jeanne confessed to her incubus, this was not enough for her judges. She had to conform to the whole witch-package, and was tortured until she confessed that she had also flown through the air, visited sabbaths and worshipped Beelzebub.

The tortures inflicted upon these poor women before their inevitable deaths show clearly the hatred of women that inspired the Craze. Weyer was appalled by what he saw in the prisons. The accused women, he insisted, were not heretics; they were poor, ignorant women who were sick and deluded. They should be treated kindly and shown the errors of their ways. Instead

> . . . these wretched women, whose minds have already been disturbed by the delusions and arts of the devil, are now upset by frequent torture, are kept in prolonged solitude in the squalor and darkness of their dungeons, exposed to the hideous spectres of the devil and constantly dragged out to endure atrocious torment until they would gladly exchange at any moment this most bitter existence for death, are willing to confess whatever crimes are suggested to them rather than be thrust back into their hideous dungeon amid ever-recurring torture.
>
> *(De Prestigiis Daemonum et Incantationibus ac Veneficiis IV, vi, b)*

The most unforgettable depiction of the suffering inflicted upon witches is given by the Jesuit Friedrich Von Spee, whose hair went prematurely gray after his experience at the witch trials in Westphalia and Franconia. He was certain that innocent people were being executed. Indeed, when he asked the judges whether it were possible for an innocent woman who was once brought into the Inquisitorial machine to be acquitted, the judges were unable to answer him. Von Spee was horrified by the way these women were treated, and wrote a brave denunciation of the injustice and cruelty of the system:

> I confess that I would at once admit any crime and choose death rather than such suffering and I have heard many men, religious and of uncommon fortitude, say the same. What then is to be presumed of the female, fragile sex? . . . I know that many die

under enormous tortures, some are crippled for life, many are so torn that when they are beheaded the executioner does not dare to bare their shoulders and expose them to the people. Sometimes they have to be hurried to the place of execution lest they die by the way.

Some women, he says, are driven to confess and then think that they have forfeited salvation for falsely confessing such a terrible crime as witchcraft, so that it "is incredible what despair they suffer in prison, unless they find someone to comfort and instruct them." He explains what gruesome reality lies behind the phrase "without torture." When judges proudly say that someone confessed "without torture," this is a piece of meaningless jargon:

> I made enquiry and learned that in reality they were tortured, but only in an iron press with sharp-edged channels over the shins, in which they are pressed like a cake bringing blood and causing intolerable pain and this is technically called "without torture."
>
> *(Cautio Criminalis,* xx)

To write so critically of the Inquisition was extremely dangerous, and Von Spee is said to have been imprisoned himself for this *exposé*.

The witchcraft craze had spent itself by the end of the 17th century; its ferocious lunacy could not survive in the cooler and more rational climate of the Enlightenment. However, in some very important sense it is still not over. We have seen that it still affects our language; men and women still choose to think about women sexually in terms of witchcraft, however thoroughly we think we have emptied the words of their original hostility. We are still uneasy about the Witch Hunts. This can be seen in the theories that keep trying to explain it away: witchcraft wasn't a hostile fantasy—there really were witches and Satanic cults; there never really was a witchcraft craze at all, it is just a myth; we mustn't exaggerate the hostility to women that the Witch Craze exhibited. If the West has been scarred emotionally by the Nazi Holocaust, the Witch Craze, which raged throughout Europe (not just in one country) and which lasted for over two hundred years, must have left a scar on Western attitudes. Men and women must still look at one another in guilt and fear, however subliminal our memory of the Craze. It shows how deeply women were ostracized in the world of Western Christianity. The extraordinary thing is that so many women managed not only to survive in this dangerous world but even managed to gain respect from men and a modicum of power. The methods they used may seem foreign to our secular culture, but in fact still affect the way women seek to liberate themselves from male dominance.

# 4

# WHY BE A
# VIRGIN?

Today women feel that they "ought" in some sense to be independent. A woman is no longer always commended for clinging helplessly to a man. Yet independence poses certain crucial problems for women. Most women, whether they like it or nor, are financially dependent upon men, if only for a certain period of their lives—when they are bearing children, for example. Financial dependency induces an emotional dependency, even if the woman is not already emotionally dependent upon her man. It is still true that the vast majority of women feel more secure and "complete" in some kind of monogamous relationship with a man. Indeed, the way society is run can make things very difficult for a woman on her own. This being so, it is surprising that the ideal of independence for women has been so quickly and firmly established during the last fifteen years. It seems that the ideal is spreading. It is no longer confined to the middle and upper classes, but is appealing to working-class women, who have always been more dependent financially on their menfolk, though perhaps their emotional dependence has expressed itself in very different ways from the dependency of middle-class women. Working-class women have not been able to afford the luxury of being delicate and clinging. In other cultures, where a woman is seen simply in her relation to her men and to her family, the ideal of female independence would be anathema. In our society it has found ready acceptance because it is not a new ideal at all but has been with us for nearly two thousand years. From the earliest days of the Church, although the overwhelming majority of women were married and dependent, Christianity kept before them the ideal of independent women who could liberate themselves from the shackles of their sex, free themselves of subjection to mere men and be fully equal to men. Later these women were the virgin saints.

Virginity very soon became a highly respected Christian ideal and the Fathers of the Church developed a theology of chastity and virginity. Inevitably these ideas filtered through to the ordinary people, through sermons, through art and through stories and song. Far more powerful than abstract ideas were the examples of the role models that were placed by the Church before all the faithful in the saints. When the Church canonizes an individual it asserts that that person has definitely got to heaven and that he or she practiced virtue to a heroic degree on earth. Obviously canonization will not benefit the saint in any way. The aim is to put before the members of the Church examples of heroic virtue and to show the ordinary Christian different ways of living the holy Christian life. There have been people who were certainly very saintly but who have not been canonized because it was felt to be inexpedient or politically inadvisable to do so. For nearly sixteen hundred years, the lives of the saints dominated the religious lives of most Christians, and in many ways they were more familiar figures to the Christian than God or Jesus.

Protestantism stamped out the cult of the saints with good reason. It smacked of paganism, and even though the Christian was officially aware that the saints were not divine, for unsophisticated and uneducated people the distinction between a holy saint and Jesus was difficult. Everybody knew the lives and legends of the saints, especially the saints of their own country or region. The saints were patrons, they would take care of you, look after your physical and spiritual interests and intercede with God for you. The cult of the saints began before the fall of the Roman Empire and people would frequent the shrines of the saints and martyrs because they were "the friends of God." Holiness was felt to be localized almost physically in these shrines and in the relics that they housed. The saint thus provided a holy place where people could be nearer to God. The idea of a patron was very important in the world of Late Antiquity. Powerful people would take a promising young man under their wing and help him on his way, just as later during the Renaissance a rich person would become a "patron" of a painter or a poet and give him money and help to advance his career. In Late Antiquity this idea of patronage was applied to the saint, who would help and guide his devotee. Later, when Christianity moved from the sophisticated Mediterranean world to the north and the barbarian nations were converted, the saints increased in importance. Their stories were more immediately comprehensible and sympathetic than many of the complicated doctrines of the church, and people would be as well acquainted with them as they were with the principal stories of the Bible or with pagan legends. Even today Catholic children often have saints whose stories are as familiar to them as those of the Sleeping Beauty or Jack and the Beanstalk. Not only were the common illiterate people very familiar with the saints' lives, they would pray to them too as much as they would pray to Jesus or to the Virgin Mary. Various saints were—and still are, in the Catholic world—considered especially helpful in different emergencies or in different circumstances. Thus you would pray to St. Antony if you had lost something, to St. Blaise if you had a sore throat or to St. Jude if you were really desperate, because he was the patron saint of hopeless cases. The legends and stories proliferated and obviously differed in the telling from one region to another. In the 13th century Jacobus de Voragine collected as many of them as he could in *The Golden Legend,* which became the first international bestseller.

The saints were more than mere characters in legends; they were real beings who had celestial powers and who would intervene in your life, and who were more immediate figures than the majestic Christ. Thus when St. Joan of Arc heard voices and was pressed by her judges to name them, it did not occur to her to think that Jesus had spoken to her; her "voices" were the voices of her favorite saints. In much the same way in our own century peasant children who have had visions at Lourdes and Fatima have seen not Jesus but the Virgin Mary, who obviously figured more powerfully in their imaginations and religious lives than Jesus Christ. During the First Crusade visions abounded, and again the people the Crusaders "saw" were the saints. If Christ appeared, it was often as a silent figure, who stood beside the saint but took no part in the conversation. An interesting feature of the Crusades is that they reveal how very local the influence of the saints were felt to be. The saints the Crusaders saw in their visions were Eastern saints, whose cults they had heard of in the West but who were not important in Europe. Instead of "seeing" St. Martin of Tours for example, who was a very popular warrior saint in the West, the Crusaders saw Eastern warrior saints who would hitherto have been very shadowy realities to them: St. Theodore, St. Demetrius and St. George. St. George became so important that when they eventually reached his birthplace near Ramleh in Palestine the Crusaders instantly created a special bishop to look after his shrine and held a service there, making up the ceremonial for the occasion. Similarly, although Pope Urban II had played an important role in the Crusade, when the Crusaders referred to St. Peter they referred to him and prayed to him as the Bishop of Antioch in Syria, not as the Bishop of Rome. In the East, Peter's powers and functions were felt to be quite different from his powers in the West. The saints, therefore, did not occupy some vague and universal celestial sphere. Their power was localized. Their presence was felt to belong to this world and to be physically present in some places more than in others. It is clearly a pagan conception. The Romans had spirits which were the "genius" of certain places and in the newly Christian mind, these genii were the saints. Clearly, to the primitive mind the distinction between the saints and Jesus was very marginal. They were both heavenly beings, but the saints could seem to be—even physically and materially—more immediate and real.

When women looked to the women saints for role models, they had lots of examples. However, women could not have failed to be impressed by one thing: nearly every single saint was a virgin. If she had unfortunately lost her virginity, as often as not she would revert hastily to celibacy in order to achieve true sanctity. The message was clear. The only serious Christian women were usually celibate and nearly always virgins. Sex and marriage did not figure as saintly attributes, but were for the second-class women of the Church. This was indeed the teaching of Christianity until the Reformation, and it was so firmly established as a Christian reality that even Calvin, who wrote very positively about marriage, found it impossible to deny that virginity was a higher vocation. Furthermore, the legends and stories began to offer quite powerful images of virginity which made the more abstruse teaching of the Fathers graphic and immediate. They were images not only of independence but of autonomy. In many of these legends the whole point of the woman saint's story seems to have been virginity. She holds on to it at all costs. Often the story seems to have been more about "How to Keep One's Virginity in Difficult Circumstances" than about the love of God. The virgin is indeed a woman who holds herself independent of man, but in doing so she becomes autonomous. The dictionary tends to define the words "autonomy" and "independence" in terms of one another, but they do have slightly different meanings. Independence, as applied to women, means that a woman is not subject to a man and can exist apart from men. Autonomy carries more of a feeling of self-sufficiency. The autonomous person could exist very satisfactorily on a desert island. This ideal of self-sufficiency is one that is much admired in our own time and indeed theologians like Don Cupitt have argued that because man today wants to be autonomous—to create a life and identity by himself instead of being weakly dependent on an omnipotent Deity—the old ideas of God are no longer meaningful to him. The autonomous person remains at some level indifferent and impervious to his surroundings. However unpleasant they might be, he remains himself; his integrity is not threatened, he is master of his own destiny and does not have to wait for circumstances to improve before he acts in the way that is characteristic of him. On a desert island or in solitary confinement he will not go mad. In a politically corrupt system he will not become venal, because he has his own standards and his own sources of motivation that do not depend on the outside world. Although such a person need not be at all insensitive, he does remain at one level impervious to the world about him. The Fathers of the Church offered women independence of men and equality with them if they embraced the holy state of virginity. The way this independence worked itself out practically in fact meant autonomy—an autonomy that could be damaging, not only because the women concerned often lacked the psychological strength to be truly and maturely autonomous but because they were forced to become impervious to realities that they should have taken into account.

The myth of virginity which Christianity imposed on the West is still with us today. Sixteen hundred years of sermons propagating the theology of virginity and sixteen hundred years of devotion to virgin saints put the ideas and images of both independence and autonomy for women deeply into the Western consciousness. Women today still strive after an independence and wrestle with the problems that both independence and autonomy impose upon them. They may not realize that they have a good deal in common with the virgins of Catholic legend and history, and that they continue to live according to the old virginal mythology. Like the virgins of old, they are seeking equality with men. Given the climate of sexual hatred and misogyny, it is obvious that virginity was a good solution for women if they wanted to gain equality with men and win their respect. If a woman before the Reformation wanted a career and did not feel that she would be satisfied by marriage and motherhood, the only way to an independent career lay in adopting the virginal state within the Church.

It might seem that the ideal of virginity was not "the women's solution" at all, but the solution imposed upon them by men. It was, after all, the male neurosis about sexuality that made it logical for a woman to give up sex and remain a virgin. Not many women could do this. Only those with money would dispense with the support of a man, and when virgins started to congregate together in convents, after monasticism had been imported into the West from the East, you needed to have a dowry before you could enter one of them. Nevertheless, by the end of the 2nd century virgins formed a distinct, élite class in the Church. By the 4th century virgins had formed themselves into a separate Order, their vows of chastity now taken for life, instead of temporarily as they had been hitherto. By the 6th century the Consecration of a virgin was such an important event in the Church that the Bishop had to do it, at a time when marriage had no special Christian ceremony. Women who renounced their dreaded sexuality gained great honor in the Church, just as in the heretical sects which abjured sex women were both powerful and respected. A woman who kept herself unsullied by sex escaped the curse of Eve: she was holy because she was sexless, as Leander of Seville says:

> Eve heard the well-deserved sentence that punished her sin: *You will be subject to your husband and will bring forth children in sorrow.* But you, wise virgin, have freed your neck of such a yoke; you will not be bowed down to the ground by the imprisoning fate of marriage, but with your head held high you look up to heaven. By her old act of presumption Eve fell from heaven, but you are allowed to climb heavenwards albeit in fear and trembling. Eve ate from the forbidden tree and lost her virginity; a virgin is allowed to marry but if she doesn't she belongs to the company of angels.
>
> *(Regula Episcopi,* Preface)

A virgin will not be subject to any man, the Fathers never tired of explaining. Only Christ is her lord. She is free of the petty confines of married life:

> And what if I ask besides, that it might seem odious, how the wife stands who hears when she comes in her baby screaming, sees the cat at the flitch and the hound at the hide, her cake burning on the stone hearth and her calf suckling all the milk, the crock running into the fire and the churl chiding?
>
> *(Hali Meidenhad,* p. 36)

The virgin knew "no pain of pregnancy and childbirth," as St. Ambrose pointed out, so she is freed of the curse of Eve, which could cost her "sorrow" and even her life. From the beginning the Church leaders were—sometimes—polite about marriage, but gave it second place to virginity and celibacy. For sixteen hundred years in our culture, married women knew that they were inferior to their virginal sisters.

Today, of course, we think that celibacy is an unhealthy way of life. Only a few people, we maintain, are natural celibates; today, with typical Christian imbalance in sexual matters, we tend to go to the opposite extreme and insist that a good sex life is essential for "salvation." Today's liberated woman is usually not a virgin; on the contrary, a necessary part of the freedom she is striving for is sexual liberation. However, like the virgin the modern feminist is striving to be independent of men. She may not care very much about the curse of Eve, but she is concerned not to be "subject" to her husband, her neck bowed under the yoke of a servile and imprisoning married life. This is a difficult ideal. Psychologists tell us that dependency poses different problems for men and women. When the boy separates from the mother and tries to attach himself to his father as a model, he has to seal himself off from the maternal world and adopt stiff-upper-lip masculine toughness because he feels rejected by his mother. The girl never has to make such an abrupt transition, but she has difficulties in another way: she finds it harder to realize herself as a separate individual. She needs to be attached, and this attachment often expresses itself as dependence. Lillian Rubin in her book *Intimate Strangers* shows that many women feel furious when they have to support their families financially for a while, and that their husbands feel emasculated. She herself found this a problem. When her husband wanted to give up his career and tried to write full time, they discussed the possibility for months beforehand. She had a prosperous career as an analyst, writer and lecturer at Berkeley, and really wanted to give her husband this chance. Yet to her astonishment she found she felt angry for the first six months of the new arrangement, even though she was convinced that she wanted to do it. Women are so deeply conditioned to expect their men to protect and support them that a rational, cerebral theory cannot stand up to their huge subconscious need to be dependent.

The bias against independence in women is strong. When we say that a man is independent it is a compliment: a "strong and independent woman," on the other hand, is often ambiguous praise, hinting at a lack of "true" femininity. Statistics show that women who are "too" independent (i.e. they feel fewer dependency needs than they "should") are less likely to make successful relationships with men than their more clinging sisters. Emotional dependence certainly goes along with the financial dependence that most women experience, and it runs very deep. Some of the women Rubin interviewed were well able to support themselves and enjoyed their ability to do so, but even so would often be struck by the "terrible" irrational thought "What would I do without him?" which they found hard to explain. Although the husbands "liked" their wives' new independence, they felt irrationally but strongly threatened by it. Since dependency seems to play such an intrinsic part in the relations between the sexes, it is interesting that the need to be independent is being felt by more and more women, despite the fact that it often brings many problems in its wake.

It is not merely feminists or middle-class professional women who no longer feel the need to be dependent and wholly subject to their men. There is a good deal of evidence that the concept is spreading. One strong indication is the flood of popular novels that are neither feminist nor highbrow which have been imposing on a large audience the ideals of female power and independence. The modern heroine is no longer the abject and passive Cinderella of the romance. Novels by Judith Krantz, Shirley Conran and Barbara Taylor Bradford, for example, show the heroine breaking into the male world with extraordinary success. These novels have been extremely popular and have reached an even wider audience by being serialized on television, both here and in Great Britain. Very often the woman who is presented as the heroine starts from a position of female inferiority and dependence; she is perhaps pregnant with an illegitimate baby or deserted in some way by her husband and in financial straits *(Lace, A Woman of Substance, Mistral's Daughter)*. Sometimes she is poor and ugly *(Scruples)*, but later sheds her layers of fat and emerges as a dazzling beauty. Sometimes she has emotional as well as financial problems *(Princess Daisy)*. Sometimes these women marry rich men, but they are not content with a purely passive role. They will either use his assets or they will capitalize on their own talents to carve out a fabulously successful career for themselves. They become tycoons with a chain of luxury apartment stores that belong exclusively to them, they become film stars, models, run model or publicity agencies, become business women, writers or corporation lawyers. These new heroines have apparently shed dependency, and despite their glamorous femininity, they break into the male world and beat men at their own game. They move from female slavery and inferiority to a position of power that was hitherto only for men.

But not entirely. At the end of each of these novels, women have to submit and accept a certain dependency in the name of "true love" or "true womanhood." They allow themselves to drop their tough business exteriors and fall in love, get married or become pregnant. At that point the novel ends, so we do not see how these tough viragos cope with the difficulties of marriage after years of success and independence. The message is ultimately a muddled one. Independence clashes with autonomy for these women, because in the end it is felt to be unfulfilling. Similarly, fashionable magazines like *Cosmopolitan* and *Company*, which tend to promote the "new" independent woman more than the housewife, are ambivalent in just the same way: articles about autonomy sit side by side with articles that tell women how to achieve a "secure" relationship, how to achieve a conventionally feminine appearance to get their men and how to fulfill traditional female tasks like cooking or home-making. The desire for autonomy is clearly felt. It informs not only feminist works and feminist novels, but popular magazines and pulp fiction. As I have said, there is nothing new in this autonomous ideal. For centuries, until the Protestant Reformation transformed and upgraded the status of marriage, women were made to feel that dependency was second best. Today we still desire autonomy. We may not be virgins, but if we wish we can be "masters" of our own body. Contraception means that even if our bodies are no longer impregnable to male desire, as were the virginal bodies of old, we can at least guard against unwanted impregnation. We can admit male invasion on our own terms without the inhibiting factor of unwanted pregnancy. Our Lady remained *virgo intacta* all her life, even after childbirth. We may not be *virgo*, but many of us, in our new independence, are seen by our men to be *virago intacta*. The only real difference is that for centuries, a "virago," a mannish woman, was a term of praise; it was what women were supposed to aspire to. The more recent cult of marriage in our culture has made a virago an ambiguous term, but the old virginal ideal has remained, despite all the difficulties, and is becoming more widespread than ever before.

One of the first of the virgin saints to act as an important role model for women was Thecla, the legendary disciple of St. Paul. Her life was recorded in the 2nd-century Encratist text *The Acts of Paul*, which, despite its heretical assertions that only by celibacy and virginity could a Christian be saved, enjoyed great popularity in the Early Church even among the Orthodox. We find Christians of unimpeachable orthodoxy, like St. Ambrose, quoting Thecla's story in a sermon as though it were well-known to every Christian. For a long time *The Acts of Paul* enjoyed the status of the Gospels and Epistles of the New Testament. Until the 4th century, Thecla was one of the most important of the holy women of Christianity. We find St. Methodius, in his *Symposium* celebrating the glory of virginity, ranking Thecla as the most illustrious virgin of the Church. Later she would lose this position to the Virgin Mary. Her story celebrates the Early Church's attitude to virginity, putting the theories of the theologians into a mythical form that the uneducated layman could easily understand. It demonstrates how virginity could bring a woman liberation as well as showing her some of the dangers the virgin would encounter in her pursuit of this difficult ideal. So perfectly did Thecla's story express the virginity myth that we find exactly the same elements being used when the lives of other virgins are written up, centuries later. Her story is still being told today. The Acts of Thecla are strongly reminiscent of novels describing how a woman frees herself of the shackles of her sex and becomes a liberated feminist. It might seem that novels by Marion French or Lisa Alther have nothing in common with a 2nd-century Christian text, but in fact the modern feminist is simply translating into a secular idiom a myth that has always exerted a strong pull on the Western imagination: the myth of the liberated independent woman. The fact that she was once called a virgin and is now called a feminist is only of minor importance. Like the feminist, the virgin is a woman who has learned to do without men. Like the feminist, the virgin claims equality with the male world and insists that privileges (like Apostleship and Ministry) that were once for men only can easily be assumed by women. Like the modern feminist, the virgin of old had to make a painful transition from dependency and acceptance of sexism to liberation, and she often makes use of the same comforts as virgins like Thecla once did.

One of the first Gentile Churches founded by St. Paul was in Iconium in modern Turkey, and it was there, *The Acts of Paul* tells us, that Thecla saw him for the first time. For Thecla it was love at first sight. She sat enraptured, listening to him telling his hearers that celibacy was the only means of being saved and that Christianity meant renouncing "filthy coitus." Thecla was instantly converted to

Christianity, although her conversion proved to be very dangerous to her. She was engaged at the time to a young man called Thamyris, but she renounced him on the spot and embraced a life of Christian virginity. Thus she not only enraged Thamyris but also her parents, who wanted her to make this fashionable match. They tried to force her to change her mind, and when nothing would dissuade her she was brought before the tribunal and sentenced to be burned alive.

Despite this heroism in rejecting and defying the male world, Thecla still has a long way to go. She is still the typical passive woman of all feminist tales before their heroines are converted to feminism. She is hormonally and emotionally dependent upon her man, the extremely reluctant St. Paul. Despite the veil of pious language it is clear that she has fallen in love with him, although he gives her no encouragement and is positively embarrassed and unpleasant about her dogged pursuit of him. For three days Thecla listens to Paul's preaching, shaken by "a strange eagerness and an awful emotion." When Thamyris gets Paul thrown into jail for inciting Thecla to rebel, Thecla visits him in prison and spends the whole night "kissing his bonds." When Paul is let out the next morning Thecla is discovered "enchained by affection . . . wallowing(!) on the place where Paul had sat in prison." During the first part of her story she hardly speaks a word but remains in a passive trance. Even when she herself appears before the tribunal she is utterly silent and has nothing to say in her own defense—no fiery and courageous proclamation of the truth of the Gospels, which is the sort of behavior we will later come to expect of Christian martyrs. Thecla simply stands there mooning over her man; "she stood looking only for Paul." Paul by this time shows so little concern for Thecla that after being released himself, he callously leaves town, so that Thecla is still looking in vain for Paul when she is led out to be burned at the stake. It is clear that Jesus is a very secondary feature in Thecla's conversion. While she stands in the arena looking desperately for Paul, Jesus has to stand in for him, appearing to her "in the likeness of Paul." Thecla may be a virgin, but she still hasn't understood the most important freedom that virginity brings with it, which is a freedom from the male world. However, she does discover some of the other benefits of virginity. When they try to light the pyre to burn her to death, her naked virginal body is enveloped modestly by

a nimbus from heaven, just as during another of her ordeals in the
stadium her body is concealed by the clouds of perfume that the
admiring spectators have hurled into the arena. The virginal body
remains inviolable, impenetrable to the lascivious gaze of men and
male hostility, so that Thecla cannot die. She is released by the bewildered Roman governor.

However, Thecla is still unliberated, and instantly sets out in pursuit of Paul, who behaves like a real male chauvinist. Whenever
Thecla really needs him he is conspicuously and callously absent.
When she catches up with him at Daphne and begs for baptism, he
refuses to baptize her because he fears that she could become "mad
after men," an attitude that we have now seen to be typical of the
Christian and Western male. Even when she is publicly assaulted by
one lustful Alexander at Antioch, Paul continues to disown Thecla:
"I know not the woman . . . nor is she mine." He then abandons
her and goes on his way, even though Thecla, because of the spite
and machinations of Alexander, is to be thrown yet again into the
arena, this time to face ordeal by wild beasts.

It is at this point that Thecla finds support in other women and so
shakes off her humiliating dependence on unworthy men. A woman,
Tryphema, takes Thecla into her house and is converted by her.
When Thecla arrives in the arena it is the women who take up the
cudgels for her against their menfolk in the audience, crying, "Evil
Judgment! Impious Judgment!" and indeed it is a lioness who defends Thecla against the male wild beasts in the arena, tragically
dying while striking a mortal blow to the most dangerous lion. It is
here, as all true feminists would expect, that once she has experienced the sisterhood, Thecla discovers her own female dignity. She
lays aside her besotted passivity and in one of the most absurd scenes
in the story she baptizes herself—she is no longer dependent upon
Paul's ministrations. She flings herself into a trough of man-eating
seals that conveniently stands near her in the arena, crying aloud the
words "I baptize *myself* in the name of the Lord Jesus!" Needless to
say, Thecla is saved from the seals by divine intervention, is released
and sets off to find Paul at Myra, dressed, as befits the liberated
woman, in a man's cloak. She coolly informs Paul that she is now his
equal: "He who wrought along with thee for the gospel, has wrought
in me also for baptism." Paul, "greatly wondering," is forced to

agree, confirms her in her mission, and Thecla goes off to preach in Paul's stead in Iconium, her home town.

In some manuscripts Thecla's story of acceptance by the male world has a rather instructive epilogue. She spends some seventy years living as a hermit in a cave in the deserts of Seleucia. However, she is still much sought after for advice and also for her healing powers, for she has a miraculous gift. Her success infuriates the male physicians of the locality, because she is taking away their trade, so they come to her cave in a body to rape the ninety-year-old virgin, convinced that if she loses her technical virginity she will also lose her miraculous powers. Thecla's position seems hopeless, but with God's help she remains *intacta* to the end. The men find (not surprisingly) that they cannot rape her so they rush forward to kill her. God miraculously opens up the rock in front of which Thecla is standing, and she disappears into it. Her invulnerable virginal body doesn't even have to die, and she remains superior to the male world and proof against its hostility to the end.

Advocates of sexual equality in the Church certainly used the story of Thecla to further their cause, for we find Tertullian writing very angrily against those who quote the case of Thecla in support of the ordination of women. The virgin may have been honored in the church from the beginning, but she was not allowed to fulfil any male tasks. She was not allowed to preach or to baptize. In the Eastern Church women became deaconesses with pastoral power, but this arose from the social conditions in the Eastern Empire, where women were traditionally segregated from men. Deaconesses could visit women and minister to them more easily than the male priests. In the West, however, where there had never been such seclusion, the virgins had no chance of becoming deaconesses. However, even though the Church would not allow her to do male jobs, the theologians were clear that the virgin became an honorary man. Thus Jerome:

> As long as woman is for birth and children, she is different from man as body is from soul. But when she wishes to serve Christ more than the world, then she will cease to be a woman and will be called man *(vir)*.
>
> *(Commentary on the Epistle to the Ephesians,* III, 5)

It is interesting that Jerome should compare women with the body. We have seen how he regarded his body as an enemy which had to be starved and brutally put to death, so that the spirit could be free. The body was responsible for the disgusting lust which bubbled forth and produced lewd hallucinations. If a woman could free herself from her sexuality, she became spiritual and masculine. Ambrose is just as clear that in order to be saved a woman has to become a male.

> . . . she who does not believe is a woman and should be desig-
> nated by the name of her sex, whereas she who believes pro-
> gresses to perfect manhood, to the measure of the adulthood of
> Christ. She then dispenses with the name of her sex, the seduc-
> tiveness of youth, the garrulousness of old age.
>
> *(Exposition of the Gospel of St. Luke,* lib. X. n. 161)

For Ambrose, salvation for a woman means shedding her femaleness and becoming fully human and fully adult, that is, becoming male. Leander of Seville makes the real point very clearly:

> . . . a virgin remains a woman and yet knows nothing of the
> drives and compulsions of her sex. Forgetful of her feminine
> weakness, she lives in masculine strength; nor has she any need
> to become a slave to her body which by natural law should be
> subservient to a man. Happy the virgin who takes her body
> from Eve but not her punishment.
>
> *(Regula Episcopi,* Preface)

Much modern feminism is equally scornful about "femininity" and urges a masculine style of dress and behavior on women. Yet to enforce "masculinity" (whatever that really means) on women is as artificial as the "femininity" that both feminists and the early Fathers denounce. It can also be a dangerous solution: Thecla found that her virginity was deeply threatening and constantly resulted in her getting thrown into the arena. Eventually her mastery of male skills caused the physicians to attempt rape and murder.

The legends of the women virgins frequently show that Christendom admired a mannish woman. We have seen how fascinated Christians were by the classical legend of the Amazons. Certain women saints, like St. Martha and St. Margaret of Antioch, are envisaged as female versions of St. George, slayers of dragons. St. Margaret's dragon was Satan himself. She was dedicated to virginity, but unfortunately Olybrius, the Roman prefect, lusted after her and had her thrown into prison when she refused him. There she encountered a much worse foe, because she was tempted by the Devil to abandon her virginity. In the 12th-century English version of her life in which Satan attacks her first in the form of a horrible dragon and then as a frightening Ethiopian, the ferocity of this saintly virago is gleefully dwelt upon.

> That mild (!) maiden grasped that grisly thing which frightened her in no way and firmly took him by the hideous hair of his head and hove him up and dusted him adown right to the ground, and set her right foot on his rough neck and began thus to speak, "Lay off now, wicked plague, at least now that you, O deceitful dark devil, afflict me no more, as my virginity has been of little help to thee!"

Certainly virginity could give a woman a truly masculine strength, and even though Olybrius finally had Margaret executed she remains triumphant over the male world in moral strength.

Another saint, St. Pelagia, illustrates another facet of the saintly virago: the transvestite. Pelagia was a rich woman of Antioch who was sometimes called "Margaret" because of the beautiful pearls she used to wear. She had a reputation for lewdness and used to dress herself up in the kind of provocative clothes that the Fathers had stigmatized. One day she was seen by the Bishop of Heliopalis, who wept bitterly because, he said, "she has arrayed herself so studiously to give pleasure to her earthly lovers, while *we* have given so little care to pleasing our Heavenly Spouse." Pelagia heard this holy Bishop preaching at Mass later that day, and was overcome with remorse at her sinful life. She begged to speak to the Bishop, who, with the usual lack of confidence in his ability to withstand the powerful sexuality of women, would only see her in the company of other people. Pelagia fell at his feet crying:

> I am Pelagia, a sea of wickedness overflowing with the waves of sin, I am an abyss of perdition I am a quagmire and a pitfall of souls.

*(The Golden Legend,* p. 611)

The Bishop baptized her, and Pelagia then set off for the Holy Land, where she became a hermit, dressed as a man and lived a holy life on Mount Olivet. She was known for her virtue and acquired a wide reputation as Brother Pelagius. Years later the Bishop went to visit her and discovered "a creature wasted and haggard with fasting. Her eyes were trenches in her face." He did not recognize her and certainly did not realize that she was a woman. This was only discovered when she died three days later, causing her mourners to cry out in astonishment: "Glory be to thee, Lord Jesus, for thou hast many hidden treasures on earth, as well female as male!"

Another version of this same story is the story of St. Margaret. She had been betrothed, but on her wedding day God inspired her to give "thought to the loss of her virginity and the sinful riotings with which it was celebrated; and prostrating herself upon the ground, and weighing in her heart the glory of virginity against the cares of wedlock, she deemed all the joys of this life as dung." Hence, that night she refused to allow her unfortunate husband to touch her, cut her hair, put on men's clothes and presented herself to the abbot of a distant monastery as Brother Pelagius. She was admitted to the monastery, where she lived such a holy life that when the abbot died she was appointed his successor. Unfortunately, this penetration of the male world brought disaster. Pelagius was also the ruler of a nearby convent of nuns, and when one of them got pregnant "he" was assumed to be the culprit, because he was the only "man" who had access to the convent. The monks therefore drove Pelagius out of the monastery and imprisoned her in a cave on a mountain, fed her on a scanty diet of bread and barley water and left her in solitary confinement. Pelagius endured this for many years "nor was troubled thereby, but comforted herself with the example of the saints." On her deathbed she wrote to the abbot explaining everything, the monks rushed to the cell but arrived too late. Pelagius was buried with great honor in the convent (ibid., pp. 613–14).

There are other versions of this story. St. Marina was brought to a monastery disguised as a boy when she was only a child. Her father had decided to be a monk, but could not bear to be separated from his beloved little girl. She lived a very holy life as Brother Marinus for years. One of her jobs was to collect supplies for the monastery in the nearest harbor, necessitating an overnight stay in an inn. A local peasant girl accused Marinus of making her pregnant, and rather than admit that she was a woman, Marinus was cast out and for five years she lived as a begger with her "son" at the gates of the monastery. Eventually she was readmitted, but made to perform all the filthiest jobs in the house and to fetch water for the latrines. Finally worn out with austerities she died and, of course, her sex was discovered amidst great consternation and remorse.

Thecla had donned male clothes to symbolize her new liberation, and these later saints followed this tradition. The 9th-century Synod of Ver indicates that this phenomenon may have been more than a pious legend when it says, "If women who choose chastity in the cause of religion either take on the clothes of a man or cut their hair in order to appear false to others, we resolve that they should be admonished and criticized, because we consider that they err through a great ignorance rather than zeal." Women plainly thought that male clothes would help them on their path to salvation which entailed becoming fully human and so male. However, in these stories of canonized saints there is no hint of censure. It doesn't matter that the policy of transvestism involves a life of lies, deception or in some cases a perversion of justice. The important thing is that the saint has shed her femaleness and thereby achieved great sanctity. Another of these transvestite monks was St. Eugenia of Alexandria, whose great virtues made her a provost of her monastery. When she revealed her sex to her monks, by baring her breasts to them, she justified her conduct in this way:

> His [Christ's] rule I have wholeheartedly embraced, and out of the faith I have in Christ, not wishing to be a woman, but to preserve an immaculate virginity, I have steadfastly acted as a man. For I have not simply put on a meaningless appearance of honor but rather . . . I have acted the part of a man by behaving with manliness, by boldly embracing the chastity which is alone in Christ.
>
> (Quoted by Marina Warner, *Joan of Arc, The Image of Female Heroism,* p. 158)

Virtue was the property of the male sex; chastity and virginity entailed becoming male because chastity was a male and not a female virtue. The male clothes were not a "meaningless appearance" but an honorable expression of the virgin's wish to shed her femininity. While transvestism for men was seen as diabolical and could lead to accusations of witchcraft, transvestism for women was, in the stories and legends about the saints, seen as a virtuous act and a way of promoting oneself on the ladder of perfection. There were many other saints, not virgins, whose conversion to the holy life involved donning male attire. St. Athanasia of Antioch, for example, separated from her husband by mutual consent, and both of them became hermits in different deserts, with Athanasia disguised as a man. Years later they met up again on a pilgrimage to Jerusalem and became inseparable friends without recognizing each other (because they were both so wasted and worn by penance). After the pilgrimage they entered the same monastery, and Athanasia's husband only discovered who she was after she had died. The pursuit of virtue justified any deception, any heartlessness if, by adopting a male appearance, a woman managed to escape her sex.

However, one of the interesting aspects of these stories is that sex is always present and dangerous. Pelagia's life of masculine penitence is a penance for her years of sexual sin. It is as though becoming male gives her an honorary virginity, just as her sanctity makes her an honorary man. Margaret may have wanted to flee the "legitimate" sex life of marriage, which is seen as a hotbed of sin, but she is accused of violating a virgin later. Margaret and Marina both suffer for sexual crimes of which they are quite innocent. It is almost as though a woman is guilty of sex, however innocent she might be technically. As Augustine said, even virtuous women were Eves and temptresses. It is also noticeable that women who enter the male preserve of the monastery may be very successful, but they are always lacerated and wounded in some way. It may be that this is only the result of excessive mortification, as in the cases of Pelagia and Athanasia. It may, however, be the result of male hostility. Again, neither Margaret nor Marina ever think of disclosing their true sex to escape the appalling punishments that were meted out to them. Marina explicitly says that she would rather suffer than admit that she was a woman and resume her true sexual identity. It is as though simply being a woman is a worse crime than any sin that a man might commit, even the sin of violating a virgin. There is also in these stories the underlying feeling that even if a woman succeeds perfectly as a man, either because of her excessive virtue or in "career" terms by becoming abbots or provosts, she has to suffer for it. Suffering and humiliation must be a woman's lot, no matter how hard she tries to shed her femininity and no matter how holy and masculine a life she tries to lead. Thecla had lived very successfully in the male world, but ultimately she encountered its hostility. However holy the virgin might be, she could never really shed her womanliness, nor the punishment that belonged to her sex. Entering the male world remained a very risky business.

The great example of the Christian transvestite is, of course, Joan of Arc, who preferred to die rather than relinquish her male clothes. The charges against her at her trial declared:

> The said Jeanne put off and entirely abandoned woman's clothes, with her hair cropped short in the fashion of young men, she wore shirt breeches, doublet, with hose joined together, long and fastened to the said doublet by twenty points, long leggings laced on the outside, a short mantle reaching to the knee, or thereabouts, a close-cut cap, tight-fitting boots or buskins, long spurs, sword, dagger, breastplate, lance and other arms in the style of men-at-arms.
>
> (Quoted by Warner, *Joan of Arc*, p. 149)

Joan insisted that God had revealed to her that she must wear male clothes. When she recanted and promised to don female dress, it was her final resumption of her male clothes that led to her arrest. When she was asked why she had resumed it, Joan answered that "she had taken it of her own will under no compulsion as she preferred man's to woman's dress. She was told that she had promised and sworn not to wear man's dress again and answered that she had never meant to take such an oath. Asked for what reason she had assumed male costume, she answered that it was more lawful and convenient for her to wear it since she was among men, than to wear women's dress" (W. P. Barrett, *Trial of Jeanne d'Arc*, London, 1931, p. 158). Even though at one point Joan claimed that the question of her dress was unimportant, the tenacity with which she clung to her male costume shows that it was in fact a matter of deep significance to her, "since it pleases God that I wear it" (ibid., p. 66). Marina Warner has shown how Joan's adoption of male clothing reveals a desire for independence of the male world. When it was suggested that a man had told her to lay aside her women's clothes, she was very indignant and denied it vehemently. Unlike the transvestite monk saints, Joan never pretended that she was a man, but called attention to her female, virgin status in her name, *La Pucelle,* the Maid. Her virginity and her clothes meant that she was shedding female dependency, as the Church had always advised women to do. Like St. Margaret, she too had once rejected a suitor chosen for her by her father, and when she ran away to join the army she had had to keep her mission secret from her father, who had vowed to kill her if she attempted any such thing. Joan's life and mission were originally a declaration of independence from the patriarchal world of power and authority. It was also, as her clothes suggested, a declaration of her equality as she successfully penetrated the masculine sphere of war.

The life of Joan shows very clearly how both sexes cooperated together in the building of the Christian myths about women. The author of the Book of Thecla was a male cleric, if we are to believe Tertullian, and later another man would preserve the lives of the saints for us in *The Golden Legend.* Yet women too had told these stories to their daughters and must often have contributed to their content. Unlike the male theologies, which preached misogynism as part of the divine order, the world of legend was probably a joint creation of both sexes. Christine of Pisan, for example, also wrote down versions of the lives of saints for posterity. Joan of Arc conceived her mission very much in terms of the Christian tradition of virginity. Her assumption of male attire was well within the transvestite myths. Similarly, the men around her contributed to the mythology. Joan presented herself to them as a Holy Virgin, and they responded to her in terms of the virginity myth. Her body, whole, unpenetrated and virginal, was seen to be as invulnerable as Thecla's had been. There was the famous occasion when she was pierced by an arrow during a battle, but rose up and continued as before, apparently unaffected by the wound. It was, her companion Dunois records, the turning point of the battle: the French were instantly heartened by this miracle and proof of divine aid, and on the other side the English were appalled by it. Again, when she was in prison, she tried to escape by leaping out of the window of her tower and— miraculously—survived this suicidal flight. However, it was not merely that Joan was impervious to pain. She was also impervious to male lust. Thus her squire, Jean d'Aulon, later declared at her rehabilitation trial:

> Although she was a young girl, beautiful and shapely, and when helping to arm her or otherwise I have often seen her breasts, and although sometimes when I was dressing her wounds I have seen her legs quite bare, and I have gone close to her many times—and I was strong, young and vigorous in those days— never, despite any sight or contact I had with the Maid was my body moved to any carnal desire for her, nor were any of her soldiers or squires moved in this way.
>
> (Quoted by Warner, *Joan of Arc*, p. 36)

He also declared that she never menstruated, which, whether it was true or not, shows that the legend building up around her was based on her intact and virginal body. It was not only Jean d'Aulon who reported on Joan's ability to repel lust. Another knight, Gobert Thibault, declared:

> In the field she was always with the soldiers, and I have heard many of Joan's intimates say that they never had any desire for her. That is to say they sometimes had a carnal urge but never dared to give way to it; and they believed that it was impossible to desire her. And often if they were talking among themselves about the sins of the flesh, and using words that might have aroused lecherous thoughts, when they saw her and drew near to her, they could not speak like this any more. Suddenly their sexual feelings were checked. I have questioned several of those who often slept at night close to Joan, and they answered me as I have said, adding that they never felt sensual desire when they saw her.
>
> (Ibid., p. 37)

Joan had instigated the cult of her virginity, but she needed the men around her to perpetuate it. Joan's calling, which had begun as a declaration of independence from and equality with men, had resulted in autonomy and imperviousness to the world about her. Her body was sealed off from the dangers and potential lust in her environment in a virginal cocoon of safety, just as Thecla's had been. If any men refused to cooperate with the myth, they did so at their own peril. René de Cériziers, a Jesuit in the court of Louis XIII, later reported the legend that "Whenever anyone looked upon her with impurity or thought dirty thoughts about her, he was immediately struck impotent *forever*" (ibid., p. 38), and an earlier story tells of a man who was foolhardy enough to voice his lecherous thoughts in her hearing and was drowned in the River Vienne an hour later.

This essential invulnerability of the virgin which constitutes her autonomy is most clearly seen in the myth of the virgin martyr. Like Thecla, all these martyrs are presented by writers like Jacobus de Voragine and Christine of Pizan as dying more for their virginity than for their faith, and it is this which distinguishes their story from the story of the male martyrs. I use the word "story" in the singular advisedly, because the legend of the impregnable virgin martyr is fundamentally always the same, no matter how many slight and accidental variations are played in the life of each saint. The virgin, like Thecla, refuses to marry. Very often the Roman prefect lusts after her and forces all manner of tortures upon her after she has refused him. Frequently he throws her into a brothel, which is a clear indication of the real view of a woman's place in the world: despite the adulation she receives, the holy virgin is still Eve, still a whore. However, nothing can hurt the virgin, who stands in the heart of all this sadistic hostility completely unharmed.

St. Agnes was probably the most popular of these early virgin martyrs. *The Golden Legend* tells us that the son of the local prefect fell in love with her, but that even though she is a mere child, Agnes answers him with undisguised horror when he tries to woo her: "Begone, sting of sin, food of crime, poison of the soul!", which hardly seems a balanced or charitable way of saying "no." However, sanctity for women is not a question of charity and balance. Agnes, the original virginal tease, rubs in her refusal by telling her suitor that she has another lover without revealing that it is Christ, quoting extensively from the official rite for the consecration of a virgin, words that are still spoken by nuns when they make Profession of Vows:

> He whom I love is nobler than thou. The sun and moon wonder
> at his beauty. His riches are inexhaustible. He is mighty enough

to bring the dead to life and His love surpasses all love. He has placed his ring upon my finger, has given me a necklace of precious stones, and has clothed me in a gown woven with gold. He has graven a sign upon my face to keep me from loving any other than himself and he has sprinkled my cheeks with his blood. Already I have been embraced by his pure arms, already his body is with my body. And he has shown me an incomparable treasure and has promised to give it to me if I persevere in his love.

*(The Golden Legend,* pp. 110–11)

This dishonest and sadistic account of her divine nuptials naturally distresses Agnes' suitor, who becomes ill. Suspecting witchcraft, his father has Agnes summoned before the tribunal, hears that she is a Christian and threatens to lock her up in a brothel if she refuses to become a Vestal Virgin. Of course Agnes refuses, so she is stripped and led into the brothel, but her hair grows miraculously and in such abundance that it covers her body and protects it from the lascivious gaze of the passers-by. When she enters the brothel there is an angel waiting for her with a vest of dazzling whiteness. Her virginity makes her physically invulnerable. It is a celestial shield that miraculously protects her and makes her quite unconscious of her environment: "Thus the place seemed for her a house of prayer, and the angel cast about her a supernatural light" (ibid., p. 111). This image of the protective shield about the virgin was so firmly established in the minds of the French soldiers that they instantly gave one to Joan. The outside world cannot impinge upon the virgin and neither can the men in the brothel sexually penetrate Agnes.

However, all this autonomy is only a prelude to death. St. Ambrose had said centuries before that virginity was a type of martyrdom, requiring a daily death to self. Eventually Agnes is stabbed in the throat, and "in this manner her heavenly spouse claimed her for His bride," writes Jacobus de Voragine, "having decked her with the crown of martyrdom." Death is the consummation of a virgin's life. That degree of imperviousness to the world is a kind of death. Agnes' body is as indifferent to the world as a corpse. Jacobus de Voragine was writing this story hundreds of years after St. Agnes had died during the Roman persecutions of the 2nd and 3rd centuries. By this time, the original stories had changed somewhat as the myth of virginity had developed. However, in the 4th century the Doctor of Virginity, St. Ambrose, had been well aware of the connection between virginity and death, and Jacobus quotes him at the end of his account in *The Golden Legend*. In his address to the virgins of his Church in Milan, he had told them the story of Agnes and ended in this way:

> This was a new martyrdom. She who was too weak to suffer was strong enough to conquer; she who could not fight yet won the crown. . . . No bride hurried to her bridal chamber as did the saint to her place of judgement, joyously, with hurried pace.

By the 4th century, therefore, Ambrose, who was so influential in shaping the myth of virginity and whose sermons were so powerful that wealthy parents used to keep their daughters away lest they vowed virginity on the spot and refused a fashionable marriage, has shown that the autonomy of virginity can be a kind of death. He tells his virgins the story of a contemporary of his, a girl who had been put into a brothel like Agnes, with much the same result: "A brothel cannot defy chastity, but chastity can purify even such a place." Lustful people had gathered around but inside "Our chaste dove," Ambrose says, was "enclosed," sealed off from the cruel and lustful "vultures" in wait outside. After being released, however, the virgin had hurried along to the stadium to offer herself as a voluntary martyr. "My body refused violation but not death," she explained. "A virgin may not accept profanation, but she may accept the blows of martyrdom." Sex is seen as literally being a fate worse than death. However, conversely, virginity can be death-bearing. It is a refusal of and a withdrawal from life and reality. The only way forward for the virgin is death.

The stories of virginity all illustrate the extreme hostility of the male world surrounding the virgin. Men want to kill her: they throw her into brothels or to the wild beasts. They cut her throat. Joan of Arc was eventually burned at the stake. But this retreat was a source of power. The virginity myth developed the image of the "whole" female body, whose hymen remains unbroken and possessed of the innocent "integrity" or wholeness that Eve enjoyed before the Fall. For, St. Augustine had explained, Eve may have had sex with Adam before she fell into sin, but technically she remained a virgin with an intact hymen:

> . . . with no loss of corporeal integrity did the husband pour out his seed into the womb of his wife. . . . At the same time that it was possible for the man's seed to enter into his wife's womb with the integrity of the female organ unbroken, just as now it is possible, with that same integrity preserved, for the menstrual flux to proceed from the womb of a virgin. . . . For as there were no groans of pain in childbirth but an impulse at maturity relaxed the female organs, so for gestation and conception there was no lustful appetite, but voluntary exercise united in both natures.
>
> *(The City of God,* XIV, xxvi)

This prurient speculation about Eve's hymen is degrading. However, that such tortuous speculation was deemed essential and worthwhile is evidence of how early in the Church's history the magical associations of the intact virgin body was established. The virginity of women like Thecla and Joan of Arc could, for a time at least, protect them from the hostile and indeed murderous male world and make them essentially autonomous. Writers spoke of the Virgin Mary as a "garden enclosed" or a "well sealed up," shut off, self-sufficient and therefore innocent and holy.

That this closed-off invulnerability can be damaging can be seen today in the number of women who remain virginal even though they have been married for years and even borne children. The virginity is not technical, of course, but many women find sexual pleasure difficult if not impossible. In sex men and women are at their most vulnerable. An essential part of sexual pleasure for many people seems often to be a balance of fear with pleasure in one's extreme vulnerability, and it seems that for both men and women trust is in some way necessary for sexual pleasure or even potency. For many people it is the only time that they can ever "let go." People feel that they can "lose themselves" in sex, that the feelings it arouses can be frightening because "who knows where they will end?" Such openness to another person means that you are giving that person the power to invade not only your body but your entire personality. To seal oneself off from all this emotional turbulence and vulnerability could certainly give a man or a woman a certain protection that would be emotional if not physical. There are married people—particularly women—who remain completely virginal in personality, not because they have not had any sexual experience, but because they themselves have remained quite unaffected by it. They have not allowed themselves to be penetrated and made vulnerable by their experience, and have put themselves into a sphere of sexual autonomy. Some people are "natural" celibates and lack a sexual dimension. Other "virgins" are simply emotionally repressed. This type of "virginity" is certainly a state of impoverishment, yet in a dangerous world this kind of virginity will ensure that a woman is not as deeply damaged by male hostility as she somehow fears she might be. The woman who is sexually experienced but who cannot enjoy sex and is frightened and threatened by passion is a common phenomenon in our culture. Even in these days of sexual liberation, sexual trust and therefore sexual pleasure are often difficult to achieve. In her novel of the 1960s, *Loose Change,* Sara Davidson explored the problems for women in a generation that had "ease with sex but difficulties with love." Men and women can very easily remain virgins in our culture because we have made sex seem such a dangerous and frighteningly uncontrollable activity.

If women still feel the need for the shield of virginity when they have intimate contact with just one man, they will feel the need of it even more when they are attempting to penetrate the male world as Joan of Arc did. Joan was able to gain male support by drawing on the strongly established popular myth of virginity, but this male support and cooperation proved to be unreliable. When Joan stopped winning battles, the French army who had so obligingly helped create her legend ditched her overnight, and for Joan as for Agnes the autonomous state was merely a prelude to death. However, Joan's career was a truly remarkable one while it lasted. Despite the dangers that were involved for a woman in the male world, there were always some women who braved that world using the protection of their virginity to gain an entrée into masculine preserves and a freedom which would have been impossible for their married sisters. Virginity could open new doors for a woman. If it made her an honorary man, then there was no reason why she should not, in theory, take a full and active part in the male world. Thus before

Joan, St. Colette of Corbie and St. Catherine of Siena both left their solitary lives to play a very successful role in the social and political worlds of their time. Catherine played quite an important part in the politics of Northern Italy and was often invited to act as a mediator in disputes. She even advised the Pope, and was popularly associated with his return to Rome after the Avignon Captivity. Yet however egalitarian the theory, in reality the men still wanted their women locked away in a separate world. They put their virgins, their career women, into enclosed convents which mirrored the state of virginity itself. Only a few women could safely venture outside the female world of home or convent and survive involvement in the great world outside. Yet they persisted in doing so. Women like Joan, Catherine or Colette were the first feminists, and the tradition to which they belonged bequeathed to the West the idea of the liberated woman who carves out for herself a successful career in worlds which have hitherto been strictly for Men Only.

For centuries, if a woman wanted to enter the male world and have a "career," the only way she could do it was to be a virgin, but it was usually the case that most virgins made no attempt to enter the male world but retreated from it in enclosed convents. So much so that when virgins started coming out of their convents and doing good works in society, this caused a scandal in the Church. Today we are used to seeing nuns scurrying round the streets, driving cars, nursing and teaching so that most people do not realize what a relatively recent development this is. One of the first of these "active" nuns was the English woman, Mary Ward, who founded the Institute of the Blessed Virgin Mary in the early 17th century. Instead of never leaving the convent grounds, Mary's nuns worked "in the world" founding schools and colleges and organizing themselves like the large religious orders of men. This called forth the wrath of the Church. A Board of Cardinals reviewed Mary's case and declared that they did not believe in "the power of women to do aught of good to any but themselves in a life consecrated to God." All a woman could hope to manage religiously was to look after herself; she was incapable of helping others. In 1631 Urban VIII suppressed the Order.

Certain women, taking the name of Jesuitesses, assembled and living together, built colleges and appointed superiors and a General, assumed a peculiar habit without the approbation of the Holy See . . . carried out works by no means suiting the weakness of their sex, womanly modesty, virginal purity . . . works which men most experienced in the knowledge of the sacred scriptures undertake with difficulty and not without great caution.

(Quoted by M. Daly in *The Church and the Second Sex*, p. 64)

Mary's real offense was that she and her nuns were running an Order as though they were men.

Women still had to remain in a separate sphere and might not come out, even in a good cause, or some terrible but unspecified danger would ensue. Since the days of Jerome, priests had been cautioned to avoid even virtuous women and leave them alone, and by Mary's time the Council of Trent had decreed that all nuns must be "enclosed." An enclosed nun must live in a convent where she has no contact with the outside world and which she never leaves during her whole life. No lay person, even other women, is allowed to enter the convent except the Parlor, where they speak to nuns through a grille. Even in church another grille separates the nuns from the lay congregation. It is an image of the segregation that the Church had for centuries desired for its women. The nun was locked away from men into a separate, wholly female world. The grille certainly reminds the visitor of prison bars, despite the nuns' cheerful reminder that the grille is there not to keep the nuns in but to keep the world out. Christianity wanted women locked away from them; Tertullian had said that they were "prisoners at the divine bar." For a nun to break this symbolic ideal of the way things ought to be was extremely dangerous, and that was what Mary Ward did.

It was obviously impossible for the nuns to carry on a serious work of education for women under the conditions of an enclosed convent, so Mary refused to accept enclosure. For twenty-six years the Institute of the Blessed Virgin Mary had spread through England, Flanders, Germany, Austria and Italy, clearly fulfilling a strongly felt need, not only for women who wanted to join the Order and lead a consecrated but active religious life, but for the girls who were flocking to be educated seriously in the schools. Nevertheless, the reprisals were severe. Mary herself had a symbolic punishment. She had refused to accept the enclosure which was the proper place for women, so she was locked up. She was literally imprisoned in a convent of Poor Clares, and because she was a "heretic" she was placed in a room apart from the community. The punishment was ruthlessly made to fit the crime in every particular. It was a real prison cell: the ceiling was very low and the two small windows were almost entirely boarded up. A dying nun had been in there and had vacated the room for Mary, so the room stank. Not surprisingly, these conditions made Mary ill, and she went down with a violent fever which brought her to death's door. She was not, however, cowed by this monstrous treatment, but wrote during her illness:

> I have never done or said anything, either great or small against his Holiness (whose holy will I have offered myself and do offer myself now, wholly to obey) or the authority of Holy Church. But on the contrary, and as far as it was possible to me, employed for honour and service of both.

(Gasquet, p. 95)

If things were bad for Mary, they were not much better for her nuns. At the time of the suppression there were between 200 and 300 sisters. The revenues of the Order were confiscated by the Church and the women were turned out of their convents, friendless, homeless and penniless. It was hard for some of the women to rejoin their families, especially the English women, for in England it was dangerous at that time to be a Catholic, let alone an ex-nun, and many convent women would have been utterly cast off by their families. The nuns of at least four of the convents had to beg for bread and were treated as criminals because they were suspected of heresy. One sister, Catherine Köchim, went to confession dressed in her habit, and the sacristan hit her and drove her out into the street.

Eventually, when she recovered from her dangerous illness, Mary managed to extricate herself from her prison and made her way to Rome to plead her cause before the Pope, who had the gall to reply in this way to her when she protested that she was innocent of heresy and a loyal daughter of the Church:

We believe it, we believe it. We and the Cardinals are well informed as to yourself, and your habits and your exemplary conduct. We and they are not only satisfied but edified, and we
know that you have carried on your Institute well. We have,
nevertheless, permitted the trial of your virtue, nor must you
think it much to have been proved as you have been, as other
Popes, Our predecessors, have done in similar cases, who have
exercised the endurance of the Servants of God.

(Gasquet, p. 105)

It is pleasant to record that Urban "pardoned" Mary and let her live
privately in Rome with a few of her most impoverished companions.
He could afford to be generous, as the Church had achieved its objec-
tive. Nuns were safely back in the cloister, where they belonged.

Yet despite the dangers of braving the male world, there were
women throughout the sixteen centuries before the Reformation who
did try to influence the world of affairs and found liberation in the
state of independence and autonomy. The Reformation of course
shut down convents and abolished celibacy as a desirable way of life.
Protestantism, however, had its drawbacks for women. The suppression of the cult of the Virgin Mary and of the female saints meant
that Christianity was now more of a male religion than ever. It also
meant that women were deprived of any official way of leading an
autonomous and independent life. The convents were certainly not a
perfect solution, but they did offer an alternative to marriage, and the
ideal of virginity did offer some women a career, whereas the spinster
and the old maid were not revered but seen as pathetic and deprived.
Still, the memory of women like Thecla did not die. In the 19th
century certain famous spinsters saw the unmarried state as a chance
to break into a new and exciting world of freedom and liberation.
Florence Nightingale, for example, compared herself to Joan of Arc
and saw her very secular career in terms of a divine calling. Like
Joan she saw visions and heard voices calling her to a special task.
When she finally realized that she was destined for the single life, she
saw it in religious terms as a new freedom: "I am thirty," she wrote
in her diary on her birthday, "the age Christ began his mission. Now
no more childish things. No more love. No more marriage. Now,
Lord, let me think only of Thy Will, what Thou willest me to do." A

year later, reviewing the year 1852, she writes, "all my admirers are married . . . and I stand with all the world before me . . . it has been a baptism of fire this year." She then began a career that took her not merely to the Crimean War but into the masculine world of government papers and committees. In 1841 Charlotte Brontë wrote enthusiastically of her friend Mary Taylor, who had emigrated to New Zealand:

> Mary alone has more energy and power in her nature than any ten men you can pick out in the united parishes of Birstall and Gomersal. It is vain to limit a character like hers within ordinary boundaries—she will overstep them. I am morally certain that Mary will establish her own landmarks.
>
> (Quoted by Nina Auerbach, *Woman and the Demon*, p. 111–12)

Mary Taylor's emigration to New Zealand and Florence Nightingale's expedition to the Crimea seem, as Nina Auerbach has pointed out, emblematic of the sense of adventure and possibility that the Victorian spinster felt. Charlotte Brontë herself, in her fictional autobiography *Villette*, recalls her journey to Brussels as an odyssey which ignored all home ties and all family obligations. Again, the Victorian feminist Frances Cobbe went to the Holy Land at the start of her career. When Charlotte Brontë received her first letter from Mary Taylor she was shaken powerfully by the idea of this search for a brave new world which reached beyond the limitations imposed on women by traditional Western society.

> I hardly knew what swelled to my throat as I read her letter . . . such a strong wish for wings—wings such as wealth can furnish—such an urgent thirst to see—to know—to learn— something internal seemed to expand unexercised—then all collapsed and I despaired.
>
> (Ibid., p. 112)

It was not only the women themselves who felt that the spinster was tapping new human possibilities. It was apparent to some Victorian men also that the old maids were becoming a new evolutionary "type" or "species." *Blackwood's* magazine denied that "the highest type of old maid" was an unfortunate and unfulfilled human being.

Rather, she has courageously refused to compromise an ideal and is fundamentally independent of the male world: "marriage as a state is not necessary to her idea of happiness. . . . She is a woman who has never met her ideal and who has never been cunningly persuaded to accept anything short of it" *(Blackwood's Edinburgh Magazine,* 12 July, 1872). Not only was she a brave and independent idealist, but an "important variation in the types of womanhood":

> The unmarried woman today is a new, sturdy, vigorous type. We find her neither the exalted ascetic nor the nerveless inactive creature of former days. She is intellectually trained and socially successful. Her physique is as sound and as vigorous as her mind. The world is before her in a truer and better sense than it is before any individual.
>
> *(Westminster Review,* 121, 1884)

This was of course the time when evolution was on everybody's lips and its concepts banded about fashionably. The spinster was seen as something new and different from anything that had existed before. However, it took a true scientist to see that the whole point of evolution is that "new" developments are simply adaptations of old types to different conditions. The myth of the virgin was reappearing, but this time not in a religious context but in a secular idiom, right at the beginning of secular Western society. Sir Charles Lyell, the geologist, told Frances Power Cobbe this at a dinner party:

> Suppose *you* had been living in Spain 300 years ago, and had a sister who was a perfectly commonplace person, and believed everything she was told. Well! your sister would have been happily married and had numerous progeny, and that would have been the survival of the fittest; but *you* would have been burnt at an *auto-da-fé* and there would have been an end of you. You would have been unsuited to your environment. There! that's Evolution for you!
>
> (Auerbach, p. 146)

Lyell could see that there was nothing new about the Victorian independent woman, but it is interesting that he identified this virago with the witch. Frances Cobbe was actually more likely to have been a virgin like Joan of Arc or Thecla.

The sense of brave new worlds opening out for women ebbs and flows: the wave of feminism in the early 20th century was succeeded by the apathy of the '40s and '50s, and the optimism of the early 1970s seems now to have waned somewhat. The brave male worlds seem rather hollow once they have been penetrated; they are still as full of neurosis and hostility as the worlds the early Christian viragos encountered. Part of the problem is the ideal of the virago. The aim of the liberated woman in the Church was to become male, even though the male worlds in both the virginity stories and in actual fact were so cruel and neurotic. Instead of seeing virginity as leading to completely different human possibilities, as the Eastern Church Fathers did, the virgin was simply invited to exchange one human limitation for another by changing sex. The Eastern Fathers saw the celibate life as being like the life of the angels, because angelic life "surpassed the ordinary possibilities of human nature." (St. Basil, *Sermo asceticus,* ii). Surely both sexes should now be seeking to transcend the old limited categories of gender. Instead, feminists still tend to see the male as the standard of equality, power and privilege just as the Christian virgins did. It is realistic perhaps to see the male world as powerful, but surely the emphasis should be on new ways of being women. Some feminists have got no further than a pathetic aping of the male world, and that inevitably brings disappointment, if not neurosis. Of the Victorian viragos we have considered, Florence Nightingale, who hated women and wanted the company only of men, was a neurotic all her life. Charlotte Brontë, whose elation over Mary Taylor's letter collapsed even while she was reading it, reneged on her earlier rebellion and married conventionally. The virago George Eliot, who had so impressed the American feminist and novelist Elisabeth Robins ("She is three parts man . . . abnormal . . . *looks* awful. Her picture frightens me!") eventually married the conservative Cross. To become a "man" is not only a disappointing experience, it is also both impossible and undesirable. The "wish for wings" is often not sufficiently imaginative and so is doomed to frustration and disillusion.

It can also be damaging and frightening. Those women who achieve independence—or a modicum of it—often find the price too high or find that it is potentially wounding. Independence may not bring us the death or persecution it brought to Mary Ward or Joan of

Arc, but it can bring us male antagonism nevertheless. It can imperil our relationships with the men closest to us, because dependency is written so closely into heterosexual relationships. Men may *say* that they want their wives to be independent, but their own deep but unexpressed dependence upon their wives makes the reality hard to take. One of the husbands interviewed by Lillian Rubin, who had urged his wife to learn to drive and get a job, felt threatened if she overstepped the mark by going out with a friend in the evening or failing to be in the house when he came home. He claimed that he liked his wife to be independent, but added, "There's such a thing as a woman being too independent, you know." In her turn, his wife tried to persuade him that they still had a valuable relationship by convincing him that she was dependent upon him, even though that was no longer as true as it had been in the past:

> I keep trying to make him understand that I'm still dependent on him. I keep telling him, "Look, I'm not independent; we do most everything together; I feel very tied to you; how can you say I'm independent?" But then I realise that those aren't the things he's talking about; I understand that now. He worries because I really am more independent inside myself, and even if I try not to let him know that, it shows and he knows.
>
> *(Intimate Strangers,* p. 155)

If, however, the wife has become as powerful or more powerful than her husband in the male world of careers and affairs, the dependency structure of a close relationship can be shot to pieces. A woman who is "too independent" or too successful can be seen as a castrating witch, as Lyell pointed out to Frances Cobbe. This male hostility can make a woman give up her autonomy and rebellion, as the heroines of novels by Judith Krantz do or as George Eliot did. There is also the danger that the male aggression she encounters may destroy something within a woman. It can destroy her personal integrity if she tries to juggle with dependence and independence together in incompatible situations.

What made a woman like George Eliot renege on her role of virago may well have been the loneliness of autonomy. We have seen that the protective shield it provides can be lethal. It can seal a woman off from realities that she ought to confront. It can mean isolation that involves not only personal loneliness but an isolation from important elements of her environment. To erect a barrier between herself and the world can mean impoverishment and damage psychologically. Not everybody has the stability or even the desire to become truly autonomous, and this can result in grave neurosis. Yet to be truly independent does involve an inner autonomy to some degree, or the independent, equal life for women becomes a mere career game, while in reality the woman is still in a state of emotional enslavement to a man, still feels that unless she *has* a man she is incomplete. Insofar as autonomy means a mature independence of one's environment and an ability to be alone when necessary, it is vital for the liberated woman.

From the earliest days of the Church virgins had been urged to withdraw from the world into a seclusion that excluded even other women. Before convents were established in the West, the virgin was encouraged to leave the world and seek solitude. Thus Jerome urges Eustochium to safeguard chastity by proud isolation:

> I would not have you consort overmuch with married women or frequent the houses of the great. I would not have you look too often on what you spurned when you desired to be a virgin. Women of the world you know, plume themselves if their husband is a judge or holds some high position. . . . Why should you, who are God's bride, hasten to visit the wife of a mortal man? In this regard you must learn a holy pride; know that you are better than they. And not only do I desire you to avoid the company of those who are puffed up by their husband's honours . . . you must also shun such women as are widows from compulsion not choice.

> (Letter 22)

The implication is that celibacy can only be maintained either by the sort of divine aid that Thecla experienced or by a quite unnatural solitude and segregation which is a refusal of reality. Ambrose is equally severe about visiting. A virgin should not even visit her relatives:

> For the younger [virgins] I think that visits, if they have to be made to parents or companions should be few. In these acts of

dutifulness modesty wears away, boldness of manner appears and levity creeps in. Modesty goes while you are trying to be courteous. If you fail to reply to a question you seem impolite; if you do reply you are caught in idle gossip.

*(De Virginibus,* III, 9)

Tertullian told virgins that they had to be a walking fortress: "Put on the panoply of modesty; surround yourself with the stockade of bashfulness; rear a rampart for your sex, which must neither allow your own eyes egress nor ingress to other people's" *(On the Veiling of Virgins).* It is a defensiveness and an embattled solitude that is reminiscent of many feminists today as they walk determinedly away from the male world.

What was a virgin supposed to do inside this fortress which saw enemies everywhere? It is here that we see the first of the dangers that threaten such a defensive female autonomy. The Fathers tell a virgin to entertain Christ, her bridegroom, who alone can penetrate her defenses. The fantasies they conjure up for their virgins are implicitly sexual and look forward to the wish-fulfillment that we saw in St. Agnes. St. Ambrose reminds the virgin that she is entertaining the spiritual and sublime Word, who existed with the Father in a totally spiritual world:

This is the way to find and hold Christ who puts his hand through your window. This window is the eye of the soul, the vision of the mind, through which we see the works of Christ. Virgin, let Christ enter through your lattice, let Christ put his hand through it; for the love of the Word not that of the body. But if the Word puts his hand through your window, make sure to prepare it.

*(De Virginitate,* 79)

It is all very well for Ambrose here to remind the virgin that he is not speaking of sexual and physical pleasure, to insist that he is not talking about the man Jesus but the mysterious and spiritual Word who dwelt with the Father from all Eternity. When he says that this Word will put his hand inside the virgin, he nevertheless plants in her mind a powerfully erotic image, especially because he is loosely quoting the *Song of Songs,* the Biblical love poem. Jerome does the same:

Let the seclusion of your own chamber ever guard you; ever let the Bridegroom sport with you within. . . . If you pray you are speaking to your spouse: if you read, He is speaking to you. When sleep comes on you He will come behind the wall and will put His hand through the hole in the door and will touch your flesh. And you will awake and rise up and cry: "I am sick with love."

(Letter 22)

Jerome himself had not coped too well with the solitude of the desert, and here, in view of the extreme seclusion that he designs for Eustochium and his opinion of the rampant sexuality of women, it seems extraordinary that he should excite her imagination with such erotic writing. It is nice to have something good to say about Jerome, and it is therefore important to remember that both in Rome and in the Holy Land he did keep his troupe of virgins fully occupied with Biblical scholarship. When he writes panegyrics of his favorite women disciples he loves to praise their intellects and to show how their keen minds constantly challenged and even outwitted him when they discussed Biblical topics. It is a pity—but not perhaps very surprising—that none of their work has survived, or we might have an interesting group of Mothers of the Church. Jerome may have kept them in physical seclusion, but he did introduce them to the masculine world of scholarship. This intellectual discipline would have helped them to guard against the perils of the solitary and celibate life.

Jerome and Ambrose had suggested to virgins that they create their own worlds in fantasy. But the fantasies that women created were often departures from reality. By the Middle Ages the men who wrote devotional works for women were no longer as careful to insist that these erotic fantasies with Christ were entirely spiritual, as St. Ambrose had been. The *Ancrene Riwle* promises the bride of Christ that she can get her spouse to do anything she wants: "stretch out thy love to Jesus Christ and you have won Him. Touch Him with as much love as you sometimes show for a man, and He is thine to do with all that you will" (p. 186). His readers were anchoresses who lived entirely solitary lives; often, like Julian of Norwich, they lived alone in a small cell built onto the Church, which they never left.

Deprived of all normal consolations and all ordinary sexuality, such advice was an open invitation to a woman to let her sexual imagination run wild. The separateness the virgin enjoyed was seen as especially conducive to a private "intimacy" with Jesus which is deeply sexual. In the 12th-century text *The Wooing of Our Lord,* the virgin is told to remind Christ: "Thou has brought me from the world to the bower of my birth. There I can so sweetly kiss and embrace and of thy love have infinite delight" (p. 33). The same text urges the virgin to contemplate not Christ, the Word of God, but Christ's physical body:

> Ah, who may not love thee, lovely Jesu? For within thee alone are all the things united that ever make any man worthy of thy love to another. Beauty and lovesome face, flesh white under clothing make many a man the rather and the more to be beloved.
>
> (p. 20)

The virgin finds herself thinking of Jesus suffering on the cross in masochistic and erotic terms: "Let my body hang with thy body nailed to the cross, enclosed transversely within four walls, and I will hang with thee and nevermore come down from my cross until I die. . . . Ah Jesu! sweet it is with thee to hang!" (ibid., p. 36). Shut up in her cell, the virgin had achieved what Virginia Woolf has said that every woman should have: A Room of Her Own. It is an image that has haunted all autonomous women. In her private female world the virgin was indeed independent of men. She could create her own perfectly legitimate sexuality for herself without them. It was even "holy" for her to have these fantasies. However, it was a lonely world, and loneliness and deprivation often creep into these fantasies, as a virgin is urged to strive to realize these fantasies physically, despite Christ's "real" absence.

> Ah, sweet Jesus, why do I not embrace thee with arms of love so fast that nothing from thence may tear away my heart? Why do I not sweetly kiss thee in spirit, with sweet remembrance of thy good deeds? Why do I not feel thee in my breasts as sweet as thou art?
>
> (Ibid., p. 3)

The reason *why* a virgin could not "really" embrace Christ and feel him in her breasts was, of course, that no such erotic relationship was possible with Christ. The virgin was being deliberately encouraged to depart from reality into an entirely imaginative world of wish-fulfillment which had no basis in fact. It would not be "sweet" to hang on the cross with Jesus; it would not be an erotic experience, and to imagine otherwise is an unhealthy self-deception. It has nothing to do with what the Christian life is supposed to be about. Christ had not invited the virgin into her own private room to satisfy her sexually. Women were encouraged to make Jesus do with them whatever they wanted, and he was often forced to go through some very strange scenarios. As the centuries wear on, many of the saints imagine wedding ceremonies with Jesus where they become his bride. Many of them, like Catherine of Siena and Teresa of Avila, claimed that he had given them a "real" ring, which was invisible to everybody else but themselves; some of them, like St. Catherine de Ricci (d. 1589), produced marks or "stigmas" on their ring fingers which looked like rings, psychosomatically acting out ther own desires. It is true that these fantasies were not doing anybody any harm and were merely giving these women a pathetic satisfaction, but by encouraging women to create these fantasies the Church was damaging them. Further, by canonizing these women, the Church put them forward as role models for other women, encouraging all women to seek a fantasy satisfaction that was impossible for them in the real world.

Women who chose the virginal life took the advice of these devotional writers. St. Margaret Mary Alacoque, who lived in France in the second half of the 17th century, had had an unhappy childhood where she had been deprived of much normal affection. When she entered her convent at Paray le Monail she withdrew into the enclosed female world of the Visitation Order. There was no reason why such a withdrawal from men should inevitably have meant neurosis. The Visitation nuns were extremely suspicious of strange mystical states and discouraged nuns from seeking them out. The way to God they sought was the ordinary road of prayer and a good life. The Foundress, Jane Frances de Chantal, had distrusted abnormal and hysterical raptures and ecstasies, so that Margaret Mary's visions and erratic behavior were strongly disapproved of by many nuns in her community. The withdrawal from the world, in Margaret Mary's case, was not caused by her entering a convent; she brought neurosis with her. The cloistered conditions, the long hours of silence and solitude, the difficulties and inevitable repressions of the celibate life certainly seem to have enhanced this neurosis and driven Margaret Mary to make a further withdrawal into her head, where she "entertained" her spouse in most dubious ways. It is to Margaret Mary that Jesus revealed his "Sacred Heart," and it is to her therefore that we owe that very strange Catholic devotion, where Christ bares his breast to reveal a bulbous heart surrounded by a nimbus of flames (of love) and a crown of thorns. The way this heart becomes separate from Jesus himself shows that for Margaret Mary love is not a part of the whole person, but a small, localized part of the person that can be split off from the rest of the personality. It clearly gives to Margaret Mary compensation for all the love she never had herself:

> I make you heiress of My Heart and of all its treasures for time and eternity, allowing you to use them according to your desire, and I promise you to use them according to your desire, and I promise you that you shall fail only to receive assistance when My Heart shall want power to give it you. You shall be for ever Its beloved disciple the sport of Its good pleasure and the victim of Its wishes. It shall be the sole delight of all your desires; It will repair and supply for your defects, and discharge your obligations for you.

(Tickell, p. 221)

Margaret Mary was imagining a "love" which would supply her with every satisfaction, "discharge all her obligations," and which made her "special" in a conventual world where women were required to submerge their individuality in the common life. Margaret Mary had always been deeply averse to sex. She tells us that the very idea of marriage was repugnant to her as a young girl; she was clearly a child of her culture and had been strongly affected by the hatred of sex that Christianity inspired. Yet the fantasies she created for herself were intensely erotic. Jesus speaks to her like an ardent lover: "Let me do my pleasure. There is a time for everything. Now I want you to be the plaything of my love and you must live this without resistance, surrendered to my desires, allowing me to gratify myself at your expense." The solitude of the cloister as well as Margaret Mary's neurotic rejection of sex, led to her creation of a perverse sexuality, where she was almost Jesus' geisha. It is pure emotional compensation which, because it is a complete departure from reality, is a form of madness. It is the deliberate adoption of a worldview that in no way corresponds to the "true" world. Margaret Mary saw the virginal life in precisely the same ways as Jacobus de Voragine had in *The Golden Legend*. She was to be impervious to the world, as impervious as Agnes in a living death. She had clearly absorbed the virginity myth in its entirety, and wanted only to be separated from reality by a shield of "indifference." On her Profession day Jesus said that she was to live a life which made her totally insensible to the world around her: ". . . all your powers and senses must be buried in Me. You must be deaf, dumb, blind and insensible to all earthly objects." She was being asked to become a "living corpse." Margaret Mary knew that a virgin was to be a defensive fortress. Yet within this fortress she enacted scenarios in which Christ was offering her a rather repulsive physical satisfaction. One day, when she had had a very bad time overcoming her nausea at the jobs she was required to do in the convent infirmary, Jesus gave her a special reward:

> The following night He allowed me for two or three hours to hold my mouth close to the Wound of His Sacred Heart. It would be very difficult for me to express what I then felt or what marvellous effects this grace produced in my soul.
>
> (Ibid., p. 192)

The interesting thing about this incident is that it is a fantasy that Margaret Mary "caught" from another virgin saint. Three hundred years before, Catherine of Siena had also had a hard day nursing an old woman. She overcame her repugnance by drinking the fetid water in which she had washed the cancerous wound, and "I assure you, father," she said to her Confessor, "never in my lifetime did I taste anything one half so sweet and delightful." The next night Jesus appeared to her and showed her his five wounds. He reached out his arms and pulled her close to him so that her lips touched the wound of his side. "Drink, daughter," he said, "drink thy fill of the Fountain of Life." The coincidence is obvious and is only one of many examples which shows how this deeply unhealthy fantasy world was transmitted from one "saint" and role model to another, crossing boundaries of time and distance and creating a special mode of behavior for women seeking the autonomous life.

When this autonomous life is as morbid as the one Margaret Mary created for herself, it is mutilating for the virgin. Margaret Mary's Christ is an appalling creation. He is neurotic, mawkish and self-pitying. In 1682 she recalls how he appeared to her just before Lent:

> . . . covered all over with wounds and bruises. His adorable Blood was streaming over Him on every side. "Will no one," He said in a sad and mournful tone, "have pity on Me and compassionate Me, and take part in My sorrow, in the piteous state to which sinners reduce Me especially at this time."
>
> (Tickell, p. 258)

What Margaret Mary was doing was inventing a Christ in her own neurotic image. She was also making him extremely "feminine." Her Jesus is completely different from the abrasive and vigorous figure of the Gospels. Yet in Margaret Mary's mind he could only be feminine. Other female solitaries also feminized Christ. Some of them have even made him into a woman. Julian of Norwich, a much more robust woman than poor Margaret Mary, saw Jesus as a kindly nurse in whose breasts we find comfort. Indeed, women were encouraged to make this transformation by the spiritual writers. Thus the author of the 12th-century English text, *The Prayer of Our Lord*, sees Jesus as a mother who is standing with outstretched arms:

> He openeth them as doth the mother her arms to embrace her beloved child. Yea, of a truth! And thou, dear Lord, goes spiritually towards us and to thy darlings with the same embrace as a mother to her children.
>
> (p. 2)

The *Ancrene Riwle* also sees Jesus as a mother, for He "plays with us as the mother does with her young darling. She flees from it and hides herself and lets it sit alone and look longingly about and calls, "Mama! Mama!" and weep awhile and return longingly" (p. 103). Women of power and strength, as well as the neurotic virgin, have made Jesus or God female. Thus as early as the 3rd century the

Montanist prophetesses claimed that they were the revelation of God in female form. Mother Ann Lee's followers made much the same kind of claim for her, and Mary Baker Eddy of Christian Science spoke of a God who was both Father and Mother. This could all be seen as a valiant attempt by women to wrest Jesus and God from the male world and translate the religion into female terms. Yet however valiant the attempt to create a female image of Jesus might be, it is a false consolation. Jesus was not a woman; furthermore, there is no evidence in the Gospels of his possessing any of the gentle and playful characteristics ascribed to him here. If this seems too literal a criticism, there is the far more profound objection that God is beyond sex and gender, just as he is beyond human categories of Good and Evil. To say that he is either Man or Woman is to limit Him. It is to make the same mistake as the old virginal and the new feminist myth makes today, by confining God and ideal reality to already established and restricted human categories of gender. Women who imagined Jesus as a woman or as a very feminine man were forced to do so because their exclusively female world made it impossible for them to see him in any other way. The virgin's seclusion had distorted her idea of God and impoverished her understanding of religion.

I am not intending to imply that in their search for autonomy women today are producing neurotic fantasies like Margaret Mary's. However, the march away from the male world by extreme feminists can produce a defensive attitude which is a rejection. The fury with which a possibly sexist remark uttered by either a man or a woman is seized upon is a rejection of the reality that these sexist habits are deeply engrained and will take a long time to eradicate. Fury is an inappropriate response, especially in cases where sexism was not intended. There is sometimes a feeling that the rejection of the male world creates a female world with intensely female preoccupations that is a distortion of reality. Certain feminists, like Mary Daly, for example, have created their own language because they feel that men and patriarchy have damaged the language far too deeply for women to use. Unfortunately, her tortuous—although very ingenious and creatively inspired—language is an impoverishment because, besides neglecting the rich resources of the English language, it also makes it difficult for a lot of people to understand her ideas, so the communication is limited. Similarly, when Christmas trees are denounced because fir trees used to symbolize the woman and the ritual slashing of women at Yule represents the male desire to exterminate the female race, one cannot help feeling that we are in the world of fanaticism. Just as the Christian virgins feminized Jesus and their religion, the radical feminist is in danger of getting a twisted view of the world by viewing and judging everything in terms of women. The view of feminists like Kate Millett that women are "superior" to men is also limiting and false. There is little evidence for it, and however consoling the idea of the superiority of women over men might be, it is again probably untrue. It is making The Female an absolute instead of transcending the neurotic conceptions of gender in our society. Neither men nor women are very great, and both sexes have great problems. The extreme feminist who rejects the male world certainly rejects a good deal of masculine corruption, but also many of the good things of life in the only world we have. To retreat to a room of their own can only confine and distort women. It is understandable that in a world which had no room for her, a woman should have desired a small space for herself: but women should now feel that they can inherit the whole world, not merely a small and limited view of it.

The modern feminist can retreat from the world as radically as the Christian virgin. Marilyn French, in *The Women's Room,* has created a feminist who moves so far away from reality that there is nothing for her but death. The character of Val, a feminist who had originally been a warm and charismatic figure, dominates the book. After her daughter's rape, however, Val severs her links with the rest of the world, saying, "All men are the enemy"; that all men are potential rapists is her ultimate truth. She withdraws herself entirely from the world of men. She also retreats from the world of politics and social concern into a female autonomy:

> . . . half the people I was trying to help were males, males who would as soon rape me or my daughter as look at us. They'd take your body if they could, your soul if they can, get you in control and then abuse you or discard you. I have been spending my life helping them! A bunch of rapists! Because there is no turning back once you've faced this. All men are the enemy!

> . . . I used to pick up male hitchhikers! No more. Let them use their own feet, fight their own fucking battles, no man, ever again, will get any help from me. Never again will I treat a man as anything other than the enemy. . . . "I'm sorry." Val glanced at Mira's face. "I know you have sons. That's good. That will keep you able to live in the world, keep you," she drawled the word sarcastically, "sane."
>
> (1978 ed., pp. 586–87)

She abandons her Ph.D. thesis at Harvard because even the world of thought and scholarship is tainted by men. She banks at a feminist bank, shops in a feminist market, she will work only in a militant feminist organization. Her former love of "pleasure, joy, fun" she sees as compromise in the light of her new realization. Her new attitude, she insists, is not an impoverishment but an enrichment:

> What you see as my deformity, I see as my purification. Hate is a great definer. You lose something, but develop something else to fullness. Like blind people learning to hear with exquisite acuteness, or deaf people learning to read lips, eyebrows, faces. Hate has made me act as I should have been acting all along. My fucking love of mankind kept me from being a friend to womankind.
>
> (Ibid., p. 588)

If the virgin was mutilated psychologically by an impoverishment, there are people who will see such an extreme feminist position as a deformity and mutilation, instead of a true vision of reality. Like the Christian virgin whose virginity has created a wall around her which makes her surroundings irrelevant, the world has nothing more to offer Val. She dies a martyr's death in a feminist cause; her body is exploded by the bullets of the male police force. For both the extreme feminist and the extreme virgin death is ultimately the only possible fate. Marilyn French has created an extreme, but the book's popularity shows that she has touched something that women recognize. Her characters have walked away from the male world just as the Christian virgin did. They may not have Christian fantasies, but their fantasies are as exclusively female and, as Val admits, they are a form of madness that has nothing to do with "the world." French means us to take Val very seriously, and indeed enthusiastic feminism must in some sense mean withdrawal.

It could be argued that a woman can make herself autonomous today, whereas once a woman had lost her virginity, there was nothing in the myth that could make her a virgin again. Once you had been penetrated by the male you could never again be truly virginal. The very early Fathers, like Jerome, would have agreed with this position. However, ways were evolved to get round this. The life of St. Margaret of Cortona shows how it was possible for a woman to achieve an honorary virginity. St. Pelagia, we have seen, managed by becoming a "male" hermit to lay aside her sinful and sexual past. Margaret of Cortona did not become a transvestite, but she did achieve autonomy which she claimed made her a virgin, although her technical virginity had certainly been lost.

Margaret of Cortona, who lived in the 13th century, had lived a sinful life before her conversion. She had eloped with a man and lived with him without being married to him. She also had a son by him. However, after nine years her man was murdered and Margaret found herself in an impossible position. Her family disowned her, as indeed did the respectable world of Tuscany. There was nothing else for it: she either had to become a saint or a professional whore. Margaret was converted and built up a great reputation for sanctity, achieving a small local influence as she intervened in the politics of her district. Her "virginity" gave her an entrée into the male world. She recovered her virginity by two standard methods. Firstly, she mutilated herself by hideous penances and by fasting. Fasting was considered the Christian way of achieving chastity. Christ told her that "no Christian can be perfect who does not restrain his bodily appetite, for without abstinence from food and drink the war of the flesh will never end; and those suffer most from the rebellion of the flesh who refuse this saving remedy" (Legend of Margaret of Cortona, by her confessor Fr. Giula, iii, 7). Margaret put herself on a lifetime's regime of strict fasting, telling Fr. Giula that until she died she could not afford to spare her body, almost as if she could fast her body back not only to chastity, but to its original "integrity." Christ commended her because

. . . thou didst begin to hate and abhor thy beauty of which hitherto thou hadst such care, and which thou hadst nurtured and sought to increase. But now by thy abstinence and macerations thou didst endeavour to destroy it, even going so far as to bruise thy face with stones and smear it with soot.

(i, 2)

The second means of recovering her lost virginity was the deliberate cultivation of autonomy, an independence of the world and an imperviousness to it, which in Margaret's case seems sometimes a callous lack of responsibility or even deliberately cultivated insanity. At the beginning of her penitential life she caused a certain scandal by sending her son away from her to leave her free for her new career:

For whilst he lived with her Margaret was unwilling to look for him lest she should lose time for prayer, and she but rarely conversed with him. "My son," she would say, "when you come home take what food you find and keep silent, for I will not spend on you the time I owe to the divine Presence."

(Ibid., i, 6)

She sent her son to the Franciscans at Arezzo, where he was probably a lot better off. It is hard, however, to forgive Margaret the occasions when she ignores ordinary human concern for other people. When her son's schoolmaster came to collect the fees, for example, Margaret was forbidden by Jesus to speak to him and the poor man had to return home to Arezzo understandably furious. There was also the night when Margaret was so overcome by remorse for her sins that she rushed out onto her balcony, crying and weeping so loudly and so long that she woke up all her neighbors. These neighbors did not seem to mind, if we are to believe Fr. Giula, but instead all got up and "grieved with her and gave thanks to God who had placed Margaret in their midst." This kind of behavior seeks an autonomy not by solitude so much as by remaining as sealed off from the surrounding world as the virgin martyrs had been. This type of autonomy is a kind of madness because it bears no relation to mundane responsibilities. However, Margaret was rewarded. Her virginity was restored. Christ tells her that her great heroine, Mary Magdalene, was the greatest virgin of all the virgins in heaven except for his mother and Catherine the martyr. It is true, Christ says, that Mary Magdalene was not a virgin technically, but she recovered her virginity by her holy penitential life. Similarly, Jesus assures Margaret that "Thy manifold sufferings shall cleanse thy soul from all attraction to sin and in thy suffering and contrition thou shalt be restored to virginal purity." After her death Margaret was promised that her "place shall be amongst the seraphim, with the virgins aflame with love." Margaret's cultivation of physical mutilation and autonomy have restored her physical integrity (iv, 3–15).

The Lord told Margaret that fasting was the only way to preserve chastity, and it was always part of a virgin's program. The virgins starved themselves so that they were sometimes unrecognizable to their nearest and dearest. If women's lust was insatiable, then excessive fasting would bank it down. Food and sex had long been connected in the Christian mind. Jerome had been quite clear when he wrote to Eustochium that fasting was an essential part of her life as a virgin: "Not that God, the Lord and Creator of the universe takes any delight in the rumbling of our intestines or the emptiness of our stomach or the inflammation of our lungs; but because this is the only way of preserving chastity" (Letter 22). Tertullian also compares the purity of the "virgin" body before a meal, when the soul is alive and sensitive, and the state of the soul after the body has been penetrated and invaded by food:

> . . . when that whole habitation of our interior man, stuffed with meats, inundated with wines, fermenting for the purpose of excremental secretion, is already being turned into a premeditatory of privies, where plainly nothing is so inevitable and natural as the savouring of lust. "The people did eat and drink, and they arose to play." Understand the modest language of the Holy Scripture: "Play": unless it had been immodest would not have been rebuked.

*(On Fasting, VI)*

The nourished body will rise up against the soul and fling a man into a violent sexual orgy, against his will and better judgment. Fasting was a particularly religious activity for women because it tamed the unruly female body. Today some form of fasting is still a major factor in the lives of the most secular women and is a cult that is growing to epidemic proportions. The devotees of the cult of slimming are often unaware that what they are doing has a strongly religious dimension.

The new slimming craze goes beyond a creditable campaign against obesity. It is especially directed against women, of course. Slimming magazines are entirely female in image and preoccupation. Men are trying to lose weight, stay trim and cut down on the cholesterol, but for women the matter of slimming is much more complex. If we can be slim, we incoherently feel, we will be loved, sexy and acceptable. It will mean that we have taken our lives creatively into our own hands and starved them into shape. We Western women are excessively self-conscious about our physical failings. We all nourish some secret disgust with some part of our anatomy: our thighs are too flabby, our noses ugly, we are too tall, too short. It sometimes staggers us to learn that even women whom the world considers ravishingly beautiful think they are fat and ugly. Today we are conscious in a way that is entirely new of our weight and calorie intake. Even in the Victorian period, when women were supposed to be weak and feeble, portraits show that they were really rather buxom. Certainly they bear no resemblance to the Twiggy models of today. We have little choice: to be beautiful we *have* to be slim. It is not always men who foist this upon us: men often like women to be more curvaceous and to be a bosomy armful. We are doing this to ourselves. The less there is of the female body, the happier we are with it. We want our female form to disappear, and we will starve our bodies with almost the zeal of a St. Margaret to achieve our aim. We regard food which is fattening with the same prurient horror as Tertullian. When we have "pigged out," as we say, and put on a few pounds, we feel guilty. It has been said that women feel guilty today about food and their weight in the same way as they used to feel guilty about sex. This is hardly surprising, because Christianity has made a connection for us between food and sex.

To say, as Susie Orbach did, that "Fat is a Feminist Issue," could be a misrepresentation of the facts. The relatively new cult of slimming is entirely due to concern with good health which affects men and women equally, a critic would say. Yet this objection seems an over-simplification. Women's slimming is not usually a matter of simple concern for healthy living. Women are bombarded with images of excessively slim models who are presented as the ideal of female beauty in a way that men simply are not. Most women may not go to an extreme of slimming enthusiasm, but to fail to live up to the images of unrealistic female perfection given to them by the models induces a guilt which the present concern with health seems merely to reinforce. However, there are signs that men are just beginning to be affected by this aesthetic guilt also in addition to their concern with health and fitness, to want a streamlined shape and to shed potbellies. The new streamlined woman is almost androgynous, and this unisex theme is of course reflected in fashion and clothes. If unisex fashion seemed to liberate women from the padded bras and boned corsets that had defined the old hourglass female shape, sadly it seems to have passed on a female guilt and obsession to men also. Anorexia nervosa used to be a disease for Women Only, but today men are developing it and dying of it too.

Religion springs from the conviction that there is something wrong with us and with the world. This conviction leads to theologies like the doctrine of Original Sin. The religious person undertakes the disciplines and rituals of a religion convinced that they will lead him or her to salvation and liberation from this imprisoning sense of restlessness and dissatisfaction. A Margaret of Cortona starved herself because she hated herself and her sinful sexuality. By ridding herself of flesh she felt that she had liberated herself from her sin and regained a former lost innocence. The zeal with which a woman today often adopts a punitive slimming regime has a religious dimension to it: by shedding those odd pounds she will cause a new slim and perfect self to appear, losing the old fat failure. The religious undertones of slimming are never far away in its pious literature, and slimming has many of the characteristics of an organized religion.

The slimming cult like a religion offers salvation and liberation and a whole new way of life: it not only offers diets and exercise but also patterns of self-discipline and self-knowledge. If the slimmer applies herself virtuously she will gain new life. In the magazines week by week the Slimmer of the Month explains how she has reached salvation and her life has changed since she was liberated from her fat self. Her husband loves her again—because of her fatness and the neuroses arising from it her marriage had been on the rocks—she is now happier and kinder to those around her, she has more friends and has reached a new peace of mind. Before, she hated herself and stuffed herself with food. Now she starves herself and she loves herself; she has become sexy and desirable to other people. She has been liberated from a prison of obesity. One woman in *Slimmer* recently was a literal prisoner, because her fatness made her agoraphobic. There is a definite religiosity about all this, and it is interesting that it should have surfaced round the old Christian shibboleths of fasting and women's bodies. The religiosity is often self-conscious. Jane Walmsley has written an article called "The Unprincipled Body: Confessions of a Lifelong Slimmer" *(Company,* June 1985) where the fact that slimmer silently rhymes with sinner says a lot about how women regard their flesh. "Thin people get more breaks than fat ones," says Jane Walmsley. (A recent edition of *Slimmer* confirmed this: people like thin people better; in fact, one employer is quoted as saying that he would not employ a heavy person because he would assume that she was feckless, lazy and without discipline and motivation.) So the answer, Walmsley concludes, is a lifelong diet, because after a short diet the fat just comes back on. "Figure control," she concludes, "requires sustained and determined effort. There's nothing moderate about it. Many women give up from time to time, but find no peace of mind. They're ever aware of a lingering aspiration left unfulfilled." The religious tone is unmistakable. It is good for us not to be overweight and to be pleased with our bodies, but when we reject "moderation" we go all out on a masochistic regime, which is becoming for an ever-increasing number of women a chronic illness.

The virgin's pursuit of autonomy and deliberate rejection of the outside world is continued today in a stark and terrible form by the woman who suffers from anorexia nervosa. This disease, which makes it impossible for a woman to eat, causes chronic loss of weight and amenorrhea, is on the increase at present. It was recently estimated that 1 in every 200 teenage girls is starving herself severely, and of these 15 percent will die of the illness. Anorexia used to be a disease that afflicted the upper and middle classes only, but working-class women are now being affected also, as confusion about the role of women spreads. The anorexic is living strictly according to the old Christian myth of virginity, and indeed many of the Christian saints

suffered from it. The anorexic is, like the virgin, deliberately rejecting
her femaleness. Her woman's shape disappears, menstruation ceases
and she becomes a neuter figure. As Sheila MacLeod says in her
prize-winning book *The Art of Starvation,* the anorexic feels the impotence and helplessness of being a woman. She wants to shed the
burden of womanhood:

> The miracle of anorexia is that this wish can be fulfilled: one
> does not have to grow up; one does not have to become a
> woman, even in the biological sense; one can reject all foreign
> substances, for which food is a metaphor, and subject them to
> one's will. This is power indeed. Once the process is under way,
> it all seems easy: the only attribute required is an initial and
> stupendous effort of will. My non-eating started from positions
> of helplessness, of hopelessness, of a barely deniable adulthood
> and an even less deniable womanhood.
>
> (p. 70)

It is a terrible parody of the rejection of the world and an imperviousness to reality that we have seen the virgin cultivating. By refusing to be nourished by food, the anorexic is striving to achieve an
autonomy which she sees as being incompatible to her femaleness.
Like the virgin, like the radical feminist, she refuses to be nourished
by the world.

Sheila MacLeod shows how the anorexic seeks to "become an
autonomous adult, and indeed an autonomous woman." However,
she sees that her sexuality makes a woman deeply dependent. She
sees that women's bodies and women's lives are invaded and penetrated by men, by babies and by vulnerability. Like the Christian
virgin she wants to cast off these female weaknesses, and become
impervious to the world about her. Her rejection of sexuality is very
deep. Statistics show that it is rare for the recovered anorexic to have
a completely normal sex life after her illness (MacLeod, p. 150).
However, she does achieve the type of invulnerablity that we have
seen the virgins achieving. She feels protected from the world by a
screen of distance and separateness. Sheila MacLeod during one of
her relapses in adulthood wrote a novel called *The Snow White Solil-
oquies,* which tells the story of a girl who endures a living death in a
glass coffin and is trailed around the country in a glass vehicle by a

motley collection of social misfits, the dwarfs of the Snow White story.

> It was only later, when I was forced to admit that, at the time of writing, I had begun to become anorexic again, that I realised in addition how closely the central character's circumstances resembled those of anorexia nervosa. Later still, my realisation was confirmed for me when I read the following statement from one of Bruch's patients: "I am completely isolated, I sit in a glass sphere. I see other people through a glass wall, their voices penetrate to me. I long for being in real contact with them. I try but they don't hear me."
>
> . . . As life in general was unreal and remote—seen through a sheet of glass—so my own suffering seemed unreal. The sight of, say, a field of corn interspersed with poppies on a sunny day didn't move me; the spectacle of a woman who had slipped and fallen in the street didn't move me—either to sympathy or to ridicule. . . . What was going on in my body was as unreal, as devoid of meaning, as were the events in the outside world. The two were part of one whole, a whole of which "I" was no part.
>
> (Ibid., pp. 107–8)

It should be obvious how the anorexic is experiencing the virginal ideal, which the story of Agnes expresses so clearly. Like the virgin the anorexic rejects the world and is protected but also impoverished by this rejection. A beautiful vision of poppies does not affect her, any more than the brothel affected Agnes. Like the virgin, the anorexic is enduring a living death in a glass coffin. If she does not recover she will die of her illness, but the world is as meaningless to her as if she were dead already. Such autonomy is mutilating physically, and the anorexic's appearance reminds us of saints like Pelagia and Euphrosyne, whose fasting and penance made them gaunt and unrecognizable. Her illness is as sexually disturbed and as psychologically mutilating as was the virgin's when she fantasized erotically about Christ. It is only fairly recently that anorexia has been recognized as an illness. Today an anorexic is treated as a sick person; a few hundred years ago she was canonized as a saint.

The legend of St. Uncumber shows us how anorexia is historically linked to the virginity myth. There were a number of saints with the same story. In Germany she was called "Wilgefortis" *(virgo fortis,* the strong virgin) and in France, Italy and Spain "Livrade," "Liberata" or "Librada," which like "Uncumber" all suggest a flinging aside of limitations, a liberation. The story is that Uncumber had dedicated her life to virginity, but her father betrothed her to a suitor of his choice. She fasted and prayed and God preserved her virginity: instead of being protected by a nimbus of flame or a celestial vest, God made her masculine—he sent her a beard. She looked so monstrous that the suitor instantly withdrew his offer and the enraged father crucified Uncumber. An article in the *British Medical Journal* has suggested that this martyr for virginity may not have been a fanciful invention of the Christian faithful but may have suffered from anorexia nervosa. Anorexics quite frequently grow a good deal of facial hair, as the hormonal balance is disturbed, and Uncumber's fasting and aversion to sexuality, as well as her desire for the virginal and autonomous state, all point to typical anorexic symptoms. It would not be surprising if anorexia were common in medieval Europe. The hatred of sexuality, of women's bodies and of femininity, together with the ideal of virginity, created perfect conditions for the disease to spread, just as the sexual confusions of today are increasing the illness.

The lives of many Christian saints show that their fasting induced chronic anorexia. This is not to deny that, unlike the modern anorexic, their fasting had a strongly religious motive. It is simply that the regime they adopted when combined with a tendency towards obsession ultimately made it impossible for them to eat. Treating your body in certain ways will bring on certain physical and psychological symptoms, whatever your original intention. Often, though, the modern anorexic's motives and compulsions overlap with the saint's. Margaret Mary was horrified by sexuality, as we have already noted. She was never tempted against purity, she writes, but she had great temptations against gluttony "of which I had a greater horror than death." The connection between sex and food could not be more neatly made. Any anorexic will recognize this syndrome:

> The Devil made me feel a ravenous hunger; he presented to my
> imagination whatever was most calculated to gratify the taste,

and this during the time of my spiritual exercises. This was a terrible torture to me.

(Tickell, p. 225)

Yet as soon as she entered the refectory she felt so sick that she couldn't eat anything. Anorexics very commonly fantasize or dream about delicious and fattening food. Ultimately Margaret Mary found eating absolutely impossible, and, like the modern anorexic, guilt seems to have played a major part in her abandonment of food. One night she had a vision of God in his purity and was convinced that she was a "sink of contempt and humiliation."

From this time eating became to me a torment. I went to the Refectory as to a place of punishment to which I had been condemned for my sins. I endeavoured to eat indifferently all that was presented to me but I could not prevent myself from always taking the least amount, and what was most in conformity with my poverty and nothingness. It was represented to me that bread and water was sufficient for me and that all else was superfluous.

(Ibid., pp. 198–99)

The question is not so much whether Margaret Mary's aversion to food was motivated religiously or neurotically but what her religion consisted in. She, like many other women of her time, was being encouraged in a false religion to see her aversion to food as holy instead of a sickness. Real religion is about the loss of the self and the quest for God. Margaret Mary's religion was self-obsessed and therefore unhealthy.

Catherine of Siena also fasted herself into anorexia, and her emaciation and inability to eat won her considerable renown and prestige. Again she was being encouraged in an unhealthy concentration on the self (which is what guilt is) away from the truly religious quest. She, like the modern anorexic, found her identity bound up with her fasting. Right up to the end of her life she vehemently refused food, leaving her confessor floundering when he timidly tried to persuade her to eat something. Emaciation was certainly a cause of her early death. Like Margaret Mary, her guilt was deeply bound up in her rejection of food, and the adulation she received which confirmed her in her suicidal path led to a certain self-exhibition. The anorexic can sometimes be just as flamboyant and defiant as Catherine, who used to call attention to her eating difficulties with a ghastly sprightliness: "Come along!" she used to cry en route to a meal, "the prisoner is now going to execution." The euphoria often experienced by the anorexic is very evident in Catherine's determined, reasoned arguments against eating. Most anorexics are now diagnosed as sick people and treated by doctors and lay people alike most unsympathetically, and cannot afford such self-advertisement; they have to resort to subterfuge. However, for both the saint and the anorexic of today, fasting is an essential part of identity and a refusal of life. Catherine was seen as holy because she was seen to be devoted to a living death and to be preserved supernaturally by God. She was seen by lay people and clerics as a walking miracle, which shows how mistakenly directed so much Christianity was at that time. She was said to live for long periods entirely on Holy Communion. Eating was always a torture to her, as Father Thomas Antonio Caffarini tells us. When he first met her in 1366 she was a young woman, but her anorexia was so engrained that already

> . . . her digestion had become so weak that she was incapable of retaining any solid food. Nevertheless to please and satisfy her parents, she would force herself to swallow something, and would call the summons to the family meal, "going to execution," so terrible was the suffering it cost her. "Nevertheless," he continues, "I always saw her cheerful."

> (Drane, p. 58)

Catherine certainly enjoyed the anorexic "high," and that her symptoms were extremely exhibitionist can be seen in the *Miracoli,* the anonymous account of her life written during her lifetime. Yet the cheerful relishing of her illness was not morbidity for its own sake. Catherine as well as her contemporaries saw her rejection of food as miraculous:

> This holy virgin always has with her two or three sisters who wear the same habit, and who never leave her; and not for her own consolation but theirs, she sits down with them to table. Her companions do not eat meat, but only herbs, vegetables and

fruit, with bread and wine, and other coarse food, cooked and raw. She takes something into her mouth, according to what may be on the table, sometimes a morsel of bread as big as a nut, sometimes a leaf of salad or an almond, or other such things, and in like quantities. She swallows nothing that she puts into her mouth, but when she has masticated it, rejects it into a little vessel, rinsing her mouth with some cold water. And this she does only once in the day.

(Ibid., p. 173)

Stephen Marconi tells us that often the artificial means she was obliged to use to reject what she had swallowed caused her to vomit blood. To inquirers she admitted that she had a "strange kind of infirmity" that made eating impossible for her because of her great sinfulness. "It is better to expiate my sins here," she would say, when urged to eat. "God sustains my life without food." However, God seems not to have done a very good job. She died when she was just under thirty years old as a result of her mortifications, wasted and emaciated.

We cannot afford to sneer at the clerics who admiringly noted all these anorexic symptoms and hailed them as miraculous evidence of sanctity. A satisfactory cure for anorexia has still not been found, and it is possible that the illness is now more rife in our culture than it has ever been before. The anorexic sums up the dangers of the myth of virginal autonomy: mutilated, and denying the world's nourishment she is slowly dying a solitary death, refusing the world, the flesh and her gender. It is interesting that the disease should be rife now that the ideal of female autonomy is also increasing. Autonomy is very difficult for women to achieve: it can literally kill them.

Nevertheless, at its best the myth of virginity speaks of new freedoms and a "wish for wings." The troubles have been caused, both now and in the past, by too limited an understanding of this liberation, and also by too violent a withdrawal from the male world. The ideal is only possible now because for centuries in our culture women knew that the dependent and married state was second best. Yet the original Christian vision of a state which brought freedom and equality to women got tangled up with the more negative aspects of the Christian sexual neurosis. Virginity, for so long the leading myth

about the free woman in the West, can give us some valuable lessons
in our struggle for liberation today. However, although it has always
been the basic woman's answer to male oppression in our culture, it
was not her only answer. We must now turn to some of the other
ways in which a woman sought and won recognition and respect in
the hostile world of Western Christianity.

# 5

# WHY BE A MARTYR?

Suffering has always been written into the heart of the Christian religion. Jesus Christ, for whatever reason, died an agonizing death. He was a victim. When St. Paul founded Christianity in the gentile world of the Roman Empire, he insisted that the Cross of Christ and its exaltation of suffering was his principal message. He had no ingenious philosophies to present to the clever Greek world, to whom the meaning of the Cross was mere folly. Later, the persecutions endured by the early Christians at the hands of the Roman Empire reinforced the message of suffering and its exaltation in the Christian mind. That cult of suffering and self-sacrifice has remained embedded in the Western world. It differs from the appreciation of bravery that one finds in other cultures because of the idealization of failure and the victim. It was inevitable that women should be as affected by this ideal as any other Christian. Indeed, they became affected by it in a way that still touches us today. The ideal of the Martyr changed over the centuries, especially when the persecutions stopped and Christianity moved to the barbarian tribes of Northern Europe. Women began to see themselves as victims and as sufferers in ways that affected the ideal of romantic love and passion in our society. Women today continue to define themselves in terms of their suffering, now not from a hostile state power, but at the hands of the male world. The martyr myth should be used with great care, however. In some of its later manifestations it is extremely unhealthy, and ultimately self-defeating for the women's cause.

Christianity has always been quite clear that to give your life for the faith is the highest of the Christian vocations. Christ died on the Cross for the sins of men, and in the Gospels he tells his followers that they have to take up their cross and follow him to death, if necessary. The martyrs had a chance to do this almost literally, and women were always included in this Christian élite and honored equally with the men who died for the faith. From the first century of its history Christians suffered at the hands of the Roman Empire, and persecutions erupted against them sporadically until the 4th century, when the Emperor Constantine was converted and Christianity became the official state religion. The persecutions made a great impact on Christianity at a formative stage of its development. Christians viewed them not as an evil scourge but as a joyful privilege. The North African theologian Origen, for example, looks back nostalgically to the reign of the Emperor Severus, who in the years 202–204 launched the first worldwide attack on Christianity:

> This was when one really was a believer, when one used to go to martyrdom with courage in the Church, when returning from the cemeteries whither we had accompanied the bodies of martyrs, we came back to our meetings, and the whole Church would be assembled there, unbreakable. Then the catechumens were catechised in the midst of martyrdoms, and in turn these catechumens overcame tortures and confessed the living God without fear. It was then that we saw prodigies. Then too the faithful were few in numbers but were really faithful, advancing along the straight and narrow path leading to life.
>
> (Fourth Homily on Jeremiah, 4:3)

There is a sense of euphoria, purpose and solidarity. It is interesting that it is the joyful aspect of martyrdom that Origen stresses. He himself as a young boy had been encouraged by his father to go and join the martyrs voluntarily, and he had been avid to do so. It was his mother who saved his life by hiding his clothes. Later generations of Christians would look back on this attitude and imagine that what Origen wanted was pain and suffering, especially in view of the fact that he later castrated himself to avoid sexual temptation and fulfill Christ's counsel and praise of "those who have made themselves eunuchs for the sake of the Kingdom." However, Origen was a complex man, and in the very complexity of his response to martyrdom and to asceticism we see the beginnings of the Christian confusion about the value of suffering. In his account of the Severan persecution there is no dwelling on the agonies of the martyrs, no grisly details of the kind that we encounter in medieval accounts of these same persecutions. The early Church looked on martyrdom differently from later Christians. Generations afterwards, most Christians totally misunderstood what martyrdom had originally meant to the martyrs themselves.

One of the first accounts of a persecution that has come down to us is the 2nd-century story of the Martyrs of Lyons, who were put to death by the local Roman authorities out of some kind of superstitious fear. Charges of cannibalism and orgies were brought up against them which were much the same as those that the Church would later bring against heretics and witches. Among the martyrs was a young slave girl, Blandina, who figures very prominently in the story and shows us that by becoming a martyr a woman instantly became one of the most honored members of the Church, superior to most men. The author declares that the story of Blandina, who was neither a beauty nor of any great rank—indeed she was of a despised caste—proves "that the things that men think cheap, ugly and contemptuous are deemed worthy of glory before God." One of the first things to notice about her is her energetic courage:

> All of us were in terror. . . . Yet Blandina was filled with such power that even those who were taking turns to torture her in every way were weary and exhausted. They themselves admitted that they were beaten, that there was nothing further they could

do to her, and they were surprised that she was still breathing, for her entire body was broken and torn. They testified that even one kind of torture was enough to release her soul, let alone the many they applied with such intensity. Instead, this blessed woman, like a noble athlete, got renewed strength with her confession of faith: her admission, "I am a Christian; we do nothing to be ashamed of," brought her refreshment, rest and insensibility to present pain.

*(The Acts of the Christian Martyrs,*
ed. Herbert Musurillo, p. 67)

The other sufferers are terrified, Blandina is not. She is filled with "power" which later martyrs will call the Holy Spirit. She is so full of this power that she becomes in some way the leader of the other martyrs. When they finally reach the arena, Blandina is tacitly compared to the mother of the Maccabees, those Jewish martyrs in the Old Testament who died for the Law under Antiochus Epiphanes. This noble mother had urged on her seven sons to martyrdom, watching them die one after the other and congratulating them on their noble end. Similarly, Blandina was the last of the martyrs to be executed:

Like a noble mother encouraging her children, she sent them before her in triumph to the King, and then, after duplicating in her own body all her children's sufferings, she hastened to rejoin them rejoicing and glorying in her death as though she had been invited to a bridal banquet instead of being a victim of the beasts.

(Musurillo, p. 79)

Her martyrdom is seen as her fulfillment as a woman—the experience is compared to what most people would consider the crowning points of any woman's life: marriage and motherhood—and yet there is nothing either mawkish or prurient about the description. Nobody is slavering with lust over Blandina's naked limbs, as they are in later accounts of the martyrdom of women, and there are no detailed and titillating descriptions of the precise tortures she endured. Apart from the references to motherhood and the bridal banquet, it is Blandina's virile qualities that are stressed, rather than her shrinking femininity. All the martyrs fight bravely and do battle in the arena with beasts and whips and fire. They cannot be overcome. Like athletes or gladiators they struggle and wrestle powerfully, but Blandina's torments are particularly distinguished:

> Blandina was hung on a post and exposed as bait for the wild animals that were let loose on her. She seemed to hang there in the form of a cross, and by her fervent prayer she aroused intense enthusiasm in those who were undergoing their ordeal, for in their torment with their physical eyes they saw in the person of their sister Him who was crucified for them.
>
> (Ibid., p. 75)

Blandina, "tiny, weak and insignificant as she was," represents Christ himself. The other martyrs as well as the other spectators in the arena see Christ in her more than in any of the other martyrs, even though she was only a woman. However, Blandina was no longer "only a woman;" she had transcended the weakness of her sex and the limitations of her status as a slave by becoming one with Christ in her ordeal. Christ was fighting in her: "she would give inspiration to her brothers for she had put on Christ, that mighty and invincible athlete, and had overcome the Adversary in many contests and through her conflict had won the crown of immortality." Blandina had transcended not only the limitations of her sex but of the human condition (Musurillo, p. 75).

Martyrdom is not seen as the passive endurance of pain. It is an active achievement. Blandina has "won the crown of immortality" in the way that an athlete in the Roman world won a laurel wreath. The martyr is not simply giving an example of human bravery and courage in enduring pain to witness to the truth of his beliefs. He is taking part in a cosmic battle. The stadium where he suffers has become the setting for another battle in a war between otherworldly powers. There was a widespread belief during the 2nd and 3rd centuries that Jesus would return very soon and that his Second Coming would be a final battle with Satan; it would be the ultimate victory in a war that Christ was constantly waging. When a martyr went to his death in the stadium he was taking part in this war with Satan that was going on all the time. Each martyrdom was thought to bring this final victory nearer. That is why people like Origen wanted to offer themselves up as voluntary martyrs—a practice to which the Church eventually put a stop. They were not rushing forward to suffer pain for its own sake. It is victory, not pain, that was the point. Indeed, there is every indication that the martyr did not feel the pain of his martyrdom. Blandina, for example, showed "insensibility in her present pain." When she was finally thrown to a wild bull "she no longer perceived what was happening because of the hope and possession of all she believed in" (ibid., p. 79). Blandina had not simply lost consciousness because of her pain. She was believed to have swooned mystically into the "possession" of Christ and her heavenly reward. The martyrs were not honored because they bravely put up with pain. The martyrs were glorified because they felt no pain at all.

When the Romans went to the stadium to watch the Christians die, they did not go to look at the spectacle of human endurance. As a nobleman explained to the Bishop of Smyrna, the Roman world was used to physical courage; they had their professional gladiators and beast hunters, who gave a much better show in that respect. What impressed the Romans about the Christians was that the martyrs seemed to suffer no pain. They offered the Roman world a particular type of religious experience. The religious world of Late Antiquity was very much a cult of different types of trance and "possession" by the gods. In his death, the Christian martyr experienced the most extreme form of trance. He passed into the next world in ecstasy, while his suffering flesh remained down below. He had already been called to the "possession of all [they] believed in" and was therefore quite indifferent to the pain. In one very deep sense "they" were no longer there to feel it. As Peter Brown in *The Making of Late Antiquity* explains, "The pain of martyrdom was thought of as irrelevant to a human body that had already turned away in trance from the ties of its human environment and was wrapped in close intimacy with Christ" (p. 56). When St. Cyprian the martyr appeared in a vision to St. Flavian, who was waiting for his own ordeal in the arena, he informed him that the martyr need not fear the pain of his death, for his spirit had already left his body: "It is another flesh that suffers when the soul is in heaven," he explained, "The body does not feel this at all when the mind is entirely absorbed in God" (Musurillo, p. 235). That is why martyrdom was seen as such a joyful experience. The martyr literally experienced "ecstasy." Ecstasy means that the soul leaves the body and becomes absorbed into the divine. Martyrdom was the supreme form of this religious experience. The lugubrious lives of the Christian ascetics like St. Jerome, who made their lives a daily martyrdom, were very different from the joyfulness of the Martyrs of Lyons as they processed proudly into the arena for their ecstatic experience:

> . . . with majesty and great beauty mingled on their counte-
> nances, so that even their chains were worn on them like some
> lovely ornament, as for a bride adorned with golden embroi-
> dered tassels, exhaling at the same time the sweet odour of
> Christ, so that some thought they had anointed themselves with
> a perfume of this world.
>
> (Musurillo, p. 73)

However, even though it is important to make the point that the cult of martyrdom was not originally a cult of suffering and pain, the bravery of the martyrs should not be underestimated. It took a lot of faith to believe that when you started being gored by a wild bull you wouldn't feel anything. Most of the Martyrs of Lyons were "terrified" at first, and it was Blandina who gave them courage. Another woman who managed to do this for her male companions was St. Perpetua, who died in the Severan persecution in Carthage in 203. She left what seems to have been a diary recording her time in prison before her martyrdom. A later editor collated her writings and added the account of her death. The *Passion of Perpetua and Felicitas,* her slave, is a moving and powerful document. Perpetua shows that she was not a tough and insensitive virago. She was both frightened and depressed when she first went into prison. She had her baby son with her, whom she was breastfeeding, and she was naturally worried about his welfare. The prison itself appalled her: "I grew frightened for I had never known such darkness" *(Passion of Perpetua and Felicitas* III). When Jacobus de Voragine retold Perpetua's story in *The Golden Legend,* however, he transforms her into a typically callous and insensitive "virgin": She spurns her father and her husband and throws her baby on the ground, clearly reflecting the virgin myth of imperviousness to the surrounding world. Even though the early martyrs felt no pain at their deaths, the martyrdom myth did not originally encourage them to be tough and unkind viragos. Perpetua was upset about her mother and her brother, who were worried about her: she "was worn out, seeing them so worn because of me." Her father, who pleads with her not to die for this terrible new faith, nearly breaks her heart. When he is struck by one of the officials at her trial she says she "grieved for my father's downfall as if I'd been struck myself" (ibid., IV). It is true that she never mentions her husband, but Dronke suggests that he may have been one of the people who betrayed the cause and did not go through with martyrdom, so that the redactor cut him out of the diary. He also suggests, quite plausibly, that the thought of her husband may just have been too painful for Perpetua to record, even in her diary.

Perpetua prepared herself and her companions for martyrdom by a series of dreams. Her companions believed that because of her dreams she was *"in dignitate,"* in a specially distinguished relationship with God. She was thus asked by her companions to see if they would definitely be martyred. That night Perpetua had a dream, she saw a high bronze ladder leading to heaven, up which Saturus, one of her companions, was climbing. He warned her about the huge dragon who was guarding the bottom of the steps, but Perpetua was not afraid and mounted to the top. There she saw a gray-haired shepherd milking a sheep, surrounded by a crowd of people in white robes. The shepherd gave her a cup of milk and everybody cried "Amen!" Perpetua woke up with a sweet taste in her mouth. She knew now that they were going to be martyred, and, she says, from that time on she and her companions renounced all hope in this world and started preparing for the next. The dream had shown martyrdom as an ascent to a higher place, as a conflict and victory over the Devil (the dragon). The milk she drank is reminiscent of the milk that the catechumens drank after their baptism. Martyrdom here is seen as a second baptism, a means of immersing oneself in the divine life, as a triumph and a victory. There is no mention of pain or masochistic relishing of torture.

As her diary continues, one can see in Perpetua's dreams how at a deep level she was striving to prepare herself for the ordeal that lay ahead. Subconsciously she was reconciling herself to her fate. The images she dreams are consoling: there is the sweet-tasting milk, the image of her brother Dinocrates who had died as a child of cancer of the face and who is now "clean, well-dressed and refreshed," the wound on his face completely healed. He is drinking from a golden bowl of water. Perpetua is given a green bough of golden apples. Finally, on the night before the "fight," as Perpetua calls it, we can see how different Perpetua is from the frightened young matron who entered the prison and who was plagued by "fearful thoughts for many days." She has a dream which envisages her martyrdom as transcending the boundaries of her sex:

Pomponius the deacon was coming to the prison gate and knocking urgently. And I went out to him and opened for him. He was wearing a loose, gleaming white tunic, and damasked sandals, and he said: "Perpetua, we are waiting for you: come!" He took my hand and we began to go over rough winding ways. We had hardly reached the amphitheatre, breathless, when he took me into the middle of the arena, and said, "Don't be afraid; here I am, beside you, sharing your toil." And he vanished. And I saw the immense, astonished crowd. And as I knew I had been condemned to the wild beasts, I was amazed they did not send them out at me. Out against me came an Egyptian, foul of aspect, with his seconds: he was to fight with me. And some handsome young men came up beside me: my own seconds and supporters. And I was stripped naked and became a man. And my supporters began to rub me with oil, as they do for a wrestling match; and on the other side I saw the Egyptian rolling himself in the dust. And a man of amazing size came out—he towered over the vault of the amphitheatre. He was wearing the purple, loosely, with two stripes crossing his chest, and patterned sandals made of gold and silver, carrying a baton like a fencing master and a green bough laden with golden apples. He asked for silence, and said, "This Egyptian, if he defeats her, will kill her with his sword; she, if she defeats him, will receive this bough." And he drew back.

And we joined combat, and fists began to fly. He tried to grab my feet, but I struck him in the face with my heels. And I felt airborne, and began to strike him as if I were not touching the ground. But when I saw there was a lull, I locked my hands, clenching my fingers together, and so caught hold of his head; and he fell on his face and I trod upon his head. The populace

began to shout, and my supporters to sing jubilantly. And I
went to the fencing master and received the bough. He kissed
me and said: "Daughter, peace be with you!" And triumphantly
I began to walk towards the Gate of Life. And I awoke. And I
knew I should have to fight not against the wild beasts but
against the Fiend; but I knew the victory would be mine.

*(Passion of Perpetua and Felicitas,* X, Trans. P. Dronke in
*Women Writers of the Middle Ages)*

Perpetua's interpretation of her dream is within the tradition which
saw martyrdom as a combat with the Devil. What is particularly
interesting is Perpetua's change of sex. The account is full of surprises: Perpetua is constantly "amazed" at what she sees and the
crowd are "astonished." Pomponius promises to be with her in her
"toil" and promptly vanishes, in the typical logic of the dream. However, her change of sex causes no astonishment to Perpetua. She
matter-of-factly sees that she "became a man." Unlike the female
transvestites of Christian legend, Perpetua doesn't dress like a man,
but really becomes male. However, she is at the same time still female, called "her" and "daughter" by the fencing master. In her
martyrdom Perpetua has become "a new creation," as St. Paul had
promised. She is truly androgynous, the true virago, man and
woman together. There is no shame about her sex. Perpetua's an-
drogyny gives her superhuman powers to defeat the Devil. Her liberation is not that she is a man but that she has become a new creature
altogether with powers that exceed both male and female strength.
She feels "airborne," fights "as if I were not touching the ground."
There is a euphoria and a sensual pleasure in the whole experience.
Perpetua suffers no Christian shame at her nakedness: she enjoys
being rubbed down by her "handsome young men." She enjoys the
liberating battle, the beautiful clothes and brilliant sandals of the
giant fencing master, the singing and jubilation of her supporters.
There is no masochistic love of suffering in martyrdom as Perpetua
sees it.

The account of her death shows that Perpetua achieved the ecstatic trance which lifted her above pain and gave her a superhuman
liberation. The night before the martyrdom her slave, Felicitas, gave
birth to a baby. While she was crying out during her labor one of the

prison guards laughed at her: "You suffer so much now—what will you do when you are tossed to the beasts?" Felicitas' reply is a classic statement of the early teaching about martyrdom: "What I am suffering now, I suffer by myself. But then another will be inside me who will suffer for me, just as I shall be suffering for him." With this confidence Perpetua and Felicitas walked into the arena the following morning. The editor writes that her face was shining "as the beloved of God, as a wife of Christ, putting down everyone's stare by her own intense gaze." Perpetua's nightly journeys into her subconscious prepared her calmly and naturally for her final dignified acceptance of her death. The two women were quite oblivious of their sufferings:

> First the heifer tossed Perpetua and she fell on her back. Then sitting up she pulled down the tunic which was ripped along the side so that it covered her thighs, thinking more of her modesty than of her pain. Next she asked for a pin to fasten her untidy hair: for it was not right that a martyr should die with her hair in disorder, lest she might be seen to be mourning in her hour of triumph.
>
> Then she got up, and seeing that Felicitas had been crushed to the ground, she went over to her, gave her her hand and lifted her up. Then the two stood side by side. But the cruelty of the mob was by now appeased, and so they were called back through the Gate of Life.*
>
> There Perpetua was held up by a man named Rusticus who was at that time a catechumen and kept close to her. She awoke from a kind of sleep (so absorbed had she been in ecstasy in the Spirit) and she began to look about her. Then to the amazement of all she said: "When are we going to be thrown to that heifer or whatever it is?"
>
> When told that this had already happened she refused to believe it until she noticed the marks of her rough experience on her person and her dress.
>
> (Musurillo, p. 129)

* The *Porta Sanavivavia*, where the victorious gladiators made their exit.

The editor, probably a man, shows that in some ways he did not understand Perpetua. This prim young woman, modestly fiddling with her tunic and fussing about her hair, is a very different woman from the one who eagerly stripped off her clothes in her dream and let her naked body be rubbed with oil in full sight of the astonished crowd. There is clearly something of the "virgin" about Perpetua; like Blandina, her experience of ecstatic martyrdom makes her insensible to her environment, but this is achieved not by magical external vests but by her own quiet interior preparation. The *Passion of Perpetua* actually stresses the womanliness of both Perpetua and Felicitas. They are mothers; Felicitas actually gives birth the night before her death and goes into the arena with her body still bleeding from childbirth and her breasts dripping milk. It is not physical integrity that provides the women with their courage when they die for their beliefs. During her days in prison, Perpetua takes control of her life so that she also owns her own death and controls it. Because the beasts could not kill the martyrs they were dispatched by the sword, but the gladiator who killed Perpetua bungled his first attempt. She then "took the trembling hand of the young gladiator and guided it to her throat. It was as though so great a woman, feared as she was by the unclean spirit, could not be dispatched unless she herself was willing." Both Perpetua and Blandina become the leaders of their companions in the ordeal of martyrdom, and for both of them martyrdom is not a masochistic seeking of pain for its own sake but a liberation from the weaknesses and fears not just of the female state but of the human condition.

However, even in the early Church there were indications of how the ideal of martyrdom would be perverted into an unhealthy ideal. Breakaway heretical groups like the Montanists believed that martyrdom was the only safe way to heaven. The true Christian, they insisted, must live a life of solitude and penance, separating himself from the world so that he does not get too embedded in its comforts. Tertullian joined the Montanists for a while, before deciding that even they were not strict enough for him. He spent his last years in the desert with a small band of Tertullianists, waiting for the Second Coming and the final battle with Satan. He was the original nonconformist Puritan, a type which has constantly recurred in Christian history, so that even though he abandoned orthodoxy his influence has never been lost. Nor did Christianity ever forget the intense experience of the Great Persecutions which stamped its early history so traumatically. The mention of Tertullian shows that adulation of the martyr ideal went hand in hand with sexual rigorism. The Montanist movement spread like wildfire during the 3rd century, idealizing martyrdom and stigmatizing sex and marriage. It is easy to see how the Montanist ascetic, in training for martyrdom and the final battle with Satan, would fall an easy prey to the antiphysical neurosis of Christianity. Origen, that other great martyr enthusiast, also makes the same point:

> Bring wild beasts, bring crosses, bring fire, bring tortures. I know that as soon as I die, I come forth from the body. I rest in Christ. Therefore let us struggle, let us wrestle, let us groan, being in the body, not as if we shall again be in the tomb in the body because we shall be set free from it, and shall change our body to one which is more spiritual. Destined as we are to be with Christ, how we groan to be in the body.
>
> (Dialogue)

Perpetua had not shown any great horror of her female body. Rather, she had in her dream positively enjoyed its new power and had displayed it proudly. In her interpretation of martyrdom, the body plays an honorable part in the struggle with Satan and is glorified rather than shaken off. However, at the time of her death she was only a catechumen. She had not had a chance to absorb the full Christian hatred of the body because she had not been a Christian very long. Later women saints would interpret the ideal of martyrdom as a daily warfare on their bodies.

Even after the persecutions ended, the early Church still retained a keen attitude towards martyrdom. The new state Church built large basilicas and the relics of the martyrs were buried there in rich shrines. These "friends of God" enjoyed special powers which they made available to their followers. The shrines of the martyrs were great centers of healing and miraculous cures. The accounts of the passions of the martyr of the shrine would be read out and it was believed that this sacramentally made the victorious martyrs present. Gregory of Tours said that when the passion of the martyr was read aloud he was really present: a sweet smell would fill the basilica and the sick and the crippled who had gathered there cried aloud, feeling the full force of the saint's healing power. The accounts of the martyrs' sufferings now became more detailed and concentrated far more on the sufferings they had endured. This was not due to an exaltation of pain for its own sake, however, rather the opposite. Peter Brown has shown that healing in the Ancient World was associated with violent pain and dislocation. Aelius Aristides speaks of the "great and strange correction" that accompanied all true healing as the sick person passed violently from one physical state to another. The accounts of the martyrs' sufferings were psychodramas, expressing the physical violence that must always accompany the passage from death to life, from sickness to health. The more gruesome the account of the passion was, the more potent the cures effected there. The early Church did not dwell on these sufferings to make Christians reproduce them in their own lives. They used these accounts of suffering precisely to effect cures and bring an end to pain. Suffering was used to end suffering.

However, when the old culture was lost and the Dark Ages descended, these subtle distinctions were lost. The alliance of martyrdom and sexual asceticism and hatred of the body was inevitable. Christians were urged to manufacture suffering—itself a contradiction in terms. To suffer means that you are passive. Pain is inflicted upon you. However, the new Christian "martyrs," deprived of the chance of actual martyrdom, tried to reproduce the martyrs' deaths by making their whole lives as painful and as unpleasant as possible. Instead of glorying in their freedom from pain, the new martyrs and Christian ascetics took pride in suffering as much pain as they could. Instead of using the accounts of the martyrs' sufferings to end pain, the accounts were used to egg ascetics on to flagellate themselves, starve themselves into an anorexic or emaciated condition and generally to mutilate their bodies.

The early martyrs' imperviousness to pain obviously had links with the myth of the virgin, even though the women concerned were not always virgins and had no "virginal" aspirations at all. It is true that the martyrs retreated from the world into ecstasy, so that they were truly invulnerable to their surroundings. It was perhaps inevitable that by the Middle Ages the martyr was nearly always a virgin, and the ideal of martyrdom had been linked to the ideal of virginity.

There is a further difference in the accounts of the early Church and medieval accounts of true martyrdom. The editor of Perpetua's *Passion* is full of admiration for the young woman, even though he does make her appear more prim and shrinking than her diary shows her to be. By the Middle Ages the Passions of the Virgin Martyrs and the legends that had developed about them show a deep hatred of women at the same time as the women are praised and glorified.

One of the most terrible things about these medieval stories is the horrible ingenuity of the way the women are tortured. There is the fiendish invention of St. Catherine's famous wheel, which was fitted out with razors which turned against one another so that whatever was between them would be sliced in two. This wheel shows what Christians would really like to do to women if they got the chance. However St. Catherine, popular and prestigious saint as she undoubtedly was for many centuries, did not have the monopoly of suffering. Other virgin martyrs suffered equally horrible and contrived torments. Thus St. Fausta had a thousand nails hammered into her head and St. Euphemia had her limbs torn off one by one by red-hot pincers. A very popular torture was one which mutilated the specifically female parts of the body. Many martyrs were hung up by their long hair or had their breasts torn off. The fact that the people inflicting these torments were wicked pagans simply set the Christian imagination free to invent still more deadly torments.

There is also a prurient motif to these stories. In the early accounts nobody is lusting after Blandina or Perpetua. In fact, when Perpetua and Felicitas were brought out naked before the crowd, Felicitas still bleeding from childbirth, the spectators were horrified and asked that the women have the dignity of clothing for their ordeal. In Thecla's virginity story, as one would expect, the prurient element is strong but is deflected by divine intervention. By the 13th century the virgin's martyrdom is depicted often as a sexual assault. The way the virgin martyrs are flung into brothels is clearly a popular male hostile fantasy. Sometimes the sufferings of the virgin martyrs read like a mass rape. Thus St. Martina refuses to sleep with the emperor and as a punishment endures tortures that read like a sexual assault:

> Thereupon the emperor had Martina stripped nude, and her lily-white body dazzled the spectators because of its singular

beauty. After the emperor who lusted after her had argued with
her for a long time and realised she would not comply, he ordered her body slashed all over and instead of blood, milk
poured from her wounds and she gave off a sweet scent. Raving
all the more at her, the emperor ordered her body to be drawn
and staked down and broken, but those who were martyring her
became exhausted because God prevented her from dying too
quickly. . . . They began to cry out, "Your Majesty, we can do
no more, for the angels are beating us with chains." And fresh
executioners arrived to torment her but they died on the spot,
and the confused emperor did not know what to do. He had her
stretched out and set on fire with burning oil. She continued to
praise God and a strong sweet odour issued from her mouth.
When the tyrants were exhausted from torturing her, they
threw her into a dark dungeon.

*(The Book of the City of Ladies,* III, 6, 1)

Needless to say, the next morning Martina is found in her dungeon
as fresh as a daisy, entertaining the angels. There is definitely a sexual undertone throughout in these 13th-century legends. The poor
benighted pagan emperor can't help his twisted fantasies, and this
enables the Christian to slaver over Martina's lily-white body. The
relays of executioners who hurl themselves upon this virginal body
and fall away exhausted or even dead are uneasily hinting at a woman's deadly and insatiable sexuality. The milk that flows from the
virginal body—a very frequent theme in these legends—reminds us
of the milk Perpetua drank in her dream, but here there are definite
touches of male fantasy about mother's milk. The sweet scent—another popular motif—that used to herald the presence of the martyr
when his Passion was read and announced the end of suffering and
pain, now only heralds a fresh round of torments for the unfortunate
woman. Above all, in each of these stories there is a deep fear of
women, which is closely bound up with the erotic. Men can try as
hard as they can to destroy them, but the women remain powerful
and indestructible, just as sexually they were insatiable and dangerous. Ultimately, the virgin-martyr triumphs over the bewildered
men, who are reduced to animals in their incoherent and savage
cruelty, which is shot through with desperation and fear.

The Church has always maintained that martyrdom is the most privileged of the Christian vocations, and the image of Christ offering himself on the Cross as a martyr of sacrificial love dominates the whole Christian ethos. However, the erotic element of martyrdom is really confined to the myth of the woman martyr. Stories of male martyrs like St. Lawrence, who jokes with his executioners while he is being roasted to death on his gridiron, telling them to turn the "joint" over and cook it on the other side, exalt the bravery and heroic endurance of the martyr. It is only women martyrs who become in Christian legend passive victims whose sufferings are somehow unpleasantly sexual. When Christians were not enduring persecution any longer, they would be encouraged to "die daily" to themselves, and the stories of the Christian saints are all too often accounts of masochistic violence and horrific and ingenious tortures. It is the women saints, however, who combine this masochism with a sick eroticism, showing how the idea of suffering and women's sexuality have become deeply linked in the Christian subconscious. We have seen already that contemplative nuns were encouraged to fantasize erotically about Jesus. When these fantasies of "love" were linked with penance, the notion of the Christian woman as a victim, suffering physical pain for the love of Jesus, becomes an important part of the ideal of female holiness.

Perhaps the most masochistic of all the women saints who made martyrs of themselves for the love of God is the 17th-century Peruvian girl, Rose of Lima, who was canonized in 1671. In Rose's life we see violence linked with sentimentality, a very common Catholic alliance. Rose's mortifications were so severe that even her confessor was nauseated by them and begged her to stop. Yet this brutal masochism was allied to a sentimentality which is almost as nauseating as her penances. Rose saw Jesus as her "true lover" who was always arranging delightful little surprises. He would murmur lovingly to her several times a day, "Rose of My Heart, My Rose, be thou My Spouse, My own." One day when she was walking in the garden she noticed that all the flowers had been picked. Then she heard Jesus explaining: "Rose, my Rose, thou art a flower. Give me all thy love, for know that it was I who gathered these flowers, for I will have no rival, no, not any creature even if it be a flower shall share with me thy heart." The sentimental lover proves to be a spouse of pathological jealousy. Yet this emotional self-indulgence is simply the prelude to a sick indulgence of self-hatred. The marriage chamber of Rose and Jesus was certainly no bed of roses. Her biographer tells us that at night she went to bed "not to sleep but to pray and macerate her innocent body with those disciplines and penances which seem to us so terrible that we can hardly understand, can scarce bear to hear of them." (See M. Summers, *The Physical Phenomena of Mysticism*, pp. 106–7.)

The spirituality of St. Veronica Giuliani, a 17th-century Franciscan nun, shows the alliance of sentimentality, pain and the erotic still more clearly. As a child she had read the life of St. Rose, who had just been canonized, and was fired with a similar zeal for suffering, whispering to herself: "If this Peruvian maiden did this why may I not do the same?" She began at once a regime of fasting and flagellation which she continued when she entered her convent. Holiness she saw at once in terms of mortification. One day she had a vision of Jesus, who murmured romantically to her: "What dost thou yearn for, Veronica?" She had of course only one answer to this: "To *suffer* all with Thee!" Christ instantly answered her prayer; her Guardian Angel crowned her with a Crown of Thorns like the one Jesus had worn during his passion. The excruciating pain of the thorns reduced Veronica to a state of orgasmic rapture. She wrote: "I felt an agony of pain not only in my head but an ache which thrilled throughout every limb, so that I was nigh to swooning." (Quoted by M. Summers, *The Physical Phenomena of Mysticism*, p. 151.) Since the very early days of the Church, virgins had been encouraged to imagine Christ as their lover in the privacy of their convent cells. Now women are using pain and suffering quite spontaneously to inflame that eroticism. When Veronica came to herself after her painful orgasm, Christ reverts to sentimental sweetness once again. In "accents of tenderest love" he told Veronica that this rapture was nothing to the delights she would experience later. Veronica cried aloud with hysterical joy: "Blessed be God! more pain! A heavier cross to come!" and staggered off to Church trembling and tearful in a state of post-coital bliss.

Five days later, Veronica developed the stigmata, the Five Wounds of Jesus, in her body. Jesus displayed his wounds to her in a vision and Veronica later wrote, "O God! O God! Such were the raptures of

Divine Love which consumed me that I can neither speak nor write of my burning desire!" As Veronica gazed at the wounds of Jesus, the heavenly court appeared behind Him. God the Father, she writes, then drew Veronica's soul to Him in mystic marriage and the Virgin Mary said to Jesus, "Let thy bride be crucified with thee." It is then that Veronica received the stigmata, and the phallic images of repeated and rhythmic penetration are an essential aspect of Veronica's experience of pain. Five rays came from the Five Wounds of Jesus, and the shafts of light formed four burning nails and a spear head of gleaming gold "which pierced my heart through and through and the four sharp nails of fire stabbed through and through my hands and feet. I felt a fearful agony of pain, but with the pain I clearly saw and was conscious that I was wholly transformed into God." Yet again Veronica was reduced to a trembling and weepy state of rapture:

> Thus my Lord and God espoused me and gave me in charge to his most holy mother for ever and ever, and bade my Guardian Angel watch over me, for He was jealous of my honour.
>
> When I came to myself I found that I was kneeling with my arms wide outspread, benumbed and sore cramped, and my heart, my hands and my feet burned and throbbed with great pain. I felt that my side was gashed open and welled and bubbled with blood. I tried to open my habit to see the wound, but I could not because of the wounds in both my hands. After a while, with much suffering, I succeeded in loosing my habit and then I saw that the wound in my side purled forth with water and blood. I wished to trace a few lines but I could not hold the quill in my hand for very agony. Whereupon I prayed to my Spouse, begging Him that my fingers might at least have power to guide the pen, since, being under obedience, I wished to write a screed for my confessor, and for him alone. And with the ink of my blood, I wrote upon a paper the name of Jesus. Then again I tried to lift the quill and I found I was unable to do so and to inscribe fair letters upon the virgin parchment.
>
> (Ibid., pp. 152–53)

The "espousals" took the form of pain and suffering. With a morbid delight in her agony Veronica recorded every pain, every flow of blood, every agony. There is the hideous touch of exhibitionism in her trying to write in her blood. Agony and Love are inseparable in Veronica's mind, just as they had been in her model's, St. Rose's.

Margaret Mary Alacoque perhaps did more than any other saint in the Catholic world to link the image of Divine Love with suffering and bleeding hearts. Her vision of the Sacred Heart of Jesus is now present in every church, convent and chapel, and is part of the imagery and psychological equipment of every Catholic woman. Margaret Mary had been enamored of penance and mortification since she was a child. Her brother Chrysostom wrote of the hair-raising mortifications she inflicted upon herself with full parental encouragement until she was eight years old. She drastically curtailed her sleep, fasted three days a week and wore a specially painful iron chain around her waist. This last caused such appalling ulceration on her side and legs that she became extremely ill. For the adolescent Margaret Mary, the "spiritual life" was synonymous with bodily mortification; as a young girl, she writes, "I did not know what spiritual life was; for I had never heard mention of it. I only knew what my Divine Master taught me and what He made me do with loving violence."

> I tied this wretched criminal body with cords full of knots, and I bound it so tight that I could hardly breathe or eat. I left these cords there so long that they buried themselves in the flesh, and I could not tear them from it except with great violence and cruel pain. I did the same with little chains which I fastened on my arms; I could remove them by taking away with them pieces of flesh. I lay during the night on a plank, or on knotty sticks which I placed in my bed, and afterwards I took the discipline.
> (Tickell, p. 29)

That Margaret Mary sees no paradox in the notion of a "loving violence" which expresses itself in self-punishment and self-mutilation is typical of the cult of suffering. Love takes the form of masochistic violence. Here the violence which Jesus "made" her do to herself is not yet especially erotic. Filled with pure self-hatred, Margaret Mary sees herself as a criminal, and the way she chooses to torture herself is in terms of painful bondage to a Divine Master.

However, once she got inside her convent she found, much to her chagrin, that the sensible rules of the Visitation Order did not allow her to continue these savage penances. Nevertheless, Love found a way. During the retreat she made before her Profession of Vows, Margaret Mary was taught by Jesus all the "mystery of his sacred Death and Passion," the upshot of which was:

> I will only say that it is this which has impressed me with so great a love of the Cross that I cannot live a moment without suffering, suffering in silence, without consolation or relief, without any one to compassionate me, sinking under the cross of every kind of insult, sorrow, humiliation and outrage, dying in fire with the Sovereign Lord of my soul. My whole life has passed in exercise of this kind. Divine Love has ever taken care to furnish me abundantly with this food, so delightful to His taste that He never says, "Enough!"
>
> (Ibid., pp. 80–81)

Jesus has an insatiable desire to see his bride both suffer and humiliate herself. It is again "Divine Love" which has engineered this "food" of suffering, so that his bride has now become positively addicted to it: "I could not live a moment without suffering," she repeats constantly; pain has to be the air she breathes.

The particular form of this Love was Jesus' revelation of His Sacred Heart, that bulbous and bleeding heart crowned with thorns which vulgarly encapsulates the Christian identification of suffering and love. So much is this the case that "a bleeding heart" has become in America the slang expression for compassionate sympathy. During the course of her long religious life, Margaret Mary developed an erotic fantasy relationship with Jesus, who shows himself full of the mawkish sentimentality that we have seen characterizing the "Spouse" of these saintly masochists. He asks her, significantly, to offer herself up as the "victim" of this love, suffering to appease the wrath of God and so redeem sinners. It was only a matter of time before her enthusiasm for suffering became an essential part of her erotic fantasies. Jesus conveyed his "love" to her in a vision of pain which is described in a manner almost overtly sexual.

> His heart opened and there issued from it so burning a flame that I thought I should have been consumed by it. I was wholly

penetrated by it, and could no longer bear it, so that I was obliged to ask Him to have pity on my weakness.

(Ibid., p. 141)

It was a pain that made her sick with a violent fever, an experience that recurred on as many as sixty different occasions during her life. This burning pain and fever nevertheless gave her such pleasure that she never complained of it. For Margaret Mary, pleasure and pain, consolation and agony were inseparable: "Never did I feel such consolation, *for* my whole body suffered extreme pain" (p. 143. My italics). She speaks of the experience as "relieving" her thirst for suffering in the same way as intercourse relieves a sexual hunger. Her erotic masochism inspires her to acts of appalling mutilation. On one memorable occasion she cut the Holy Name into her breast over her heart with a penknife, and later burned the scars into her flesh with a lighted taper. It was an emblematic identification of the "heart" of romantic, sentimental love with destructive suffering. Love and self-mutilation were for women like Margaret Mary, Rose and Veronica seen as identical. You expressed your love by injuring yourself. The pain itself became pleasure. When one day Margaret Mary "disobeyed" Jesus, who had told her to keep this self-inflicted wound as a secret, by showing it to the Infirmarian in the convent, Jesus punished her sadistically. He kept her "under His sacred feet for five days." Trampled on by her man, Margaret Mary is a Christian image of the Western woman who expresses her "love" by allowing men to degrade her.

It is possible that the woman in the pornographic movie who crawls about loaded with chains or is beaten and trodden underfoot by men is a tired secular relic of this Western tradition of Christendom which links female sexuality with pain and humiliation. The alliance of pain and punishment with women and sex is clearly in line with the sexual disgust that informed Christian emotion. Men have been taught in our culture to take pleasure in the sight of a woman suffering; suffering is seen as a female virtue and it is also, obscurely, seen as sexy. Alongside the legends and real lives of the women saints, purely secular myths of women suffering the onslaught of male hatred surfaced to reinforce this Christian neurosis. Thus the tale of Patient Griselda, told by Boccaccio, Petrarch and

Chaucer, is a classic study of a woman as victim. Walter, Griselda's husband, decides to test her virtue and obedience to his will: he takes away her children from her, implying that he is going to have them killed, and for some twelve years she sees nothing of them; he decides to send her back home to her father's house wearing only her underwear; he gets papal permission to repudiate Griselda and begins to make preparations for installing a new wife—Griselda being summoned from her father's hovel to supervise the wedding. Throughout all these years of suffering, Griselda's compliance and cheerful submission to Walter never fail. Suffering after suffering is laid upon her in Walter's elaborate charade, for he is completely convinced of her virtue and loyalty, and when at the end of the story Griselda is reunited to her children and reinstated as Walter's wife, there is in her rapture no censure of Walter's sadistic behavior. Shakespeare has also presented us with memorable women victims: the most obvious is Kate in *The Taming of the Shrew*, who has to be broken and her will crushed to make her a fit wife for Petruchio. To prove her love a woman has to suffer, often unjustly like Ophelia or Desdemona. The alliance of loving with victimhood is peculiar to Western society, and is a clear relic of Christianity.

That this suffering is often deeply sexual is clear in the writings of de Sade, one of whose heroines, Justine, actually has the name of a famous virgin martyr. Like the virgin martyrs, Justine is morally superior to her persecutors, but this is of no help to her—like the martyr, she suffers torment after torment and finally dies. The "Christian" trappings of de Sade's nightmare world, with its monasteries and convents and churches, are an essential ingredient of the story, not just a titillating backdrop. Without the background of Christianity, de Sade's madness would have been impossible. The way his sick fantasies have taken root in the Western imagination, so that he has given his name to a sexual perversion that sees sex in terms of suffering, is astonishing given the frightening nature of his vision. De Sade's picture of pain and humiliated women has clearly touched a nerve in Western consciousness, canalizing and naming a strong neurosis—it is not the private raving of a diseased brain. Similarly, novels like Samuel Richardson's *Clarissa* partake fully of the old Christian legends of the virgin martyrs. Clarissa is the ultimate victim—she is imprisoned, abused, isolated and finally raped. At one point, like the virgin martyr she is even put into a brothel by her male tormentor Lovelace. Like the virgin martyr she remains superior and the moral victor of the story, even though some two thousand pages are devoted to the depiction of her victimhood and death. It is most unlikely that the Protestant Richardson had ever read *The Golden Legend*, but his mastery of the old myth shows how deeply the idea of woman as the victim of male lust—and also men's terror of these indomitable victims—had penetrated the Western mentality.

The ideal of the woman as the victim continues to be found in the worlds of love and sex. Germaine Greer has noticed how novelists like Norman Mailer and Mickey Spillane show that the proper fate for a woman is death at the hands of her "lover." The woman is either killed or murdered, or she dies a metaphoric death of orgasmic frenzy and obliteration. Thus Mailer's hero in *An American Dream* (1966) strangles his wife. She asked for it—she got it:

> She smiled like a milkmaid and floated away and was gone. And in the midst of that Oriental splendor of landscape, I felt the lost touch of her finger on my shoulder, radiating some faint but ineradicable pulse of detestation into a new grace. I opened my eyes, I was weary with a most honorable fatigue, and my flesh seemed new. I had not felt so nice since I was twelve. It seemed inconceivable at this instant that anything in life could fail to please.
>
> (p. 36)

Germaine Greer notes that killing your woman is seen as a ritual of manhood, like killing a bear or a mythical monster. The world is purged of woman (and evil): "It is a man's world once more" *(The Female Eunuch,* pp. 226–27). Both man and woman find joy and transcendental peace in this killing. The religious tenor of the language is also noticeable: Mailer's hero feels his disgust turn into a "new grace"; killing his woman is a redemptive act, and he has recovered his lost innocence. It is certainly true that in our culture more men than is often supposed are turned on by whips and bondage. They have been taught to associate pleasure with female pain and humiliation, and it is also true that many women cooperate with this sadism and themselves find pleasure in being beaten and hurt. The snuff movie, where a girl is actually killed in front of the cameras, is an extreme example of this male sexual desire to hurt and degrade their women. It is a neurosis that men have inherited from Christianity.

Even if men and women remain untouched by Sadism in our society, they will not escape the myth of the Grand Romantic Passion. The word *passion* has a complicated history and is deeply ambiguous. It is surely interesting that we use the same word now to describe extreme sexual emotion that was once used to denote suffering even unto death. The Passions of Christ and of the martyrs did not refer to their great love affairs but to their physical agonies and their deaths as victims. From the beginning, of course, these "passion" stories were seen to be associated with love. Blandina was compared to a bride and a loving mother, and Perpetua was seen as the beloved "wife" of God. Later the medieval version of her "passion" would see St. Agnes' betrothal to Christ in a far more explicitly sexual way, and prurience crept into the "passions" of the virgin martyrs which found their consummation in death. It is true that our use of the word "passion" is not a straight inheritance from its older meaning of "suffering," as the witch words were directly transferred from the language of the Inquisition to the vocabulary of sexual attraction. Nevertheless, the complex of suffering, love and death that exists in our culture is neatly expressed by our adoption of the word *passion.* Women as well as their menfolk expect to suffer for love. The popular romance thrives on this vision of women as passive victims of male sexual "love." The shrinking woman is "crushed" to the breast of her macho lover; his "violent passion" terrifies her; her lips are "bruised" by his kisses. For women in these novels, sexual passion means the passive endurance of a fervid attack. It is a notion that is deeply written into the hearts of both men and women.

The most famous story of Romantic passion in the English-speaking world is perhaps *Wuthering Heights.* Emily Brontë was the daughter of a Protestant clergyman, and if her sister Charlotte's neurotic anti-Catholic prejudice is any indication of the atmosphere of the Brontë home, it would seem unlikely that Emily was influenced directly by the old Catholic myths of women as loving victims. Like Richardson, she had simply absorbed the old Christian neurosis in a purely secular way. The pain and suffering of women at the hands of men in the name of Love and Passion runs powerfully through the novel. Catherine constantly tells her lover, Heathcliff, that she is his victim: "You have killed me and thriven on it, I think. How strong you are!" During their last meeting, when Catherine is dying their love is seen as a brutal and savage violence:

> At that earnest appeal he turned to her, looking absolutely desperate. His eyes, wide and wet, at last flashed fiercely on her; his breast heaved convulsively. An instant they held asunder, and then how they met I hardly saw, but Catherine made a spring and he caught her, and they were locked in an embrace from which I thought my mistress would never be released alive: in fact, to my eyes, she seemed directly insensible. He flung himself into the nearest seat, and on my approaching hurriedly to ascertain if she had fainted, he gnashed at me and foamed like a mad dog, and gathered her to him with greedy jealousy. I did not feel as if I were in the company of a creature of my own species:
>
> (Chapter XV)

It is the same old pattern. In the grip of that uncontrollable sexual passion, which Christianity had taught the West was an irresistible force, men became savage beasts. It is a force which is destructive to both the man and the woman. The man here, seen through the eyes of two women, Emily Brontë's, and her narrator's, is seen as no longer fully human, but in the grip of a destructive passion, just as the Roman emperors of the Christian legends were reduced to helpless savagery before the passive but impenetrable virgin martyr. Where men like Norman Mailer see the murder of their women as a liberating "grace," women like Emily Brontë see women as the dying victims of male passion. Again, Heathcliff's wife, Isabella, becomes the slave of a romantic "delusion" which she sees as love and which morally destroys her. Healthcliff speaks scornfully of her willful blindness in:

> . . . picturing in me a hero of romance, and expecting unlimited indulgences from my chivalrous devotion. I can hardly regard her in the light of a rational creature, so obstinately has she persisted in forming a fabulous notion of my character and acting on the false impressions she cherished. But, at last, I think she begins to know me: I don't perceive the silly smiles and

grimaces that provoked me at first; and the senseless incapabil-
ity of discerning that I was in earnest when I gave her my
opinion of her infatuation and herself. It was a marvellous effort
of perspicacity to discover that I did not love her. I believed, at
one time, no lessons could teach her that! And yet it is poorly
learnt; for this morning she announced, as a piece of appalling
intelligence, that I had actually succeeded in making her hate
me! . . . She cannot accuse me of showing one bit of deceitful
softness. The first thing she saw me do, on coming out of the
Grange, was to hang up her little dog; and when she pleaded for
it, the first words I uttered were a wish that I had the hanging of
every being belonging to her, except one: possibly she took that
exception for herself. But no brutality disgusted her: I suppose
she has an innate admiration of it.

(Chapter XIV)

Love, hatred and brutality are mixed inexorably into a self-destructive complex. Isabella has become an abject and helpless dupe of her
man's hatred, thinking that what she feels for him is love.

With all the images of female pain that *Wuthering Heights* contains, it is surprising that women and men persist in seeing the novel
as the ultimate expression of a desirable Romantic Passion. In the
popular mind, Heathcliff is seen as an ideal sexual hero by both men
and women. Through suffering women achieve a new transcendence
and a new freedom. When Catherine has died and is laid out, the
narrator describes her as though she were a saint who had died a
holy death instead of the imperious, spoiled and often frankly unlik-
able young woman she really was:

Her brow smooth, her lids closed, her lips wearing the expression of a smile; no angel in heaven could be more beautiful than
she appeared. And I partook of the infinite calm in which she
lay: my mind was never in a holier frame than while I gazed on
that untroubled image of Divine rest. I instinctively echoed the
words she had uttered a few hours before: "Incomparably beyond and above us all! Whether still on earth or now in heaven,
her spirit is at home with God!"

(Chapter XVI)

Emily Brontë's usually hard-headed narrator, Nelly Dean, here allows herself the comfort of sentimentality—a comfort which is easily obtained but superficial because it is false. In Emily Brontë's world, love usually means an assault and a declaration of ceaseless war rather than a holy peace. The novel is full of images of the pain which men inflict on women. From the moment when the sterile and sentimental Lockwood dreams that he takes the wrist of Catherine's ghost and rubs it over the jagged glass of a broken window "till the blood ran down and soaked the bedclothes," we are in a world where women suffer at the hands of men. Often this suffering is given the name of love. It is significant that men and women who have perhaps never even read the novel continue to accept its reputation for being the ultimate English romance. Romances which are not classic masterpieces make a similar alliance of passion and pain.

It is often said that *Wuthering Heights* is uncharacteristic of the Victorian period. Yet it seems that it is quintessentially Victorian, and it was genius in Brontë to grasp the cruel truth that lay behind the pallid myth of decorous Victorian love. It is a commonplace that the Victorian age was an age of sentimentality. It is also a commonplace that men of the period speak of women particularly with sickly sentiment. Yet the thousands of Victorians who wept over the death of Little Nell in Dickens' *The Old Curiosity Shop* had followed avidly the month by month account of her suffering and martyrdom. Little Nell sacrifices herself that others may thrive; hers is a picaresque path of sacrificial love. The Victorians loved to see their women suffer. At night they loved to see their virginal child brides endure their brute sexual passion. They thoroughly enjoyed their easy tears over the spectacle of female pain. Victorian fiction is full of suffering women: Florence Dombey, Esther Summerson, Lady Dedlock, Amelia Sedley, Mrs. Gaskell's Ruth, Tess of the d'Urbervilles and Sue Bridehead. Victorian taste was informed by a sentimental sadism directed at women at the same time as women were exalted for their virtue.

For all our attempts at sexual liberation today, many women are still—even consciously—unable to separate pain from passion. Edna O'Brien sees pleasure and pain as inextricably entwined, and her novels have continued to perpetuate the old Christian myth. When

Miriam Gross questioned her recently about this she admitted the connection:

> It's not something I'm proud of, but it is something that has happened in my own life more than once, so it can't be accidental. I think it links with your earlier question about religion. Probably for me pain has a socket of pleasure in it, and pleasure likewise must carry a load of pain to be thrilling.
>
> ("The Pleasure and the Pain," *The Observer*,
> 14 April 1985)

This linking of passion and pain she sees as something directly connected with her Catholic upbringing. Her religion makes it impossible for her to view passion as leading toward anything but death and an often violent estrangement.

> Yes, I think my preoccupation with death, both the death in the life of relationships and actual death, is partly due to the loss of my original religious fervour. One seeks the kind of love that is as much spiritual as it is physical, and of course the twain do not meet, it's an impossibility. I see the end, so to speak, in the beginning. However, I think that there are other reasons for these feelings than religious . . . I have a rather marked degree of anxiety about relationships which I think was instilled in me as a very young child, because I grew up in a world in which relationships, and especially marital relationships, were violent and hurtful.
>
> On top of all that I have an incurable romantic disposition—I seem to be espoused to all those myths about tragic love and star-crossed passion. What first appealed to me in my fantasy— and, as we know, our fantasies are stronger than anything that will ever happen to us—was the idea of love as ultimately thwarted.
>
> (Ibid.)

The romantic and erotic relationship is a complex knot of violence, cruelty, estrangement and death. We have seen already that when in the West "love" takes the form of idealizing women this act of love is in fact an act of hostility and alienation. Similarly, when men and women in our culture view the romantic and passionate love relationship, they envisage it frequently in terms of warfare. To enter on a love affair can involve the deliberate quest of pain and death, because ultimately Christian love is shot through with Christian hatred.

However, it is not only in the spheres of passion and love that the Martyr myth has influenced and continues to influence Western women. Paradoxically, suffering was seen by women as an act of self-assertion and self-definition. This is paradoxical because the mortifications and masochistic tortures that women perpetrated on their bodies were inspired by self-hatred. It was to make the self die with Christ on the cross that these penances were undertaken. Yet however strong the self-hatred of a Margaret Mary, her penances can also be seen as a pathetic act of self-advertisement. Her lacerated breast, slashed with her knife, is an attempt to mark her out as somebody special: her vocation as the loving "victim" of Jesus is also asserting that she is not just an ordinary nun in her convent but has a unique and noble destiny. Throughout the history of Christian women we see them suffering. The transvestite saints, for example, were often only able to make themselves pass as men because their penances had ravaged their bodies and made them unrecognizable as women. Sometimes these mortifications took on an erotic dimension, but that was not always the case. Some women simply made saintly careers for themselves by their prodigious penances. A suffering and emaciated body was the badge of the holy woman. It made her stand out physically from other women, rescued her from anonymity and won her the respect and admiration of men. It was in an important way a hallmark of liberation, an essential part of female holiness. When Perpetua had been martyred, though, she had been fighting an external enemy. Very often the later woman ascetic was simply fighting herself, her struggles turned inward. Deprived of the means of expressing her religious devotion in the external world of affairs, her mortifications took on a different quality from that displayed by male ascetics, for whom suffering could be the mere background of a rich active life directed outside himself. Most women saints who embarked on their religious careers found that they had to make a career out of suffering in itself.

That a life of mortification was a means of self-expression can be shown very clearly in the life of the 14th-century freelance ascetic,

Angela of Foligno. In the account of her life in *The Book of Divine Consolation,* she gives us a clear picture of the way in which a woman could get started on a career in sanctity. Angela had been married with a family, so she was off to a bad start. Precisely *because* she was afflicted with a family, she tells us, she "did not feel much love for God." Marriage and true sanctity were clearly incompatible in her eyes. However, Angela had a break. "By the Grace of God," she says, her family all died one after the other, first her mother, then her husband, and "likewise in a very short space of time also died all my children." Angela was delighted: "And because I had commenced to follow the aforesaid way and had prayed to God that He would rid me of them, I had great consolation of their deaths, although," she adds rather as an afterthought, "I did feel some grief." Because God had answered her prayers and caused all her family to die, she was now free to pursue her vocation as an autonomous and holy woman (pp. 4–5).

Angela had learned very thoroughly the lesson Christendom taught her about the despicable nature of women. She was so consumed with self-hatred that she felt "possessed" by demons. Her self-hatred felt like a powerful force coming from outside herself and compelling her to acts of destructive violence aimed against herself. "Oftimes was my rage so great that I could scarce refrain from rending myself and beating myself most grievously, thus causing my head and all my limbs to swell" (p. 15). Like Catherine of Siena and Margaret Mary, Angela also had a vision of the suffering Jesus and was invited to "Put thy mouth into the wound in My side." After her vision, Angela instantly wished that she could die a martyr's death for Christ. Martyrdom was still the highest vocation. Yet beneath conventional expressions of humility in saying that she was not worthy of this honor, there is a definite self-assertion:

> I did desire that for His love all my members should suffer affliction and death more vile and more bitter than the Passion. Wherefore I bethought me and did seek to find one who would put me to death, in order that I might suffer for the sake of His faith and love. But I knew that I was not worthy to die as the holy martyrs had died. Nevertheless, I did desire that He would cause me to die, and by a death more vile and more slow and

more bitter, I could not bethink me of a death as vile as I did
wish for, or one that would differ from the deaths of the saints—
for I did surely deem myself unworthy of dying their death.

(pp. 8–9)

Here is the usual identification of pain and love: suffering is the only
possible response to the love of God. Angela doesn't just want the
honor of witnessing (the word "martyr" originally means "witness")
to the truth of Jesus as Perpetua had done, she wants a more horrible
death: "more vile and more slow and more bitter." Instead of seeing
this mortification as a way of getting rid of self, Angela sees it as a
way of asserting her individuality. She wants a death that is different
from the deaths of other saints. She wants to be more distinguished
in suffering than Jesus was himself. By her suffering she would define
herself and make herself special.

Angela gives us some kind of insight to the problems that many of
these women ascetics must have had. It is not natural to deprive
yourself of sleep, to starve yourself to anorexia and flagellate yourself
daily. There were bound to be times when, however devoted she was
to the cause, the trainee ascetic felt like giving up. There may have
come a time when such practices became second nature to her, but
until then there must have been many temptations to take an extra
few hours' sleep, or sneak the odd illicit meal. Angela clearly had
this difficulty. She was, she explains, studying hard "how that I
might obtain the fame of sanctity," and one of the ways of acquiring
this fame was by proclaiming loudly that you were living a life of
mortification. It was no good performing nameless acts of un-
remembered love. You had to be seen to be fasting and sleepless.
Before she had adapted to this way of life, there were times when
Angela used to "cheat," and she confessed her failure in a most
interesting way.

. . . in order that I might make known my dissembling and my
sins, it came into my mind to go throughout the cities and open
places with meat and fishes hanging about my neck, and to cry:
"This is that woman, full of evil and dissembling, slave of all
vices and iniquities who did good things that she might obtain
honour amongst men! And especially when I caused it to be told
unto those whom I had bidden to my house that I did eat nei-

ther fish nor meat, and when—being the while full of greediness, gluttony, and drunkenness—I did feign to desire naught save what was needful. I did diligently make an outward show of being poor, but I caused many sheets and coverings to be put there where I lay down to sleep, causing them to be taken up in the morning in order that none might see them."

(pp. 18–19)

Angela's way of atoning for her cheating was by blatant self-advertisement, which would have greatly aided her ambition of acquiring a reputation for sanctity. Walking through the towns and countryside of Italy, telling everybody that she had conned them into thinking her a saint, she proclaimed loud and long that because of "the hidden iniquity of mine heart I have deceived many." People would certainly notice her and remember her. After all, it isn't every day that you see a woman wandering around with stinking, rotting fish and meat slung round her neck. They would tell their friends about her. Even in the act of denying that she was a saint she was establishing a widespread reputation for sanctity. It was a shrewd career move. Angela used even her failures to escape anonymity. Despite her loud protestations of humility and unworthiness, she actually had quite a high opinion of herself. In one of her visions, Jesus told her that he loved her more than he loved anybody else in the Spoleto valley and that she understood him better than anybody ever had, even his own apostles when he was on earth (p. 161).

The life of mortification had special dangers for women because of the isolation of their lives: most women ascetics were either shut away from the male world in enclosed convents or lived retired lives with their families, as Catherine of Siena did. The freelance ascetics like Margaret of Cortona or Angela of Foligno, who influenced worldly affairs, were less common. The way women particularly identified themselves with suffering can be seen in the strange phenomenon of the stigmata. While it is perfectly true that many of the male saints lived very mortified lives and were probably as savage to their bodies as Margaret Mary or Angela, the overwhelming majority of stigmatics have been women. When in 1894 Dr. Imbert-Gourbeyre produced his scholarly but gullible book *La Stigmatisation,* he discovered 321 stigmatics since the time of St. Francis of

Assisi produced the first stigmata. Of these only 41 were men and 280 were women. Women were particularly drawn to "love" the suffering Christ. However, even the male saints who had particular devotion to the Passion of Jesus, like Ignatius Loyola, Philip Neri or the Curé of Ars, did not produce stigmata. They were all very busy men. When they had finished meditating on the sufferings of Jesus, they went about their work of attending to parishes, hearing vast numbers of confessions, founding religious orders and canvasing in Church politics. They hadn't got time to develop a morbid obsession. Also, they could direct their zeal and emotional identification with Christ creatively outside themselves. Women, on the other hand, living far more limited lives, did not have that outlet; their fervid desire to "suffer" had to be expressed inwardly. Just as the anorexic saint cut herself off from the world by rejecting all nourishment and in doing so damaged her body, so did the stigmatic externalize her emotions by producing painful and disfiguring wounds.

Even ardent champions of stigmatics, like Dr. Imbert-Goubeyre or Fr. Thurston S.J., do not deny that many stigmatics have had a history of emotional disturbance before they received the stigmata. Just as the anorexic has to have a certain type of personality, the stigmatic has to be deeply suggestible, as was the contemporary stigmatic, Cloretta Robertson, who had the stigmata until recently when she was "cured" by hypnosis. Cloretta developed the stigmata when she was only ten years old, after having read a very emotional book about the Passion. Her hands started to pour with blood while she was sitting in class, and her teacher reverently stored the blood in a vial (he still displays the dried blood) and then paraded her through the school, making her show her hands to all the other children. She plainly lived in an environment that encouraged this type of phenomenon. Cloretta continued to produce the stigmata for ten years, especially on Good Friday. She believes that the wounds were sent by God "to make people believe in him." However, Cloretta is unusual in that as a stigmatic she does not lead a full-time religious life, nor did she ever make the stigmata the focus of her life. Apart from involvement in the New Light Baptist Church, in Oakland, California, Cloretta lived a normal secular life and often found the stigmata an embarrassment. At first she had suffered no pain, but later she described the sensation as a "horrible" feeling. Cloretta had no desire to suffer. Often her hands started bleeding in difficult circumstances: once she went out on a date, and when the bleeding started she had to lock herself in the women's room, leaving her bewildered escort behind.

Usually stigmatics have lived intensely religious and very secluded lives. Most of them have been very simple people. In the 19th century there was an "outbreak" of stigmatics like Domenica Lazzari, who were peasants. The Tyrol produced quite a crop of wounded women, and that part of the world often goes in for particularly realistic, life-size crucifixes. The image of the grotesque sufferings of Christ were embedded in the religious imaginations of the people, making stigmatization a "natural" outlet for the religious emotions of many young girls.

Perhaps the most famous of the recent stigmatics was the Bavarian woman Theresa Neumann, who died at the age of sixty-four in 1962. Theresa had a background of neurotic illness before she developed the stigmata. As the result of a trauma when she was involved in a fire, she developed hysterical symptoms of blindness and paralysis. Previously she had been a loud, robust and rather insensitive girl whose ambition was to become a missionary nun, but the blindness and paralysis, which she suffered for years, caused her to withdraw entirely from the world. She was bedridden in her father's house in Konnersreuth. Her hysterical withdrawal made her unable to walk out into the real world or even to see it. She lived entirely in a room of her own inside her head. However, Theresa was cured by a vision of her namesake, St. Thérèse of Lisieux, also called the Little Flower, to whom Theresa had a special devotion. She heard the Little Flower say the words "Through your suffering more souls will be saved than through the most brilliant sermons." The words came from her patron's autobiography, *The Story of a Soul,* which was just beginning to enjoy a great vogue in the Church. The Little Flower went on to tell Theresa:

> The sufferings that appear to the eye [i.e., Theresa's blindness and paralysis] will diminish, but in its place more suffering will come. No physicians can aid you, and in the end the suffering will affect you both externally and internally, even your soul. . . . Your entire self-renunciation and willingness to suffer

pleases us . . . you will have to suffer much, but you need not
fear, not even the interior suffering. Only thus can you co-oper-
ate in the salvation of souls. But you must always die to yourself.

(Teodorowicz, pp. 145, 147)

Her suffering will lead Theresa to "die to herself," while at the
same time it makes her special. Certainly it brought Theresa fame
and notoriety, a fame that she would never have achieved as a missionary nun. Every Friday, Theresa would retreat into a visionary
state of ecstasy, and would watch the course of Christ's Passion from
the Agony in the garden in Gethsemane to the final crucifixion. She
would often, spectators claimed, speak aloud in Aramaic. All the
time, blood would pour from her hands, feet and side and also from
her eyes. She would suffer excruciating pain. Around her bed sat
more and more eminent priests, theologians and bishops, who were
glued to this very distressing spectacle. Theresa would give a running
commentary on her visions. One of the interesting things was that
while she was in this state, she apparently "forgot" the story of the
Passion of Christ. She kept thinking that she would be able to rescue
"the Savior," as she habitually called Christ. Week by week she was
always amazed and horrified when Christ was not rescued, did not
escape and was at last nailed to the cross. In her book on Theresa,
Hilda Graef has commented that Theresa's visions were, therefore,
deeply untheological: the sufferings of Christ that she "saw" every
week were not informed by any notion of their purpose: to save the
world. Theresa was not interested, if that is the right word, in the
reason *why* Christ was suffering the torments she witnessed. She had
visions of suffering for suffering's sake. Yet when she was conscious,
Theresa did see her own sufferings as being redemptive. Like Margaret Mary, she saw herself as a victim and would "offer up" her
sufferings for needy souls, as Catholic children are still taught to do.

There was nothing erotic in Theresa's experience of Christ's suffering. On the contrary, Theresa's visions and stigmata seem to have
been some kind of regression back to the world of childhood. While
she was in ecstasy, she would "forget" not only the major doctrines
of the Church, but also the meanings of quite common words like
"bishop" or "doctor." She very often spoke in a childish tone of

voice, and giggled like a coy toddler. One day when she was lying in bed, chatting to her confessor and three other priests, she fell into a trance and had a vision in which she saw episodes from the life of Mary Magdalene. Christian legend has it that the Magdalene ended her life as a hermit near Marseilles, and when Theresa saw her cave, she started speaking to Christ with the vocabulary and intonation of a five year old: "She begged Him to give her the 'little room' that was Mary Magdalene's. After all, she didn't need it any more. It would suit her exactly. To be sure one would have to get a stove, a table, a bed . . ." (Thurston, p. 113). Just as Theresa had retreated from the world into blindness and paralysis, her later stigmatization was also a means of retreat. It was a retreat from knowledge, from the burdens of adulthood and the rational world into a "little room" of her own. The motif of withdrawal, which has always characterized a good deal of female sanctity, is also evident in the stigmatic. Teodorowicz, who was Theresa's biographer, admirer and Archbishop of Lemberg, picks up this motif of withdrawal and retreat from the male world. "The stigmatisation destroyed her life's dream of being an active missionary nun. The joyous activity of a strong masculine will was forced into passive suffering" (p. 293). Stigmatics have usually been women because their active desires have been "forced" by the Church into passivity and lives of enclosure and retreat. However, I would differ from the Archbishop in one important respect. Theresa was not prevented from being a missionary by her stigmatization. With her history of hysterical illness, no religious order would have taken her. It is as though Theresa knew somehow that she lacked the emotional stamina that the life of a missionary required, and so chose illness and retirement from the world of activity. She incapacitated herself and made her life's dream impossible. It is interesting also that the Archbishop equates the active life with the masculine world. Joy is also the prerogative of the male world; by implication, suffering and passivity are the lot of women.

One of the extraordinary aspects of the phenomenon of the stigmata is its circus element. It may happen to women, but it affects droves of men. A very strange assortment of male celebrities found their way to the obscure village in Bavaria to see Domenica Lazzari, including the Earl of Shrewsbury, the Archbishop of Sydney, T. W. Allies, Dr. Wendell and Conan Doyle. To the annoyance of Theresa's family, Konnersreuth became an even bigger center of pilgrimage. Priests and clerics flocked to Theresa's bed and spent hours listening to her "childish prattle," watching her ecstasies, gazing lugubriously at the blood that poured from her every Friday. We have seen that the spectacle of suffering attracts men sexually in our society, driving some of them to "snuff" movies and violent sex shows. However, other men simply enjoy the sight of a woman in pain, even where there is absolutely no sexual element. The circle of men round Theresa's bed shows that many men will travel for miles to watch a woman retreat into a suffering world of her own. The descriptions of Theresa's admirers is portentous with reverence for female endurance to the point of absurdity. Thus Fr. Hermann Joseph, who had missed a passion ecstasy, made the most of his glimpse of Theresa when he was vesting for Mass:

> Suddenly the door was opened very forcibly from the outside. Involuntarily I turned my head. I beheld a countenance so full of pain and interior sorrow such as I have never seen before, not even in the dying. The eyes reminded me of a person parched with thirst using up his last bit of energy to reach a fountain of water, before he sinks down powerless. It was Theresa Neumann coming to receive Holy Communion.
>
> (Teodorowicz, p. 13)

This ludicrous, histrionic description shows the delight Fr. Joseph felt in the picture of female suffering. It is as suspect an enjoyment as that of the Archbishop who had relished Theresa's "childish prattle." The life of self-sacrifice which makes a career out of laying aside the self, lays aside also the duty of responsibility and the pain of being fully adult—a trap that sometimes catches the woman-martyr —saint or secular.

It is interesting that Theresa chose Thérèse of Lisieux as the patron who foretold her stigmata and gave her a mission of suffering. When the church canonized Thérèse in 1925, it was to stress that people did not need to seek extraordinary religious experiences to be holy. Thérèse died in 1897 aged twenty-four, having done nothing extraordinary in all her life except become a Carmelite nun at the very early age of fifteen. Her "Little Way" had become very popular with the publication of her autobiography. It consisted in making the most of the small things of life, as a means of reaching God. When she describes her religious life, the "sacrifices" she is talking about are on a very different scale from everything we have considered up to now:

> One evening after Compline I went to look for my cell lamp on the shelf where such things were kept, and it wasn't there; the Great Silence had started, so there was no chance of getting it back; obviously one of the other sisters had picked it up by mistake for her own. I needed it badly, but somehow I didn't find myself repining over the loss of it; I counted it as a privilege because, after all, I said to myself, poverty doesn't just mean going without luxuries, it means going without necessities. All was dark around me, but there was a fresh infusion of light from within. It was at this time that I developed a positive taste for ugly things and inconvenient things, so that I was really delighted when somebody took away the pretty little jug that used to stand in my cell and replaced it by a big one that was badly chipped. . . .
>
> I tried my best to do good on a small scale, having no opportunity to do it on a large scale; I would fold up mantles which the sisters had left lying about, and make myself useful in ways of that sort.
>
> *(The Autobiography of a Saint,* Chapter XXVI)

Clearly this is much more healthy than the masochism of a St. Rose of Lima. Like the Visitation nuns, the Carmelites at that time did not allow extravagant mortifications. Thérèse was far better employed tidying up mantles than carving herself up with a penknife. It is easy to sneer at her exaggeration of the trivial here. Anybody who has spent any time in an institution which stresses uniformity, like a convent, boarding school, prison or the army, knows how disproportionately upsetting this type of incident is. Your own possessions somehow distinguish you from everybody else, so that the loss of them can be obscurely threatening. However, it is sad that the service of God should have entailed a retreat into the trivial for women. In an important sense, Thérèse did resemble Theresa Neumann in her retreat back to childhood. In religion, her name was Sister Thérèse of the Child Jesus, and she used to be fond of calling herself

Jesus' little plaything. She was like a ball which the Child Jesus could play with when he felt like it and could then forget and leave lying around in some dark corner for days at a time. In other words, she was something totally unimportant and unnecessary, a mere distraction from the serious and important things of life. Thérèse was simply expressing in religious terms what was happening to women in the West. Having been excluded from the masculine world of joyous activity, women were becoming the mere toys of men, shorn of power, adulthood and a real place in the world. That many men continue to regard women as pretty but insignificant extras in their lives is a point too obvious to require elaboration.

The cult of St. Thérèse spread with an extraordinary rapidity throughout the Catholic world, so that she is now one of the most famous and beloved women saints. Little Thérèse, the Little Flower, and her Little Way tells a Catholic woman that she is little: she cannot hope, as Thérèse said herself, to do good in a "larger sphere." To cut a woman down to the size men imagine her to be can be as destructive as encouraging her to starve herself into anorexia. Both are urging her to be smaller than she should be. Catholic women are often warned not to be presumptuous enough to imitate Teresa of Avila, who is called the "Great" St. Teresa to distinguish her from the "Little" Flower. Even the redoubtable Mother Teresa of India, surely the embodiment of practical and active Christianity today, has taken the Little Flower as her patron, lest she appear to take "greatness" to herself. At the same time as the Catholic Church was cutting women down to size, the secular world also was encouraging women to stay in the secular shrine of the Home in a world of perpetual childhood. Later this overgrown and retarded child would become the "nice" girl, something that Teresa of Avila was certainly not.

Inevitably, the cult of suffering must mean some form of damage to the woman, either physical or psychological. To deny the self is something that is still expected of women. In the Victorian period, novelists wrestled with the problems this Christian inheritance had left to women. In *The Mill on the Floss* George Eliot makes Maggie Tulliver adopt a career of self-denial in a traditional Catholic way. She discovers Thomas à Kempis' classic *The Imitation of Christ* and sets about systematically destroying her ego, as the book suggests, finding in this self-abnegation a strange fulfillment and relief. When she encounters love and passion she gives them up in order to sacrifice herself to the happiness of her crippled fiancé and her cousin Lucy, who is engaged to Maggie's lover. Her career in self-sacrifice finds its consummation when she is drowned with her brother, who has for years made her life a misery and spurned her slavish devotion. The wild little girl that Maggie was once, who did not fit into traditional female roles and who rebelled against the restrictions of a girl's life, has been suitably quenched. Jane Eyre, another rebellious girl-heroine of the period, however, continues her rebellion in adult life. She too makes her sacrifice an act of self-assertion: when she gives up Rochester and refuses to compromise her standards, she cries, "I care for *myself!*" insisting upon her equality to her lover and her own self-respect and dignity. It is interesting that at the end of the battle that engages Jane and Rochester throughout the novel it is not she who is wounded and mutilated by love, but Rochester, who has been blinded and has lost a hand when he plunged into a burning house to rescue his mad wife. The equilibrium between the lovers is achieved at the cost of a maiming, but this time it is the woman who is the victor.

The nice girl is encouraged not to assert herself; women are taught to sacrifice themselves and are prepared for the vocation of wife and mother by being trained to suppress too clamorous an assertion of their identity. To have an individual life of one's own is regarded still by many women with as much distaste as a hundred years ago Mrs. Gaskell expressed in her letter to Tottie Fox. "If self is to be the end of exertions," she wrote in the good old Christian tradition, "these exertions are unholy, there is no doubt of *that*—and that is part of the danger of cultivating the individual life." The Christian ideal of self-abnegation has been put before men and women alike, but it is to women that it has been most rigorously applied in reality. Nobody would ever warn a man against the unholiness of self-definition and the pursuit of individuality. It is one of the main burdens of the feminist song, of course, that women have been trained not to cultivate the self but to suppress it. Women, however, define themselves in terms of this self-sacrifice—indeed the men in their lives often call them "martyrs," irritated by the burden of guilt that this constant self-sacrifice lays upon them. We watched our mothers tiptoeing around our fathers, keeping to the periphery of their lives. We heard how our mothers had sacrificed "everything" to bring us up, though what this "everything" consisted of was left vague. Germaine Greer pointed out in *The Female Eunuch* that women think this sacrifice is part of some unspoken bargain, which will insure them against their husbands' desertion or infidelity. When a woman cries, "How could you do this to me!" her outrage implies that her man has broken the agreement. She has sacrificed herself for him and the children and become a less interesting person, perhaps, in the process. Now her husband does not see her any more because she has made herself invisible. His part of the bargain was fidelity. Sacrifice is still seen as the real mission of women. Even today unmarried women are often told that their lives are "selfish," something that people would not necessarily say to a male bachelor whose life is often envied. Yet in reality, the life of the wife and mother is just as selfish as that of the single woman who is "cultivating the individual life." It is today very unlikely that anybody forced the wife to the altar against her will. She married not because it was her duty but because she wanted to. It was a selfish desire. If she stays married, she will find satisfaction in this life of self-abnegation and define herself through this.

We have seen that one of the wounds of a life of self-sacrifice is a psychological regression back to an infantile state. If the self is to be denied and made to disappear, the burdens and responsibilities of being a mature and self-aware adult disappear and the woman fails to grow up. It is often much easier to defer to someone else and say, "I'm quite easy—do whatever *you* want" than to state our desires honestly. It is often more difficult and more adult to discover what our desires actually are than to pretend that we haven't got any. The life of self-sacrifice which defines the way a woman functions in the male world can be not only infantile but damaging to other people. It can be a ferocious form of blackmail and a destructive assertion of the rights and claims of the ego, reasonable or not, at the very moment when such claims are being loudly denied and relinquished. In their individual lives far too frequently women are still encouraged and trained to be martyrs.

It remains true that women still tend to use their sufferings publicly as a means of self-assertion. The Suffragettes, for example, used precisely the old images of martyrdom and masochism that have been burned into our culture to gain the Vote. One woman actually threw herself under the King's race horse at the Derby, becoming a literal martyr. When Suffragettes chained themselves to railings, they were using the same imagery of bondage that had haunted the female Christian imagination for so long. When they submitted to forcible feeding they were again back in a very familiar role for women in the West:

> The sensation is most painful . . . I have to lie on the bed pinned down by wardresses, one doctor stands on a chair, holding the funnel end above the level and then the other doctor, who is behind, forces the other end up the nostrils.
>
> (Mary Leigh's description to her lawyer, 1909)

Yet again a woman is the victim at the hands of the male world, passively submitting to an ordeal that has all the overtones of a rape. At a time when women were campaigning for an active place in the male world, the images they often used to press their claim and raise the consciousness of the nation was of woman as the passive victim, in bondage, the sex object of male sadism. There is a passivity that was not present in Perpetua's struggle. Victorian feminists had idealized this very passivity of women, in terms that are again extremely familiar. In 1840 the French feminist Flora Tristan recorded her impressions of the sufferings of prostitutes in *Promenades dans Londres,* and concluded that the prostitute was a true victim and martyr:

> . . . surrendering herself! annihilating both her will and her bodily feelings; sacrificing her body to brutality and suffering and her soul to contempt! The prostitute is for me an impenetrable mystery. —I can see in prostitution a horrible folly, or else it is so exceedingly sublime that my human self cannot comprehend it. Risking death is nothing—but what a death awaits the prostitute! She is engaged to suffering, vowed to abjection! Physical tortures increasingly repeated, a moral death each instant! *And self-contempt as well!!!*

The description could almost be applied word for word to the Christian martyr or to the ascetic saint: the prostitute has transcended the human condition becoming an impenetrable "mystery" which human reason cannot understand. The language is overtly religious; it

reproduces that of popular works of devotion—self-surrender, anni-
hilation of the will, sacrifice, sublimity. Just as the men of the period
were evolving a myth that banished all prostitutes into a state of ruin
and despair that meant either death or transportation, so feminists
were creating another myth that bore no relation to reality, but
which consoled by appeals to language that was traditionally felt to
transfigure reality with a new and sublime meaning. Some of the
painters of the period also caught something of this inflation of the
Fallen Woman into the highest and most powerful reality. Thus Ford
Madox Brown's picture *Take Your Son, Sir,* shows the fallen woman
with the illegitimate baby in her arms as another Madonna. Her
form, clad in virginal white, fills the painting, and her pathetic se-
ducer appears only huddled before her majesty as a shadowy reflection in the mirror, which frames the woman's head with a halo.

Even in today's far more aggressive climate women still appeal to
their sufferings when they claim total equality with men. Marilyn
French's novel *The Bleeding Heart* completely identifies woman with
suffering, just as Archbishop Teodorowicz had done when writing
about Theresa Neumann. Her heroine's name, Dolores, would make
the point sufficiently, even if she were not writing a thesis about
women and pain. Her lover's name, Victor, reinforces the traditional
view of a war between the sexes. Their affair takes place in an ambience of pain, as they both, Dolores especially, howl and weep over
the sufferings that men inflict upon women. It is certainly true injustice has to be recognized before the relations between the sexes can
improve, but by reinforcing the old martyr myth there is a danger
that women will merely reproduce old sterile and unhealthy patterns.
Men are used to the spectacle of women's suffering. For centuries in
the Christian West they have found it sexually titillating, spiritually
exalting or emotionally reassuring. In their turn, women have mutilated and destroyed themselves psychologically by eagerly embracing
the role of victim. This unhealthy war of sadomasochism must cease.
The point about martyrdom is that it is voluntary. At some point the
martyr must choose her own death, or she is not a martyr. Perhaps
we should cease to define ourselves to ourselves and call attention to
our rights by appealing to the male world in terms of our suffering.
Flora Tristan had exalted the spectacle of the female victim, but
twenty years later, in 1860, another French feminist, Maria

Devaisnes, declined the role of victim and martyr and firmly removed herself from the arena of suffering. Perhaps she had something important to say:

> Of all women's enemies, I tell you that the worst are those who insist that woman is an angel. To say that woman is an angel is to impose on her, in a sentimental and admiring fashion, all duties, and to reserve for oneself all rights; it is to imply that her speciality is self-effacement, resignation and sacrifice; it is to suggest to her that woman's greatest glory, her greatest happiness is to immolate herself for those she loves; it is to let her understand that she will be generously furnished with every opportunity for exercising her aptitudes. It is to say she will respond to absolutism by submission, to brutality by meekness, to indifference by tenderness, to inconstancy by fidelity, to egotism by devotion.
>
> In the face of this long enumeration, I decline the honour of being an angel. No one has the right to force me to be both dupe and victim. Self-sacrifice is not a habit, a custom; it is an *extra!* No power has the right to impose it on me. Of all acts sacrifice is the freest, and it is precisely because it is so free that it is so admirable.
>
> (Quoted by E. A. Hellerstein, *Victorian Women,* p. 140)

The heroine of Margaret Atwood's controversial novel *Surfacing* puts the same point rather more succinctly but with a slightly different emphasis. At the end, having achieved her liberation, the heroine decides:

> This above all, to refuse to be a victim. Unless I can do that I can do nothing. I have to recant, give up the old belief that I am powerless and because of it nothing I can do will ever hurt anyone. A lie which was always more disastrous than the truth would have been.
>
> (p. 191)

To perpetuate the myth of the victim and martyr is to abdicate responsibility. It is a denial of truth because it tells women that they are helpless and have no control over their fate. This denial of responsibility makes women less than human. Like Perpetua, the Christian martyr, Atwood's heroine achieved her liberation by the third solution that women have found in the West: mysticism.

# 6

# WHY BE A MYSTIC?

It will by now be clear that both the martyr and the virgin very often shared certain mystical experiences. The virgin claimed to have had visions and revelations; the stigmatic's agony is usually accompanied by a visionary or an ecstatic trance, and the early martyrs claimed not to feel their pain because they were so absorbed in the Spirit. All religions have had their mystics, but in most religious traditions mysticism has been a predominantly male activity. In the Christian West, however, it is not only the case that many of the most distinguished mystics have been women, but that in the popular mind mysticism is seen as a female activity. The voices of Joan of Arc and Bernadette Soubirous' visions of the Virgin Mary at Lourdes are far more famous than the equally illustrious visions of some of the male saints. Francis of Assisi was a mystic and a stigmatic, but he is more famous for his preaching to birds and animals and for founding the Franciscan Order than for his visions. Similarly, we remember Ignatius Loyola far more as the founder of the Jesuits than as the solitary mystic in the cave at Manresa. The figure of Teresa of Avila is more well known in the popular mind than her beloved colleague, St. John of the Cross, and few people today have even heard of her great teacher St. Peter of Alcantara, who was a mystical legend in his own lifetime. The woman visionary or ecstatic resurfaced again in the Protestant world, far more clearly than the virgin or the martyr who had to find submerged means of survival. The female Protestant visionary was not suspected of Popery because Protestantism valued individual religious experience very highly. Through her mystical experiences and ecstasies a woman was sometimes able to break into the male world and escape the limitations of ordinary female existence. She could challenge the male world because she could claim to be directly inspired by God. This mystical process could be very dangerous; it could not only bring her obloquy and persecution, but also lead the woman into certain psychological dangers. Nevertheless, the female mystic shows us one of the most positive ways in which a woman could develop and achieve liberation in the hostile male world and may still have something to teach women today, even if women will not necessarily have visions of the Virgin Mary or the Sacred Heart.

In all religions mystics are the "stars." They are achieving what every ordinary religionist thinks he should be doing. The Moslems say that ultimately every good Moslem has to be a Sufi because the Sufis (the mystics of Islam) achieve on earth that absorption in God which every Moslem will experience in the next world. In all religions the phenomena of mysticism seem to be much the same. Mystics fall into trances, they feel that they have achieved a state where the "soul" leaves the body and is absorbed in a greater reality which some mystics have called God. This state they call ecstasy. While in ecstasy the mystic is totally impervious to his surroundings and to pain. Hindu gurus can walk on sharp spikes and cast their hands into fire without being burned. They can be buried in the earth and survive, remaining quite unconscious of the experience because they are locked into a higher state of consciousness. Sufi dervishes whirl themselves into ecstasy; Christian mystics, like the martyrs, have claimed to be as impervious to pain as the Hindus. In all religions people claim to have been possessed by the gods or by demons; they speak in strange tongues, feel "inspired" to prophesy the future or to give special messages to the community. It seems that whatever the intellectual beliefs and differences of the various religions, the nature of the mystical experience itself remains the same. Thus a Buddhist who denies belief in a personal God describes his absorption in Nirvana in very much the same way as a Christian or a Sufi speaks of union with God. By a disciplined process of meditation, mystics of all religions strive to get above the selfish ego and achieve a "higher" state of being and a sense of bliss and peace. Often when the mystic descends into the depths of his mind by practicing certain meditative techniques, he feels as though he encounters a "presence" there which is different from him-"self," and this occurs whether he is a Christian who claims that this presence is God or Jesus, or an atheistic Buddhist. Recently psychologists have done a good deal of research into mysticism, and many of them now claim that the mystical experiences are not supernatural, but quite normal human activities for which some people have a special talent. The mystic has the ability to do certain things with his mind which is akin to the ability other people have to write poetry or compose music. Not everybody has this mystical ability, just as not everybody has the "gift" of writing poetry. It also seems at present that it is the scientists, who have for the last century been seen as the main enemies of religion, who believe more strongly in mysticism than the average religious person, who may feel that it is unhealthy rubbish. The scientist will interpret the experiences of Teresa of Avila or John of the Cross in a way that is very different from the way the saints themselves would have done, but he will take their experiences seriously and deny that they are delusions or fantasies.

Perhaps one of the reasons why mysticism is so often associated with women in our culture is because our society has valued the rational and the intellectual activities of the brain more highly than the more receptive states of mind, which are characterized by quite different brain rhythms and which can produce a mystical experience on the one hand and a poem or a completely original idea like Archimedes' principle on the other. The male world has traditionally been seen as rational, while the woman's is patronizingly seen as the world of the intuition and the heart. Both men and women have suffered from this sharp division of activities and experience. Men often remained emotionally retarded because their feelings were not cultivated as much as their brains. Women, on the other hand, denied for centuries the benefits of education, remained intellectually undeveloped, unable to express themselves rationally or judge their experience critically. They have been in danger of remaining intellectual cripples, subject to uncontrolled and inchoate bursts of feeling or to fey, vaguely "spiritual" and irrational experiences. Teresa of Avila constantly complains in her writings that women are not "learned." They are therefore, she says, subject to delusions and are prey to all sorts of idiotic notions because they have no means of assessing or analyzing them. The mastery of the techniques of meditation demands considerable mental power; all cultures would agree that mindless stupidity is not the order of the mystical day. Thus a Margaret Mary clearly lacked the intellectual discipline and strength that mysticism required, and became prey to neurosis and idiocy. Lack of education made the mystical path extremely perilous for women.

While it is true that we tend to be skeptical about mysticism today, there seems at the same time to be a rush toward ecstatic experience in one form or another. In the Christian Churches charismatic movements have mushroomed in nearly all denominations. People who reject Christianity are turning more and more to the Eastern mystical religions, especially Buddhism, which is enjoying a great flowering at present in the West. People experiment with drugs which can induce states that are apparently mystical, though somebody on a "trip" lacks the control over his experience that the talented mystic achieves. Other people seek a false euphoria and immunity from stress in tranquilizers. Rock concerts propel the young into a state of tranced frenzy. It seems that we seek the bliss and invulnerability of the mystical states as much as ever we did in a more religious world. However, mysticism is not for everybody. The Zen practitioners have always said that a neurotic person coming to meditation to be cured will only become sicker. Meditation centers should carry a government warning in their prospectuses: meditation can seriously damage your health. To confront the subconscious demands considerable mental and emotional robustness, and not all mystics are able to cope with what they discover in themselves. LSD, for example, can produce a nightmarish "bad trip." Rock concerts can produce mass violence and a temporary madness.

Ecstasy and trance were present in Christianity from its very beginning. On the feast of Pentecost the Apostles of Jesus spoke in tongues and felt "possessed" by the Spirit. Paul shows how common the trance of ecstasy and prophecy was in the early Church in his epistles. The Greco-Roman religious world at that time was ecstatic and sought out strange and exotic states of consciousness, and Christianity was no exception. However, because ecstasy was so "normal," it meant that there was nothing very exceptional about it. In *The Making of Late Antiquity,* Peter Brown has shown that contact with the Divine in the 2nd-century Church was not seen as something special or dramatic. You encountered God in the heart of your own personality, just as Perpetua received "Divine" messages, as she thought, peacefully and naturally in her dreams. By the 4th century this had all changed: the way to God had become fraught with difficulty and struggle, possibly because of the growing horror of and struggle against sexuality and the increasing Christian guilt. Augustine's *Confessions,* with their gloomy regrets, dramas, tears and guilt, show that we are in a very different world from the world of Perpetua's diary. In the 2nd century the state of trance or the religious experience did not set the mystic apart from his fellow Christians. These experiences were for the whole community—St. Paul is very strict on this point—not for the individual's private satisfaction and fulfilment. Perpetua experiences her dreams not just for her own consolation but for the consolation of her companions, who approach her and ask her for a Divine message. However, as religious experience became more dramatic and was seen as a supernatural battle with the self and the Devil, it inevitably became more self-involved, with the mystic seeking out a solitude that set him apart in the Church. Women, we have seen, were urged to retire from the world into their own heads, if they wanted to lead the virginal and autonomous life. This meant that the challenge that the female visionary could pose to men was neutralized: she never saw any men to challenge.

In all cultures the aim of mysticism is loss of the self. It offers a means of achieving liberation from the demanding and self-destructive ego. Some Christian women mystics, alas, proved that they were not capable of this. They got stuck and more deeply embedded in their neurotic egos than ever. For many of these women mystics, ecstasy was simply another means of retreating from the world. It was flight instead of quest. Instead of achieving ecstasy slowly as part of a controlled process of meditation, ecstasy fell on the visionary unawares, out of the blue with often ludicrous results. Thus Cardinal Jacques de Vitry, writing in the 13th century, describes a phenomenon in Liège in a way which makes the religious lives of the Béguines seem like a game of musical statues; the women "froze" in ecstasy whenever the Spirit moved them, and retreated into a hysterical paralysis. They would, the Cardinal admiringly recalls, fall into a trance for "practically the whole day," so deeply that "they could not be aroused by any noise, no, however loud or clanging it might be, nor could they be hurt by any buffet or knock upon their bodies. Even pricking them sharply again and again had no effect whatsoever." Ecstasy, which is only a flight from the world, is not true mysticism. The great mystical traditions are all adamant that after his enlightenment the mystic must return to the world. As the Buddhists say, he must "return to marketplace" in compassion and love. The aim of the Béguines' kind of mysticism was simply to retreat and achieve not compassion but an unnatural invulnerability. The Cardinal continues:

> I myself have seen a religious who frequently fell into Ecstasy, yea, very often, as many as five-and-twenty times in the space of one short day. I have seen her in Rapture and that for a long while together. Whenever the Rapture fell upon her she remained stationary, motionless and immobile, until she returned to herself. Yet, however unusual a position she was in, however ill-balanced and precarious for the moment, she never tottered nor fell, but was supported most wonderfully by her Guardian Angel. Sometimes if the Rapture overwhelmed her as she was stretching out her hand far, it would remain steadily in that awkward and difficult gesture. And when she came to herself the limb was not stiff and benumbed, but lithe and lissom, nor was she in the least weary, rather she was active and nimble, and her heart full of a great joy.

(Prologue to the *Life of St. Mary of Oignes*)

The circus element that we noticed in the phenomenon of stigmatism is just as evident in the lives of the women ecstatics. Wherever a mystic falls into ecstasy, there male observers like the Cardinal are to be found, taking notes, sticking pins into the ecstatic woman, hitting her to observe her lack of response and marveling at her complete absence from the world.

This quest for immunity from pain continues in purely secular ways. Women swallow tranquilizers to escape from the unhappiness of life. The numbers of women addicted to drugs like Valium is a worrying indication of our spiritual barrenness as a society where people have no internal resources against pain. Other people get frozen into a state of depression, which does not express itself emotionally, but which becomes an inability to feel. The heroine of Doris Lessing's novel *The Golden Notebook* is told by her analyst that most women turn to psychiatry because they can no longer feel. Margaret Atwood's heroine in *Surfacing* discovers, before her mystical illumination, that she can no longer feel.

> I realised I didn't feel much of anything. I hadn't for a long time. Perhaps I'd been like that all my life, just as some babies are born deaf or without a sense of touch; but if that was true I wouldn't have noticed the absence. At some point my neck must have closed over, pond freezing or a wound, shutting me into my head; since then everything had been glancing off me, it was like being in a vase or the village where I could see them but not hear them because I couldn't understand what was being said.
>
> (pp. 105–6)

This joyless "ecstasy," where the woman is raptured or snatched away from feeling and can experience neither joy nor pain, is all too common and has become symptomatic of a society which has lost touch with the inner self and has imprisoned people in sterile and over-rational systems, ignoring the emotional dimension.

The woman described by de Vitry, who was blacking out twenty-five times a day, was spending nearly all her life in an unconscious state. This is clearly a very sick phenomenon, but when we read the lives of the women mystics of Christianity we find that it is extremely common. Catherine of Siena's ecstasies or raptures used to descend upon her with such suddenness that on one occasion when she was preparing a meal she fell into the oven. Needless to say, her trance rendered her immune so that she was not burned. When she went to Communion in the Cathedral she always fell into ecstasy as soon as she received the Host and would stay, rapt and oblivious, for hours after Mass. Eventually when it was time for the Sacristan to lock up he found that he could not do so, because Catherine was still there, immobile and unconscious. After waiting about impatiently for a while he would have to pick her up, cart her outside the Cathedral and dump her in the gutter. There she stayed, kicked at by scornful passers-by, until she came to herself and returned home, muddy and disheveled. This is clearly not healthy behavior, but by now it should be clear that it is part of the essential path of female sanctity. The virgin retreated from the world into a safe and invulnerable cocoon. She had been urged to separate herself from the world, so she obliged and often did so in a way that protected her from the world's hostility. The men who are so fascinated by this phenomenon are, at a deep level, also pleased to see that the woman has withdrawn from them so radically. The mystics described by de Vitry and Catherine of Siena have not left the self behind. They have simply escaped from the world and have become frozen in a neurotic autonomy which refuses to be open to the realities about them. They have become more deeply imprisoned in themselves than ever.

Another story of St. Catherine of Siena shows the plight of a woman who wanted to take up a career in mysticism, but who received no help at all about the basics of the spiritual way and was encouraged in unhealthy neurosis by her confessor. Catherine had been talking to her friend Father Bartholomew in the Cathedral one day, describing one of her visions. The story is told by her contemporary, Raymund of Capua, who had the story from Father Bartholomew himself:

> It chanced that her own brother, Bartolo, who was in the church, passed by, and his shadow, or the noise he made in passing attracted Catherine's attention so that for a moment she glanced aside to look at him. Instantly recovering herself, she broke off her words and began to weep in silence. Fr. Bartholomew waited for a time till she should speak again, but finding that she remained silent, he bade her continue. "Ah! wretch that

I am!" she said, "who will punish me for my fault?" "What fault?" he asked. "How!" she replied, "did you not see, that even while our Lord was showing me his great mysteries, I turned my eyes to behold a creature?" "Nevertheless," said the confessor, "I assure you the glance of your eye, of which you speak, endured so short a time I did not perceive it." "Ah, father," she said, "if you knew how sharply our Blessed Lady rebuked me for my fault, you would surely weep and lament with me." And so saying she would speak no more of her revelations that day, but she retired to her chamber sorrowing and doing penance for her sin; and she declared afterwards that St. Paul had also appeared to her, and reproved her so roughly for that little loss of time, that she would rather suffer all the shame in the world than abide such another rebuke at the apostle's hand. "And think," she added, "what a confusion and shame that will be which all wicked and unhappy sinners shall suffer at the last day, when they shall stand before the majesty of God, seeing the presence of only one apostle is so dreadful and intolerable."

(Drane, pp. 101–2)

This is sheer lunacy. Instead of freeing the mystic from the destructive self, this kind of mysticism is simply embedding her in her own neurosis. Buddhists call guilt an "unskillful" state because it can only hinder Enlightenment, and this story shows us why. Guilt makes the self far too important. One involuntary glance requires a series of celestial delegations to stress its magnitude. St. Paul has to appear to Catherine again, after she has wept for three hours, to cheer her up. Guilt, we have seen, is part of Catherine's neurosis, and also part of the makeup of Western women, and this story may give us another clue about why women encourage guilt in themselves, even when, as here, it is entirely misplaced and inappropriate. Guilt makes a woman feel she is important and that her actions count and have a significance which in reality—where women are so often thrust on to the sidelines of life—they simply do not have. We need our guilt perhaps, because without it we might accept the estimate of many of the men in our lives—that nothing we do really matters. Another important component of this story is Father Bartholomew.

He is supposed to be Catherine's spiritual director, guiding her steps along the spiritual path. In fact, he is totally ineffectual. He is probably very ignorant about mysticism—which was, after all, quite an esoteric study—and clearly does not see that this indulgence of guilt is absolutely contrary to true mysticism. He offers a few half-hearted words of consolation, which Catherine sweeps impatiently aside. Often, when reading her life story or the story of many of the other women saints we see that their spiritual directors are no match for them in neurosis, but, also, they are no match for the women in intelligence. Catherine is often seen wrapping her male "directors" round her little finger because she is too clever for them. Constantly in the lives of the women mystics we see the poor saints receiving very bad advice and encouraged in practices which would make any true mystical adviser—like John of the Cross or Peter of Alcantara—extremely angry. Left to their own devices and neuroses with no education to qualify their limited insights, and guided by inadequate men, women mystics were very likely to get stuck in a way of life which was both destructive and unhealthy.

The life of Mary Magdalene de Pazzi, a 16th-century Carmelite nun who was canonized in 1669, is a very clear example of the dangers of plunging into pseudo-mysticism. Mary was certainly an intelligent woman with a good deal of determination and spunk, but she was also, alas, very neurotic. Her story shows her ignoring the advice of her Reverend Mother and the half-hearted remonstrations of her confessor, Fr. Puccini, and becoming quite deranged by encouraging strange, "mystical" states of mind. Like Catherine, she is full of guilt and makes her Prioress beat her in front of the other sisters. She ties herself blindfolded to the altar rail and lies prostrate so that the other nuns can walk over her—behavior which was surely damaging not only to her but to the other sisters whom she forced to participate in this.

One can only feel deeply sorry for Mary Magdalene's community. When the poor nuns were singing the Office in Choir, Mary often used to climb up into the Rood loft, unscrew the figure from the Crucifix, "with incredible agility," as Fr. Puccini admiringly records. Then she used to sit, rocking this life-sized statue of Christ in her lap. Taking off her veil, she would attempt to dry the blood and sweat painted on it. To say the least, this wild behavior would have been most distracting. Her mystical "prayer" induced a hyperactivity which used to make her rush frenetically round the convent, shouting, "O Love, O Love!" at the top of her voice, seizing her sisters by the hand and asking them if they had seen Jesus recently and whether they really loved him. Then she used to rush up into the belfry, clang all the bells and shout "with a loud voyce; *O you Soules, come love, come love this love by whome you are so much beloved*" (Puccini, p. 54).

This hysterical self-advertisement is characterized by the cry she used to make when she was rapt in ecstasy and, for once, rooted to the spot. She used to cry to God, significantly, *"Adsum, adsum, adsum!"* Here I am! This "mystical" behavior is constantly crying out "Look at me!" It is the frantic exhibitionism of a woman who has never found her true place in the world. It must have been a perfect nightmare to have had her in the community; she was clearly not suited to the communal life, where it is a matter of principle for the religious not to make themselves "singular." Everybody eats the same food, wears the same clothes, does the same thing at the same time and makes a point of not asking for any exemptions from the Rule. This uniformity is to help the religious to lose herself and to pay as little attention to the greedy ego as possible. Mary Magdalene's visions, on the other hand, were all designed to do precisely the opposite. Jesus told her to wear special clothes, to go barefoot, to follow a special diet and to obey twenty special rules which were for her alone, because she was his favorite. When her Superiors objected, Mary used to vomit publicly in the refectory, and she became paralyzed so that her long-suffering sisters (while they may have had a rest from her frantic rushing about the convent) found that they now had to carry her up to Communion. On each occasion the Superior had to give in. Nobody knew enough to restrain her, and so she was allowed to drive herself virtually insane. We have all met women like Mary Magdalene de Pazzi. Usually not enough thought has been given to their education, or they find that while there is plenty of scope in the world for men, there are still not enough paths for women. Bored wives embarrassing their husbands because they feel trivial and exhibitionist daughters of famous men whose antics we read about in the gossip columns every week can be seen as secular equivalents to Mary, who wanted a career and notoriety but was

quite unsuited to the only career open to her. The desperate behavior
of the exhibitionist is apparently "liberating" because she is doing
what she wants and is, certainly, unique in her "freedom" from con-
vention. In fact, however, there is no liberation, simply a deeper
imprisonment in one's old problems. The mystical journey is traditionally supposed to help the mystic to find himself by losing himself.
It can bring about healing and liberation, but when it is misdirected,
as in Mary's case, indulgence of strange, twilight states of mind dangerously encourage basic personality disorders.

However, though many women were encouraged on dangerous
mystical paths and were damaged by it, not all women were as unfortunate as Mary Magdalene de Pazzi. Many women used their mystical talent to break into the male world and win an authority and
respect that would otherwise have been impossible for them. Thus
Perpetua's dreams gave her an authority over her male companions,
who looked to her for leadership. From the very earliest days of the
Church, direct religious and mystical experience gave women an
equality with men. In the *Acts of the Apostles* the four daughters of
St. Philip who were prophetesses are mentioned as well-known and
important personages. The prophet claimed to receive a message for
the community directly from God, and we have seen that St. Paul's
nervous and defensive censures about the women prophets in Corinth who were not wearing their veils suggest that they challenged
the traditional sex roles of superior men and dependent, subservient
women. The prophetess not only showed the early Church that
women were equal to men, because they received inspiration and
divine gifts just as men did; it showed also that women were autonomous. If Jesus had direct contact with a woman, it showed that she
was quite independent of male religious ministry. If women didn't
need men in the religious world, then they could have started to
express this independence in other new and alarming ways.

Throughout Christian history certain women not only claimed autonomy and equality to men, but some of them actually assumed
Christian leadership. Thus the 3rd-century Montanist prophetesses,
Appolonia and Priscilla, who both claimed to be female manifestations of the Divine, were both ecstatics, claiming a Divine revelation
as the source of their authority and power in the movement. In the
late 18th century Mother Ann Lee claimed leadership of the Shakers

on the strength of her visions, and so did the leader of the Amana Inspirationists, Barbara Heinemann Landmann, who founded another of the celibate movements of 19th-century America. Unlike the Shakers, the Amana movement was generally very oppressive to women for all the usual Christian reasons, but Charles Nordhoff, who was researching the communal movements in America at that time, says that Barbara Landmann was seen as an incarnate vehicle of the Holy Spirit: "They regard the utterances, while in the trance state, of their spiritual head as given from God." A woman's claiming of religious inspiration did not always bring her power and obedience, however. Anne Hutchinson, who led a rebellious faction against the leaders of the New England colony in its very earliest days, claimed that she received an "immediate revelation" from the Spirit which had inspired her criticisms of the Boston Church. She was summoned to appear before Governor Winthrop in 1637, accused of stirring up dissension in a way that was "a thing not tolerable nor comely in the sight of God nor fitting for your sex." She had claimed that the New England Church had become concerned only with external conformity and that the liberty of the Spirit had been taken away from the people. Her claim of hearing an "immediate voice" was seen at once by Winthrop as a challenge that could undermine the whole political balance of the colony because it would value the "inspiration" of individuals more than the authority of the leader of the theocracy:

> The ground work of her revelations is the immediate revelation of the Spirit and not by the ministry of the word. And that is the means by which she hath very much abused the country that they shall look for revelations and are not bound to the ministry of the word, but God will teach them by immediate revelations and this hath been the ground of all these tumults and troubles. And I would that those were all cut off from us that trouble us, for this is the thing that hath been the root of all mischief.
>
> (Heimert and Delbanco, pp. 156–61)

Accordingly, Anne Hutchinson was banished to Rhode Island, where she lived with her family and followers until the death of her husband in 1642. She died in New York the following year at the hands of the Indians during the Dutch-Indian War, and never once allowed Winthrop and the Bay Colony to see her spirit broken. "Her *Repentance* is in a paper," complained the Deputy Governor, "but . . . not in her countenance." Women could, therefore, lead people of both sexes away from orthodoxy. They could attract a loyal and devoted following, even in a society like New England that was oppressive to women. The source of their authority and leadership was an immediate contact with the Divine, which bypassed the usual male hierarchical channels that the orthodox believed that God should take when he wants to get in touch with us. Direct contact with the Divine especially when accompanied by celibacy could justify the "unnatural" phenomenon of female leadership not only to the men who followed these mystics, but to the women themselves.

For a woman to claim authority over men was such a revolutionary and extraordinary thing to do that it required of a woman something quite outside all her previous experience. The courage necessary for this original act must have involved a plumbing of all her available resources, psychological and spiritual. The Divine vision or inspiration was a familiar metaphor for a conviction or insight that came to her with such force that it seemed to come from outside herself. Thus Joan of Arc was inspired to her extraordinary mission by strange internal and mystical experiences that later, at her trial, she came to call the "voices" of her favorite saints. At first, however, she spoke of these experiences in terms of light as well as sound. They were not voices in the normal sense: they could be "seen" as well as heard and they gave her great comfort. It was only the third time Joan experienced this light and this "voice" that she "realized" that it must be an angel. Bursts of light are often experienced by mystics of all traditions and of all religions when a spiritual breakthrough has occurred. Joan's decision to go and save France was just such a breakthrough for her in psychological and imaginative terms. She had left behind her previous life and all the basic assumptions of her time and conceived an astonishing new idea of herself. Only much later, when pressed by her judges, did she begin to give her voices names and identities. She gave them the names of saints who had "inspired" her to act as she did by force of their example: St. Michael, the great angel warrior; St. Margaret of Antioch, the virago who had fought so bravely with the Devil; and St. Catherine of Alexandria, who by defeating 120 great philosophers in argument and converting them to Christianity had also succeeded in the male world. These saints were role models for her, but the moment of her vocation demanded a psychological breakthrough that required her to pass beyond the normal and established concepts with which she was familiar. The courage and initiative required of her went beyond the ordinary imitation of saintly heroes. She had to summon up all her imaginative reserves in a way that caused a mystical or psychological explosion. At first, however, she insisted that her voices were not her exclusive property. They were heard also by the King and some other members of the court. These consoling and affirmative experiences were shared by her closest associates, who were having to make as huge a psychological effort as she did to accept Joan's original and at first sight ludicrous mission.

Catherine of Siena, who was a more articulate woman than Joan (to whom concepts and words did not come easily), described her vocation to participate in the male world in a far more detailed way. For years she had lived as a member of the Third Order of St. Dominic; that is, she was not a regular nun living in an enclosed convent, but she lived a retired but independent life in her father's house. Consequently she had more freedom of movement than an enclosed nun, and, after years of the solitary life, she decided that she was called to a more active role. Her contemporary and biographer Raymond of Capua told the story of her vision. Christ appeared and said that he wanted her to take a more active part in the world of men and affairs.

> In vain did she in her humility and simplicity represent her unworthiness for such a function, whether by the weakness of her sex or other infirmities. "How can I, a poor and miserable woman, be able to do any good in Thy Church?" she would say; "how shall I instruct wise and learned men, or how will it be even seemly for me to live and converse with them?" But He [Jesus] made her to understand that in the counsels of His wisdom He had chosen her, a weak woman, to confound the pride of the strong. Her mission was to exhibit to a world "lying in wickedness the power of the Divine Word, made known to them by the feeblest of human instruments."

Catherine was clearly aware that she was about to do something extraordinary and needed to create a Divine backing for her decision. It would mean going against all the rules that governed the relationships between the sexes. She would be assuming a superior role, even though she could neither read nor write at this stage. Women were supposed to occupy a separate sphere from men, but Catherine was now proposing to "live and converse with them" in a way that might seem unseemly and even wrong. Many of the men she would be advising would be men of learning and sophistication. Yet Christ's reply was directly in line with an old Christian tradition. St. Paul had said that God had chosen the weak and contemptible things of this world to confound the strong and learned, to show the world that God's wisdom was infinitely superior to mere human learning. As Catherine was in contact with God directly and inspired directly by Him, her being a "poor and miserable woman" would teach the Church a much-needed lesson in humility. Christ elaborated this point:

> I have determined that those men who are wise in their own conceits should be made ashamed by seeing weak and frail women, whom they account as things vile and abject, to understand the mysteries of God, not by human study, but only by infused grace, confirming such doctrine by many marvellous signs above the course of nature.
>
> (Drane, p. 56)

Catherine's very despised femaleness was a positive asset to God: it turned the natural order on its head. St. Paul had continually stressed that God's wisdom put Him right outside purely human categories, and in this he was merely reiterating the Old Testament prophets, who had proclaimed that God's ways and thoughts were as high above man's as the heavens were above the earth. The Cross of Christ and the whole Christian life was against the natural order: death and defeat were seen to be victorious; humility the only source of pride; poverty the only true riches. Consequently, when God did as unnatural a thing as sending a mere woman, whom men regarded as vile and abject, to instruct men, he was acting "above the course of nature." Catherine's whole life would be a miracle. Already she was famous because of her extraordinary fasting: she was able to sustain herself only on Holy Communion. Now, without any education, she would show how well she understood the "mysteries of God," not by any natural means, but by "infused grace." She would skip the normal laborious means of acquiring knowledge, because God would teach her himself. One thing he did was teach her how to write, Catherine claimed. Her whole life was unnatural; she was nourished intellectually and physically by no normal means. Hers was an intellectual and spiritual as well as a physical autonomy, and as such it was a "miracle."

Catherine may have been a disturbed woman, and certainly her mysticism did nothing to liberate her from her neuroses, but she was also extremely intelligent. This is a brilliant justification of her position: it seizes the nettle of female "vileness" and "abjection" and turns it into a strength. She had grasped for herself the essence of Paul's words about human strengths and weaknesses—words which she couldn't have read for herself but only heard quoted occasionally in sermons and devotional talks—and given them a new interpretation which was deeply challenging to the male position. Her "supernatural" intellectual acquirements were probably the result of a strong and intuitive intelligence, which, because of her lack of education and because she was a woman who was not supposed to have any intellectual abilities, must have seemed miraculous to herself as well as to her contemporaries. It was this miraculous quality which Scipio Ammirato, the Florentine historian, saw as the reason for Catherine's political and social success:

> The Florentines knew for certain that she had remained many days without food than the Blessed Sacrament, though that was impossible in the natural order; they were aware that she had passed most of her life in solitude; they were convinced that it was by the particular design of God that she had exchanged the contemplative for the active life; and hearing that with no knowledge of Latin she yet explained the most difficult passages of Holy Scripture, and that she had learnt to read by no human means, all her words and actions came to be regarded as Divinely inspired. Hence she was continually implored to reconcile enmities, to deliver the possessed, to console the afflicted and to come to their help.
>
> (Drane, p. 300)

Catherine's neurosis shows her often straining her mind beyond the safe limit, but she did overcome extraordinary disadvantages to gain an authority that would have been envied by most of the men of her day. Her vocation to this life she justified to herself in the form of a vision, as Joan of Arc did, because what she was doing must have seemed so extraordinary that her mind could only explain it as a miraculous, as a Divine vision.

Other women, like Angela of Foligno and Margaret of Cortona, we have also seen enjoying a certain political celebrity, because of their lives of visions, austerity and autonomy. It was not only Catholics who used the vision and the notion of divine inspiration to justify their involvement in politics. The English Civil War saw an outbreak of female prophetesses, like Lady Eleanor Davies, who were able to get a hearing and a following by claiming Divine inspiration. These women were probably all totally sincere. Their political convictions came to them with a force and a compulsion that seemed to come from outside themselves and which were therefore in those days of extreme religious fervor easily attributable to the Divine. Over the Atlantic, Anne Hutchinson had also felt this touch of the Divine. Puritanism had claimed to dispense with an intervening hierarchy and institution which came between God and the individual. In the male-dominated society of Cromwell's England, the role of the prophet was the only means a woman had to get herself heard, and Cromwell himself favored these prophetesses when they pushed through the crowds to speak to him. They expressed a fundamental truth about Protestantism which stressed the importance of individual religious experience rather than an authoritative Church. However, for centuries Catholic women had found that same method of breaking through the barriers of hierarchy and prejudice into the male world.

What the ecstasy at its best represents is a huge imaginative breakthrough for a woman into a new world of experience. It required her to lay aside all her old presuppositions and prejudices and forge ahead into frightening and unknown territory, where it was all too probable that she would encounter a good deal of hostility. Similarly, the truly creative thinker has to lay aside all previous habits of thought and modes of knowledge to break really new ground. Thus Darwin wrote of ideas that they come "we know not *how* nor *whence."* They are not, he insists, "voluntary acts." To be sure, Darwin researched his ideas for a long time, but when the research fused together in a way that was truly original, the new ideas seemed to come to him "in a flash." It is no use sticking to pure rationality and aggressively intellectual striving if you want to produce an idea that nobody has ever thought of before. To do that means simply that you are embedding yourself in forms of thought and ideas that have already been established. We have all had the experience of an idea that has come to us quite out of the blue, when we were doing something quite different. Usually when we relax and allow our minds to become receptive is the moment the various elements of the ideas that we have been struggling with for a long time come together at once in a new "vision." The most obvious example of this is Archimedes, whose famous principle "came" to him while he was relaxing in his bath, when it had long eluded him in his study. It came upon him with such force that he leapt out of his bath crying *Eureka!* He had "found" something which was so clear and obvious that it seemed to have existed before him, quite independently of him even though he was its real creator. In this the creative thinker is just like the mystic. I have written elsewhere that they seem to be having much the same kind of psychological experience. Thus the scientific atheist Einstein claimed to be a mystic:

> The most beautiful emotion we can experience is the mystical. It is the sower of all true art and science. He to whom this emotion is a stranger . . . is as good as dead. To know that what is impenetrable to us really exists, manifesting itself to us as the highest wisdom and the most radiant beauty, which our dull faculties can comprehend only in their most primitive forms— this knowledge, this feeling, is at the centre of all true religiousness. In this sense, and in this sense only, I belong to the ranks of devoutly religious men.
>
> (Quoted by M. Laski, *Ecstasy,* p. 201)

To hear Einstein call his faculties dull and say that the source of all true knowledge is emotional not rational is a shock to our intellectual prejudices. Keats also insisted that the "dull brain" of the poet could only "perplex and retard" the progress towards vision and imaginative insight. This denigration of mere knowledge has always been the hallmark of the true mystic in all cultures. The mystic claims to go by a path of constant disciplined deprivation, away from what he knows already toward what he does not. The mystic can never tell you what God is, but only what he is not. He is an agnostic —so much so that the Sufis always claim that after they have been "touched" by the Divine, the usual intellectual divisions and prejudices of creed and religious sectarianism are completely irrelevant. The Sufi can claim to be as much at home in a Christian Church as a Mosque; he is no longer bound to any purely human category, so he is neither a Moslem, a Jew, a Christian or a Buddhist. As St. Paul says, he is a "new creation." John of the Cross also speaks of this disciplined walk towards agnosticism:

> . . . the soul must journey by knowing God through what He is not, rather than through what He is, it must journey, insofar as possible, by way of the denial and rejection of natural and supernatural apprehensions. This is our task now with the memory. We must draw it away from its natural props and capacities and raise it above itself (above all distinct knowledge and apprehensible possession) to supreme hope in the incomprehensible God.

> *(The Ascent of Mount Carmel,* 2, ii)

The mystic and the creative thinker are both journeying away from prejudice and already established categories toward something inconceivable and apparently incomprehensible.

Though it may seem a far cry from Joan of Arc and Catherine of Siena to Einstein and Darwin, all four of them had in common the mystical impulse to break new ground. To the Christian mystics this supreme achievement of the imagination expressed itself in Christian imagery, but Darwin and Einstein both use religious terminology and evoke the mystery and uncertainty of true creativity. Thus for women the vocation of mysticism could be liberating in a more deeply imaginative way than any of the other myths of autonomy. If she were strong enough mentally and in personality, she could achieve not only a new status but a new intellectual power which bypassed dependence upon men and set her free in a far larger world than would otherwise have been available to her. It was a dangerous vocation. Joan of Arc was burned at the stake, and other mystics were not psychologically strong enough to escape damage. However, occasional women showed a shrewd insight into how to cope with the male world and expressed a natural "genius" in religious and Christian terms.

Perhaps the most remarkable of these "creative" visionaries who were able to transcend the limitations of their sex was the 12th-century prophetess St. Hildegard of Bingen. During her lifetime Hildegard enjoyed considerable prestige. She corresponded with three Popes, with rulers of the status of Conrad III, Henry II of England, Eleanor of Aquitaine and Frederick Barbarossa, and re-buked them, if necessary, in good round terms. A Pope and Chapter guaranteed the authenticity of her visions; clerics of the status of Odo of Paris wrote asking her advice about complicated metaphysi-cal disputes, even though she had absolutely no philosophical or theological training. She went several times on preaching tours and tried to exorcise people "possessed" by demons—both offices nor-mally reserved for the priesthood. Hildegard's talents and their range are quite extraordinary. Her voluminous writings cover topics as widely diverse as cosmography, medicine, ethics, mystical poetry and music. She was not merely a theoretical musician, but wrote songs and music herself which are of considerable power and beauty. It has been said that only the Arab thinker Avicenna equaled this diversity and originality in the Middle Ages, and that she can be profitably compared with Goethe. Yet Hildegard has a certain ambiguous view of herself. Constantly she calls herself, without a shadow of irony, a "poor little woman" even when she is being particularly autocratic and is exercising her power in the male world with most confidence. There is nothing contradictory, however, in her attitude. Without her visions Hildegard would most certainly have been a poor and powerless individual precisely because she was a woman. It was her inspiration by God Himself which lifted her above normal female limitations.

Hildegard may have been canonized, but in many respects she is no saint: she is a snob (admitting only the highest-born women into her convents), a manipulator and had all the makings of a megalo-maniac. There are certainly incidents where she gives a ruling in a dispute without any revelation at all but is still quite happy to claim that God is definitely on her side, even though it could seem that she is acting purely out of self-interest. Nevertheless, there is a warmth and spontaneity in Hildegard which is attractive, and also a sound degree of sanity, which is rare in women saints and mystics. Given the stress her position must have entailed, and its very real loneliness, she manages to survive mentally intact, even though she certainly suffered a good deal from physical illness, which she seems to connect very intimately with her visions.

Hildegard's visions are more like Joan's "voices" than the other visions of Jesus we have considered in this book. In the first place, she claims that she never has ecstasy. She never loses consciousness, but her visions take place "in her soul" night and day, when she is wide awake and in full possession of her senses. When she "saw" or "heard" things, she explains, she did not see them with the eyes of her body and the voices she heard did not speak through a voice. We are clearly talking here about insight and a creativity which Hildegard, because of her particular circumstances as well as because of the times she lived in, interpreted as Divine Light. Because she does this, it gives her a freedom extraordinary in her time. In an age that was intellectually obsessed by "authorities" and where established positions always had to be deferred to, Hildegard, because she believed that her own insights were Divine revelations, could take absolutely no notice of prevailing opinions or authority. She could simply be original and strike out entirely on her own. Yet even though her writings show enormous confidence and enjoyment of her ideas and insights, the gift did not come easily to her. She grew up very fearful about these "visions" of hers, and was not easy until they had been ratified and approved by the appropriate Church authorities. Hildegard was no early feminist. She believed that women were intrinsically weak and feeble, but that she, by some special grace, had been lifted above the lowly lot that would certainly have been hers had she been left to her own powers and talents.

Hildegard grew up in a very religiously charged atmosphere. She tells us in her *Vita* that she was born in the year 1100, a time when there was a widespread sense of the wickedness of the world, which seemed to have grown spiritually sluggish and cold. Her parents were certainly depressed by the spiritual apathy of their time and dedicated their daughter to God when she was still "in my mother's womb." It was then, Hildegard believed, that "God raised me up with the breath of life, he fixed this vision in my soul." At the age of eight she was formally offered to God. As a very young child she was aware of "seeing" more than the ordinary people around her, things which she could only express "in a simple way," but which still staggered the people around her. But then Hildegard got worried. Perhaps if she had had normal ecstasies she would have been happier with these visions of hers, but as it was her experience seemed unique and therefore deeply frightening:

> Then I too grew amazed at myself, that whenever I saw these things deep in my soul I still retained my outer sight, and that I heard this said of no other human being. And, as best I could, I concealed the vision I saw in my soul. I was ignorant of much in the outer world, because of the frequent illness that I suffered, from the time of my mother's milk right up to now; it wore my body out and made my powers fail.
>
> Exhausted by all this, I asked a nurse of mine if she saw anything save external objects. "Nothing," she answered, for she saw none of those others. Then, seized by great fear, I did not dare reveal it to anyone; yet nonetheless, speaking or composing, I used to make many affirmations about future events, and when I was perfused by this vision I would say many things that were unfathomable to those who listened. But if the force of the vision—in which I made an exhibition of myself more childish than befitted my age—subsided a little, I blushed profusely and often wept, and many times I should gladly have kept silent had I been allowed. And still, because of the fear I had of other people I did not tell anyone *how* I saw.

(Dronke, p. 145)

What is striking is Hildegard's fear of the outside world. It is a fear that kept her silent about her visions until she was forty years old, when "I was forced by great pressure of pains to reveal what I had seen and heard." But even then she was still "very much afraid." She would herself have preferred to stay shut up in her enclosed convent, away from the world of men as befitted a mere woman like herself. It is clear that her illness is deeply bound up with this vision. Her illness had not only kept her separate from the world, but it seems to impel her first to seek advice from her nurse. She is "exhausted by all this," she says, seeming to refer to her illness as much as to her worries about her visions. What she "sees" is not Jesus having long conversations with her, but Light in various manifestations. It is a great brightness, flashing lights, lights shooting and falling like stars. It has been suggested that she suffered from crippling migraine, and this could well have been the case. What is remarkable about Hildegard is that she was able to use her illness creatively, and that the solitude it imposed upon her did not make her unbalanced (despite the constant worry about the nature of her vision) but creative and original. For it is quite clear that Hildegard was, without any formal education, a natural genius whose insights came to her with all the force of a vision. The content of her visions so impressed the monks and bishops, as well as Pope Eugene when they were brought to his attention, that he could only conclude that her "visions" came from God. What she experienced in vision was pure intellectual originality:

> In that same [experience of] vision I understood the writings of the prophets, the Gospels, the works of other holy men, and those of certain philosophers, without any human instruction, and I expounded certain things based on these, though I scarcely had literary understanding, inasmuch as a woman who was not learned had been my teacher. But I also brought forth songs with their melody, in praise of God and the saints, without being taught by anyone, and I sang them too, even though I had never learnt either musical notation or any kind of singing.
>
> (Ibid., p. 145)

When she was an old woman of seventy, with a full thirty years as an accredited prophetess behind her, she wrote to one of her most ardent fans, the monk Guibert of Gembloux, and her account of this "vision" is unchanged. There is no ecstasy, no voices or sights that belong either to the "heart's thoughts" nor to the five senses. What she sees is "like a sparkling flame and a cloud moved in pure air" as well as in the things about her "in changing forms of clouds and other created things." What she experienced was an extraordinary intuitive grasp of reality which enabled her to understand things that most people have to acquire laboriously through a long, disciplined education. Einstein said himself that he was a mystic, that his insights appeared to him in truly mystical form, and Darwin said that ideas came from mysterious and unfathomable sources. Hildegard's ideas and music also came from no obviously human source: they just arrived in her mind fully formed. Her education was entirely received from these visions—what doesn't come to her in vision, she claims, is a closed book to her:

> Whatever I have seen or learnt in this vision, I retain the memory of it for a long time, in such a way that, because I have at some time seen and heard it, I can remember it: and I see, hear and know simultaneously, and learn what I know as if in a moment. But what I do not see I do not know, for I am not learned.
>
> (Ibid., p. 168)

We are clearly here in a very different world from that of the neurotic mystic. Vision is not a mere projection of the mystic's fears and fantasies; it is a creative insight, which was so astonishing in women that it could only be interpreted in the 12th century as a direct revelation of God.

It was no mere intellectual gift, however. The experience of this insight brought to Hildegard a complete liberation from the lowly state of womanhood which would otherwise have been her fate:

> Then how could it be that I, poor little creature, should not know myself? God works where he wills—to the glory of his name, not that of earthbound man. But I am always filled with a trembling fear, as I do not know for certain of any single capacity in me. Yet I stretch out my hands to God, so that, like a feather which lacks all weight and strength and flies through the wind, I may be borne up by him. . . . And as God wills in this vision my spirit mounts upwards, into the height of the firmament and into changing air, and dilates itself among different nations, even though they are in far-off regions and places remote from me.
>
> (Ibid., p. 168)

Without her gift she would have had only a tiny sphere of influence in her convent. As it is, she has been caught up to a breadth of knowledge and experience that most men would have envied. Like

Einstein, she sensed a Vision and a Reality that were independent of anything she could create herself and which was the source of a liberating consolation and peace:

> And in that same brightness I sometimes, not often, see another light, which I call "the living light"; when and how I see it, I cannot express; and for the time I do see it, all sadness and all anguish is taken from me, so that then I have the air of an innocent young girl and not of a little old woman.
>
> (Ibid., p. 168)

For Hildegard ecstasy did not mean a "failing loss of consciousness," as she explains, when she became impervious to external reality. As confidence in her own "vision" grew, she came to disapprove of these more spectacular raptures. For her vision meant abundance of life, not an anesthetic retreat from it. Her "ecstasy" included an increasing joy in her femaleness, which became something young and innocent—an extraordinary thing for a woman to claim amid the misogyny of the 12th century. Hildegard believed that women should express this confidence proudly. She used to make the nuns in her convent wear elaborate and symbolic tiaras, to illustrate their virginal dignity. They also wore white veils, not black ones, which were the garb of *ancillae,* of servants and handmaidens. Women were to regard themselves as royal personages. She longed to see incarnate in the women around her the radiant, celestial beings she "saw" in her visions who symbolized Wisdom or the Church. Because Hildegard's vision had enabled her to liberate herself from the restrictions usually imposed on her sex, she could not bring it upon herself to despise it even though she would never say that men and women were "equal." Ecstasy was not an abandonment of her femaleness but its enhancement.

Hildegard was aware of some kind of connection between her ill health and her visions. It is not clear whether she obtained any alleviation from her sickness during her life, though her extraordinary output and her busy life once she became an accredited prophetess could be indicative of some kind of improvement. However, the most famous of all women Christian mystics, St. Teresa of Avila, certainly found that her practice of mysticism improved her health, both mentally and physically. Like Hildegard, she too attained a lightness and a robust joy, where before she had been ailing and unhappy. This inner liberation enabled Teresa also to enter the male world of affairs. She began her life in a truly terrible state. She had appalling health— it has been suggested that she was epileptic—and on one occasion her life was despaired of and they had even dug her grave in the convent cemetery. She was filled with such self-hatred that she undertook hideous penances, like crawling into the refectory on all fours carrying a basket full of boulders on her back. She was also prone to raptures and ecstasies of the "frozen statue" type. Later, her companion and mentor John of the Cross would warn her and all other mystics about the dangers of such undisciplined blackouts. In addition to this, Teresa was terrified of Hell. She had only entered a convent to get a foolproof ticket to Heaven. For twenty years she was completely miserable in the religious life. The convent she had entered was full of well-intentioned but worldly women, and there was nobody there to teach her to meditate or to make real and not neurotic progress in the mystical life. Like Mary Magdalene of Pazzi, who was her contemporary, or like Catherine of Siena, she could all her life have remained neurotic, ill and without a sense of vocation and purpose.

Teresa's story is interesting because it shows how mysticism *can* liberate some women from their inhibiting neuroses and channel their energies into completely new and unexplored paths. As soon as Teresa met St. Peter of Alcantara her life was, little by little, transformed. He was a master of the mystical life and taught her to meditate properly, so that she was no longer dependent upon stupid men like Father Bartholomew and Father Puccini, or floundering about in neurotic desperation like Mary Magdalene. Encouraged away from her former unhealthy practices, she was taught the proper mental disciplines and techniques which enable the mystic to enter into his mind and, if he has the basic mystical talent, to heal himself. The real turning point came years after she had started meditation when she had a vision of Hell:

> I realised that it was the Lord's will that I should see the place which the devils had prepared for me there and which I had merited for my sins. This happened in the briefest space of time, but even if I were to live for many years, I believe it would be

impossible for me to forget it. The entrance, I thought, resembled a very long, narrow passage, like a furnace, very low, dark and closely confined; the ground seemed to be full of water which looked like filthy, evil-smelling mud, and in it were many wicked-looking reptiles. At the end there was a hollow place scooped out of a wall, like a cupboard, and it was here that I found myself in close confinement.

*(Life,* Chapter XXXIII)*

Theologians have often said that Hell is not, as it were, another country or a physical locality, but rather the eternal and unalleviated endurance of the Self in all its petty and limiting egotism. This would perfectly tally with Teresa's vision, and she stresses the claustrophobic nature of the confinement she experienced:

In that pestilential spot, where I was quite powerless to hope for comfort, it was impossible to sit or lie, for there was no room to do so. I had been put in this place which looked like a hole in the wall, and those very walls, so terrible to the sight, bore down upon me and completely stifled me.

(Ibid.)

Teresa was experiencing the imprisonment of the ego. It was a "vision," she tells us, that she never forgot. At one time it would have plunged Teresa into a horrifying bout of destructive penance, and probably into a clinical depression. Now that she has been freed from this unhealthy behavior, she uses this vision creatively. It spurs her on to take positive action. If this was Hell, she reasoned, people had to be saved from it. The only way women could help with the salvation of souls at that time was by praying for them in enclosed convents. However, as Teresa knew only too well, the convents were not always helpful places for their nuns. New convents were needed where the sisters could learn about the mystical life properly and understand its techniques and disciplines. She herself had been full of good will as a young nun, but there was nobody in the convent who had been able to help her. The vision of Hell reinforced in her the horrors of the self from which she was, slowly, being rescued by means of proper instruction and discipline. Teresa decided, therefore, to reform the order of Carmelites to which she belonged to provide a proper environment for nuns—and later friars—to live a profitable and healthy mystical life without any of the dangers that she had encountered. To reform an order, if you were a woman, was not an easy enterprise, and Teresa encountered enormous hostility. Nevertheless, she persevered with indomitable courage, placing herself alongside the great male reformers of her age—Luther, Calvin and Ignatius Loyola. From this point until the end of her life, Teresa traveled ceaselessly around Spain, founding her reformed convents and transforming monasticism for the women of her time.

Like Catherine and Hildegard, therefore, Teresa's mystical experience enabled her to transcend the limits usually imposed upon women and take up a role—that of reformer—which was considered to be strictly for men only. However, there is a difference between Teresa and Catherine of Siena. Catherine achieved "liberation" externally; her political activities gave her power and equality with men. Yet internally there was no liberation, she remained locked in her anorexia and the guilt that was the product of the hostile Christian misogyny of her time. Teresa also suffered from the sickness that male attitudes could inflict upon women. Yet unlike Catherine, she had the good fortune to meet with people who were strong enough and expert enough to guide her out of the hell of her fears. Her vision of Hell shows that Teresa's liberation was a twofold one: she was delivered from her "self," and at the same time achieved an external liberation into the male world of affairs. Teresa's life shows women that some kind of inner journey may be necessary, and for her internal health accompanied her new freedom in the outside world. Like the other mystics, Teresa needed a mystical justification for leaving her enclosed life and venturing into male spheres of action:

> It seemed to me that, considering what St. Paul says about women keeping at home (Titus, 2:5) (I have already been reminded of this and I had already heard of it) that this might be God's will. But he said to me, "Tell them [i.e. Teresa's critics] that they are not to be guided by one part of Scripture alone, but to look at others; ask them if they suppose they will be able to tie my hands."

*(Spiritual Relations,* XIX)

If Christ was not to be constricted by men's rules and insights, neither were the women in Teresa's convents. Her vocation to the life of
a reformer had been the result of a vision of Hellish confinement.
Teresa did not want her nuns hampered or limited by any pettiness.
Indeed, liberation from anything small or "womanish" is a constant
theme of her writings for her nuns. She doesn't want them to be silly
women, she tells them in *The Way of Perfection,* and so she forbids
them to have sentimental friendships, as women tended to do at that
time, and use sloppy phrases like "my life," "my soul" and "my
darling." It was not that Teresa disapproved of friendship—on the
contrary, she was an extremely affectionate and warm woman—but
simply the weak expression of it, that most people considered "womanly." Teresa rejects trivial and feeble expressions of femininity as
sharply as does the feminist of today. She told her nuns that women
were not "little" beings, but she wanted them "to resemble strong
men; and if you will do what lies in your power, the Lord will make
you so virile that you will astonish the menfolk" (ibid., VIII). Anything that tied a woman's hands, her nuns were to despise. She warns
them against fussing about "the little weaknesses and ailments of
women, forget to complain of them; for sometimes the devil makes
us imagine these ills; they go and come; if you do not give up the
habit of speaking of them, and you complain of everything unless it
were to God you will never end" (ibid., XII).

Above all, Teresa was concerned to guide her nuns away from the
hysterical mysticism that we have seen to be rife amongst women
and which was so damaging to them. She herself had been too near
the brink to be anything but suspicious of a good deal of female
mystical states and she valued true mysticism too much to condone
this kind of behavior:

> It happened not in a convent of our Order but in a Cistercian
> house. There was a nun who was not less virtuous than those I
> have referred to. By dint of much discipline and fasting she had
> become so weak that, whenever she communicated or had occa-
> sion to be enkindled in devotion she would fall to the ground
> and remain there for eight or nine hours: both she and the other
> nuns thought it was a case of rapture. This happened to her so
> often that, if she had not found relief, I think she would have

come to great harm. The fame of her raptures spread through the whole town: for myself I was sorry to hear of this for the Lord was pleased to reveal to me what the matter was and I had misgivings as to what might come of it. Her confessor who was a great friend of mine, came to tell me about it. I gave him my opinion—that she was wasting her time, for these fits could not possibly be anything else but the result of weakness. I told him he must forbid her fasting and discipline and provide her with some distraction. She was obedient and did as he said. Soon she became stronger and stopped thinking about raptures.

*(Book of the Foundations,* VI)

It is good to hear the voice of common sense at last, but it is interesting to note that yet again the priest was at a loss and needed Teresa to put him right. Teresa is quite certain that such raptures can be dangerous. She wanted women to stay clear of morbid or sentimental states of mind and body that would damage the strong and virile women that she envisaged in her convents.

Her own new liberation from neurosis is clear in the later writings. She can now control her ecstasies, she says, so that they are no longer noticeable to other people. When she finds herself sinking into depression and destructive thoughts, she has discovered a simple but effective mental exercise, after which, she writes, "my soul and body become quite quiet and calm and my understanding grows quite clear, and I have as much fortitude and as many good desires as usual." The practice of meditation had actually improved her health:

For more than six months past I have felt remarkably well as to bodily health, and during this period I have experienced a number of raptures. Sometimes the improvement has lasted for over three hours, while at other times I have been much better in health for a whole day. . . . When I am recollected in this way, therefore, I am not afraid of any illness.

*(Spiritual Relations,* I, 1560)

Instead of inspiring her to further displays of self-hatred, she is becoming more at peace with herself. The "raptures," which are no longer the spectacular "frozen statue" kind but quieter experiences, calm her nerves and make her physically better.

The *Spiritual Relations* is a diary where Teresa occasionally made notes about her spiritual progress. Twenty years after the last entry, in 1581, she writes that she is now much more careful of her health and her body and "less mortified as to food and in doing penance" (VI). She is quite certain that mortification can produce a self-indulgent pleasure which is not helpful to the mystic, and that it is far more important and a far more mature attitude to preserve one's health. Teresa feels that she is now more at peace with herself and no longer suffers the violent "interior feelings which used to torment me when I saw souls being lost and wondered if I was committing some offence against God" (VI). The gusts of guilt and terror that had made her miserable and physically sick have now been stilled. She has learned to be kinder to herself:

> I had read in a book that it was an imperfection to have nice pictures so I did not want to keep one which I had in my cell. Even before reading this I had thought it a sign of poverty to have no pictures of any kind. Once however, when I was not thinking about this at all I heard the Lord say that this mortification was not good. For which, He asked me, was better: poverty or charity? If love were better, I must not give up anything that awakened love in me, nor take any such thing from my nuns.
>
> (XXX)

The young nun who had once tortured herself with boulders of guilt has been able to transcend this masochistic neurosis. She has declined to be a victim. Mysticism is dangerous for some people, but Teresa was blessed by a very strong intelligence and a sense of humor, which helped her to use the meditative techniques therapeutically and creatively. It is her strong and robust common sense and her humor which endear her to her reader. She has learnt to laugh at herself and at suffering. She teases her nuns out of their neurotic worries and declines the histrionics of the virginal life. On one famous occasion during one of her marathon journeys, her cart overturned and the nuns found themselves stranded in the midst of a ravine flooded with water and a raging storm. Instead of maundering on mawkishly about being a Victim of Divine Love, Teresa bellowed into the warring elements: "Lord! if this is the way you treat your friends, no wonder you've got so few!"

Like Teresa, Protestant women have also found that ecstasy not only gives them new ideas, but a new dimension of personal confidence and mission. It was certainly the case that the more emotional and charismatic forms of Christianity, like the Quakers, gave women an important and equal place in the movement. It was also true in the Great Revivals of 19th-century America. Thus Ellen White, the Seventh-Day Adventist Prophetess, reveals a process whereby the woman broke through the barriers of her normal inhibitions. This millenarian movement, which expected the Lord's imminent return, not only tolerated women speaking and prophesying at meetings, it positively expected women to pray and prophesy aloud and ecstatically. This used to worry Ellen a great deal. She "drew back from the duty," she says, "fearing that if I should attempt to pray I would be confounded. Every time I went before the Lord in secret prayer this unfulfilled duty presented itself, until I ceased to pray and settled down in a melancholy state and finally in deep despair." This vicious circle of depression could only be broken by the kind of violent experience that later psychiatrists would call abreaction or Primal Scream Therapy. Ellen had come to the limits of her normal resources and needed some breakthrough which was deeper and more instinctual than mere cerebral promptings to do her duty or an intellectual appreciation of the importance of prophecy. The abreaction occurred during the emotionally charged occasion of a prayer meeting that took place at Portland, Maine, in 1842:

> . . . when others knelt to pray, I bowed with them trembling, and after two or three had prayed, I opened my mouth in prayer before I was aware of it, and the promises of God looked to me like so many precious pearls that were to be received by only asking for them. As I prayed, the burden and agony of soul that I had so long felt left me, and the blessing of God came upon me like the gentle dew. I gave glory to God for what I felt, but I longed for more. I could not be satisfied till I was filled with the fullness of God. Inexpressible love for Jesus filled my soul. Wave after wave of glory rolled over me, until my body grew still.

Everything was shut out from me but Jesus and glory and I knew nothing of what was passing around me.

I remained in this state of body and mind a long time, and when I realised what was around me, everything seemed changed. Everything looked glorious and new, as if smiling and praising God. I was then willing to confess Jesus everywhere.

(Ruether and Keller, *Women and Religion in America*, p. 80)

Ellen had achieved the type of religious ecstasy which makes her blank out from the external world, descend into the depths of her psyche and emerge with a new "vision" of the world. This vision of a world where everything is seen as new and glorious is a very common one, and is shared by religious mystics and purely "secular" mystics in all cultures. It is known as "Adamic" vision, because the world appears as it must have appeared to Adam before the Fall. Often it seems to be triggered by a shock or by the mass emotion (or hysteria) of a Revivalist prayer meeting. For Ellen the world *was* new: she had acquired another dimension of confidence and peace. Ecstasy was extremely liberating for her, forcing her beyond the traditional restraints that society had imposed upon women.

Men had always been aware of the power that mysticism could give to women. There is a wariness in the attitude of a Father Puccini and a Father Bartholomew as well as an inadequacy. "Mystical" women like Catherine of Siena were slightly alarming. Men were both satisfied that the women had left this world and retreated into another one and, at the same time, rather in awe of the extraordinary freedoms—healthy or otherwise—that the tranced ecstasy seemed to give to women. Nineteenth-century women like Ellen discovered new power in a purely religious ecstasy, but in the same century, men were celebrating the power of the ecstatic woman in purely secular ways. Rossetti, for example, saw the tranced woman as brooding and menacing with a hidden smoldering power. His *Beata Beatrix'* trance is erotic and blazes with a power which is achieved quite independently of any man. So deeply had Christianity associated women's mysterious power with the mystical, that the image of the ecstatic woman permeated purely secular society. Painters constantly depicted Tennyson's Lady of Shalott in ways that hint of strange menace. Waterhouse sees the Lady rearing herself up as though she has achieved some frightening new perception, and Holman Hunt paints her as struggling powerfully like a witch with her magic web. Writers also celebrated the ecstatic woman. Du Maurier's Trilby may be the mere creature of Svengali, hypnotized trance-like into a talent which is beyond her normal powers, but both the descriptions and the illustrations show her towering over all the men in the novel, including Svengali himself, in a way that is superior and frightening. Alice in Wonderland, that famous dreamer, seems to be terrorized by her visionary world and is forced, like all Victorian Angels, to pacify it by "good little girl" manners, but ultimately all the power is hers. By waking from sleep and shouting, "You're nothing but a pack of cards!" she can shatter the whole of Wonderland. Finally, Madame Tussaud created a powerful image of woman about to wake up from sleep. Her famous waxwork of the Sleeping Beauty (which breathed) drew vast crowds. It might seem that she had created the typical Victorian woman, passively asleep needing to be woken up by her Prince. However, it is also true that once the Sleeper has woken up, the whole Palace will be galvanized into activity. No one can wake from their trance until she does. For centuries Christianity has presented women as powerful ecstatics, achieving talents and influence quite independently of men. In the 19th century, when women were otherwise so powerless, men feared the hidden reserves of the woman ecstatic.

The 19th century was also the great age of women writers, and many of them seem to see the creative process as a form of ecstasy. Thus Mrs. Gaskell speaks of the "hidden world of art" as a "refuge for women" which takes women away from morbidity and triviality "into the land where King Arthur is hidden and soothes them with its peace." George Eliot certainly "encountered" strange presences or powers in her mind when she was writing. It was of her that Richard Simpson wrote in 1863. Women, he says, have:

> . . . almost the monopoly of the emotional nature—of the passions, which are the elements of life; a bubbling and fermenting source of power, whose impulses seem like the acts of external force, instinctive, indefinite, vague, involuntary, but rich and mighty, like a Divine energy within us. Perhaps she does not

think that women possess it more really than men, but that in
the woman it is not overlaid with all the unreasonable products
of manly reason; with overlogical feats and over honeycombed
brain.

(Quoted by Elaine Showalter, *A Literature of Their Own*,
p. 149)

Creative mystics like Hildegard had had a positive advantage in not
getting bogged down in the intellectual limitations of the 12th century. Similarly, although the women of the 19th century often longed
for the education that their brothers had, the educational standards
of the time could in fact be a positive hindrance. Eliot created a
powerful picture of academic impotence in Casaubon, the dried up
scholar-husband of the glowing Dorothea. Simpson was right that
gifted women were lucky not to be hampered by the aridities of poor
Victorian scholarship. They had easier access to the more instinctual
and creative powers of the mind, which were seen as powerful indeed
—almost "Divine." It is of course true that to profit from this educational exclusion you had to be a very exceptional woman indeed, and
that most women were crippled by intellectual impoverishment. Still,
Simpson was surely right that the deeper "involuntary" powers of
the mind are creative and that men often have difficulty of access to
them because of their over-rational approach to life. Keats urged the
poet to adopt a means of stilling or controlling the rational faculty,
to gain access to the creative imagination. He called the gift "negative capability" which exists when the mind is capable in "resting in
doubts and uncertainties" without any "irritable" reaching out for
"facts and reason." If he could stay in this mystical darkness—an
image Keats often uses—the poetic imagination would transport him
to quite a different world of vision and reality.

If women writers have been enthusiastic about a woman's mystical
powers, most women have abandoned ecstasy as an ideal in our own
century. There are many reasons given for this abandonment. Ecstasy and mysticism have led to neurotic and hysterical states.
Women have now become educated and more "rational." They now
tend, like many men, to distrust their more creative and receptive
aspects. Also, to dabble in mysticism and see it as an ideal for women
can reinforce the old myths about women being incapable of rational

thought and suitable only for the role of Earth Mother. There is a good deal of truth in this. However, to confine creativity to artists and writers only is surely a dangerous trend. There have been three women writers who have recommended Ecstasy and Trance as something desirable for women, and it may be that they have something important to say to us.

Virginia Woolf was quite clear that to be creative was to be mystically receptive. "The whole of the mind must lie wide open if we are to get the sense that the writer is communicating his experience with perfect fullness. There must be freedom and there must be peace," she writes in *A Room of One's Own*. The "writer must lie back and let his mind celebrate its nuptials in darkness. He must not look or question what is being done." Within the mind, "some marriage of opposites has to be consummated." Only then can there be the birth of a new creation. Once the writer has entered this Keatsian darkness, the mystical dark night of the soul, he or she is liberated from the normal confines of his gender:

> If one is a man, still the woman part of the brain must have effect; and a woman also must have intercourse with the man in her. Coleridge perhaps meant this when he said that a great mind is androgynous. It is when this fusion takes place that the mind is fully fertilized and uses all its faculties.
>
> (p. 97)

Elsewhere she writes of creation as "a state of trance." She pictures the writer sitting "sunk in dreams on the verge of a deep lake . . . letting her imagination sweep unchecked round every rock and cranny of the world that lies submerged in the depth of our subconscious being." *(Professions for Women)* Sadly, like Catherine of Siena, Virginia Woolf was never able to achieve this creative liberation and freedom in her personal life, whatever she did when she was writing her novels. Far from coming to terms with her subconscious, her neurosis destroyed her and led her to suicide. It is not every nature that can stand such intense exposure to the subconscious. It is no wonder that women fight shy of vision and ecstasy. "Ecstasy" and "madness" used to be synonymous words in our language a few hundred years ago.

Doris Lessing, another great champion of "mysticism" for

women, also shows that this process can bring about temporary derangement. Her purely secular mystics roll around on the floor weeping, they hit their heads against the walls, chew their fingernails till
they are permanently bleeding, wander round the streets at night
hallucinating and raving, mutter and gibber uncontrollably during a
performance in the theatre. They look terrible: their hair becomes
wild and crazy; their bodies are frighteningly emaciated. Often they
become physically ill or are inmates of mental hospitals. Similarly,
Margaret Atwood's mystical heroine in *Surfacing* rejects the human
race totally and wants to become an animal. She prowls round the
forests naked, scrabbles in the earth for roots and plants to eat,
checks constantly to see if she is growing any fur. If this is what
mysticism does for you, who needs it?

Lessing is careful to bring her mystics out of this derangement,
however, into a richer existence and a new sanity. The derangement
is a temporary but necessary stage. Modern life and the role of
women are seen as so unhealthy that only through psychic violence
can a woman break through her conditioning and achieve true humanity. Women are conditioned, Lessing says, constantly to placate,
to charm and to appease. We have seen how and why this is so. To
gain a real knowledge of self and a new liberation, the transition
from this placating state is bound to be violent. It involves inner
journeys into the subconscious and confrontations that are frightening and terrible. Thus Kate in *A Summer Before the Dark* escapes
from the demands of her grown-up family after years of service, and
during a summer adopts several different new roles. She begins to
have a serial dream, where she finds herself carrying a dying seal
over bleak and terrible terrain to save its life. She knows that until
she has finished the dream and liberated the seal she cannot return to
her family. Her dream is showing her at a level beneath the rational
that all is not well with her life; just as Perpetua dreamed her way
through to a courageous control of her life and her death, so too does
Kate. In *The Four-Gated City* the mystical vision is seen as an end in
itself, not just as a necessary and liberating stage. After taking her
heroine with the symbolic name of Martha Quest through all the
main stages of a woman's life in a marathon series of five novels,
Lessing ends her journey with the mystical life. Martha marries,
bears a child, has lovers, gets involved in politics, spends some time

as an Earth Mother managing and controlling a large household. She does not discover her full potential, however, until she develops her "mystical" ability to go on inner journeys away from the conscious and rational world. This leads her to expand the powers of her mind, so that she becomes clairvoyant and telepathic. Elaine Showalter has perceptively remarked that in this novel Lessing has reversed the *Jane Eyre* story. In *Jane Eyre,* the mad wife is kept in the attic. In Lessing's novel, the mad wife, who is also the greatest mystic in the novel, lives in the basement, and Martha, her husband's lover and housekeeper, descends into the basement and joins Lynda in the "madness" which leads to new vision. The basement shows the more fundamental powers of the subconscious mind. Upstairs in the upper regions of the conscious mind, Mark, the husband and lover, inhabits the male cerebral world in his study which he tries to make an emblem of his purely rational—and ultimately inadequate—vision of and solution to the world's problems.

Margaret Atwood's heroine in *Surfacing* has damaged herself and become frighteningly inhuman and dissociated from her environment. In her mystical journey she has to come to terms with her past, plunge into the depths of her psyche, confront death and realize how she has lied to herself. It is only when she has descended below the rational level, which her overly rational father told her was All, that she can understand what has happened to her and achieve a true liberation into a rich and emotional appreciation of the world around her. Like her father, she has "discovered new places, new oracles, they were things he was seeing the way I had seen, true vision; at the end, after the failure of logic" (p. 145). For neither Atwood nor Lessing is the mystical quest a traditionally religious one, but the path their heroines take is essentially the same. Both writers see that until women have made this journey in some sense they will remain impoverished human beings whatever professional success or equality with men they may achieve. "Liberation" can be a soulless and cold achievement, concerned only with external circumstances. Thus Atwood's heroine is certainly a "liberated" woman at the outset of the novel: she has freed herself from the limitations of her parents' lives, has left her husband and child, takes lovers and lives a trendy and conventionally interesting life with a "creative" job. However, she is dead inside herself, sealed off from reality.

One of the reasons why women reject mysticism today may well be that it offers too extreme an autonomy for most women. Mystics like Catherine of Siena and Hildegard of Bingen were able to be quite independent of the world of men, but most women are neither capable of this autonomy nor do they want it. Writing of the mystical vision, T. S. Eliot said that "human kind cannot bear very much reality." John of the Cross warned the mystic that he would have to leave his former props and supports behind and step into a dark night where nothing was familiar and where there was no easy consolation. Lessing and Atwood offer to the potential mystic a very bleak and lonely future: their heroines have sought not a man but a vision. More to the taste of most women is the less radical solution offered by feminist novelists who describe women's social liberation —writers like Marge Piercy, Alix Kates Shulman and Lisa Alther. Like the mystic, these writers are also clear that there has to be a period of social dislocation when the women painfully peels away from herself if true liberation is to be achieved. This means going out on a limb like the mystic, and facing loneliness. At the conclusion of these stories of women's liberation the heroine is often left without an official mate. However, the loneliness is qualified: very often the heroine has some form of love, and has nearly always acquired a new circle of close (often women) friends. The liberation achieved does not mean the absolute autonomy of the mystic.

Yet whether or not women choose the mystical path toward liberation, the women mystics—Christian or post-Christian—are useful to use. Life, we know only too well, is different from the world of fiction. To set out on the road to liberation is lonely at the start, and there are no guarantees that you will not be lonely at the end. It is possible that having abandoned a former dependent mode of life, a woman may *not* discover, for example, a convenient, warm circle of supportive friends to raise her consciousness. The possibility of the Dark Night has to be faced when changing one's life. A woman has to be ready to accept the bleakness of the mystic, because independence necessarily demands a self-reliance that brings some loneliness with it. This raises the question that every woman has to ask herself. How independent does she really *want* to be? Does she simply want financial independence, for example? Is she prepared for the fact that such independence can jeopardize the emotional dependency of a relationship? Does she want to retain some measure of emotional dependency? And if so, how much? It is important to handle these and related questions in a very clear-sighted way. Women's liberation and the raising of the feminist consciousness means more than attacking male oppression and working for eternal change. It demands some degree of inner liberation, some new inner independence, and this will demand some kind of inner journey. Inevitably this will mean pain of some kind. The mystics provide us with an extreme image of absolute autonomy against which each woman can measure the independence that she wants and can realistically achieve.

It is interesting and perhaps ironic that the only form of ecstasy that most women consciously seek today is sexual ecstasy. It is now a commonplace that we have made a religion out of sex, especially since the 1960s, and invest orgasm with ultimate, transfiguring significance. That we have transferred words like "ecstasy" and "rapture" from the world of mysticism to the world of sex is itself revealing. Words that once described a woman's most radical withdrawal from the male world now describe her moment of strongest connection with a man. Perhaps this shows us the unease we still subliminally feel about intimacy and closeness between the warring sexes. Even when we are speaking most enthusiastically about sexual intimacy and experience "ecstasy," perhaps at that very moment of sharing the sexes want to retreat from one another. Perhaps at some level a man and a woman still desire some degree of distance from each other even at the moment when they are supposed to be most deeply connected. Indeed, it is a commonplace that sexual pleasure can make a man and a woman even more conscious of the gulf that really separates them—*post coitum omne animal triste.* It is also ironic that ecstasy once provided a woman with the most independent experience; now her sexual ecstasy is envisaged as a deeply dependent experience. Because women are so often ignorant about their bodies, they are frequently more dependent on their men for their pleasure than ideally they should be, and it never occurs to many of them to take the initiative in procuring some pleasure for themselves or their partners. As Germaine Greer put it in *The Female Eunuch,* since the recent Cult of the Orgasm sex has become for women "a mystical experience which is a grace from men, as Teresa of Avila was granted ecstasy by God" (p. 218). At the very time when women are seeking new independence they have created for themselves a new myth of extreme sexual dependency, as they wait for their men to "give" them orgasm, seeing it as the man's sole responsibility. Similarly, psychoanalysis offers a form of ecstasy in the sense of a deep interior journey into the heart of the mind, which unleashes repressed energies and, ideally, leads to liberation from neurosis. It offers a myth of secular enlightenment. It is very popular among women, especially in the United States. However, this also involves deep dependency. This is not just because psychoanalysis largely depends upon the insights of male thinkers like Freud and Jung, so that women are yet again running to men for their ideas about themselves. Dependency upon the analyst is an essential part of the whole process. Women claim that they want to be independent and free of subservience to men, and very often the women who make this claim the loudest are the very women who seek orgasmic dependency or plunge into the dependency of analysis.

We may not wish to embark on the deep mystical journey into the psyche. We may not have the psychological robustness to expose ourselves to such a journey. Scientists have made it clear that not everybody is able to produce the right type of brain rhythms to achieve the receptive state that is the essence of mysticism. However, the contrast between a St. Catherine of Siena and a Teresa of Avila points to the importance of achieving some kind of interior freedom, instead of relying solely on gaining liberation in the external world vis-à-vis men. Today we no longer think of the tranced woman as a source of strange independent power. Men have fairly recently abolished this ideal for women. On his study wall, Freud used to keep a photograph of the hypnotist Charcot treating a hysterical woman. It is an image that is by now familiar to us. The woman is in a paralyzed trance, rather like de Vitry's frozen statue mystics. All around her, gazing at her intently, are men, Charcot's pupils. However, this circus of men is no longer regarding the ecstatic with wonder and reverence. Charcot is about to pull this woman back into the world out of her trance. Men have penetrated this last resort of women's minds. Freud was fond of remarking that hysteria seemed to have declined among women during his lifetime. It is as though once men had penetrated into defense and invaded their inner territory, women no longer sought this method of escape. Freud and Charcot were right to pull women out of this unhealthy retreat, but mysticism, we have seen, does not have merely to mean neurotic withdrawal.

A study of all the great mystical traditions shows that the true mystic is deeply agnostic. If you ask a mystic who this God is that he is supposed to have encountered, he will always tell you that he does not know, that "God" is so far above limited human conceptions that he is above human definition, concepts and terms. Whether a mystic is a Sufi, a Christian or a Buddhist, he is aware that ultimate reality is indefinable and at some level beyond human certitude. The creative mystic like Einstein also moves from the known to the as-yet unknown in a similar process of mystic agnosticism. There is at present between the sexes a good deal of aggressive rationalization and dogmatic prejudice. Men make sexist remarks about women; women vilify men. Many of the dogmatic assertions on both sides are at best only half-truths, because we simply do not know enough about the real personality differences between the sexes. A little mystical agnosticism would not come amiss here. Both sexes are stuck in neurotic and hostile patterns of behavior toward each other. Constantly we repeat the myths of our Christian past in ways that are often unhealthy. Instead of repeating old myths and getting stuck in prejudiced ruts, men and women need a new vision, beyond what we know and have experienced already. Instead of wearily reproducing old modes of behavior and old emotional prejudices, we should be content to wait in Keats' state of "negative capability," or John of the Cross' Dark Night. We cannot see clearly at present, and prejudice and aggression are not the right way to arrive at new imaginative vision. If we are to arrive at new solutions, then we need to cultivate the receptive as well as the aggressive analytical part of the brain.

# 7

# THE FOUR FACES
# OF EVE

In the West men declared war on women and excluded them from
their world. The good woman was one who was independent of men
and lived in a sealed-off female world. The atmosphere between the
sexes was hostile. However, we have seen that there were women
who could, even in the heat of the sex war of Europe, command the
respect of Christendom. Women who were virgins, martyrs and mystics were esteemed. A career of sanctity usually involved one of those
three paths. However, once the path was taken, the three modes of
female goodness in the West became one. A woman saint might spe-
cialize in one particular discipline—thus St. Margaret of Cortona
was devoted to the path of autonomous virginity, St. Perpetua to
martyrdom and St. Teresa of Avila was preeminently a mystic—but
to take on one of these three ways of life meant that you had, in some
sense, to take them all on. Thus every woman had to be a virgin in

one way or another, even if her virginity were only honorary. The sex hatred of Europe demanded that. However, we have seen that virgins usually undertook the hair-raising penances that belong to martyrdom to tame their unruly bodies. You could not be a successful saint unless you suffered. Moreover, virgins and martyrs both had intensely spiritual experiences of Jesus, which could loosely be called mystical. The mythologies of each of these three states overlap, as the myths develop. Thus the autonomy of the virgin is very similar to the autonomy achieved by the mystic, when she is sealed off from the world. As the martyrdom myth developed, women martyrs were seen more and more as virgins dying to preserve virginity, and many of the stigmatics and ascetics had erotic mystical experiences that characterized the virginal Bride of Christ. In its earliest days martyrdom was simply the most extreme form of Christian mysticism; thus Perpetua and Blandina go into a mystical trance and do not feel their sufferings, and though Perpetua may not be a virgin herself, her dream foreshadows the virago myth of virginity. What we have here, therefore, are not three means to sanctity for women, but one composite and complex means. The good woman of the West is Virgin/Martyr/Mystic. Men had declared that women were evil; each one of them was Eve. If Eve was to be redeemed by sanctity, therefore, she had to undergo a threefold discipline. She had to be Virgin/Martyr/Mystic all at once. Each woman was Eve, but if she were a saint she had three faces, three aspects.

However, in fact, as the mythology of the redeemed, Christianized ideal woman developed, the redeemed Eve turned out to have not three faces but four. Not only did women see themselves as Virgin/Martyr/Mystic, men saw them this way too, but however much they praised this holy woman saint they were often threatened by her. In the late 15th century the sex war of Europe would begin its most intensive assault on women, in the Witch Craze. However, the castrating witch had appeared in the Christian emotions before that. The holy saint was also often seen as frightening and castrating to men. Underneath the praise of her holiness, it is possible that the men who told her story saw the witch. Eve then is Virgin/Martyr/Mystic/Witch, a tight, complex knot whose strands are inextricable.

During the previous four chapters, I have traced each strand of the Christian myth of female goodness separately. This chapter will show how the four apparently separate myths merge and melt into one. So deeply had the myth of Eve with her four faces sunk into Western ideals of women, that long after the Reformation tried to abolish the cult of the saints, it persisted in its fourfold form and even found secular expression.

One of the very first women to be held up as ideal was St. Thecla, the legendary companion of St. Paul. Her story idealizes virginity, but already it had jelled with the ideal of martyrdom. We are constantly seeing Thecla flung into the arena to face suffering and death. It is precisely in the arena that she discovers her autonomy and becomes independent of Paul. She baptizes herself—no longer needing Paul's ministrations—by an act of voluntary martyrdom when she flings herself into the trough of man-eating seals. Virginity and martyrdom are deeply linked in the Christian mind. When Ambrose, the great Doctor of Virginity, tells Thecla's story he introduces it by saying: "Let Thecla show you how life can be sacrificed" *(De Virginibus,* II:19). It was Ambrose who told the story about the virgin he knew who was locked into a brothel by the Romans and who, once she escaped, rushed off to sacrifice her life in martyrdom. Virginity he sees as inseparable from suffering and death. "Virginity," he says, "is not praiseworthy because it is found in martyrs, but because itself makes martyrs" (ibid., I:10). Virginity was itself a type of martyrdom. Ambrose sees St. Agnes as a Victim and a Virgin, pursuing a double vocation of virginity and suffering. "You have then in one victim a twofold martyrdom, one of modesty and one of religion. She remained a virgin and achieved martyrdom" (ibid., I:19). If you want to be an autonomous and independent virgin, the next step was, in some sense, death. A virgin is essentially also a martyr.

It might seem that at first the women martyrs who were revered by the Church were not virgins. Blandina, Perpetua and Felicitas, we have seen, were viewed as wives and mothers. Yet Perpetua's famous dream of becoming an androgynous "man" in the stadium is clearly connected with the transcendence of sexuality which was virginity, and with the virago ideal. To become a virgin meant that you left the limitations of your gender behind, as Perpetua does in her fight with the Devil. Perpetua becomes a virago in the act of martyrdom. Yet Perpetua didn't suffer any pain, and here the third element of the complex appears. Because she is in a state of Ecstasy and Trance she achieved an invulnerability and an imperviousness to pain that is precisely what virginity was also supposed to give a woman. Later in the 13th century Jacobus de Voragine's *The Golden Legend* showed that martyrs were virgins who felt no pain and could not be subdued by any of the appalling tortures that were devised to make them suffer. Thecla also had felt no pain and could not be killed. Her virginity put a shield around her which made her invulnerable to the hostilities of the outside world. The virgin and the ecstatic both cultivate an autonomy that is impervious to the world.

Catherine of Siena is a clear medieval example of the triple ideal existing in one person. She was a virgin who had fantasies of divine nuptials with Jesus and who produced the virginal disease of anorexia nervosa. She was also a martyr who not only killed herself by her fearful austerities, but who also developed the stigmata. Finally, she was an ecstatic whose ecstasies prompted her to break into the male world and live an active life. Yet it is not merely that women following the career of sanctity followed three separate routes to sanctity. The ideal itself was basically one. Virginity and ecstasy both give invulnerability, so that St. Agnes' body is covered by a celestial vest in the brothel and the Béguines in their ecstasies cannot feel it when Cardinal de Vitry sticks pins into them and beats them. Virginity also is a form of martyrdom because it spells death to a woman's gender. Ecstasy too is a martyrdom: in the early days of the Church martyrdom was simply seen as the final type of ecstasy when the soul finally passed away into God in a ecstatic swoon. Writing of ecstasy in her autobiography, Teresa of Avila says that it is a martyrdom. When the soul seems to lose consciousness and becomes absorbed into God, "It seems as though it were on the threshold of death, save that this suffering brings with it such great happiness that I know of nothing with which it may be compared. It is a martyrdom, severe but also delectable" *(Life,* XX).

Yet these invulnerable, autonomous women were also very threatening to men in the atmosphere of the sex war. Women who didn't need men because they could baptize themselves, receive independent vocations and missions, and have direct contact with God in ecstasy were clearly worrying. Even as early as the 2nd century we can see this male hatred of the autonomous virgin surfacing in the Thecla story, when the male physicians come up to rape and murder

her in her cave. Later Joan of Arc, the virgin and virago par excel-
lence, was burned as a witch. An ecstatic who was a contemporary of
St. Teresa of Avila narrowly escaped the same fate. María de la
Visitación, the Portuguese nun, was a typical "saint" of the type we
have been considering. She was virginal, a stigmatic and had ecstasies and raptures—all the hallmarks of sanctity, in fact. These
credentials won her respect in the male world and she was constantly
consulted by churchmen and politicians—Philip II of Spain even
asked her advice about the Armada. However, she became too powerful and was denounced to the Inquisition as a witch. She threw
herself on the mercy of the Pope, confessed that she had had an
incubus as a child and because of her sincere repentance she was
publicly humiliated and imprisoned in a convent of Poor Clares,
where she died a saintly death. The Witch Craze was then at its
height, so it would not have been surprising if some of her dreams
and ecstasies had taken witchy forms and her "confession" was probably quite sincere. Ecstasy was dangerous for women: some people
had erotic relationships with the Devil in dreams and visions, and
others had erotic relations with Jesus. It could go either way. Teresa
of Avila was constantly being examined to see if her visions were
inspired by the Devil. The saint, however holy, was sometimes seen
as a witch; her independence and power seemed diabolic.

Even when women were not pilloried and persecuted as witches
but revered as saints, the frightening witch is often latent in the
powerful virgin. The medieval virgin-martyr stories are full of terrifying tales of these women who are clearly dangerous to have around
and fatal to men. St. Catherine's famous wheel disintegrated and
killed all the executioners. When St. Martina was taken to the Temple to be sacrificed to idols, the devils living in the idols were so
terrified by her virginal presence that the idols collapsed and killed
all the priests. The story of St. Barbara, as it is told by Christine de
Pizan, is a typical story of these dangerous women:

> Because of her beauty, her father had her shut up in a tower.
> She was inspired by faith in God, and because no one else could
> baptise her, she herself took water and baptised herself in the
> name of the Father, the Son, and the Holy Spirit. Her father
> sought a noble marriage for her, but she refused all offers for a

long time. Finally she declared herself a Christian and dedicated her virginity to God. For this reason her father tried to kill her, but she was able to escape and flee. And when her father pursued her to put her to death, he finally found her through information provided by a shepherd, who immediately was turned to stone, he and his animals.

The father brought her before the prefect who ordered her to be executed with excruciating tortures because she had disobeyed all his commands. And she said to him, "Coward, are you unable to see that tortures will not harm me?" Whereupon, flying into a rage, he commanded that her breasts be torn off, and in this state he had her led through the city. During the entire time she praised God, and because of her shame at having her virgin body seen naked, our Lord sent his angel who healed all of her wounds and covered her body with a white robe.

After she had been led around enough, she was taken back to the prefect, who was beside himself with rage when he saw her completely healed and her face radiant like a star. He had her tortured again until her torturers were exhausted with tormenting her. She prayed to God to help all those who would entreat Him in her memory and who remembered her passion. And when she had finished her prayer a voice was heard, saying, "Come, beloved daughter, rest in your Father's kingdom and receive the crown and all that you have asked will be granted you." After she had climbed the mountain where she was to be beheaded, her criminal father cut off her head himself, and as he was coming down from the mountain, fire from heaven struck him down and reduced him to ashes.

*(The Book of the City of Ladies,* III, 9, 2)

St. Barbara is a typical woman, walled off from men because of her sexuality into her separate sphere. Shut up in her tower, she has no contact with the male world. She becomes completely autonomous in her seclusion. Like Thecla she baptizes herself, and like Thecla again, Christianity for her means virginity. She will suffer not so much for her faith, as for the affront and the challenge her virginity offers to the male world. She no longer has to be subject to any man, and she will suffer "excruciating tortures" simply because she refuses to obey her father. Her virginity has rescued her from the normal state of female dependence and subservience. Virginity also gives her complete invulnerability. Her wounds are healed and she is given the celestial robe, as Agnes was, which seals her virginal body off from the world. In the end she is triumphant. The unfortunate shepherd and his totally innocent sheep are turned to stone for betraying her. The executioners are exhausted and the prefect reduced to impotent fury. Her womanhood becomes impregnable to them; her breasts grow back on and her body remains fresh and tireless when male "passion" has expended itself upon her. She even taunts the emperor for being an impotent and ineffective coward. Clearly she is the ultimate castrating bitch. Finally her father himself is killed. Her death is a parody of the sacrifice of Isaac: she goes up the mountain like Isaac to be killed by her own father, but she is the heroine, not the Patriarch. When the father is coming down from the mountain, like Moses descending from Mount Sinai where God had spoken to him amid thunder and lightning, his triumph is short-lived: he is struck by fire from heaven. Virginity is destructive of traditional patriarchy. The witch also was protected by a defensive shield of either glamour or charm, which is at the same time destructive and castrating to men.

This autonomous and invulnerable woman is often a dangerous and castrating witch at the same time as she is a saint. The story of María de la Visitación is classic in this respect. It is no accident that the medieval legends often have the virgin-martyr accused of being a witch and an enchantress. Women themselves were sometimes quite conscious of the threat that this complex vocation presented to the male world and how deeply challenging it was. Thus in the 9th century, the nun playwright Hrostvitha used some of these legends as bases for her plays. Virtue, she says, is shown as especially triumphant when "womanly frailty emerges victorious, and virile force, confounded, is laid low." This might well be true, but the men of the Court who watched Hrostvitha's plays would have felt rather alarmed by their virile force being laid low by poor, frail women. One of her characters, the Virgin Martyr, Hirena, reveals herself as a real virago when she jeers at her persecutor's impotence:

Unhappy man! blush, blush, Sisinnius, and groan at being vanquished ignominiously: for you could not defeat a tender little girl's youth without a panoply of arms. . . . You shall be damned in Tartarus; but I, about to receive the palm of martyrdom and the crown of virginity, shall enter the etherial bedchamber of the eternal King.

(Dronke, p. 78)

If men were threatened by these dangerous viragos, the women themselves were shown exulting in their triumph. Hildegard of Bingen may have talked about herself, quite genuinely, as a frail and worthless woman, but when her will was crossed in any way she could become a real harridan. Because she was a Prophetess, her views were greatly respected and there were certainly occasions in Hildegard's life when she claimed in no uncertain terms a Divine backing for what was really a scheme of her own. It cannot have been easy for her, told by the Church that she was inspired by God, to make the distinction between the "Divine" and her own "human" vision. Thus when she decided that she was going to leave the prosperous Abbey of Disibodus and make a foundation of her own, the reaction of her Abbot was hostile. Hildegard was a prestigious subject, and she would be removing from the Abbey, with her nuns who would take with them all their dowries and revenues. Hildegard wrote this letter in answer to his objections:

If you are determined to go with your perverse proposals, raging against us, you will be like the Amelicites and like Antiochus, of whom it was written that he despoiled the Temple of the Lord. If some of you, unworthy ones, said to yourselves: Let's take some of their freeholds away—the I WHO AM say: You are the worst of robbers. And if you try to take away the shepherd of spiritual medicine [i.e. Hildegard's personal adviser] then again I say, you are sons of Belial, and in this do not look to the justice of God.

(Ibid., p. 153)

It is excellent that women like Hildegard were able to defy men and get their own way, but her very ready identification of her own will with the Divine is slightly disturbing, and one cannot help feeling she was exploiting her position by putting a curse on her Abbot. He was plainly alarmed by this threatening of the Divine displeasure and hastily gave in. As Hildegard puts it: "And when I, poor little creature [!], had with these words petitioned [!] the Abbot and his confrères for the freehold of the site and domains of my daughters, they all granted it to me." We are only a step away here from the curse that a witch was supposed to put upon men. The witch was clearly inherent in the way that both men and women regarded the holy and autonomous virgin.

"The Lady of Shalott" is often scorned today by literary critics, but in this poem Tennyson clearly caught the imagination of the Victorians, and its popularity has persisted into the 20th century. The Lady of Shalott has even captivated the attention of the contemporary novelist Muriel Spark in her most famous novel, *The Prime of Miss Jean Brodie.* It is not surprising that the poem has so much appeal. Tennyson managed to find a secular form for the old myth of Western woman, with her four faces. The Lady of Shalott encapsulates in herself the fourfold way the West had come to view women. Thus she is shut away from the ordinary world and enclosed in the tower of Shalott, like St. Barbara. Isolated by a "curse" which means that she may not even look at the world, the Lady is just like the Christian woman, who was ostracized and condemned arbitrarily by Christianity because she was Eve, and enclosed in a world of her own. Inside her tower, the Lady is a mystic because she is creative, weaving her vision of the world into her tapestry. She is also a virgin, though a reluctant one because she finds herself longing for love. When she falls in love with Sir Lancelot she is, as the victim of romantic passion, at once destroyed. She becomes a martyr, and venturing out into the world which was forbidden her causes her death. The world of Christendom was a dangerous place for women, and they did better not to try to break into it. As she goes to her martyrdom, the Lady continues in the traditional ecstasy "like some bold seer in a trance." Holman Hunt painted her like a witch. She completely embodies the woman that Christianity had taught itself to venerate and fear in a myth which it developed during the nineteen centuries of its history.

Today the complex vision of women bequeathed to the West by Christianity is still with us. One face of Eve quickly becomes another. Thus some women claim that they want independence and go about winning it by presenting themselves as passive martyrs, entirely dependent upon their tormentors, men. The virgin thus becomes the martyr. Certain women like Marilyn Monroe presented themselves as glamorous castrating witches during their lives, and after their death they were seen as martyrs. The powerful viragos of the Krantz-Conran style of fiction are also witches, because they very often castrate men, using them for their own ends. Other women confuse power with the role of victim in a damaging exercise of power through a display of helplessness. The way that women often view the witches of the 16th and 17th centuries shows signs of the same muddle. Some feminists like to call themselves witches because they see themselves as powerful rebels against the establishment, but in fact the real witches were suffering victims. Most feminists like Mary Daly who encourage this view would probably despise the castrating glamorous and charming "witches" of today, who are the true heirs of the *Malleus*.

The biggest muddle perhaps exists in our attitudes toward men. Are we supposed to deride them, as the virgin-martyr St. Barbara did, egging them on to further displays of impotent rage? Or are we supposed to placate them and sacrifice our lives to them? When the ideal has always been separateness, autonomy, defensive self-protection and defiance, then what happens to the new ideal of togetherness and marriage? The Protestant Reformation exalted marriage for the first time and promoted the ideal of Holy Matrimony. The new ideal woman was to be dependent on her husband, and, as that had always been an economic fact of life for most women, it was an ideal that was easily accepted. Are we supposed to be autonomous or dependent? Ultimately the two ideals are mutually exclusive. Which to choose? When women have always been told that marriage is second best, how will they adapt to the new married idea? When the old ideals become part of the new ideal of the dependent wife and mother, then a fresh muddle occurs. A woman will now be told to sacrifice her life not to God but to her husband and children. Sometimes she will be told that even though she is sexually experienced and has children, she is really a virgin, and physically and psychologically impervious to male lust. Later she will be told that she can have an independent life and career. She can live her own life, like the independent and autonomous virgin, even though she is emotionally dependent upon her husband and has children dependent upon her. She will be told that she will have a transfiguring experience not when she has a vision of God, but when she falls in love with a man. She cannot have independent ecstasy but only dependent orgasms. The old ideals of autonomy have now been taken right into the heart of the dependency ideal creating what is possibly the most difficult muddle of all.

# 8

# THE PROTESTANT SOLUTION: WIFE AND MOTHER

The vast majority of women have never been professional virgins, martyrs, mystics nor witches but wives and mothers. In most cultures a girl's whole life is simply a preparation for marriage, and no other destiny occurs to her. In the Christian West, on the other hand, there has always been the ideal of the independent and autonomous woman, even though, in practice, this ideal was only possible for very few women. Today the rising divorce rate and the quest for alternative ways of family life show a rejection of marriage which

would be unthinkable in other cultures, where there is, for women at least, no life outside the family, and certainly no "higher" glory than being a wife and mother. The feminist movement, which continues the ideal of virginity in a secular mode, is often virulently opposed to marriage, and more and more women in more and more sectors of society are feeling that although they want to be married and want to have children, marriage and the family are not enough for them. They have rejected Luther's axiom, which was so vigorously championed by the Victorians, that a woman's place is in the home. Like the holy women of old, they want now to break into the male world and have careers instead of simply living vicariously through their husbands and children. It is not surprising that marriage is encountering such fundamental criticism, because as a valued ideal in the West it is a new institution. It was always important for the wealthy and landowners because it was a means of forming political alliances and increasing possessions. For the humbler peasants and artisans, marriage was similarly important in providing both men and women with helpmates in the struggle with life. However, the Church did not concern itself with marriage, and married people thought that their marriages were their own business, not that of the Church. In an age dominated by religion, marriage was seen, by both Catholics and by Protestants, as a purely secular arrangement, even as something religiously regrettable for the also-rans of this life. It was the Protestant Reformation which slowly evolved the ideal of Holy Matrimony which still survives. However, the older ideals of celibacy and independent lives for both men and women persisted alongside the growing adulation of dependent marriage for women, to find forcible expression in our own day.

We have seen that from the very earliest days of Christianity marriage and the family were not given the value and respect that they certainly had in other cultures. Both Jesus and Paul seem to have viewed marriage as a very secondary factor in the Christian life. If you could not manage without it, then it was permissible and acceptable, but, given the factor of Jesus' imminent return and the fact that "the things of this world are passing away," it was seen as better for men and women to remain unattached if they could. Both men and women had to wean themselves from the absorbing responsibilities and preoccupations of family life. Women were no longer to find

their fulfillment in motherhood and domesticity. Like the male Christians, they had to learn new priorities and to put "the Lord's affairs" first. Men and women were seen ideally by Jesus and Paul as equal partners, living celibately if they possibly could, but in independent equality and mutual respect. However, we have also seen that even in the New Testament there is a change in the later scriptures. Misogyny and sexual fear have crept into the First Epistle to Timothy, and in the post-Pauline Letter to the Ephesians we have a very different view of the relationship between the sexes:

> Give way to one another in obedience to Christ. Wives should regard their husbands as they regard the Lord, since as Christ is head of the Church and saves the whole body, so is a husband the head of his wife; and as the Church submits to Christ, so should wives to their husbands, in everything. Husbands should love their wives, just as Christ loved the Church and sacrificed himself for her to make her holy. He made her clean by washing her in water with a form of words, so that when he took her to himself she would be glorious, with no speck or wrinkle or anything like that, but holy and faultless. In the same way husbands must love their wives as they love their own bodies; for a man to love his wife is for him to love himself. A man never hates his own body, but he feeds it and looks after it; and that is the way Christ treats the Church, because it is his body and we are its living parts. *For this reason, a man must leave his father and mother and be joined to his wife, and the two will become one body* (Genesis 2:24). This mystery has many implications; but I am saying that it applies to Christ and the Church.
>
> (Ephesians 5:21–32)

This passage has been used in very different ways. Christian apologists have used it to point to the essentially positive view of Christian marriage as found in the New Testament: never mind St. Paul's preference for the celibate life in 1 Corinthians, here we see that Paul really valued both sex and women. Here married sex is compared to Christ's love of the Church—what could be better than that? Similarly, women are compared to the Church itself by St. Paul, who clearly, therefore, sees women as essentially noble and holy, whatever later, more unbalanced, Christians may have said about femi-

nine evil. On the other side, critics of St. Paul have seized on this passage to prove Paul's ultimate chauvinism: women may be compared to the Church, but really Paul sees them as essentially impure —look at all the washing the bride has to do before she is fit for her husband, and for all Paul's remarks elsewhere about the essential equality of men and women, it is clear here that women are really deeply subservient to men. However, to attribute this Epistle to St. Paul is probably a mistake, as it seems to have been written some fifty years after his death, in about A.D. 100. The critics of the passage are right to see women portrayed here as dependent beings, and this is yet another instance of the progress of Christian thought into ideals that would have been strange to both Paul and Jesus. The author of Ephesians has picked up St. Paul's view of the Church as the body of Christ, but he has radically altered this image. Paul had seen the Church and Christ as an inseparable unit: each Christian had a special function in the Church; just as each member of the human body has a special function and are all dependent on one another, no function or gift in the Church is superior to any other. Again, all the members *are* Christ in some way. Because they *are* the body of Christ, they cannot be separated from him in any way at all. By the time Ephesians was written, the Church is seen as separate from Christ: the Institutional Church is emerging to stand between Christ and the individual Christian, and will subordinate some members of the Church to others—clergy over laity, celibate over married people, men over women. This is fundamentally opposed to Paul's egalitarianism. Christ is no longer identified inseparably with a Church but is superior to it and independent of it, as a husband is independent of and superior to his wife. The author of Colossians will see this same separation between Christ and his body, the Church:

> Now the Church is his body,
> he is its head.
>
> (1:18)

Because the author of Colossians conceives of the Church as inferior to Christ instead of one with him, he sees the Christian life in terms of subordination of one Christian to another. Slaves are to be obedient to masters, children to parents and "Wives," the author urges,

"give way to your husbands as you should in the Lord" (3:18). It is a far cry from Paul's advice to married couples where wives were seen to enjoy equality with their husbands, because all Christians were one in the Lord and there were now no further distinctions of race, class and sex once Christians had become part of Christ's body. Thus already in the New Testament the family life of a Christian is seen to have conflicting ideologies: there is the earlier ideology of equal partnership between the sexes opposing the later ideology that women were dependent upon men and inferior to them. It is a conflict that persists in our own day and which persisted throughout the transformation of marriage into a Christian vocation.

Christianity has followed the author of Ephesians in making the Church female. It might seem that this habit of speaking of the Church as "she" and as our "Holy Mother" can only benefit women, just as the adulation of the Virgin Mary would. However, the essential inferiority and dependency of women was written into the image of the female Church right from the very beginning. It certainly did not affect the way men viewed women. Similarly, Christian art may have filled our Churches and art galleries with images of motherhood, with Mary carrying the child Jesus, but always this was a virgin motherhood, which bore no relation to motherhood as it affected the ordinary Christian woman.

Had things remained stable at this point, it would simply have meant that Christian marriage and the position of women within it would have resembled the position of women within other cultures: she would merely have lost the equality with men and essential independence from them that Jesus and Paul had offered her. However, things did not stop there. The Christian message was absorbed into the pagan world of Late Antiquity and absorbed, in a way quite peculiar to Western Christianity, a sexual neurosis. For the Fathers of the Church with their hatred of sex, marriage cannot be a true and valuable Christian vocation even though they may oppose sects like the Encratists and the Manichees who say that marriage is sinful. Ideally, because sex was evil, marriage should be shunned. "I praise wedlock, I praise marriage," wrote Jerome, "but only because they produce me virgins" (Letter 22). This "praise" of marriage was hedged about with the self-deceptions of Christian doublethink: In the same letter Jerome could write, "Do you dare to disparage wedlock, a state which God has blessed?" So far, so good. But then, inevitably: "It is not disparaging wedlock to prefer virginity. No one can make a comparison between two things if one is good and the other evil." Because sex is so deeply linked with sin and evil in the Christian mind, evil is brought right into the heart of every marriage, for all God's "praise" and "blessing." Tertullian saw this when he saw that marriage "consists essentially in fornication" *(An Exhortation to Chastity)*, and he is delighted to seize upon St. Paul's words and interpret them in a way that would have astonished Paul, but which was entirely expressive of Tertullian's Christian neurosis: Paul had said that *"it is good for a man not to touch a woman.* It follows that it is evil to have contact with her; for nothing is contrary to good except evil" *(On Monogamy,* iii). Again, when he refers to Paul's famous words about it being better to marry than to burn, Tertullian comments grimly: "Better it is to lose one eye than two" (ibid., iii). The Fathers view sex very differently from Paul, and this colors the way that they interpret his view about marriage—a view which would hitherto be seen through their eyes in the West. Marriage must be an evil and should, therefore, be avoided. It might be objected that the Fathers could not have wished marriage to die out because this would mean that the human race could not continue. That was no problem to the Fathers, for procreation was by no means seen as a Christian duty. "Leave that to the pagans," Tertullian said tersely. Cyprian, Bishop of Carthage, a great admirer of Tertullian, said that the first commandment given to men was indeed to increase and multiply, but now that the earth was full there was no need to continue frenetically this process of multiplication. Augustine was clear that if everybody stopped marrying and having children that would be an admirable thing: it would mean that the Kingdom of God would return all the sooner and the world would come to an end. By continuing to propagate the human race, we were simply holding up Christ's glorious return.

This negative view of marriage was reflected in the complete lack of interest in it shown by the Church authorities. For one thing, no special ceremonial was devised to celebrate Christian marriage. The Church very quickly produced its own liturgy of Eucharist, Baptism and Confirmation, but nothing was done about marriage. It was not important for a couple to have their nuptials blessed by a priest.

People could marry by mutual agreement in the presence of witnesses; they could have sex at once, and there was no need to wait for the Church's blessing. This system, known as Spousals, persisted after the Reformation and endured well into the 18th century. Very often the couple married in the church porch. Thus Chaucer's Wife of Bath tells the Canterbury pilgrims that she had had five husbands "at the Church door." Augustine and Aquinas may have said that marriage was a sacrament, but no ceremonial was devised to celebrate this sacrament. At first the old Roman pagan rite was used by Christians. Clearly it had to be modified, but the modifications were purely superficial: the Holy Spirit and Christ were substituted for the names of pagan gods. Thus there was no special Christian marriage service for centuries. The first detailed account of a Christian wedding in the West dates from the 9th century, and it was identical to the old nuptial service of Ancient Rome. For all the insistence of the Scholastics that Christian marriage was something essentially different from marriage between pagans, this sacrament had to wait centuries before receiving Christian baptism.

The wedding is now so firmly entrenched in our Western consciousness that it is difficult for us to realize how very new the wedding mythology really is. A young girl is taught, traditionally, to look forward to her wedding as the high point of her life. Clad in virginal white, she will float down the aisle to pledge her life to her husband. This will be her fulfillment as a woman. Love, that deeply Christian virtue, is now seen to be inseparable from the ideal of marriage and human fulfillment in family life. Today men and women who are not Christians, who have no real Christian beliefs and never enter a church normally, will still often want a Church wedding. Marriage and Christianity somehow seem inseparable. Because marriage is now seen as a union of Love, it has become something "sacred" to us, and a purely secular celebration is seen as unworthy by many people. It does not matter that the young couple may have ample evidence for the fragility of married love; they usually buy the whole wedding package. Unmarried people are urged to the altar by their married friends with as much zeal as the Fathers once urged virginity. Therein lies a person's whole fulfillment, they insist, in one of those violent swings of opinion that characterizes the Christian neurosis. Yet this coupling of love and marriage is relatively new. From the time of the Troubadours, love was seen to be quite independent of marriage, and in the 12th century a very famous pair of lovers felt that marriage would inevitably destroy their love.

Abelard and Héloïse have assumed a romantic status that is usually given only to the lovers of legend, like Tristan and Isolde. Theirs was a *cause célèbre* of the 12th century. Abelard was the leading scholar of his time. He had a towering reputation. From all over the known world people flocked to hear him teach and lecture all his life. They would follow him into the "wilderness" after the catastrophe and camp around his poor little oratory, the Paraclete, building themselves huts made of twigs and daub. Abelard was not primarily a religious teacher nor a theologian: his theological studies tend to be rather conservative. He was really a philosopher and a logician, but it was not possible to separate the two spheres of secular and religious. Philosophy was the "handmaid of theology," and toward the end of his life the theological implications of his philosophical conclusions caused him to be shamed and denounced by the Church in the person of St. Bernard.

Abelard was no religious rebel, however. It is perhaps difficult for us to appreciate fully the pervasive power of the Church in the medieval world. All the universities were run by the Church. The only way you could get an education was by becoming a clerk, or taking at least minor orders (the lower ranks of the priesthood). It is not clear whether or not Abelard was a priest, but there is every indication that he simply took minor orders when he decided to become a scholar. He led a devout and chaste life until he reached a peak in his career, when he fell in love with Héloïse. Héloïse was an extremely intelligent woman, the niece of Fulbert, one of the Canons of the Cathedral, who lived with him in his house. Abelard got himself into Fulbert's household without difficulty. Fulbert was as infatuated with the brilliant and charming young man, as was everybody else. Abelard also had no trouble seducing Héloïse: as she herself says in one of her letters, he was physically very attractive to women, and he could make up songs and sing them beautifully. Abelard gave Héloïse lessons, and she fell deeply in love with him. Their love affair continued for months, right under the nose of the unsuspecting Fulbert.

If Fulbert was unaware, however, the rest of the world was not. Abelard became so infatuated that he became lackadaisical in his teaching and his studies, and mooned around like a typical lover, composing love songs to the beautiful Héloïse. His pupils and colleagues became first worried and then incensed. It was only a matter of time before somebody enlightened Fulbert and he caught the lovers *in flagrante delicto*. From that moment events started to gather for the tragedy. Héloïse became pregnant and was spirited out of Paris into the country to have their son, whom Abelard called, rather oddly, Astralabe. By this time Fulbert was out for Abelard's blood, and to pacify him Abelard promised to marry Héloïse.

It was then that Abelard panicked and caused Fulbert to wreak his terrible revenge. There was absolutely no reason why, legally, Abelard could not get married. It is often supposed today that because he was a priest marriage was impossible for him. This is not true. Even if, for the sake of argument, we admit that Abelard was a priest, celibacy for the clergy was not yet obligatory. It would be some eighty years before Innocent III was able to impose celibacy on the clergy at the Lateran Council. It was at that time never even mooted for the minor orders, among whose ranks Abelard was almost certainly placed. However, although it might have been legal and valid for Abelard to marry her, this brought no joy to Héloïse. A modern girl with an illegitimate baby might be overjoyed to get married to the father of her child, especially if he was one of the great celebrities of his day. But Héloïse was appalled at the idea, precisely because he was a celebrity. She argued fiercely with him against this marriage. For a careerist like Abelard marriage would be as damaging in the 12th century as the discovery of an illicit love affair would be to a politician like Cecil Parkinson today. It would have been much more acceptable for Abelard to have kept Héloïse as his mistress. The status of marriage was so low that it could blight a rising young man.

In a long letter written to a "friend" but which was probably a circular letter for concerned people, Abelard sets forth *The Story of My Calamities* and gives several pages outlining Héloïse's arguments against the marriage. In one of her later letters to Abelard, Héloïse confirmed that she had been against the marriage and that she found the title of Mistress or Whore much more desirable than Wife. She knew perfectly well that marriage would not "make an honest

woman of her," as we would imagine today. She would be blamed
for ruining Abelard's career. She herself—and in her letters as well
as in the arguments she used to dissuade him we see what a very
good pupil of Abelard's she was—intelligently and passionately
shows Abelard that marriage is beneath him. It is a state to which
somebody of his caliber should never sink. The Fathers of the
Church are quoted copiously by both lovers, especially St. Jerome,
and clearly their scorn of marriage had informed public opinion in a
way that seems incredible to us, for whom marriage gives a rising
young man or woman the seal of respectability. Héloïse was adamant
that marriage could only bring disgrace to them both, and in the
event she was proved quite correct:

> What honour could she win, she protested, from a marriage
> which would dishonour me and humiliate us both? The world
> would justly exact punishment from her if she removed such a
> light from its midst. Think of the curses, the loss to the Church
> and grief of philosophers which would greet such a marriage!
> Nature had created me for all mankind—it would be a sorry
> scandal if I should bind myself to a single woman and submit to
> such base servitude. She absolutely rejected this marriage; it
> would be nothing but a disgrace and a burden to me.
>
> *(Historia Calamitatum)*

Later in one of her letters, Héloïse laments in very conventional
but heartfelt terms the way that women can only bring shame upon
men who are foolish enough to get involved with them. She quotes
the examples of the great temptresses of old, like Delilah and of
course Eve, for "she who had been created by the Lord as [Adam's]
helpmate became the instrument of his total downfall." Héloïse is
deeply and emotionally convinced of the Christian myth of feminine
evil. Long before the *Malleus Maleficarum* was written, she sees
herself literally as a castrating witch. Abelard's tragedy was her fault
because she was a woman and because her sin was the female sin of
sexuality: "I yielded long before to the pleasures of carnal desires,
and merited then what I weep for now. The sequel is a fitting punishment for my sins." For Héloïse the great mistake was that she and
Abelard decided to get married:

For while we enjoyed the pleasures of an uneasy love and abandoned ourselves to fornication (if I may used an ugly but expressive word) we were spared God's severity. But when we
amended our unlawful conduct by what was lawful, and atoned
for the shame of fornication by an honourable marriage, then
the Lord in his anger laid his hand heavily upon us."

(Letter 3)

Héloïse was an entirely orthodox young woman, and though later
Abelard would be denounced by the Christian establishment, on the
subject of sex he went entirely along with the Church. Abelard and
Héloïse were not a young couple in love who rebelled against conventional views with a fine careless rapture. Both believed that they
were sinners because of their relationship, and that they richly deserved their appalling fate. Yet despite their orthodoxy it is interesting to note that Héloïse views here are exactly the same as those of
the Catharists, who were being persecuted for their views by the
Church. The Cathars also felt that marriage was shameful because it
attempted to make something essentially evil honorable and respectable, and advocated that a couple should not get married if they
could not do without sex and asserted that promiscuity was preferable to wedlock. Yet again, the "heresy" of heretics on this matter of
sex is seen as identical with the views of devout, orthodox Christians.
The Devil, Héloïse adds well within the orthodox tradition, knew
very well that "men are most easily brought to ruin by their wives,
and so . . . he attacked you by means of marriage when he could
not destroy you through fornication" (ibid).

For Héloïse there was nothing honorable about marriage. She set
before Abelard a long list of authorities—Paul, Jerome and Augustine figuring importantly—to show why marriage was an unworthy
state for a great man. In the *Historia Calamitatum* Abelard recalls
the strong arguments she used to dissuade him from taking this
disastrous course: as a philosopher, she urged, Abelard had a sacred
vocation. To sully himself with the ignoble and unworthy state of
marriage should be beneath him. There is no talk of the sacrament of
marriage, no talk of its being an image of Christ's love for the
Church, no mention of it as an "honorable estate," provided for
man's comfort in the Garden of Eden by a loving God. For Abelard

to stoop to "the unbearable annoyances of marriage" was an appalling thought. The philosophers had always taught that philosophy is a full-time pursuit, demanding that a man despise the world and give himself up to it wholly. Philosophers "have cut themselves off from their fellows because of their singular chastity or austerity." Marriage is such a sordid state that it is impossible for the philosopher who requires a "dignified way of life":

> What harmony can there be between pupils and nursemaids, desks and cradles, books or tablets and distaffs, pen or stylus and spindles. Who can concentrate on thoughts of Scripture or philosophy and be able to endure babies crying, nurses soothing them with lullabies, and all the noisy coming and going of men and women about the house? Will he put up with the constant muddle and squalor which small children bring into the home? The wealthy can do so, you will say, for their mansions and large houses can provide privacy and, being rich, they do not have to count the cost nor be tormented by daily cares. But philosophers lead a very different life from rich men, and those who are concerned with wealth or are involved in mundane matters will not have time for the claims of Scripture or philosophy. Consequently, the great philosophers of the past have despised the world, not renouncing it so much as escaping from it, and have denied themselves every pleasure so as to find peace in the arms of philosophy alone.
>
> *(Historia Calamitatum)*

There is never a moment when Héloïse thinks that she could enhance his life as his wife. It is either the stylus *or* the spindle: married life and philosophic dignity are mutually incompatible. It never once occurs to Héloïse that marriage is a noble and fulfilling vocation which can lead them to God. It can only suck him down to depths of uncontrollable emotion where reason is lost in the chaos of concupiscence:

> But if pagans and laymen could live in this (celibate) way, though bound by no profession of faith, is there not a greater obligation on you, as clerk and canon, not to put base pleasures before your sacred duties, and to guard against being sucked

down headlong into this Charybdis, there to lose all sense of shame and be plunged forever into a whirlpool of impurity.

(Ibid.)

Héloïse was not pulling out of the love affair. What will pull Abelard forever into this irretrievable and shameless impurity is not the sin of fornication, but legalizing the sin by marriage. By publicly setting himself up as a married man, Abelard was telling the world that he was having sex. The final arguments Héloïse uses against marriage sound surprisingly modern:

> Héloïse . . . argued that the name of the mistress instead of wife would be dearer to her and more honourable for me—only love freely given should keep me for her, not the constriction of a marriage tie, and if we had to be parted for a time, we should find the joy of being together all the sweeter the rarer our meetings were.
>
> (Ibid.)

But it was no use. Abelard was adamant and Héloïse had to give in, with none of the tremulous joy we associate with blushing brides but with a sense of doom: "amidst deep sighs and tears she ended in these words: 'We shall both be destroyed. All that is left us is suffering as great as our love has been' " (ibid.).

Héloïse's fears were totally justified. Abelard also knew that a marriage could only harm his career, and when he offered to marry Héloïse he insisted that "the marriage should be kept secret so as not to damage my reputation." The wedding was furtive, and after it the unhappy pair separated and "went our ways unobserved." Abelard was trying to atone for his sin and give his son legitimacy, but the stigma attached to marriage was too great for him to acknowledge Héloïse publicly as his wife. Fulbert was now so angry with Abelard that no marriage ceremony would calm him down. It would be nice to think that Fulbert was concerned about his niece, but that does not seem to have been the case. He had taken so little notice of her before her pregnancy that she had been able to sleep with Abelard right under his nose. He was furious because of "the dishonour done to him." His mode of revenge, knowing just how detrimental this could be to Abelard, was to spread the news of the marriage, break-

ing his oath of secrecy. Héloïse, far from being proud to be acknowl-
edged as Abelard's wife, cursed him and swore publicly that they
weren't married, causing Fulbert in exasperation to hurl abuse at her.
Abelard panicked. He packed Héloïse off to a convent in Argenteuil
and, despite the fact that there was no thought at this stage of her
becoming a nun, made her wear the religious habit. It must have
looked as though Abelard were trying to disguise the fact that she
was his wife, and it gave to Fulbert the excuse he needed for his
famous act of revenge. He broke into Abelard's lodgings one night
and castrated him.

All around Abelard and Héloïse more ordinary souls were getting
married, but they do not seem to have been "falling in love" to do so.
Until the mid-18th century love remained confined to poetry and
later to novels. Even when the increase of literacy and the rise of the
popular novel made the notion of love rise to the forefront of a
woman's consciousness, it was still considered inexpedient to marry
for romantic passion. Marriage was seen as a practical partnership.
A young peasant would not have the energy or leisure to "fall in
love." He would need a woman who was a good worker. Although
among the wealthier classes there was, during the 17th century onward, an increasing tendency to allow young people to choose their
own mates, passionate love and desire were not seen, even by the
couple themselves, as a sign of a promising relationship. It was not
until the 19th century that the ideal of marrying for love took real
root in the popular mind in practice as well as in literature. This does
not mean that people were mercenary or soulless. Life was hard and
serious for the poor, and love a luxury that they could not afford.
Similarly, the mortality rate made such a notion as "till death us do
part" have a very different ring. Even in the 16th century the average
life expectancy was not much greater than it had been in the paleo-
lithic era. The average age at death was between twenty-five and
thirty. Thus marriage could not be seen in such "world-without-end"
terms as it has been since. It was probably regarded, by both men
and women, as a rather transitory state. A young woman could be
twice married and twice widowed before she reached the age of
twenty, and a child might have two or three stepmothers *and* stepfa-
thers between birth and adulthood. This, historians like Lawrence
Stone suggest, affected the emotional climate. It was just not good

sense to invest too much emotional capital in a relationship which was most unlikely to last for long. The emotional climate warmed appreciably during the 18th century—novelists like Laurence Sterne write of feelings and "sentimental" love, and love creeps into the correspondence between spouses and lovers more frequently and more warmly. The fact that by this time the mortality rate had so improved that a moderately affluent Englishwoman could expect to live until she was fifty must have made a great difference to the freedom a young couple felt to make a strong emotional commitment to each other. But even to put the life expectancy at fifty is still to feel its brevity. To blame the frequency of divorce today is unrealistic. Marriages never lasted so long as they did in the late 19th and early 20th century, until divorce became common. The divorce rate could be said simply to have replaced the death rate of previous centuries.

To say all this is not to say that no married couple ever loved each other. The ideal was not so much that love would strike before marriage, as grow after it. But even then we are talking about a love of companionship and esteem. A woman in 16th-century England and before was usually a companion and partner to her husband, helping to manage his estates, his business or working alongside him in the fields. By the Victorian period, it became fashionable to prove that you were wealthy enough to manage without a working wife, and women became delicate, decorative, and married because of "love" rather than utility, a debilitating and weakening state of affairs for a woman because it deprived her of an equality that she had gained as a practical partner to her husband.

The second point that has emerged is that marriage was seen as something essentially secular. It may have been a sacrament, but the wedding was not usually celebrated in Church. The "sacred" character of Western marriage is a relatively new phenomenon, whether we mean a "secular" or a conventionally religious "holiness." Héloïse did not see marriage as being valuable religiously; she has absorbed too well the teaching of the Fathers whom she quotes to Abelard. If the Reformers tried to build marriage up as an ideal, this did not mean that Protestants regarded marriage in a religious light. Luther denied that marriage was a sacrament. It is a purely secular matter for him, a business arrangement, something that is essential to a healthy life like food, clothing, house and land, which may be necessary to men but is not holy in itself. It is, he insists, for the state to decide what does or does not constitute a legal marriage, and the Church has no rights at the wedding; it can only enter the "ceremony" if invited. Marriage does have its Christian aspects, but only because the couple are Christians, living, in other respects, a fully Christian life. Later, too, the Puritans would also see marriage as a secular affair with no religious connotations. All this might seem quite healthy. After all, it meant that the Churches, whose influence on the lives of ordinary people could be rather disastrous, were being encouraged to leave married people alone. Apart from the Roman Catholic Church's concern to try and limit the sex lives of married couples to a near-celibacy, she was quite content to leave the marriage laws in an extraordinary disarray. In the 9th and the 13th centuries the Church did try to discourage illegitimacy and polygamy by making laws about inheritance, but it seems unlikely that this legislation had much effect. What did and what did not constitute a legal marriage was never defined very clearly, and by the beginning of the 17th century in England, the marriage laws were in great confusion. Desertion and polygamy seem to have been rife, and fidelity backed up by no really effective secular coercion. It was the Puritans who instituted proper legislation about marriage and who began a Registry for Births, Marriages and Deaths which was effective, even though this was a secular activity. Until this point it seems, from the scanty evidence available, that ordinary people regarded their marital arrangements as their own affair and of little interest to the governing authorities.

For marriage to be considered a simply secular affair may, in our more secular society, seem no very great disability, but in an Age of Faith like the Middle Ages, where there was nothing that was entirely secular, such an attitude meant that marriage was pushed to the sidelines of life. Luther's attitude about the essentially secular nature of marriage again degraded it as a Christian vocation in an age of extreme religious fervor, and in a theocracy, like the Puritan State in New England, a secular concept of marriage meant that the sex lives of ordinary people were not seen as having any real religious value. Luther and Calvin stamped the Augustinian neurosis firmly on Protestantism, and in such a climate of sexual distrust marriage was unlikely to be seen as something "sacred." One might, as Luther declared, be propelled toward marriage inexorably by the force of one's uncontrollable lust and concupiscence, but this did not make marriage holy for him. He did abolish the celibacy ideal, but this was simply because he felt that celibacy was impossible because of man's uncontrollable lust. It is a very negative view of marriage: it is not a vocation that is lovingly chosen—rather, there is no escape from it. To Wolfgang Ressenbusch, who was dithering about whether to get married or not, Luther wrote that he had absolutely no choice in the matter, so he should stop agonizing:

> It must, should and will happen in any case. Stop thinking about it and go to it right merrily. Your body demands it. God wills it and drives you to it. There is nothing you can do about it.

For Luther with his extremely negative views about sex all marriage can do is be "a hospital for sick people." Celibacy, he knew, could lead to a breed of very "peculiar" people, and all Christian marriage can hope to achieve is to provide a remedy for a man's dangerous sexuality so that "God winks at it." The baptism of marriage does not happen with Luther, although his denigration of celibacy as a superior state is one move toward the acceptance of marriage as a worthwhile step in the Christian mind.

With Calvin we are very much nearer to the Christianization of marriage as an integral part of the Christian life. Calvin is the first Christian theologian to speak really well of women, even though he distrusts sexual pleasure as Christians had always done, and he still maintains that celibacy is a higher state than marriage. Marriage in Calvin's view was not created by God simply for procreation but to provide man with a necessary companion. Without women, men are incomplete—something entirely new to the Christian view of the creation of woman. Slowly, other Anglican and Reforming divines would pursue this ideal of companionate marriage. Thus William Tyndale would be horribly traditional in his view of marriage as beneficial for the woman because it could "control her lusts and wanton appetites," and yet he does allow the wife to have an important Christian role in the family, equal to her husband's. She may, in certain cases of necessity, baptize, preach and administer the Lord's supper. Admittedly these cases of necessity are few and far between, but in principle woman is seen as a companion to man here. The famous divine Jeremy Taylor says that marriage was the best of friendships, "a union of all things excellent." The husband should be "paternal and friendly, not magisterial or despotic," though the wife had to be duly subservient to this friendly father figure. Sex must not be immoderate in Taylor's view, but one of its purposes was certainly "to endear each other." Slowly, in however qualified a manner, a woman is beginning to be seen as a companionable, if still submissive, presence in the life of man and a force for good in his life, with a few intimations of equality about her.

However, we must not take these intimations too seriously. This new Protestant ideal of the companionate wife was not the force which has propelled Western women in our century to demand independence and equality. The Protestants may have begun to baptize marriage, which was the way of life for the vast majority of Christian women, but this ideal of togetherness went strongly against the whole Christian tradition. Just as the apparently positive imagery of the Church as female actually wrote dependency and inferiority into the female position, so too were the old Christian neurotic habits of alienation and sexual hatred written into the beginnings of the theology of marriage. It was absolutely right and good that the vocation of most women was now creeping into a central and positive place in the Christian life instead of being accorded a place on the sidelines, but the Reformation was not an unmixed blessing for women. Calvin's praise of woman as a complement to man instead of an evil influence did not make him in practice any different from the Catholics. Geneva was a very male state indeed, and women were definitely accorded a subordinate place in the Calvinist world, separate from the male world of affairs. Of the Reformers, it is Luther who most forcibly makes women lonely outcasts, ostracized from the world of men in a "Christian" marriage. For Luther, far from giving dignity to women by promoting marriage as obligatory, sees marriage as a woman's punishment:

> This punishment too springs from original sin; and the woman bears it just as unwillingly as she bears those pains and inconveniences which have been placed upon her flesh. The rule remains with the husband, and the wife is compelled to obey him

by God's command. He rules the home and the state, wages
war, defends his possessions, tills the soil, builds, plants, etc.
The woman, on the other hand, is like a nail driven into a wall.
She sits at home . . . the wife should stay at home and look
after the affairs of the household as one who has been deprived
of the ability of administering those affairs that are outside and
concern the state. . . . In this way Eve is punished.

*(Lectures on Genesis,* 3, 16)

Nothing has changed. Luther may have quarreled doctrinally with
Rome, but we have frequently seen how the tradition of the Christian
neurosis is unaffected by intellectual dogmatic difference. A woman
is still Eve. She still has to be banished to a world apart from men.
The extraordinary image of a woman as a nail driven into the wall is
revealing. She is helpless, driven, hammered into her role of wife and
mother, not lured or wooed into a cosy marital intimacy. There *is* no
intimacy. She and her husband inhabit separate worlds. She is kept a
prisoner at home in a state of deprivation, while her husband engages
in the great world outside. At the very beginning of the history of
"Christian" marriage, therefore, there is no love, no equality and no
togetherness for men and women.

However, it took a while for the sexual neurosis to "take" in Europe under Catholicism. It would also take a while for the Protestants to Christianize marriage in the West, which had for so long
been kept as a purely inferior and secular vocation, outside the mainstream of life. Historians of the family, like Ralph Houlbrooke,
maintain that the religious world of Europe did not affect the lives of
ordinary married people. Neither Catholics nor Protestants saw marriage as a truly religious affair, but the Protestants, particularly the
Puritans, were efficient proselytizers and by the 19th century would,
disastrously, have succeeded in impressing the Christian neurosis
onto married life—the Victorian neurosis that still affects us today.
We have seen that as far back as the New Testament there was a
conflict about the role of women in marriage. Was she to be equal to
her husband in all respects, as Paul and Jesus said, or was she to be
dependent and consider herself as an inferior partner as the later
New Testament writers had insisted? What was to be the role of sex
in marriage? How would married people, now that marriage was

being Christianized, be able to square traditional Christian misogyny and the new ideal of married love? These questions would not receive their final unfortunate answer until the Victorian period, but previous Protestant generations had wrestled with these problems and attempted answers.

In the first place, it could be said that Protestant promotion and control of marriage was a bad thing for women, even though it tried to come to terms with the lot of most women and rescue them from the irrelevant margins of the Christian life. It is true that under Catholicism women had had a very bad deal and that most women had no choice about their vocation. The virginal career was only for the wealthy few. Nevertheless, the cult of virginity had provided women with images of female autonomy and independence, and women knew that members of their sex could be powerful beings, superior to men and even feared by them on occasion. The Reformers banned these stories and the cult of the Virgin Mary and the saints, and so took these images away. Christianity became more of a male world than ever. Not only did it deprive the Christian imagination of powerful images and myths and thus made it a cerebral, emotionally impoverished and narrowly masculine affair, on a more basic level the only important people and "gods" now were all men. Also, the communal life of Catholicism with its festivals and feasts, its liturgy and processions had made religion a very sociable affair. Puritan Protestantism took away these public liturgies and made religion a private, internal affair of the heart. The life that had been allowed to women in the community and her own religious involvement was now taken away from them, and in purely religious ways they became deeply dependent upon their husbands. Nailed in her home, the woman was even more isolated than before.

In Catholicism, as in Judaism, women had enjoyed a certain power in controlling the domestic rituals of feasting and fasting, rituals which no longer happened in the Protestant regime. The Catholic woman also had and has a confessor whom she can consult privately, and thus, in theory at least, she has a counter-balance to domestic tyranny. In the Reformed Churches it was the husband who was the guide of her conscience and of her religious life. The Protestant doctrine of the priesthood of all believers made the husband and father of the family a priest in his own home. In a Puritan household it was the father who led the family prayers, a function that had a great emotional impact upon his family: it was he who interceded for them, he who spoke to the Almighty. Husband and wife were no longer kneeling side by side, while a priest, distinct from them both, stood at the altar. It has been said that patriarchal tyranny rises and falls in England with the rise and fall of the practice of family prayers. The father became a bishop in his own house. He could punish his family in the name of God and exact obedience as from God himself. Because Protestantism revived Augustine's pessimistic and terrible doctrines of Original Sin (which in Catholicism were being, slowly, replaced by less frightening theories), the father felt it his duty to flog Original Sin out of his children: Elizabethan England, of course, was a great age of flogging. Also, as the practice of religion became less a matter of evocative and symbolic liturgy and more concentrated on the Word and private Bible study, women became deeply dependent upon their husbands because of the wide educational gap that existed between men and women at this time. Most women were unable to read in Elizabethan England. Only a very few women were educated to as high a level as men during this period. One thinks of Queen Elizabeth herself and, earlier, of Thomas More's daughter, Margaret Roper. This was, however, a privilege offered to a tiny minority. Women and men no longer learned their religion together by joining in the services of Catholicism, where the liturgy and the religious art surrounding them in the Churches and great Cathedrals offered them a religious education. In England, as in the Protestant countries of Europe, it seems that there was a decline in the status of women after the Reformation, and it is difficult to believe that Protestantism is not at least partly responsible for reinforcing a trend of repression of women or even creating it. There was of course the "monstrous regiment of women rulers" like Queen Mary and Queen Elizabeth; a female in power would certainly have had some effect on the consciousness of men and women about the status of women. Yet in fact, despite these powerful and learned women, there is evidence that women were less well thought of after the Protestant Reformation than before it.

The Protestants were very anxious to gain control of the family, since they could see that this was the place to start weaning the ordinary people away from their doctrinal or emotional loyalty to the old faith. There are indications that this took some time, because people were just not used to having their marital arrangements and family lives directed by authority, apart from hearing ceaseless admonitions on the evils of sex and the advantages of abstinence. The new concentration on the Word meant the sermon became more important than ever. Sermons were of course published and read during the somber Protestant sabbaths. Later the Puritan habit of introspection led to the beginnings of autobiography. People would read accounts of the strivings for salvation of prominent Christians. Because many people's conversions were of the "twice-born" variety, there is the usual Christian twice-born inability to come to terms with sexuality, especially the sex that happened prior to "salvation." Thus the young 17th-century Puritan minister Oliver Heywood, who wrote one of the pious journals which became such a vogue, could write this pure Augustinianism:

> Though my parents were saints, yet my birth and my nativity was in sin, and so was my conception, for they were instruments to bring me into the world not as saints but as man and woman. . . . Therefore I am by nature . . . a limb of Satan . . . with propensity to sin.
>
> *(The Diaries of Oliver Heywood,* ed. J. H. Turner, 1883, pp. 153–54)

It is a classic definition of the way Original Sin is passed on. Sex has nothing to do with holiness; his parents created him not as "saints" or as saved people but as man and woman. It is obvious what Heywood would have been telling his parishioners in Yorkshire about the role of sex in their married lives. Furthermore, Heywood thinks about sex in the old Christian way—as something monstrous and uncontrollable. He embraced marriage in the spirit of Luther, not as a matter of conscious choice but out of grim necessity. "My necessities within and without put me on seeking a suitable yoke-fellow" (p. 154), he writes. It is quite clear that one of these inner "necessities" was sex, which in the manner of the twice-born Christian he regarded as evil and irresistible:

> From my childhood and youth my natural constitution exceedingly inclined to lust. . . . Temptations, backed with strong so-

licitations, have been so violent upon me that I look upon it as a miraculous mercy that God hath not left me to stain my profession and be a perpetual blot to myself and friends by some notorious act of prodigious uncleanness.

(p. 168)

It is unlikely that this prim young Puritan was possessed of such a "prodigious" sexuality, but the important thing is that he saw himself as a sexual monster, his appetite held in check only by an unnatural "miracle." The twice-born experience was, of course, extremely common in the Puritan brand of Christianity as it has been in later forms of Protestantism like Methodism. Luther and Calvin were both "converted" by sudden, blinding experiences, and both of them distrusted sexual pleasure and held sex as a concupiscent and irrepressible force against which man was helpless. The anti-sexual neurosis of such "sick souls," an apparently essential part of the twice-born experience, meant that Protestantism provided a very fertile ground for the continuation of the old Christian emotional hatred of sex, despite the "break" with the old Catholic dogma. The tradition of neurosis continued to be passed on in outpourings like Heywood's and in sermons. However, like Luther, the Puritans were realists. Sex had to be held in check and sermons and writings constantly harped on the importance of self-control, even though everybody knew that sex, alas, was a fact of life.

Even writers who, like Tyndale, preach positively about the position of women continue to be wary of sex. It is also true that whatever the Protestant preacher might have to say that is positive about the companionship of men and women, the old suspicion of women remains. Women who listened to the sermons and read the pious books would have carried away from them a very clear picture of their dependent and inferior status. Protestantism went back to the Bible, and this didn't just mean the New Testament. Examples from the Old Testament were sought to provide the reformed Christian family with suitable images of family life and proved to be much more fruitful than the New Testament. The holy family of Mary, Joseph and Jesus was a most unusual family because Mary and Joseph never had sex and the child Jesus was divinely conceived. The Puritan and Anglican preachers therefore turned to Abraham, Isaac and Jacob for inspiration. This was not helpful to women, however, as the wives of these Patriarchs seem little better than slaves. Thus William Gouge could write that "the extent of wives' subjection doth stretch very far, even to all things." A husband "in regard to his place and office" was the representative of God, he "beareth the image of God" simply because he was a husband and father, even though he personally might be "the image of the Devil." (See Lawrence Stone, *The Family, Sex and Marriage in England, 1500–1800*, pp. 197–98.)

Woman had been told for centuries that they were the image of Eve. They were sexually insatiable and lured men away from their pure and lofty spiritual selves. They were wicked and powerful. Now, with the stress on a woman as a wife the emphasis shifted away. Woman was not evil, she was just weak and inferior. As Gouge said, this was the direct result of the Fall: "We cannot think that the woman was made before the Fall that the man might rule over her." The Fall meant that she lost her power and independence. Luther had seen her imprisoned in her husband's home as a punishment; Gouge is kinder, but equally damaging. A wife must be subject to her husband for a good reason: "that she who first drew man into sin should now be subject to him, lest by the like womanish weakness she fall again." It was a new twist to the Eve myth. Instead of powerfully leading men to their spiritual doom, the new Protestant Eve is not exactly wicked; she is just so weak and so spiritually enfeebled that she hasn't a hope of salvation unless guided by her husband. The old misogynism remained. Some Anglicans make nice noises about women from time to time, but always women need guidance and correction. From 1562 onward, parsons were ordered to read every Sunday a homily on marriage, which said that:

> . . . the woman is a weak creature not endued with like strength and constancy of mind; therefore they be the sooner disquieted, and they be the more prone to all weak affections and dispositions of mind more than men be; and lighter they be and more vain in their fantasies and opinions.
>
> (Stone, p. 198)

Woman is the "weaker vessel, of a frail heart, inconstant, and with a word soon stirred to wrath." Protestants still continued to burn witches until the end of the 17th century, as the old myth of the evil insatiable woman was far from dead, but alongside it grew this image of woman as deformed, weak and inferior in her very nature. Women accepted this estimate of themselves. Thus even the valiant New England rebel Mrs. Anne Hutchinson admitted "woman's ignorance and weakness of judgement, which in the most knowing women is inferior to the masculine understanding of man" (ibid., p. 199).

Women were now presented as lonely dependents. The nuclear family which causes us such trouble today seems to have been the creation of Protestantism. The extended family of the Mediterranean in the Muslim and Catholic worlds is entirely different. From 1500 to 1700 the family became smaller and more self-contained. The Reformation swept away all the old support practices of Catholicism, which had tided people over crises. Confession, the doctrine of Purgatory, Miraculous Shrines, Novenas, Processions had all kept alive, however spuriously, a feeling of hope and a strong sense of community. Man now stood alone before his maker with his Bible in his hand, deprived of all the old psychological props and collective rituals that Catholicism had provided. There was now only the family, and written into the family was the principle of wifely subordination. In New England the Puritan governments of the 17th century officially denied to women the independence of any religious life at all. Even Cotton Mather, who was sympathetic to women, told them that the best way to avoid errors (to which women are especially prone) was to follow the example of virtuous men. The idea of men learning from women, as Catholics had sat at the feet of women saints, was now anathema. In some of its practices the Protestant Church underlined the doctrine of the inferiority of women. Thus in the Anglican community of Virginia in the 17th century the authorities were faced with a problem that caused a conflict between wifely subordination and heresy. George Walker was a Quaker, and therefore a heretic. Alice, his wife, was an Anglican and should have been considered a more suitable person to instruct and control their children. However, the court that was asked to intervene in this case of female "rebellion" chose to uphold George's authority in his own home, thus seeing patriarchy as more Christian and important than orthodoxy. Protestant women would appear to have lost any ideal of individual dignity and independence that Christianity had offered them.

However, this does not seem to have been the case entirely. It is certainly true that during the 17th and 18th centuries women lost a good deal of power and respect in Europe, and certainly the Church's preaching of wifely dependence and authority did nothing to improve her lot. Yet it has been argued that the real villain in this swift cult of female dependency was not Christianity but Capitalism. The rise of a capitalist economy, Alice Clark has argued in *The Working Life of Women in the Seventeenth Century,* deprived women of many of her traditional powers and areas of authority. By stressing the commercial aspect of landownership and making estate management a male-dominated enterprise, women were denied a real role in family life and were made mere consumers in the bourgeois world of the towns. Whatever Christians may have said before about men and women occupying separate spheres, in practice the average wife and mother had had a strongly productive role and the Churches, both Catholic and Protestant alike, had, until this century, not much concerned themselves with the inferior, and in some sense evil, state of married life. Now an economic change was driving women back from the outside world away from men, depriving her of her productive power and making her a mere dependent with her husband no longer playing an integral part in the life of the home. This new dependency was certainly backed up by Protestant and Counter-Reformation teaching about marriage, but it may well be that as yet the Christian West was still not used to being instructed about marriage by the Christian authorities, and that this dependency change was largely secular. Christian teaching may only have been reinforcing a purely economic change.

It may be that in the 17th century at least, especially in New England, the Christianization of marriage did not make itself felt in the dependency but in the independence of women. The Colonies were a much more favorable environment for women at that time. Women there were not yet affected by Capitalism, as they were desperately needed as workers and the shortage of women meant they were sought after as wives. Puritan Church organization was, we have seen, very patriarchal, and yet Protestantism with its stress on the individual conscience meant that women in fact played a very important role in the life of the community and that in theory they were considered the equals of men. There was a certain conflict, which the fundamentalist, Bible-inspired Puritan community must have seen in the New Testament, where there was a similar disagreement about the woman's role. The preachers there preached patriarchy and wifely submission, as it was found in Ephesians and Colossians, but they were well aware that a woman also had to wrestle with her own salvation: it was no longer possible for her to get by simply by being a member of the Church. The Protestant and Puritan Churches had developed in opposition to establishment Christianity, so what built into their view of religion was a questioning and independent spirit which would be difficult to handle when they themselves became the establishment. This too would affect the position of woman, who had in the old fighting days often been encouraged to "rebel" from establishment before her husband, just as in Elizabethan England Catholic women had been encouraged by the Church to stay true to the Old Faith when their husbands had conformed to the New. That the Puritans of New England, who had been great rebels in the old country, were aware of the conflict in their attitude to women is shown by the remark of the preacher Jonathan Mitchell in Cambridge, Massachusetts, 1671: "Woman," he said, "is lastly (i.e. ultimately) and as *Homo* (or one of mankinde) for God; but nextly and as *Mulier* (in her proper place and sex) for the man" (R. Thompson, *Women in Stuart England and America*, p. 86). Expressed in slightly different terms is the old contradiction that had persisted in the Fathers. As *virgo* a woman had become a man, in their view, but when faced with real viragos they had found it difficult to be consistent.

Women in New England clearly found Puritanism attractive. By the end of the 17th century more women attended the Churches than men. The Church was careful to maintain that a woman could be more spiritually advanced than her man, and this must have given women's self-image a useful boost. Thus a number of women were made Members of the Church of Boston before their husbands. This was not a superficial matter. To be a full Member was to be one of the Elect; it was not a human state but divine, the difference between Heaven and Hell in the next world. If the Church admitted you as one of the Elect, it meant that you were predestined by God for salvation. Thus in Dedham, Massachusetts, in 1637 the Church was electing seven "pillars" of the newly established Church from a shortlist, among whom were Joseph Kingsbury, an important member of the community, and his wife. Joseph was rejected because he was found, when examined, to be "too much addicted to ye world," "stiff and unhumbled" and was finally guilty of "distempered flying out" in his examination. He was rejected not only as a "pillar," as one of the Elect, but was barred from more ordinary Church membership which entailed a loss of citizenship. However, his wife was admitted to Membership among the first intake. She was "a tender harted soule full of feares and temptations but truly breathing after Christ." As Roger Thompson has pointed out in his book *Women in Stuart England and America,* this must have affected the domestic life of the Kingsburys and been to the other women in Dedham a living example of their essential equality and perhaps their individual superiority to their men (pp. 84–86).

New England calls to mind not mere equality but independence and female leadership in the person of Anne Hutchinson. Her example, together with the example of other women who had defied their men in New England, acted as an intoxicant for 17th-century colonial women, as the hostile Edward Johnson writes:

> In the new community of rebels on Rhode Island whither Anne and her family had been exiled there were extremists among whom there were some of the female sexe, who (deeming the Apostle Paul to be too strict in not permitting a woman to preach in the publique Congregation) taught notwithstanding; they have their call to this office from an ardent desire of being famous, especially the grand mistress of them all, who ordinarily prated every Sabbath day, till others, who thirsted after honour in the same way with herself, drew away her Auditors, and then she withdrew herself her husband and her family also, to a more remote place.
>
> (ibid., p. 91)

Puritanism could inspire and revive, even within a climate that did not exalt female celibate autonomy, the myth of the emancipated woman. Its doctrines may not have permitted them the cult of independent women saints, but they did revive against savage male hos-

tility the Christian ideal of the woman who could claim not merely equality but even superiority to the men around her. It was not necessarily the case that these women were rebels. Thus the New England poet Anne Bradstreet, a contemporary of Anne Hutchinson, had originally been shocked when she first arrived in the Colony by the apparent tyranny of the Church there and its determination to enforce belief. Yet this did not hinder her developing her own religious insights, quite separately from the men around her, even when these insights or questionings led her into speculation which the official church would have condemned. Thus in a letter that she left for her children we see a personal search and quest that is entirely independent:

> Many times hath Satan troubled me concerning the verity of the Scriptures, many times by atheism how I could know whether there was a God. I never saw any miracles confirm me, and those which I read of, how did I know but they were feigned? That there is a God my reason would soon tell me by the wondrous works that I see, the vast frame of the heaven and the earth, the order of all things, night and day, summer and winter, spring and autumn, the daily providing for this great household upon the earth, the preserving and directing of all to its proper end. The consideration of these things would with amazement certainly resolve me that there is an Eternal Being. But how should I know He is such a God as I worship in Trinity, and such a Saviour as I rely upon? Though this hath thousands of times been suggested to me, yet God hath helped me over. I have argued thus with myself. That there is a God, I see. If ever this God hath revealed himself, it must be in His word, and this must be it or none. Have I not found that operation by it that no human invention can work upon the soul, hath not judgments befallen divers who have scorned and contemned it, hath it not been preserved through all ages maugre all the heathen tyrants and all of the enemies who have opposed it? Is there any story but that which shows the beginnings of times, and how the world came to be as we see? Do we not know the prophecies in it fulfilled which could not have been so long foretold by any but God Himself?

> When I have got over this block, then have I another put in
> my way, that admit this be the true God whom we worship, and
> that be his word, yet why may not the Popish religion be the
> right? They have the same God, the same Christ, the same
> word. They only enterpret it one way, we another. . . .
>
> (Heimert and Delbanco, pp. 140–41)

She toys with atheism and with Popery with an astonishingly free
and independent spirit of inquiry, in a way which neither her husband nor the Church could have countenanced. Anne Bradstreet was
a very exceptional woman with a good marriage. Her own excellent
mind enjoyed the responsibility that Protestantism and Puritanism
gave to the individual to work out his or her own salvation. Instead
of finding it inhibiting, Anne Bradstreet found it liberating.

The story of Catharine Beecher, another American woman, gives
us some idea of both the difficulties and freedom that Calvinist family life provided for women. Catharine was the eldest daughter of the
New England preacher Lyman Beecher, and in early 1822 she became engaged to a young Yale professor. Dr. Beecher decided it was
time to precipitate in his daughter some kind of religious awakening
before her wedding. In order to be a good wife and mother she had
to be "converted" and see the light for herself. However, his efforts
met with little success. They seemed to have been characterized by
sadistic terrorism that drove Catharine into a state of prostration as
he wrestled with her soul. Thus he wrote to his son Edward:

> Catharine has been sick three days, the first in acute distress. I
> had been addressing her conscience not twenty minutes before.
> She was seized with the most agonizing pain. I hope it will be
> sanctified.
>
> (Hellerstein and Offen, p. 102)

The little session with Catharine's conscience sounds horrific, but
worse was to come. A month later, in May 1822, Catharine's fiancé
was drowned in a shipwreck. Beecher then told his daughter that this
was all her fault. Her fiancé had died because she had not been
converted; he was a martyr to her lack of faith. Catharine expresses
the isolation women have so often felt in a letter to Edward. If it
were not enough that she has lost her fiancé, there is the terrible fact

that "now that I have nowhere to go but to God, the heavens are closed against me and my prayer is shut out." It is not that Catharine was rebelling against her religion or her father. She had not stood out against his terrifying assaults on her conscience out of pride. She wanted to believe, but she could "feel no realising sense of my sinfulness, no love to the Redeemer, nothing but that I am unhappy and need religion." However, need is not belief. The Calvinist born-again Christian has to *feel* that he loves God, *feel* that he is saved, *feel* that he is a terrible sinner. This Catharine could not do. Her father may have beaten her into the ground so that she became ill, but she still could not say that she had "got religion" because she knew that it was not true.

This tenacious clinging to the truth made Catharine proof also against the new assault launched by her father. For nearly a year the Reverend Beecher laid siege to her soul, trying to induce in his daughter a proper sense of her guilt. He called in a Brother Hawkes; he confessed himself at his "wit's end," but still Catharine was unable to lie either to him or to herself:

> I see nothing but the most debasing selfishness and depravity in my heart, and this depravity equally displayed in all the actions of my past life.
>
> But alas! this extenuating feeling blunts the force of conviction. I see that I am guilty, very guilty, but I cannot feel neither can I convince my understanding that *I am totally and utterly without excuse.* . . . . I feel that I am guilty but not as guilty as if I had received a nature pure and uncontaminated. I can not feel this; I never shall, by any mental exertion of my own.
>
> (Ibid., p. 103–4)

If God has given her this sinful nature, Catharine argues to herself and to her brother, then how can she be wholly to blame? She can see that this feeling is "contrary to the whole tenor of the gospel," but she cannot give it up: "But is there not a real difficulty in the subject?" She cannot get beyond this difficulty. "The more I struggle the less guilty I feel," she says desperately. Despite her grief and bereavement, despite her loneliness and alienation from her father, Catharine could not take the easy way out. Finally she writes in February 1823 that she and her father will have to agree to differ.

The difficulty and the guilt consist in this consciousness of inability. The truth to be proved, then, is that, in certain cases, we
must not rely upon our own consciousness, but trust to the
interpretations that are given by fallible men of the Word of
God.

If I say that I can not perceive that emotions of affection are
at the control of the will, you say that, as you understand the
Bible, God does require these things. Now, which is easiest: to
abandon confidence in my own consciousness or in your interpretation of the Bible?

(Ibid., p. 105)

Anne Bradstreet and Catharine Beecher showed that within the
new nuclear family of the Puritan world, a woman could preserve
independence of spirit if great-hearted. The stress Protestantism
placed on individual salvation could force a woman like Catharine to
discover an irreducible reality within herself, and a strong personal
integrity. It is also true that two centuries before Catharine's time,
the women who were burned during the Salem witch hunts behaved
on the whole with considerably more dignity than the men. Yet mere
mention of the witch hunts throws into relief the real hatred that
could flare up in New England Puritanism. Anne Bradstreet had had
a loving marriage, but she lived and pursued her spiritual quest in an
atmosphere of potential misogyny. Anne Hutchinson had certainly
felt its full force and so, two hundred years later, did Catharine
Beecher in the heart of her own family. Anne Hutchinson was supported by her own husband, even though she was condemned by the
men of the Colony. In the witch hunts men were ready to accuse
their own wives in the general hysteria and see them go to their
deaths. Two hundred years later, the struggle that Catharine encountered was more hidden and private. The power she showed was an
internal one. Unlike Anne Bradstreet and Anne Hutchinson, she did
not rebel by breaking into the male worlds of poetic creation and
religious leadership, but rebelled in her own conscience. The position
of women had so declined by the 19th century, even in the New
World of America, that the power enjoyed by these early women
Puritan settlers was no longer open to Victorian women, however
brave. For Catharine even the experience of falling in love and be-

coming engaged to be married is turned, by her father, into a battle. Men and women are still at war, even in the Christian world of love.

The position of women declined still further in the West during the 18th century. In England the rot set in earlier than it did in America. The power that many women had enjoyed during the Civil War and the religious authority that a few women discovered in the Puritan Churches stopped at once with the restoration of the monarchy and the demise of Puritanism. Restoration comedy gives a picture of powerful women, manipulating their men, for example, by dictating very strict terms of marriage. However, there is no evidence at all that women enjoyed such power in reality, and it is far more likely that such scenes were in fact a satire and derived their humor from the real picture of women's helplessness. What is much more true to life is the hatred that subsists between men and women in these plays. The sexes are at war, even when they make "love." Husbands and wives are always in a state of hatred. Women who are mistresses suffer at the hands of their lovers and endure their cruel humiliations, sometimes with witch-like vitriolic revenge and witty, articulate hatred, but sometimes, too, by expressing sheer pain and vulnerability, which cuts through the glittering artificiality of the world of Restoration drama with a gasp of raw reality. The plays of Congreve, Wycherley and Etherege, for all their presentation of powerful women, vibrate with the hatred. Also, for all the apparently "godless" world of these plays, for all their deliberate rejection of Christian values and cult of secular practice, the view of women and their relationship with men is entirely Christian. Even when a society thinks it is rejecting Christianity, it is deeply enslaved by the Christian neurosis. These women are sexually insatiable. A woman will rape a man with her husband in the next room; once initiated she cannot get enough of it; she will use sex to manipulate her husband and humiliate him. There is no such thing as an innocent woman, in Wycherley's view. Even the "country wife" is a shrewd, sexy little vixen, and women will form together in cabals like witches to plot against their men.

Neurosis went underground in the more apparently reasonable age of the Enlightenment, only to surface again, violently, during the Victorian period. The explosion of sexual fear and hatred that erupted during the 19th century, especially in England and in Eastern America, produced, as an essential part of the neurotic package, the old neurosis about women. Because in the anti-Catholic environment of England at that time a revival of celibacy was impossible, the virginity myth was revived in a more submerged form. Women, like the Virgin Mary, became virgin wives and mothers. Marriage in fact depended on the existence of prostitutes, and brothels mushroomed in Victorian London. The myth of the evil woman actually supported the myth of the Angel Wife, just as in reality a man could resort to prostitutes and mistresses and save his wife from too many onslaughts of his foul lust. The good woman had to be a sexless one. Other more intrepid Victorian virgins revived the old virago myth and felt a new freedom and independence, but in general the Protestant climate succeeded in enforcing the notion of dependency very successfully. For the last two centuries Christian preachers had been urging the notion of the compliant woman, and now the ideal really took root, despite the independence and equality written into Protestantism. Thus the Evangelical writer Elisabeth Sandford could write in her treatise *Woman in her Social and Domestic Character:*

> . . . there is something Unfeminine in independence. It is contrary to Nature and therefore it offends. A really sensible women feels her dependence; she does what she can, but she is conscious of her inferiority and therefore grateful for support. . . . In everything women should show their consciousness of dependence.

The Evangelical writer Hannah More also urged this ideal on her fellow women: "Women in this respect are something like children," she wrote, "the more they show their need of support the more engaging they are." Where for centuries the notion of the independent virgin, who had retired from the world of men into a female autonomy, had been pressed on the West, and was being tentatively expressed by women like George Eliot and Florence Nightingale, the ideal virgin in the neurotic atmosphere of Victorian England was now a wife. Locked up in her home, and pressed by unrealistic myths of female perfection into a marginal position in society, women found that their world had truly shrunk. Alongside the old myths of virginity, the other faces of Eve reappeared obediently as an essential part of the complex neurosis. Coventry Patmore's "Angel in the House" is a familiar figure:

> A rapture of submission lifts
> Her life into celestial rest;
> There's nothing left of what she was;
> Back to the babe the woman dies,
> And all the wisdom that she has
> Is to love him for being wise.

Patmore was a Catholic, so it is hardly surprising that he should speak of the new Virgin-Angel in terms of the old Catholic saints. Yet despite the violently anti-Catholic feeling in England at the time, the poem was immensely popular. The Angel in the House is a mystic. Her rapture, however, is no longer absorption in God, but submission to a man. She dies to herself, regressing back into infantilism, but this new mortification is again directed not to God but to her husband. The new ascetic has an indomitable will, like the ascetics of old, but "Her will's indomitably bent On mere submissiveness to him." The world of women has contracted alarmingly. Her rapture, her martyrdom is now entirely for her husband. As the famous Unitarian Harriet Martineau said: "The sum and substance of female education is training women to consider marriage as the sole object in life, and to pretend that they do not think so." The Victorian writer Anne Richlieu Lamb in her book *Can Women Regenerate Society?* made the same complaint, and showed the fundamental impossibility of a woman's life:

> Treated at one moment as a child, at another as a plaything, if fair as an angel—for a while! Then wearied of, as the child, thrown away as the toy, and beauty varnished, stript of her angelic splendour and forced to tread the miry paths of life in the way she best can. Such is woman now: trained from childhood to believe that for man and for man alone she must live, that marriage must be not only her highest, but her only aim on earth, as in it is comprised the whole of her destiny.
>
> (p. 13)

Clement Scott's song, which was so frequently sung at American weddings in the late 19th century, shows that marriage was a wom-

an's destiny not only in this life, but that it is almost the Beatific
Vision of God: women have again been isolated from men and put on
a superhuman pedestal. Beatrice showed Dante paradise, but he had
never had the chance of being married to her, and so disillusioned.
The wife is the new Beatrice:

> Oh promise me that some day you and I
> Will take our love together to some sky
> Where we can be alone and faith renew
> And find the hollows where these flowers grew,
> Those first sweet violets of early spring,
> Which comes in whispers, thrill us both and sing
> Of love unspeakable that is to be;
> Oh promise me! oh promise me!
>
> Oh promise me that you will take my hand,
> The most unworthy in this lowly land,
> And let me sit beside you, in your eyes
> Seeing the vision of our paradise;
> Hearing God's message while the organ rolls
> Its mighty music to our very souls
> No love less perfect than a life with thee
> Oh promise me! oh promise me!

Marriage has been transformed into an earthly paradise; expectations
are raised for both men and women that cannot possibly be fulfilled.
For women particularly, as marriage is her only world, this is cata-
strophic. God has faded away, but she has still to fulfill all the old
religious duties. She has to be a mystic, whose special and spiritual
perceptions are a guide to her husband, and yet she is to allow herself
to be guided directly and absolutely by him. She is to deny herself
sexual pleasure. She will always be virginal, because she is incapable
of real penetration. She will always remain aloof from the man with
his dark, bestial urges which he cannot control. And yet she has to
endure sex without pleasure and as virgin-mother bear as many children as possible. She is a martyr because she has to die to herself
daily, and is not allowed to achieve a personal fulfillment, but to
serve and love her husband. It was a life that was impossible, and

that mutilated women as much as the old images of alienation and hostility had ever done.

It was inevitable that, given such a brief, women would suffer. The 18th-century woman had been robust and healthy. In an age of relative sexual and domestic freedom she had flourished. Nailed back into the home, however, Victorian women became delicate. Partly this was because to have a delicate wife was socially *chic*. However, the frequent "declines" into which women fell were genuine enough, if psychosomatic. An anonymous woman author of a book called *The English Matron,* which was published in 1846, writes of the sufferings of women: "How many suffer, or say they suffer from debility, headaches, dyspepsia, a tendency to colds, eternal sore throats, rheumatic attacks and the whole list of polite complaints." Yet she concludes that "the two prevailing diseases among females in this country are hypochondriasis and hysteria" (p. 133).

By the Victorian period there was the worst of all Christian worlds. The old sex fear was back in full flood, and women had lost the autonomy that they had once possessed, if only ideally. The man and the woman marry for love but in fact this "love" is shot through with hatred. Even the ideal Angel in the House is seen as an inimical figure in Patmore's poem: This "child" of a woman, who "prattles like a child at play," has actually an iron determination under her soft exterior:

> And evermore, for either's sake,
>     To the sweet folly of the dove,
> She joins the cunning of the snake,
>     To rivet and exalt his love;
> Her mode of candour is deceit;
>     And what she thinks from what she'll say,
> (Altho' I'll never call her cheat,)
>     Lies far as Scotland from Cathay.
> Without his knowledge he was won;
>     Against his nature kept devout;
> She'll never tell him how 'twas done
>     And he will never find it out.
> If, sudden, he suspects her wiles,
>     And hears her forging chain and trap

> And looks, she sits in simple smiles,
>     Her two hands lying on her lap.
> Her secret (privilege of the Bond,
>     Whose Fancy is of either sex),
> Is mine; but let the darkness guard
>     Mysteries that light would more perplex.

The hostility that exists beneath the surface of this ideal of married "love" is extraordinary. A woman is seen as an amoral manipulative little liar. She may "exalt" a man by her love, but at the same time she "rivets" him against his will, forging a chain of slavery. Although she is wreathed in demure "simple smiles," the woman is still Eve, even while she is an angel. The "cunning of the snake" attracts her just as much as it attracted the mother of all the living. She is still trapping man by her wiles; powerful in weakness, she still seduces him, if not sexually, but "against his nature" and without his knowledge. Man is the prisoner of his beloved wife, trapped by a creature he doesn't want to understand. The success of Patmore's poem shows that he struck a deep feeling in England at the time, and that for all its idealization of married love, men and women hated one another as much as ever. The only difference is that now they cannot even express this hatred openly, but have, helplessly, to call it "love." Throughout Christian history men had thought of women as deformed monsters. The Angel in the House is also a moral monster:

> If none but her dear despot hears,
>     She prattles like a child at play.
> Perchance, when all her praise is said,
>     He tells the news, a battle won,
> On either side ten thousand dead.
>     "Alas!" she says: but, if 'twere known,
> She thinks, "He's looking on my face!"

Unfortunately, the Angel in the House is still a familiar figure. We all know these cunning little kittens whose narrow outlook dooms them to appalling triviality. The interesting thing here is that this was precisely the Victorian ideal. Women were creatures that men loved —and still love—to hate. She is still Eve, the enemy of man.

Beneath this idealization of women and blissful married life there was therefore great unhappiness. In America this unhappiness surfaced in the explosion of sects and experiments that rejected the traditional notion of the Puritan nuclear family. Either these groups rejected sex and marriage completely, like the Shakers or the Amana Inspirationists, or they experimented with communal living and free love, as did the Oneida Perfectionists, who did away entirely with the normal sex roles and tried to live lives of total sexual equality. There were no permanent sex bonds at Oneida, and each member of the group could, in theory, have sex with any other member. It was seen not as sexual license but as freedom from possessive selfishness. Noyes, the founder of the group, devised a means of sexuality which inhibited ejaculation, which not only acted as a desirable contraceptive but which was reminiscent of the sexual practices of Tantric Buddhism, where ejaculation is withheld to enable the adept to transcend himself. The Oneida group enjoyed considerable success, and again we have to see that the unhappiness and frustration with traditional marriage must have been great in America at the time if so many men and women were willing to embrace communal lives which were such a challenge to all their conditioned responses. The Mormons also revolutionized conventional marriage patterns, and the fact that men and women were not only ready to accept polygamy but were also ready to follow Brigham Young on the perilous migration to Utah speaks volumes for the growing dissatisfaction with the Christian family.

In both the Oneida and the Mormon experiments, women flourished. It is easier to understand that women would thrive in the liberating atmosphere of Oneida, where women were allowed to do traditionally male work as well as experiment with sexual freedom. The Mormon system of polygamy certainly produced traumas of jealousy in some women, and most women found the whole idea, when Joseph Smith originally introduced it, deeply shocking. However, some women did find it liberating. One woman state senator put it this way: "A plural wife isn't half as much a slave as a single wife. If her husband has four wives, she has three weeks of freedom every single month" (A. de Riencourt, p. 324). The traveler Richard Burton claimed that:

. . . incredible as the statement may appear, rival wives do dwell together [in Utah] in amity. . . . They know that nine-tenths of the miseries of the poor in large cities arise from early and imprudent marriages, and they would rather be the fiftieth "sealing" of Dives than the toiling single wife of Lazarus.

*(The City of the Saints,* London, 1963, p. 483)

Mormon leaders like James Strang, who had at first bitterly opposed polygamy, justified the system by claiming that it benefited women: monogamy claimed to give women freedom in choosing their mate, but in fact the pressures of the marriage market meant that in practice a woman often had to take any man she could get. This meant that strong and talented women often found themselves bound to puerile men who are inferior to them in every way. Polygamy, he claimed, gave women a better choice. Mormon women certainly felt that they were the equals and friends of their husbands in a way that the conventional American woman of the period did not. It was not only that the frontier conditions in Utah and the long absences of the husbands on preaching expeditions gave the women more power and freedom, but also that the polygamous system undercut romantic love for men as well as for women. The sheer mechanics of the large household where there were several wives made the expression of romantic love impractical, but even more simply the "harem" completely destroyed the idea that everybody had One True Love, which is the essence of the mythology of romantic love. This freed women from the masochistic rituals and absurd idealizations that existed elsewhere in the 19th century. The Mormon women were also advised not to allow themselves to become emotionally dependent upon their husbands, because otherwise the polygamous life was impossible. Even though Salt Lake City was clearly a male world and the men got the best of the bargain (women were not allowed to have several husbands), it did prove to be liberating for many of the Mormon plural wives. Certainly the fact that Utah granted suffrage to women in its first state constitution and that there were more professional women in Utah at the end of the 19th century than almost any other state says a good deal for the confidence and the autonomy that Mormonism gave to its women.

The new cult of loving togetherness then was fraught with difficulties, as it cut across the habits of centuries. Constantly we find old neuroses cropping up in marriages that are quintessentially Christian. Sex, which is still often a problem in secular marriages, remained very problematic in religious marriages. We can see this with the many people who joined celibate movements like the Shakers and Amana groups. The 18th-century Boston preacher Cotton Mather, who was obviously a highly sexed man, became deeply worried about his sexual life with his wife at the end of his life. Mather was married three times and had fifteen children. His intimate diary shows no worries about married sex, but only fear of extramarital sex and the strongly felt need to replace one wife with another very quickly to inoculate himself against temptation. However, later in his life he became very worried that he was enjoying sex too much. Both Protestants and Catholics were fond of quoting Jerome's remark that to make love to your wife with too much pleasure (so that you would still want her even if she were *not* your wife) was adultery. Mather had picked up a very old neurosis, even though he clearly thought that marriage itself was "holy." A "holy" pair who have been presented in the Catholic Church as the example of what a Christian marriage should be were the 19th-century French couple Louis and Zélie Martin, the parents of St. Thérèse of Lisieux. This happy pair hated sex so much that after their wedding they did not consummate their marriage for ten months and had every intention of remaining perpetually celibate in imitation of the Holy Family. However, they were persuaded by a priest to do their marriage "duty" and produced many children, of whom five girls survived. Despite her frequent rhapsodies about the joys of family life and motherhood, Zélie was constantly bemoaning the fact that she had not been able to be a nun, and was always longing for the cloister. Both she and Louis had applied to religious orders and been rejected. Marriage was for both of them only second best. Zélie always claimed that her wedding day was the unhappiest day of her life: "I cried as I have never cried in my life and was never to cry again." She spent the day after the ceremony with her sister, who was a Visitation nun: "I compared my life with hers and the tears flowed more than ever" (S. J. Piat, *The Story of a Family,* p. 38). If she was not allowed to be a nun, she was determined that all her daughters would be. She used to tell her daughters about the superior state of virginity, and when her eldest girl, Marie, stood out against her (refusing, for example, to say the Prayer to St. Joseph that begins "Protector of Virgins"), Zélie began a campaign of retreats and lectures until Marie gave in. All her daughters did become nuns; four were Carmelites and one a Visitation nun. That the Catholic Church has constantly pushed this family story before the faithful as an example of what a Christian family should be shows that things haven't changed much.

The Martin home was filled with "love," which was expressed with all the cloying sentimentality of the late 19th century. They loved God and Jesus, but also loved one another with great emotional fanfares. Yet this model family could also be unbelievably unkind, even cruel. Zélie clearly disliked her third daughter, Léonie, who was neither as healthy, pretty or as intelligent as her sisters. She constantly slighted Léonie, and taught her other daughters to do the same. When the sister of Zélie who was a Visitation nun was dying, Zélie wrote this to her:

> As soon as you are in Paradise, go and find Our Lady and tell her: "My good Mother, you played a trick on my sister when you gave her that poor Léonie; that was not the sort of child she asked you for, and you must mend the matter. Then you are to go and find Blessed Margaret Mary, and say to her: Why did you cure her miraculously? It would have been better to have let her die: you are bound in conscience to remedy the evil.*

(Ibid., p. 205)

That the good Fr. Piat, who has written the fullest account of the edifying family life of the Martins, can print this without ever thinking that something was wrong with this loving home speaks volumes for the way Christian love is so often and so acceptingly seen to coexist closely with cruelty. Zélie was not joking; she meant every word of this. Her letters are full of complaints about Léonie, who "could never be a credit" to her like her other children. Today Léonie would be sniffing glue or shoplifting. All she could do then was withdraw completely from family life, going off to the kitchen after meals to sit with the servant Louise and haunting Zélie with pathetic pleas for love, which were constantly rejected. Just before Zélie died

---

* Léonie had been cured of a dangerous illness by a novena made to Margaret Mary.

it was discovered that for years Léonie had been engaged in a sado-masochistic relationship with Louise. Nobody had bothered to see what had been going on right in the heart of this loving family.

Throughout this book I have tried to show how easily Christian love can sometimes become hatred. The love of a good woman, whether the woman was the *Domna* of the Troubadours or the Victorian Angel, could become in some cases an act of alienation. It is not simply in the relationships between men and women that Christian love explodes easily into Christian hatred in the West. The Christian ideal of love is very difficult, even impossible. How can one love one's enemies without them stopping, ipso facto, being enemies at all? Yet love is the most important of the Christian commandments and the essence of the Christian life. The neurotic suppressions of the West have meant that this love usually expresses itself more by a banding together against outsiders than in positive warmth which radiates outward to the "enemy" outside. Thus Lawrence Stone has pointed out the violent tenor of 16th- and 17th-century life where one's "friends" were not one's dearly loved companions but simply one's controllers and financial backers, as the word is used at that time. The most clear example of the hatred that surrounds Christian love was of course the phenomenon of the Crusades. Popes and saints preached the idea of Crusade as an act of the love of God *and* love of neighbor. Yet they resulted in the violent slaughter not only of infidel Moslems and Jews in thousands, but also of the massacre of fellow Christians in Byzantium and Syria. The fears and insecurities that Christianity has so often imposed on the West can only erupt irrationally and violently, and hatred is never very far away from "perfect love."

It should not then be surprising that the enemy woman comes in for similar hatred, even within the confines of what is supposed to be a "loving" marriage. The historian of the English Family, Ralph Houlbrooke, says that very few families seem to have been happy in the period 1400 to 1800. Certainly in our own day marital unhappiness is a constant and very familiar phenomenon. The battered wife is an obvious example, but in the West, especially the Protestant West, there is a real tendency to make an enemy of the wife. In Cockney rhyming slang "wife" is translated "trouble and strife." The nagging and tyrannical wife is a constant stereotype, and while she made a figure of fun in soap opera and sit. com., the fun is edged with real male hostility. The stag night, where a prospective groom indulges in an all-male orgy of freedom, still celebrates the male feeling that in marriage one is abandoning one's real friends (men) and getting sucked in by the enemy. Similarly, the bored and weary way men traditionally talk about "the wife," and are encouraged to do so, shows that no matter how much money has been spent on a romantic, orange-blossom, Christian-style wedding, the reality is, more often than not, a state of war. Men and women have been urged for too long to keep away from one another in our culture to sink easily into cosy loving intimacy within a marriage. It is interesting that the ideal of Christian marriage really "took" in the 19th century at a time when the hold of Christianity was beginning to be loosened and science and technology were suggesting a different world-view. Women at that time were alienated and ostracized by being identified with goodness and with a religion that their men were leaving behind them. In an Age of Faith marriage was considered secular and religiously irrelevant, even religiously unworthy. In the Age of Doubt it is made a sacred reality and the wedding at last begins to come into its own. Always marriage in the West has been outside the main preoccupations of the period, a marginal activity. Whatever lip service had been paid throughout the Christian centuries to marriage as a sacrament, it was only truly Christianized through and through, emotionally drawn into the main mythology of Christendom, when Christianity was beginning for the first time to be seriously doubted. Just as women were made to stand in for a religion that men like the great Victorian Leslie Stephen had outgrown, and damaged by having an impossible idealism imposed upon them, so too the ideal of married love is tacitly regarded as an impossibility by being invested with the trappings of a religion which more and more people in our culture were rejecting. The reality, in the Victorian period as now, is that women and men have traditionally felt marriage to be a battleground in the Christian West.

The "formal" wedding today often looks as though the marriage myth is no longer seriously believed in. In our age which idealizes simplicity and informality and which feels that extravagance is no longer merely unwise financially but morally wrong in view of the starving millions, the expensive wedding with everybody dressed up to the nines and processing to a Church they never otherwise visit is right outside the real ideology of our time. People even look as though they are in fancy dress: the bride, virgin or not, is in an incredible confection of white with a veil and style of dress that bears no relation to her normal clothes. The dress usually costs a fortune and can never be worn again because it is so obviously a wedding dress and would be totally unsuitable for any occasion that the bride might attend in her normal life. The men have often had to hire Morning Dress, which often smells subtly of moth balls because the suit has been unworn for so long. It is not uncommon for the main participants—the happy pair and their families who are footing the bill—to find the whole affair to be an extremely traumatic occasion. Nerves run high with the strain of it all. And yet the large formal wedding continues to be chosen as the way that married people commit themselves to one another. While the divorce rate rises and the validity of marriage is more and more questioned, the formal wedding gets bigger and bigger. In our century, which has been more secular than any other, the Wedding Myth has reached a crescendo. The marriage of H.R.H. Prince Charles and Princess Diana was arguably the biggest national event we have had in Britain for decades. In the United States, which has deliberately eschewed monarchy, thousands of people sat up all night to watch the ceremony on television. The Archbishop of Canterbury said that the wedding and affair was a "fairy tale." He made a point that was truer than he realized. Just as the fairy-tale world expresses dreams that we *know* cannot be fulfilled but which we continue to repeat as some kind of compensation for unsatisfactory reality, so too do we cling to the cult of the wedding ever more firmly, making it ever more extravagantly deny the realities and values of our life not only as compensation but, with the logic of the fairy tale, perhaps, to try and "magic" the reality into being by celebrating the ideal. The zeal with which the press pounced, shortly after The Wedding, on signs of marital discord between Charles and Di and on Di's possible anorexia and frequent bad temper show that however much they may have raved on the day about Royal Romance, both they and their public were only too well aware of the difficulties that marriage brings to any couple, royal or not.

The media too, which did The Wedding so proud, also present

weekly for our delectation sagas of marital strife and disharmony in the series *Dynasty* and *Dallas.* Both present the family as solid and united against outsiders (in the tradition of Christian love), but really the families seethe with hostility. In *Dynasty* the women tend to be glamorous and castrating witches. They are the powerful ones. Most of them have little clout outside the family—with the grand exception of Alexis—but within it they do pretty much what they want, and know how to manipulate and control their men. Even the soft-spoken, breathy Krystle gets her point across pretty sharply when she wants to. In *Dallas,* on the other hand, women are seen as family victims. The power resides with J.R. and the male world. Women are powerless martyrs, endlessly suffering helplessly and passively, their lives rarely extending beyond the confines of the home. In a recent episode one woman was in prison, another a chronic case in a mental hospital, another deserted by her husband and pregnant, another pining for love of her husband who has rejected her, another cruelly ignored by the man who had just married her, and Sue Ellen, as usual, driven by J.R.'s manipulations to drink and alcoholic misery. The enormous popularity of *Dallas* does not show a very good picture of marriage outside the Ewing ranch. It means that women must recognize in this picture of female family suffering something that they can identify with and that men must enjoy seeing women put in their "proper place." In *Dynasty* men are continually turned on by the glamorous and castrating witches whom they can lust after and at the same time justifiably condemn for their evil sexiness, while the women enjoy identifying with the displays of female power.

There is no need to stress the fact that in the West we are increasingly troubled about the future of marriage and the family, and the popularity of *Dallas* and *Dynasty* underline that unease. New pressures like the growing equality and independence of women have been added to the old stresses and strains of married life, when it was definitely seen to have an inferior status in society. The same insecurity that made Abelard hide his marriage from the world is evident today in the doubletalk going on about marriage. On the one hand, it is still extolled as the only healthy way of life, while on the other the vocabulary of married or monogamous "relationships" is hostile, bearing very little resemblance to the "caring" ideal of nurturing love. Rosalind Coward shows this in her essay "What Is This Thing Between Us?":

> The language of the emotions bears startling resemblance to descriptions of the economic activities of the capitalist system. It describes losses, gains, outlays, investments and returns. And it is, in essence, aggressive. Take the very goal of a *committed* relationship. The ultimate goal is *security* and *trust,* two specifically capitalist modes of holding property. The greatest disaster for a relationship is *loss,* a *wasted* effort. We talk of *commitments* to one another; we take *risks* that don't *pay off;* we seek *assurance* from one another. If we are fortunate we have a *rewarding* relationship. Personal behaviour too is described in these terms. Protagonists are accused of being *possessive* or *dependent,* and are praised for being *self-sufficient.*
> This is the language of economic competition and survival. Implicitly, it refers to the issue of who will support whom, who is dependent upon whom, who owns the other person. It speaks of a desire to profit from experience, of a desire to have material gains, and of the economic base line of sexual relations. The aggression implicit in the language is obvious. It speaks of a system where dog eats dog and only a few succeed. But the aggression implied here is mild compared with the other great metaphor for emotional life, that of warfare. Protagonists in a relationship can be described as *triumphant victorious,* or *defeated.* We talk of *peaceful* or *destructive* or *devastating* experiences. We talk of people *surrendering,* or *resisting* or behaving *defensively.* Relationships are described as being *dangerous* or *explosive. Reconciliations* or *truces* are sometimes achieved between *warring* forces. And if that happens we call ourselves *survivors.*
>
> *(Female Desire,* p. 128)

There is nothing very surprising in the idea of relationships being seen in economic terms. Marriage was always an economic arrangement before Christianity baptized it. However, the aggressive edge should not surprise us either. It is not simply that Coventry Patmore wrote of love in terms of bewildered hostility in "The Angel in the

House" just over a hundred years ago. The coexistence of hatred as the obverse of love is a very old complex in our culture.

Slowly and very late in the Christian West the ideal was evolved of marriage as a union of two loving partners who would cherish one another throughout their lives. The fact that we still feel uncomfortable about love between the sexes institutionalized and made, in secular terms, "holy" is shown not only in the agressive jargon which has sprung up in the rhetoric of relationships recently, but in the very self-conscious ways we speak in jargonese about relationships at all. We analyze and worry and discuss; we take our "problems" to counselors and to psychiatrists. We see the relationship, whether we are talking about marriage or about its secular offspring, the monogamous couple who are "living together," as something problematic. We cannot accept it as simply an institution of our culture. We have to "work at it," be "imaginative" and "seek out new forms." We do indeed. We are not yet used to the ideal of the sexes being loving partners. In our culture they have been enemies, and when we endlessly chew over the "problems" we have in our "relationships" we are constantly using language that acknowledges this subliminally.

Throughout Christian history we have seen that it is separation which has been the dominant motif, not togetherness. Men have pushed women away from them, and women have withdrawn. Women have erected protective defences around themselves to make them invulnerable to male attack. Men and women have wounded and castrated one another. Mutilation has been the motif far more than the loving embrace. We have seen how between the sexes that love has quickly modulated into hatred and sometimes springs from hatred. No matter how firmly we believe that love is an ideal, love has proved to be a double-edged weapon. No matter how much we tell ourselves that we long for married love, we know that the Christian family has often been cruel and neurotic; that love often expresses itself with hatred. We know also that though the sexes want to live together, togetherness is the difficult ideal. It may be that the reality is that the sexes are continuing their long Christian tradition of withdrawing from one another.

# 9

# THE FUTURE: EXODUS?

In 1971 for the first time a woman was invited to preach at the principal Sunday service in Harvard Memorial Chapel. It seemed a breakthrough. Not only was a woman being asked to preach—something which is traditionally seen as a male privilege in Christianity—but a woman was penetrating the ultramale preserve of Harvard University. However, the woman preacher, the feminist Mary Daly, saw the occasion rather differently. Her sermon was a bitter attack on the sexist structures of institutional Christianity. Her solution was the new model that she called "Sisterhood," which stressed the prophetic and healing aspects of the Christian life. Finally Mary Daly ended her sermon with an appeal:

> Sisters: the sisterhood of man cannot happen without a real Exodus. We can this morning demonstrate our exodus from sexist religion . . . we cannot really belong to institutional reli-

gion as it exists. It isn't good enough. . . . Our time has come.
Let us affirm our faith in ourselves and our will to transcendence by rising and walking out together.

She then descended from the pulpit and headed a mass departure
from the Chapel. She has never returned to the Church. As the
Christian feminist Sara Maitland has said, she has become a mystic
in the desert. The occasion had seemed auspicious: a woman was
being invited to enter, however transiently, the male world. Yet the
woman concerned chose to retire into a world of her own. As
Maitland points out, Daly's action is symbolic, but it does nevertheless express a widespread withdrawal by women from mainline
Christianity: "The very existence of women's 'heretical' groups, from
Mary Daly's 'post-Christian feminism' to witches, Mother-Goddess
worship and various pantheistic nature cults is itself a demonstration
that women feel radically disgusted by the Church" (A Map of the
New Country, pp. 139–42).

Men are also making their own Exodus from the Church. The
decision of the General Synod of the Church of England to admit
women to the priesthood has compelled alarming numbers of clergy
and laity to withdraw into more chauvinist churches. Many are going to the Greek Orthodox Church and, still more significantly, to
the Roman Catholic Church. The British have a deeply ingrained
prejudice against Catholicism. Hugh Trevor-Roper, the historian,
suggests that Catholics and the Pope are to the British what Jews are
to Germans or Communists are to Americans. Yet the fear of women
invading the male preserve of the priesthood is strong enough to
impel them into the arms of this ancient enemy. Even if men are not
actually joining the exodus from the Church of England, very many
of them deeply oppose the Synod's decision. The attitude of Christians to this question is interesting. Few male Christians, of whatever
denomination, would be prepared to denounce women as did St.
Jerome or Tertullian, but, however incoherently, they share the same
essential misogyny. In the West today women have invaded the male
world. They attend universities, even traditionally male preserves
like Harvard or the Oxbridge colleges, which were formerly for men
only. Women are members of Parliament. In Britain there is even a
woman Prime Minister. It is also against the Law in England to

exclude women from jobs on the grounds of sex. It is generally recognized that women are as intellectually capable as men and that the old prejudices that excluded women from certain professions were ill-founded. Yet in the midst of this widespread social change, women are still denied entry to the priesthood in some churches and encounter huge opposition in those to which they are admitted. The ingrained Christian prejudice against women is deep indeed.

Throughout this book we have seen the gradual Christian creation that led to this neurotic shunning of the female. Women were urged to withdraw, and were only too glad to retreat from this hostility if they got the chance. The women's novel shows that for a long time women have continued this tradition in quite secular ways, seeing women as seeking liberation by withdrawing into a room of their own. Olive Schreiner presents such a retreat in her novel *From Man to Man*. The heroine Rebekah retires from the frustrations of her marriage into an extraordinary little room that is rigged up in her children's bedroom:

> The room was a small one, made by cutting off the end of the children's bedroom with a partition. She had had it before as a study for herself where she could always hear the children call if they needed her at night. It was hardly larger than a closet, but there was a window in it and a small outer door, and both looked out on to the rockery and the plumbago hedge but on nothing else and there was a small door close beside the window which she had put in that at any time she might run out and work a little in the garden.
>
> (London, 1926, p. 171)

This room is certainly womblike, but with its image of the Madonna and its tiny confines it is also reminiscent of a nun's cell. Rebekah retires here to sew, to meditate and to write. It is a place which she can call her own, a symbol of her autonomous self which is as free as she can make it from the demands of the family. Yet the outlook is limited: all she can see is a hedge and a rockery and, Schreiner is careful to tell us, "nothing else." In it Rebekah paces up and down like a prisoner: "On the brown carpet on the floor was a mark like a footpath where the nap had been worn off running right around the desk. This was where she walked round and round, because the room was not large enough for her to allow walking up and down." The icon of the Virgin, the autonomous woman who created a child without being invaded by a man, as well as the meditation that Rebekah performs there show her to be creating, like the contemplative nun, an ambience where she is a prisoner but in some sense free and independent.

Sarah Grand, the feminist novelist, also makes her heroine discover a secret room in *The Beth Book*. Again it is an extraordinary and pathetic place; a woman can only achieve a niche for herself in this world with great difficulty and contortion. Beth has to crawl into it on her hands and knees because it has no proper door. Here she plans to write novels in a search for creative ecstasy like Rebekah's meditation:

> Her mind which had run riot, fancy-fed with languorous dreams in the days when it was unoccupied and undisciplined, came steadily more and more under control and grew gradually stronger as she exercised it. She ceased to rage and worry about her domestic difficulties, ceased to expect her husband to add to her happiness in any way, ceased to sorrow for the slights and neglects that had so wounded and perplexed her . . . and learned by degrees to possess her soul in dignified silence so long as silence was best, feeling in herself *that* something which should bring her up out of all this and set her apart eventually in another sphere, among the elect.
>
> (London, 1980, p. 370)

Beth is exploring her mind in her cell like a mystic, and through this meditation she learns autonomy. She is no longer dependent emotionally upon her husband, but is independent of circumstance and has discovered a personal integrity deep within herself. She sees it as a salvation almost in religious terms. Her ecstasy will rapture her away from the domestic difficulties which engulf her; she will be "among the elect," but in "another sphere." That sphere is entirely feminine. Beth's novels will be For Women Only:

> . . . not for men. I don't care about amusing men. Let them see to their own amusements, they think of nothing else. Men entertain each other with intellectual ingenuities and Art and Style,

while women are busy with the great problems of life and are striving with might and main to make it beautiful.

(Ibid., p. 376)

Beth sees that the only possible liberation is an Exodus from the world of men. Like Mary Daly she sees in Sisterhood creativity and charismatic depth. Mary Daly had seen Sisterhood in terms of the meditative and mystical process of prophecy, and Sarah Grand *(The Beth Book* is an autobiographical novel) also urges this polarization between the aggressively intellectual arrogance and selfishness of men and the nurturing creativity of women. It is a noble vision for women, but is it true? It seems that the room became a symbol for women of peace and vision, whenever they sought refuge from the male world. Thus in *The Tree of Heaven,* May Sinclair's suffragette heroine attends a celebratory banquet in honour of her release from prison. The women's Marseillaise is sung and

> The singing had threatened her when it began; so that she felt again her old terror of the collective soul. Its massed emotion threatened her. She longed for her white-washed prison-cell, for its hardness, its nakedness, its quiet, its visionary peace.

(London, 1917, p. 225)

Again that contradiction that we have noticed before in the suffragettes: when they sought an active place in the male world they sought victimhood, and now they long for retirement and imprisonment. Elaine Showalter has shown how in the 19th century the image of the room of one's own constantly recurs. Even in children's literature it appears in novels like Mrs. Molesworth's *The Tapestry Room* and Frances Hodgson Burnett's *The Secret Garden* and *The Little Princess.*

It is still a potent image for women novelists. Thus Booker prizewinner Anita Brookner's timid and defeated heroines, who are continually excluded from the male world of love and normality, find themselves walled into strange flats that are either sterile and meticulous or gloomy and abnormally ugly and archaic. Doris Lessing's heroines constantly take themselves off to basements or to private rooms that are quite separate from their normal lives to undertake their mystical voyages of self-discovery. From these rooms the only possible exit is by some kind of ecstasy or recovery of the self, by a vision which takes the heroine through the walls of the room or through the barriers of time and space, or finally by death. In her short story *Towards Room 19*, Lessing's heroine in flight from her domestic life takes a hotel room where she can be alone. Her husband thinks she is having an affair, and when it seems that discovery is imminent she goes to her private room and kills herself. Marilyn French's feminist novel *The Women's Room* begins with the heroine retreating from the frightening male world of Harvard into the women's lavatory—the only place she feels at home. It ends with her isolated and alone, set apart even from her women friends, pacing up and down a beach in Maine, muttering madly to herself. Like Lessing's visionary heroines, she seems to have lost touch with reality, because she is in the grip of a vision that puts her quite apart from the normal (male) world. Madness and isolation end the book with an image of a room she dreamed about in a nightmare:

The sky grows icier day by day; it is large and vacant and mindless.

Some days I feel dead, I feel like a robot, treading out time. Some days I feel alive, terribly alive, with hair like wires and a knife in my hand. Once in a while my mind slips and I think I am back in my dream and that I have shut the door, the one without a handle on the inside. I imagine that tomorrow I will be pounding and screaming to be let out, but no one will hear, no one will come. Other times I think I have gone over the line, like Lily, like Val, and can no longer speak anything but truth. An elderly man stopped me the other day as I was walking along the beach, a white-haired man with a nasty face, but he smiled and said, "Nice day, isn't it?" and I glared and snapped at him, "Of course, you have to say that, it's the only day you have!"

He considered that, nodded, and moved on.

Maybe I need a keeper. I don't want them to lock me up and give me electric shock until I forget. Forget: lethe: the opposite of truth.

I have opened all the doors in my head.

> I have opened all the pores in my body.
> But only the tide rolls in.

In women's fiction, then, the picture is a depressing one. The only way a woman is seen to achieve autonomy and self-respect is by withdrawing totally from men into a lonely isolation. Yet this retreat is not the whole picture. If in the Churches men and women seem sometimes to be withdrawing from one another, in the secular world, now that women have managed to break into what were hitherto wholly masculine worlds, there is a new contact between the sexes. By working together men and women are learning to see one another differently, even though the number of women who have complete equality with men in their work is relatively small. By seeing men in a working environment instead of a purely domestic and social one, ... them more fully and men must be learning ... competently ... within marriage ... common for fathers to take a more active ... to help with housework and cooking. In this respect things ... are improving, even though inevitably old prejudices flare up from time to time.

There seems to be one sad legacy that has been bequeathed to us from Christianity that might threaten these promising signs. For centuries the teaching and propaganda put about by Christianity was misogynistic. Men castigated the female sex as evil and dangerous. There is no equivalent for the word misogyny which means hatred of men, though some people have recently taken to using "homophobia." Whatever we choose to call it, this feminist tendency to berate and even hate men is as deeply prejudiced as Christian misogyny ever was. For a long time in our culture the uneasy tension between the sexes led to a hatred which has now spread so that women feel that the way forward to liberation is prejudice and aggression towards men, the enemy. It is true that although Christianity was dedicated to spreading love and compassion between people, all too frequently it spread bitterness, suspicion and hatred. Jesus had told his followers to love their enemies, but Christianity made a virtue out of creating enemies—first outsiders like Jews and Moslems, and then other Christians. The Inquisition, Reformation and Counter-Refor-

mation continued the old tradition of hunting out "enemies," who
were presented as lurking in the midst of the Christian community,
torturing them and murdering them. Informers and spies planted by
Inquisitors and Church/State authorities spread suspicion and fear
in the community. In the Victorian period Christianity was very
often used to ignore callously grave social and political injustice.
Hatred is very much the traditional ambience of Christianity. When
early missionaries set out in the 14th and 15th centuries to evangelize
the Moslems, so deeply had the habit of crusading been burned into
Western consciousness that it seems that their preaching consisted in
bitter and violent invective against Islam, instead of a peaceful presentation of the case for Christianity. Some women today are continuing this tradition of Christian hatred. They are creating Man, the
stereotyped enemy, in as blinkered and prejudiced a way that the old
Christian stereotypes—Jew, Moslem, Witch
Those old images, we have seen, b
were quite irrational. However, the prejudice was deeply nee
Many women seem to need to hate men in order to gain a new
appreciation of woman, just as Christians have traditionally defined
themselves in terms of aggression and hatred. The first collective and
self-conscious act of Europe as she crept out of barbarism was the
slaughter of the Crusades. Women would often say that the women's
movement is a "Crusade" for a better world, but they should be
aware of the appalling cruelty and violence that that word "crusade"
hides so blandly.

This kind of aggression and creation of enemies is certainly part of
our Christian heritage. Far from leading to liberation, it all too often
involves a narrowing of horizons and a deeply sick refusal to look at
reality which is always too complicated for the stereotype. The ag-
gressions or homophobia of some women today is creating in many
men new prejudices against women and a new irritation or anger. In
their turn, men are beginning to create a stereotype of the Feminist
as the Enemy. Crusades simply evoke new Holy Wars in the Enemy,
in a vicious circle. Until this Christian sickness is overcome, there is
no real hope for men and women peacefully inhabiting the same
world.

Christianity has always preached love, which is a very difficult
virtue to put into practice. It is much easier to love our neighbors by

defining and hating our enemies. It would seem to me impossible for Christianity to rid itself of this neurotic habit of prejudice which, I believe, has scarred the West and, in Protestant countries, has made us dogmatic and aggressive with opponents. Even today, fundamentalist or Born-Again Christians are quite happy to ignore the immense wisdom and insight of many of the Eastern religions and say that all such religions are inspired by the Devil. For certain American fundamentalists, as, I suspect, for our present Pope, Communism is not just an undesirable political system, Communists are in league with Satan. We cannot hope that Christianity can help us to transcend this tendency to hatred and prejudice. As its truths become increasingly marginal, it seems to become even more aggressive. The charismatic and fundamentalist groups which have mushroomed in all the Churches and have attracted numerous converts nearly all have this dogmatic and intolerant prejudice toward whomsoever they see as enemies, clinging proudly to their irrationality. Their aggression, of course, betrays and fans a deep insecurity as does the new homophobia of the 20th century and the new misogyny it gives rise to. Men and women today need to extricate themselves from the old habits of suspicion and invective.

Christianity has also preached the virtue of detachment, at least for mystics. Detachment ideally does not mean a chilly indifference to the world, but an ability to stand back from oneself, to check in ourselves the neurotic clinging to the ego which makes us express our insecurities in fruitless ways, and, finally, to free oneself from old, unproductive habits of thought and action which merely embed us further in our insecurity. When men and women are able to detach themselves from old unproductive patterns of behavior and cease to define their sex by hating the other, there will be an end to the sex war.

Western women are spearheading the liberation of women from male oppression, and we have seen that this has been possible in the West because of the long Christian tradition of idealizing the independent woman. At the very beginning of its history the gospel Christianity offered to women was positive. Later the myths of virginity, martyrdom and mysticism often went sour and produced destructive neuroses in the women who attempted to escape the anonymity of femaleness. Christianity certainly has bequeathed many problems to both men and women. If women have trouble being the offspring of Thecla or Catherine of Siena, then (in the matter of male-female relationships) it is no joke for a man to be the heir of Jerome, Augustine, Sprenger or Luther either. Yet however bad things were between men and women, there were always women who accepted the challenge Christianity offered them and did embark on lives of independence. Often they made a mess of it, and this is not surprising. This book has often had to chart the failures of these women, and it could be objected that because I have dwelt only on these rather exceptional women my account has been biased. Women who opt for independence and who challenge the old sex prejudice of the West have always been a minority, but today more people than ever before are questioning the old mythologies of the sexes. It is not surprising that many women fall into old Christian traps today just as they have always done. However, many of the women in this book show that it is possible to use the Christian myth creatively to obtain a new and healthy freedom. They started from a much worse position than we do today. It should be possible for us to use those aspects of our heritage to carry us a long way forward.

# BIBLIOGRAPHY*

ACTON, William. (i) *Functions and Disorders of the Reproductive Organs.* London, 1857. (ii) *Prostitution,* London, 1870.

AMBROSE, St. *The Nun's Ideals: De Virginitate and De Virginibus.* Dublin, 1963.

ANDREWS, Edward Denning. *The People Called Shakers: A Search for the Perfect Society,* new ed. New York, 1963.

ANNAN, Noel. *Leslie Stephen.* London, 1951.

APTER, Terri. *Why Women Don't Have Wives: Professional Success and Motherhood.* London, 1985.

AUCLAIR, Marcelle. *St. Teresa of Avila.* London, 1953.

AUERBACH, Nina. *Woman and the Demon: The Life of a Victorian Myth.* Cambridge, Mass., 1982.

BAILEY, D. S. (i) *Homosexuality and the Western Christian Tradition.* London, 1955. (ii) *The Man-Woman Relation in Christian Thought.* London, 1959.

BAKER, Derek (ed.). *Medieval Women.* Oxford, 1978.

BATAILLE, Georges. *Eroticism* (trans. Mary Dalwood). London, 1962.

BERGER, Peter L. (ed.). *The Other Side of God: A Polarity in World Religions.* New York, 1981.

BESTERMAN, Theodore. *Men Against Women: A Study of Sexual Relations.* London, 1934.

BOASE, Roger. *The Origin and Meaning of Courtly Love: A Critical Study of European Scholarship.* Manchester, 1977.

BROWN, Peter. (i) *Augustine of Hippo: A Biography.* London, 1967. (ii) *Religion and Society in the Age of St. Augustine.* London, 1972. (iii) *The Making of Late Antiquity.* Cambridge, Mass., and London, 1978. (iv)

* Citations in the text refer to the British edition.

*The Cult of the Saints: Its Rise and Function in Classical Antiquity.*
London, 1981. (v) *Society and the Holy in Late Antiquity.* London,
1982.

BUGGE, John. *Virginitas: An Essay in the History of a Medieval Ideal.* The
Hague, 1975.


CARTER, Angela. *The Sadeian Woman: An Exercise in Cultural History.*
London, 1979.

CHRISTINE de Pizan. *The Book of the City of Ladies.* London, 1983.

CLARK, Alice. *The Working Life of Women in the Seventeenth Century.*
London, 1919.

COCKAYNE, O. (ed.). *Hali Heidenhad.* London, 1866.

COHN, Norman. (i) *The Pursuit of the Millenium, Revolutionary Millenari-
ans and Mystical Anarchists of the Middle Ages,* London, 1970 (3rd ed.).
(ii) *Europe's Inner Demons: An Inquiry Inspired by the Great Witch-
Hunt.* London, 1975.

COLE, W. G. *Sex in Christianity and Psychoanalysis.* London, 1956.

COLET, John. *An Exposition of St Paul's First Epistle to the Corinthians*
(trans. J. H. Lupton). London, 1874.

COWARD, Rosalind. *Female Desire: Women's Sexuality Today.* London,
1984.

CUTHBERT, Father, O.F.C. *A Tuscan Penitent: The Life and Legend of St.
Margaret of Cortona.* London, 1907.

CYPRIAN, St. *The Writings* (Trans. Re. R. Ernest Wallis). 2 vols. Edinburgh, 1869.


DALY, Mary. (i) *The Church and the Second Sex.* London, 1968. (ii) *Beyond
God the Father.* London, 1979. (iii) *Gyn/Ecology: The Metaethics of
Radical Feminism.* Boston, 1978. (iv) *Pure Lust: Elemental Feminist
Theology.* London and Boston, 1984.

DAVIES, W. D. *Paul and Rabbinic Judaism.* London, 1948.

DAVIS, Charles. *Body as Spirit.* London, 1976.

De BEAUVOIR, Simone. *The Second Sex* (trans. H. M. Parshley). London,
1953.

De ROUGEMONT, Denis. *Passion and Society* (trans. M. Belgion). London, 1956.

DINGWALL, Eric John. *The American Woman: A Historical Study.* London, 1956.

DOOLEY, W. J. *Marriage According to St. Ambrose.* Washington, 1948.

DOUGLAS, Mary. *Purity and Danger: An Analysis of Concepts of Pollution
and Taboo.* London, 1966.

DRANE, A. T. *The History of St. Catherine of Siena and Her Companions.*
London, 1880.

DRONKE, Peter. *Women Writers of the Middle Ages: A Critical Study of*

*Texts from Perpetua (d. 203) to Marguerite Parete (d. 1310).* Cambridge, 1984.

DRYSDALE, George. *The Elements of Social Science.* London, 1854.

EDWARDS, Susan. *Female Sexuality and the Law.* Oxford, 1981.

FIELDING, William J. *Love and the Sex Emotions: Their Individual and Social Aspects.*

FOSTER, Lawrence. *Religion and Sexuality: Three American Communal Experiments in the 19th Century.* Oxford and New York, 1981.

FOUCAULT, Michel. *The History of Sexuality,* vol I (trans. Robert Hurley). London, 1981.

FRASER, Antonia. *The Weaker Vessel: Woman's Lot in Seventeenth-Century England.* London, 1984.

FREND, W. H. C. *Martyrdom and Persecution in the Early Church: A Study of the Conflict from the Maccabees to Donatus.* Oxford, 1965.

FRIDAY, Nancy. *My Mother/My Self: The Daughter's Search for Identity.* Glasgow, 1979.

FRIEDAN, Betty. *The Feminine Mystique.* London, 1963.

GASQUET, Rt. Rev. Abbot, O.S.B. *Life of Mary Ward, Foundress of the IBVM, Compiled from Various Sources.* London, 1909.

GRAEF, Hilda C. Mary. (i) *A History of Doctrine and Devotion.* 2 vols. London, 1965. (ii) *The Case of Therese Neumann.* Cork, 1950.

GREER, Germaine. (i) *The Female Eunuch.* London, 1970. (ii) *Sex and Destiny: The Politics of Human Fertility.* London, 1984.

HANDY, Robert T. *A History of the Churches in the United States and Canada.* Oxford, 1976.

HARRISON, Fraser. *The Dark Angel: Aspects of Victorian Sexuality.* London, 1977.

HAYS, H. R. *The Dangerous Sex: The Myth of Feminine Evil.* London, 1966.

HEIMERT, A. and DELBANCO, A. (eds.). *The Puritans in America: A Narrative Anthology.* Cambridge, Mass., 1985.

HELLERSTEIN, E. A., and OFFEN, K. M. (eds). *Victorian Women: A Documentary Account of Women's Lives in 19th Century England, France and the United States.* Brighton, 1981.

HOUGHTON, E. *The Victorian Frame of Mind.* London, 1957.

HOULBROOKE, Ralph A. *The English Family, 1450–1700.* London and New York, 1984.

HUIZINGA, A. J. *The Waning of the Middle Ages.* London, 1924.

JACOBUS, de Voragine. *The Golden Legend* (trans. G. Ryan and H. Rippergen). New York and London, 1984.
JONES, Ernest. *On the Nightmare.* London, 1931.

KIRK, E. E. *The Vision of God.* London, 1931.
KIRK, Rev. John. *The Mother of the Wesleys.* London, 1876.

LASKI, Marghanita. *Ecstasy: A Study of Some Secular and Religious Experiences.* London, 1961,
LASLETT, Peter. (i) *The World We Have Lost,* London, 1965. (ii) *Household and Family in Past Time.* London, 1972.
LEA, H. C. (i) *History of Sacerdotal Celibacy in the Christian Church.* Philadelphia, 1932. (ii) *Materials Toward a History of Witchcraft,* (arr. and ed. A. C. Howland). 3 vols. Philadelphia, 1939.
LEANDER of Seville. *Episcopi Regula, sive de Institutione Virginum et Contemptu Mundi ad Florentiam Soro Liber.*
LEWIS, I. M. *Ecstatic Religion.* London, 1971.

MACK, F. M. (ed.). *Seinte Marhete the Meiden ant Martyr.* London, 1934.
MacLEOD, Sheila. *The Art of Starvation.* London, 1981.
MAITLAND, Sara. *A Map of the New Country: Women and Christianity.* London, 1983.
MARTIN, Thérèse. *Autobiography of a Saint* (trans. Ronald Knox). London, 1958.
MAY, Geoffrey. *Social Control of Sex Expression.* London, 1930.
MIGNA, J. P. (ed.). *Patrologia Latina.* Paris, 1864–1884.
MITCHELL, Juliet. (i) *Psychoanalysis and Feminism.* London, 1974. (ii) *Women: The Longest Revolution,* London, 1984.
MOREWEDGE, Rosemarie Thee (ed.). *The Role of Women in the Middle Ages.* London, 1975.
MUSURILLO, Herbert (ed. and trans.). *The Acts of the Christian Martyrs.* Oxford, 1972.

O'FAOLAIN, Julia, and MARTINES, Lauro (eds.). *Not in God's Image: Women in History.* London, 1973.

PAGELS, Elaine. *The Gnostic Gospels.* London, 1973.
PARRINDER, Geoffrey. *Sex in the World's Religions.* London, 1980.
PEARSALL, Ronald. *The Worm in the Bud: The World of Victorian Sexuality.* London, 1969.
PIAT, S. J., O.F.M. *The Story of a Family: The Home of the Little Flower.* Dublin, 1947.
POLLARD, A., and CHAPPLE, J.A.V. *The Letters of Mrs. Gaskell.* Manchester, 1966.

POMEROY, Sarah B. *Goddesses, Whores, Wives and Slaves: Women in Classical Antiquity.* London, 1976.
POWER, Eileen. *Medieval English Nunneries.* Cambridge, 1922.
PUCCINI, Vincentio. *The Life of the Holy and Venerable Mother Suor Marie Maddalena de Patsi.* London, 1619.

RADICE, Betty (trans. and ed.). *The Letters of Abelard and Heloise.* London, 1974.
RIENCOURT, Amaury de. *Sex and Power in History.* New York, 1974.
ROSENBERG, Rosalind. *Beyond Separate Spheres: Intellectual Roots of Modern Feminism.* New Haven, 1982.
RUBIN, Lillian B. *Intimate Strangers.* London and New York, 1983.
RUETHER, Rosemary Radford. (i) (with E. McLAUGHLIN) (eds.). *Women of Spirit, Female Leadership in the Jewish and Christian Traditions.* New York, 1979. (ii) *Sexism and Godtalk: Towards a Feminist Theology.* London, 1983. (iii) (with Rosemary Skinner Keller) *Women and Religion in America: A Documentary History,* vol I. San Francisco, 1981.
RUNCIMAN, Steven. *The Medieval Manichee: A Study of the Christian Dualist Heresy.* Cambridge, 1960.
RUSKIN, John. *Sesame and Lilies.* London, 1865.

SANDERS, E. P. *Paul and Palestinian Judaism.* London, 1977.
SARSBY, Jacqueline. *Romantic Love and Society.* London, 1983.
SCOTT, Donald, and WISHY, Bernard (eds.). *America's Families: A Documentary History.* New York, 1982.
SCUDDER, V. D. *St. Catherine of Siena as Seen in Her Letters.* London, 1905.
SHAHAR, Shulamith. *The Fourth Estate: A History of Women in the Middle Ages* (trans. Chaya Galai). London and New York, 1983.
SHOWALTER, Elaine. *A Literature of Their Own: British Women Novelists from Brontë to Lessing.* Rev. ed. New York and London, 1982.
SIMPSON, Alan. *Puritanism in Old and New England.* Chicago, 1955.
STEEGMAN (trans.). *The Book of Divine Consolation of the Blessed Angela of Foligno.* London, 1909.
STONE, Lawrence. *The Family, Sex and Marriage in England, 1500–1800.* London, 1977.
SUMMERS, Montague. (i) (trans. and ed.) *Malleus Maleficarum.* London, 1928. (ii) *The Physical Phenomena of Mysticism.* London, 1950.

TANNAHILL, Reay. *Sex in History.* London, 1980.
TAYLOR, G. R. (i) *Sex in History.* London, 1953. (ii) *The Angel-Makers: A Study in the Psychological Origins of Historical Change.* London, 1958.
TEODOROWICZ, Rev. Jósef (trans. Rudolph Kraus) *Mystical Phenomena in the Life of Theresa Neumann.* St. Louis and London, 1940.

TERTULLIAN. *The Writings.* 3 vols. Edinburgh, 1870.

TERESA of Jesus. *Complete Works.* 3 vols. (trans. and ed. Allison Peers). London, 1944.

THOMAS, Keith. *Religion and the Decline of Magic.* London, 1971.

THOMPSON, Roger. *Women in Stuart England and America: A Comparative Study.* London, 1974.

THOMPSON, W. M. (ed.). *The Wohunge of Ure Lauerd.* London, 1958.

THURSTON, Herbert, S.J. (i) *The Physical Phenomena of Mysticism.* London, 1952. (ii) *Surprising Mystics.* London, 1955.

TICKELL, George, S.J. *The Life of Blessed Margaret Mary.* London, 1890.

TREVOR-ROPER, H. R. *The European Witch-Craze of the 16th and 17th Centuries.* London, 1969.

TRUDGILL, Eric. *Madonnas and Magdalens: The Origins and Development of Victorian Sexual Attitudes.* London, 1976.


VANCE, Carole, S. (ed.). *Pleasure and Danger: Exploring Female Sexuality.* Boston and London, 1984.


WARNER, Marina. (i) *Alone of All Her Sex.* New York, 1976. (ii) *Joan of Arc: The Image of Female Heroism.* London, 1981.

WELSH, Alexander. *The City of Dickens.* London, 1971.

WILLIAMS, N. P. *The Ideas of the Fall and of Original Sin.* London, 1927.

WOOLF, Virginia. *A Room of One's Own.* London, 1970.

WOODHAM SMITH, Cecil. *Florence Nightingale.* London, 1950.

WOODS, Richard (ed.). *Understanding Mysticism.* London, 1981.

# INDEX